THE WORKS OF
THEODORE ROOSEVELT

NATIONAL EDITION

VOLUME XV

THE NATIONAL EDITION
OF ROOSEVELT'S WORKS

State Papers
as Governor and President
1899-1909

By
Theodore Roosevelt

New York
Charles Scribner's Sons
1926

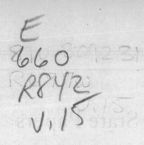

CONTENTS

CONTENTS

CONTENTS

CONTENTS

x

CONTENTS

CONTENTS

CONTENTS

CONTENTS

CONTENTS

CONTENTS

CONTENTS

CONTENTS

CONTENTS

CONTENTS

CONTENTS

CONTENTS

EDITOR'S NOTE

THE State Papers of Theodore Roosevelt as Governor of New York and as President of the United States are so voluminous that it is possible in this edition of his works to include only the most important of the documents of his administrations. In this volume will be found his annual messages and his three inaugural addresses. The reader is referred to the bibliography at the end of the volume for information concerning more complete collections of Mr. Roosevelt's public papers.

H. H.

ROOSEVELT AS PRESIDENT

By Gifford Pinchot

IT may be that wise men speak truly when they say that balanced and accurate history can be written only after the lapse of years. I do not know. But of this I am sure—that unless we who knew Roosevelt set down as best we can the essentials of his great spirit as we saw them, and so supply to the colder and more distant judgment of the historian, who must guess at objectives, reconstruct situations, and imagine motives, whose documents are documents and nothing more, the best descriptions we can formulate of the great soul we loved, as well as the most illuminating facts about the great man we admired, much will be lost that otherwise would live, much perish of which the world could make good use. It is, I think, in such personal light as this that his writings can best be read.

Roosevelt's state papers are the product of a knowledge of domestic and foreign affairs and of executive detail which taken together were unapproached by any other President; of a degree of contact and co-operation between himself and the men and women best informed on each subject that is without example; of the original workings of his own penetrating, brilliant, and aggressive mind; and of long-continued and painstaking care in preparation. They hint at, if they do not completely describe, his wise and forceful, careful and fearless, controlled and abounding personality.

Whether we have ever had in high public life a man more forehanded and less sudden than Roosevelt in matters of this kind is doubtful. An outstanding illustration was his completion, during the strenuous final months of his presidency and before he went to Africa, of the address to be delivered at the Sorbonne after his return from the Dark Continent. I had the pleasure of reading that address in final form some little time before he left the White House.

It is fair to describe Roosevelt's customary method of preparing a state paper of importance, provided we remember that his mental make-up was too adventurous, too vigorous, and too little bound by the past to fall easily into fixed habits. That he had a few such habits there is no gainsaying, such as his invariable ending of the dictation of a letter with the spoken words, "Sincerely yours, Theodore Roosevelt." Nevertheless, it would be unsafe to say that his method of dealing with any particular problem was always thus or thus.

It was Roosevelt's custom, then, beginning several months before the date set for the completion of an important paper, to work out by consideration in his own mind and by discussion with others a rough outline, then to dictate a first draft, and then to put that draft in a certain drawer of his working desk. Thereafter for weeks or even months, as the case might be, he took it out whenever there came into his room (and he saw to it that they came often) a man or woman competent to advise him.

To such visitors he read, or asked them to read, the passages upon which their advice was desired. Thereupon he would correct, and usually add to, the draft with interlineations so small yet written with so coarse a pen as to be the despair of the copyist. As time went on one clean-written draft followed another until, in some cases at least, the final document embodied the results of discussion literally with hundreds of the best-informed individuals in America. Naturally a document so produced was almost impregnable.

The high technical accuracy and comprehensiveness of Roosevelt's discussion of foreign and domestic affairs led often to the question how one man could be professionally expert upon so many and such various matters. The answer lies partly in the fact that Roosevelt knew with the knowledge of the expert and saw from the point of view of the expert more branches of human knowledge than almost any man of his time. It lies also in his habit of consultation with specialists. Roosevelt respected expert opinion and made use of it to a degree which was unmatched among the public men who were his contemporaries.

Men of small caliber in public office find scorn of expert knowledge a convenient screen for hiding their own mental barrenness. So true is this that one of the best measures of his own breadth and depth of mind is the degree to which a public man acknowledges the value of expert knowledge and judgment in fields with which he himself, in the nature of things, cannot be familiar. By this standard Roosevelt stood at the very top.

No public man has ever lived who would have been capable of dealing wisely and effectively, through his own unsupported knowledge, with all the multitudinous and intricate affairs of the Government of the United States. It is not only the right but the duty of every President to seek and accept assistance of every sort and from every source that will make his work in office more useful to the nation.

In what mind the point of view expressed in a President's message first was formulated; who first gave utterance to the policy it sets forth; from what expert came the facts by which its conclusions are supported—these are questions of hardly secondary importance. It is the President's adoption or rejection of facts, policy, and point of view that counts. What he has adopted is thenceforth his own, and he becomes solely responsible to the public for the accuracy of the facts, for the wisdom of the policy, and for the breadth and soundness of the point of view.

Accordingly Roosevelt's state papers—and it is vastly to his credit—were as a rule composite photographs of the best knowledge and judgment of his time, moulded, directed, and given force and carrying power by the originality of his own mind, the depth of his knowledge, the richness of his experience, and the fervor for public service of his own soul. None the less for that reason were they Roosevelt's very own.

The personality which underlay Roosevelt's writings was always of greater interest to me than the writings themselves. I would rather try to point out what gave its power to the written word than to discuss and comment on the text itself. Of such comment and discussion there has been and there will doubtless be no lack.

Much of the quality and content of Roosevelt's state papers came directly out of his unsurpassed ability and experience as a public administrator. For while Theodore Roosevelt was the greatest preacher of good morals and good citizenship, he was also the greatest executive of his generation. He led men's thoughts toward sounder views of life and duty and good citizenship. He led also in putting theory into practice—in getting things done.

Roosevelt's achievements as a public administrator have failed of their due share of public appreciation. His powers and his accomplishments in this respect were fully as remarkable as what he did in the field of international statesmanship or as the leader of public thought in America. His management and direction of the government machinery gave evidence of qualities as exceptional as those which made him the unquestioned leader among advocates of personal and civic righteousness.

As a public administrator Roosevelt gave proof of genius in the selection of his assistants, in the formulation of great governmental plans, and in securing a degree of efficiency in the conduct of the public business unmatched either before or since.

The corps of public officials whom Roosevelt drew around him during his presidency was probably without a parallel in the whole history of government administration. They came from every walk of life, and with every sort of background and training. But whether they were public servants already in office when he became President, cowboys, college graduates, frontiersmen, professors, gunmen, writers, scientists, or professional executives, each one was distinguished by intelligent loyalty to the government and to the ideals of the President, and by that combination of devotion to duty and efficiency in service which produces genuine results. Lord Bryce, certainly a competent judge, said of them that he had never in any country seen a more eager, high-minded, and efficient set of public servants, men more useful and more creditable to their country.

Roosevelt used the whole Government of the United States consciously, and with the most conspicuous success, as a means of doing good to the people of this country. The government to him was always a means to an end—never an end in itself—and he made use of it, as he would of any other tool, for the accomplishment of very specific purposes, holding that whatever the people needed, and the law did not specifically forbid, he could do and ought to do.

In his own personal capacity to turn out work Roosevelt stood alone. Nothing, to my mind, illustrates it more completely than the fact that, at the end of years of such effort as would have cost the life of an ordinary man, and in spite of the prodigious rush of the closing weeks, he left the White House with every task accomplished and every letter answered. I was with him when he passed out of its door as President for the last time, and I know.

Roosevelt's undefeated mental endurance made it possible for him to work at high speed and efficiency long after the power to produce at all would have deserted a less hardy and resilient mind. After a day that would have left most men in collapse I have often heard him call for his secretary at ten or eleven o'clock at night and begin the dictation of an important document.

What Roosevelt required of himself he required also, in their degree, of others. In consequence, the actual service rendered to the voters for each dollar of tax expended was immeasurably higher under Roosevelt than under any other of the seven national administrations with which I have been familiar. The driving power of the man at the head; the high and difficult standards which he set for himself; the generosity of his recognition of good work in others; his intimate acquaintance, not simply with the heads of departments, but with the work of subordinates throughout the Government Service; his unequalled power to arouse enthusiasm and command the very best each individual could produce—all these combined to transform, reanimate, and uplift the Government Service until it reached a point of efficiency where, in certain cases at least, government organizations had nothing to fear from comparison with the most effective organizations in the business world.

Roosevelt made it worth while to work for the people of the United States. He was the greatest of public administrators not only because his knowledge of the government was unrivalled, not only because he set in his own person a perfect example of effective work, not only because he was a great master of organization, but because he had the power to establish high ideals of public service, and to inspire in others the same devotion to the public good which illuminated his own life. Roosevelt never said: "Go you and serve the public while I watch you." He said: "Come on, let's do the job together."

For Roosevelt was a leader first of all. The gift of leadership belonged to him in paramount degree. His mind, robust, alert, and bold, led him naturally and inevitably to take the foremost place in every matter with which he had to deal. Among the endless services to his people and his time for which all humanity has profound reason to be grateful, his power to lead supplied, in my judgment, the most essential and the most beneficent.

Knowledge of public opinion, sense of proportion, practical common sense, high daring, and magnetic personality were all developed in Roosevelt to the point that made him the foremost leader of the people of the time in which he lived. Foresight, courage, strength, and skill were not only his as individual characteristics, but they were blended and ripened in the fire of his passion for righteousness until the sum and essence of his whole nature was focussed and expressed in his power to lead. This was the centre in which Roosevelt's innumerable qualities and capabilities met and combined. This was the supreme gift which made him the power he was. More than that, it gave him the undying leadership we are still following to-day.

Leadership implies a following, and a following is impossible, in public life, unless the followers consent to be led. To consent they must be convinced. Beyond any other man of his time,

ROOSEVELT AS PRESIDENT

Roosevelt had the capacity of speaking the public judgment on public issues even before it was fully formed. He was continually seizing and expressing in papers, speeches, essays, and articles the public opinion of the American people when it had not yet quite reached the surface—public opinion still in the bud until he brought it to blossom. What he thought to-day the nation would think to-morrow.

It was this instinctive knowledge of what the rest of the people were thinking, combined with the God-given ability to express it accurately at just the moment when it needed expression, and combined also with his boundless sympathy, that gave the men and women of the nation that feeling of comradeship for him which was the basis of his strength. He felt what they thought, and they knew it was right when he spoke it for them. Roosevelt was the leader of the people because he moved in advance of them, yet never without intimate contact and complete understanding with the great body of his followers.

On our walks together we often discussed this question of leadership, and together developed what we called "the theory of the next step." It was concerned with the fundamental truth that he who goes in advance of public opinion and expects it to follow him must move forward but one step at a time. If his advance is so rapid that the people cannot keep up with him; if they fail to see their way from one foothold to the next; if the gap between the place where they stand now and the place where the leader asks them to stand with him is too broad to be crossed in a single step—contact is broken and the leadership fails.

A leader worth his salt must have courage, for without it the people will despise him. Roosevelt had it to the limit of human endowment. He must have instant perception of an issue and the willingness to grasp it instantly, for otherwise the people will leave him behind. Roosevelt had both. He must have that fine sense of righteousness which sifts the wheat from the chaff and accepts only those things which are eternally right, for otherwise the people eventually will refuse to follow. He must have that mental and moral balance which detects the extremist, rejects the unsound doctrine, and having weighed all things, holds fast that which is good. Finally, he must have the power to speak for the people, to express their thought, to demand that their desire shall be accomplished. He must seize and give voice to their aspiration almost before they are conscious of it themselves.

Roosevelt had all this and more. He never failed to speak his mind, never let the golden moment pass, never left the people without a leader to call forth the best that was in them. The people followed him gladly because he went ever before them on the road which their profoundest convictions declared to be right.

While the people were his friends, during his lifetime Roosevelt's enemies were legion. To-day those who question his greatness are few and far between. But Roosevelt wore his greatness with a difference. His size and elevation among his fellow men were not like those of an icy and inaccessible mountain peak, standing rigid and alone among the lesser elevations of common life. Roosevelt was rather like a great plateau, a land higher and more productive than the levels below it, breathing a finer and more stimulating air—altogether a better land—but one where every inhabitant of the lower levels who came to live within its influence might breathe deeper, work better, think higher thoughts, and live a worthier life.

The people loved Roosevelt because he was like them. In him the common qualities were lifted to a higher tension and a greater power, but they were still the same. What he did plain men understood and would have liked to do. To millions he was the image of their better selves.

The people loved him because his thoughts, though loftier, were yet within their reach, and his motives were always clear in their sight. He was larger, stronger, of greater breadth of vision and larger scope, but nevertheless a man whose impulses and achievements, whose sympathies and antagonisms, whose purposes and ideals, were all of like nature with their own. He was like the rest of us, except that there was so much more of him.

No man is great unless his point of view has greatness. Roosevelt's physical and intellectual powers were not without example. I have known a man or two whose memory equalled his; a man or two whose breadth of knowledge might be compared with his; a man or two at least his equal in mental acumen; a man or two the versatility of whose mind did not suffer greatly in contrast with Roosevelt's. But none of us has known a man whose extremely rare endowment of great faculties was at the service of a spirit so gallantly eager to play the whole of a man's part in the world.

His own explanation of his unusual physical achievements well illustrates this view. It was his custom to regard himself as without exceptional physical equipment (in which judgment he was somewhat less than just) and to say: "Physically, I am no better than the average—the difference is that I do things with my body which other men could do just as well but which they do not think of doing."

Where other men faltered Roosevelt never lost his fighting edge. Harassed as he was at times by the treachery of trusted friends; checked as he was at times by the opposition of powerful enemies; baffled as he was at times by the deadly indifference of those upon whose support he had the right to count, he never lost his cheerful courage or the zest of life. He loved his work; he loved the people for whom he spent his fighting life as they loved him. There are few sayings of his that hold for me so much of him as this: "Aggressive fighting for the right is the noblest sport the world affords."

Roosevelt was a gallant man. That describes him better than any other adjective I know. We who knew him at work marvelled at the blitheness of his spirit under the strain of bitter struggles, at his eagerness to meet each new call upon faculties alert to the limit of human vitality and overflowing with the joy of life. What other man with such and so many conflicts on his hands, such daily disillusioning contact with the baser sides of human nature, such overpowering labor in the service of humanity (and for much of it at the time such scant recognition and reward) was ever so buoyant as he? Surely in no man of our time but Lincoln did the essential kindliness of a most kindly nature throughout a life of such enormous pressure, such absorbing warfare, such venomous attack, remain so genuinely unspotted from the world.

Few though there be who believe it, Roosevelt had true humility of mind. Pride of opinion was utterly foreign to him. The final test with Roosevelt was always—Is it right? And when he had concluded what was right in any given set of circumstances his action followed simply and certainly. Yet, having acted, if he could be shown that for any reason whatever his action had been wrong, no matter how far it had been carried, he was always willing to reverse himself.

This view of himself as a servant of righteousness was thoroughly characteristic of Roosevelt. So was his consistent refusal to accept credit that could by any reasonable possibility be assigned to some one else. To receive approval that he had not earned, to fail in acknowledging what others had done, or to graft upon the personal achievements of others, was so repugnant to him that at every stage in his career he gave to others the praise for achievements that really were his own. There can never have been a leader more generous to his fellow workers than he, and deeply was he loved because of it.

Abundance of life was the wellspring of his power—life at its warmest and fullest and freest, at its utmost in vigor, at its sanest in purpose and restraint, at its cleanest and clearest, life tremendous in volume, unbounded in scope, yet controlled and guided with a disciplined power which made him, as few men have ever been, the captain of his soul. Alert, glad, without meanness and without fear, free from arrogance and affectation, with few hesitations and few regrets, slow to promise but ardent to perform, delighting in difficulties, welcoming danger, sensitive to the touch of every phase of human existence, yet dominated by standards more severely set for himself than for any others, sustained by a breadth of knowledge and of sympathy and by an endurance, both physical and mental, which belonged to him alone, Roosevelt lived with a completeness that lesser men can never know.

STATE PAPERS
AS GOVERNOR AND PRESIDENT
1899-1909

AS GOVERNOR OF NEW YORK

I

INAUGURAL ADDRESS [1]

A VERY heavy responsibility rests upon the governor of New York State, a State of 7,000,000 of inhabitants, of great wealth, of widely varied industries and with a population singularly diversified, not merely in occupation, but in race origin, in habits of life, and in ways of thought. It is not an easy task so to frame our laws that justice may be done to all alike in such a population, so many of whom have interests that seem entirely antagonistic. But upon the great and fundamental issues of good government there must always be a unity of interest among all persons who wish well to the Commonwealth. There is much less need of genius or of any special brilliancy in the administration of our government than there is need of such homely virtues and qualities as common sense, honesty, and courage. There are very many difficult problems to face, some of which are as old as government itself, while others have sprung into being in consequence of the growing complexity and steadily increasing tension of our social life for the last two generations. It is not given to any man, or to any set of men, to see with absolutely clear vision into the future. All that can be done is to face the facts as we find them, to meet each difficulty in practical fashion, and to strive steadily for the betterment both of our civic and our social conditions.

[1] Delivered in the Assembly Chamber at the Capitol, Albany, New York, January 2, 1899. In response to a brief greeting by the retiring governor, Mr. Roosevelt prefaced his address with the following words: "I appreciate very deeply all you say, and the spirit that prompts you to say it. We have the same ends in view; we are striving to accomplish the same results; each of us, according to the light that is in him, is seeking to advance the welfare of the people."

We must realize, on the one hand, that we can do little if we do not set ourselves a high ideal, and, on the other, that we will fail in accomplishing even this little if we do not work through practical methods and with a readiness to face life as it is, and not as we think it ought to be. Under no form of government is it so necessary thus to combine efficiency and morality, high principle and rough common sense, justice and the sturdiest physical and moral courage, as in a republic. It is absolutely impossible for a republic long to endure if it becomes either corrupt or cowardly; if its public men, no less than its private men, lose the indispensable virtue of honesty, if its leaders of thought become visionary doctrinaires, or if it shows a lack of courage in dealing with the many grave problems which it must surely face, both at home and abroad, as it strives to work out the destiny meet for a mighty nation.

It is only through the party system that free governments are now successfully carried on, and yet we must keep ever vividly before us that the usefulness of a party is strictly limited by its usefulness to the State, and that in the long run, he serves his party best who most helps to make it instantly responsive to every need of the people, and to the highest demands of that spirit which tends to drive us onward and upward.

It shall be my purpose, so far as I am given strength, to administer my office with an eye single to the welfare of all the people of this great Commonwealth.

II

ANNUAL MESSAGE[1]

To the Legislature:

The people of New York, like the people of every other State in the Union, are to be congratulated, because during the past year the nation has carried to a brilliant triumph one of the most righteous wars of modern times. When last spring it became evident that the interests of humanity and of national honor alike demanded that we should drive Spain from the western hemisphere, and free from her tyranny the subject peoples of the islands of the sea, New York responded with eager zeal to the call for volunteers, and in the Cabinet, in Congress, and in camp, her representatives did all they could to insure the success of the American policy. We are not merely New Yorkers. We are Americans; and the interests of all Americans, whether from the North, the South, the East, or the great West, are equally dear to the men of the Empire State. As we grow into a mighty nation, which, whether it will or not, must inevitably play a great part for good or for evil in the affairs of the world at large, the people of New York wish it understood that they look at all questions of American foreign policy from the most thoroughly national standpoint. The tropic islands we have taken must neither be allowed to lapse into anarchy nor to return under the sway of tyranny. War is a grim thing at best, but the war through which we have passed has left us not merely memories of glory won on land and sea, but an even more blessed heritage, the knowledge that it was waged from the highest motives, for the good of others as well as for our own

[1] Dated, Executive Chamber, Albany, January 2, 1899.

national honor. Above all, we are thankful that it brought home to all of us the fact that the country was indeed one when serious danger confronted it. The men from the East and the West, from the North and the South, the sons of those who wore the blue and of those who wore the gray, the men of means and the men who all their lives long had possessed only what day by day they toiled to earn, stood shoulder to shoulder in the fight, met the same dangers, shared the same hardships, and won the same ultimate triumph.

In our domestic affairs, the State is to be congratulated on the gradual return of prosperity. Though temporarily checked by the war this return has been, on the whole, steady. The capitalist finds constantly greater business opportunities; the wage-worker, in consequence, is more steadily employed; the farmer has a better market.

TAXATION

No other question is of such permanent importance in the domestic economy of our State as the question of taxation. At present our system of taxation is in utter confusion, full of injustices and of queer anomalies. It is an exceedingly difficult subject, one well worthy the attention of our best men, the men with most highly trained minds and the broadest practical experience; men who are able to approach the subject from the standpoints alike of the farmer, the merchant, and the manufacturer. Not only is it necessary to consider whether any kind of tax ought, if practicable, to be levied, but whether it is in fact practicable to levy it. We should discourage the building up of non-taxable interests, and yet we should discourage driving property out of the State by unwise taxation, or levying a tax which is in effect largely a tax upon honesty. I most earnestly commend the whole matter to your special attention.

CANALS AND COMMERCE

New York State took the lead in this country in the promotion of a canal system, and the operation of the Erie Canal has been of incalculable benefit, not merely to Buffalo, New York, and Brooklyn, and the cities of the Mohawk Valley, but to all of the State; for, when a part of it is benefited, the benefit is shared ultimately by the whole.

Of recent years the city of New York has fallen off relatively to other cities as regards the increase of her commerce, and in exports there has been a positive decrease. Under my predecessor a commission was appointed to examine into the causes of this decline. I recommend that this commission be allowed ample additional time to close its work, the subject being one of such vast importance, and that it be given all needful aid.

The canals at present are in such condition that the money already expended will avail nothing if the work is discontinued. As a chain is only as strong as its weakest link, so the navigability of the canals is determined by the shallowest sections. While I do not now recommend the voting of any large amounts of money, yet in fixing up those different parts, expenditures that can be clearly made within the constitution should be authorized.

It is essential to the State no less than to the city of New York that our commercial supremacy should be maintained. With this end in view the canals should be administered economically and with an eye single to the welfare of the whole people. Any man, whether public servant or contractor, who in any way defrauds the State or perverts the business of the State to his private gain must be dealt with as rigorously as the laws will permit.

The Canal Investigating Commission, appointed by my predecessor pursuant to the provisions of Chapter 15 of the Laws of 1898, has completed its work and made its report. Its work has been of great service to the State. The act provided that

the commission should serve without pay, but should receive
the actual and necessary expenses incurred in the performance
of its duty. The commission was also authorized to employ
counsel, experts, engineers, and such other assistants as it
might deem necessary. The time for making its report was
extended by my predecessor to the latest date authorized by
law, and the investigation made was broad in its scope and
searching in its nature.

In addition to the report of the commission required by law,
which is herewith transmitted to you, a supplemental report
of the commission's expenses has been made and filed, by
which it appears that the appropriation made for the expenses
of the investigation has been exhausted, and that it will require
an additional sum of eleven thousand eight hundred and sixty-
nine and fifty-one one-hundredths dollars to discharge the
obligations of the commission properly incurred in the performance of its duty. I recommend that the further sum of
$12,000, or so much thereof as may be necessary, be appro-
priated without delay, for such purpose.

I shall later communicate with you further on the subject
of the canals, and as to the exact course to be followed in
regard to them.

LABOR INTERESTS

Of late years there has been a tendency to extend the sphere
of State action in various directions. This is a tendency which
may readily be carried too far, and the State should give expression to it only when the good to be achieved is undoubted,
and when there is no reasonable probability that it will be
counteracted by harm. Nevertheless, much good has resulted
in the past from such State action. In bygone ages, when
wrong most frequently took the form of brutal violence, the
aid of the State was invoked to shackle force; and exactly as
we have shackled force in the past, so it may be necessary more
and more to shackle cunning in the present. The right to interfere against the individual who does wrong by craft is, of

course, as great as the right to interfere against one who does wrong by open violence; though it is a much more simple matter to interfere effectually in the one case than in the other. Great care, however, must be exercised in the interference. The machinery of business is delicate and complicated, and if it is improperly disarranged or interfered with, the harm, which at first falls on the business men of greater or less wealth and on the corporations, will ultimately be distributed throughout the community at large.

In dealing with the interests which we have grown to group together as the interests of labor, we must always keep in mind the fact that ultimately each man's salvation rests mainly with himself, and that no amount of legislation or of combination can supply the lack of individual initiative—the lack of individual energy, honesty, thrift, and industry. Yet this capacity for individual self-help can, and should, be generally supplemented by that form of self-help that follows on organization and association, as has been shown by the careers of many of the trade-unions and labor federations; and sometimes it can be supplemented by the direct action of the State itself.

The development in extent and variety of industries has necessitated legislation in the interest of labor. This legislation is not necessarily against the interest of capital; on the contrary, if wisely devised it is for the benefit of both laborers and employers. We have very wisely passed many laws for the benefit of labor, in themselves good, and for the time being sufficient; but experience has shown that the full benefit of these laws is not obtained, through the lack of proper means of enforcing them, and the failure to make any one department responsible for their enforcement.

At present the enforcement of the law regulating the hours of labor of minors under fourteen years of age and of women employed in mercantile establishments, and the sanitary condition of stores and buildings used for similar purposes in large cities, is left to the board of health. If the city government fails to furnish the proper appropriation and appoint the necessary officers to carry out the law, as is at present the case in New York City, it is practically a dead letter.

Another important statute of this character relates to providing secure scaffolding in the erection of new buildings. The law on this subject is all that could be desired, but this enforcement is left to the city police, and, as a matter of fact, practically no provision is made for carrying it into effect. In New York City, where this law is most needed, police officers are unacquainted with the character and requirements of the law. Most of them, indeed, are not aware that the enforcement of this law is any part of their duty.

The law regulating the hours of labor on surface railroads is also an excellent provision against the tendency to work the men an almost unlimited number of hours. The enforcement of this law is left to the railroad commissioners. As they have no active force to use for such a purpose the law fails by default, except when individual citizens undertake the prosecutions. The employee himself will rarely or never complain for fear of being discharged.

In order that the desire of the people, definitely expressed in this wholesome legislation, shall be made effective, I recommend that the enforcement of the entire body of legislation relating to labor be placed under the Board of Factory Inspectors. This would simplify the whole question of labor legislation and place the responsibility for its enforcement where it properly belongs, and would also give the maximum efficiency of service with the minimum cost to the State. With a slight increase in the general force of factory inspectors, this work can be done for the whole State, and the object of the legislation be satisfactorily secured to the people. I recommend that the legislature provide for additional factory inspectors, so as to bring the total number up to fifty, and also that the governor be empowered to appoint unsalaried deputies.

Another very important phase of this subject is the sweat-shop system, which is practically the conversion of the poorest class of living apartments into unwholesome, pest-creating, and crime-breeding workshops. Laws have been enacted by the legislature to suppress this vile phase of industrial life in our large cities, by prohibiting the use of dwellings for the purposes of manufacture. Although the law is quite explicit, and the intention of the legislature obvious, great difficulty has been experienced in its effective enforcement. It is everywhere agreed that this tenement-house, or "sweat-shop," system is degrading to the unfortunate individuals engaged in it, and to the social and moral life of the community in which it exists. How to enforce the law on this subject has perplexed the statesmen of other countries and States as well as our own.

The most effective and uninquisitive means yet devised for accomplishing this end is that recently adopted by Massachusetts, viz.: providing that buildings used for manufacturing purposes must have a permit or license, such license or permit to be granted only on condition that the appointments of the building fulfil the requirements of the law for manufacturing purposes. These permits or licenses ought to be granted by the Board of Factory Inspectors, who should be held responsible for the proper inspection of the buildings and the enforcement of the law.

There are several reasons why this simple method would be effective. It would at once classify buildings used for manufacturing purposes, as a building so used without a permit would be violating the law. It would prevent much friction, because all requirements of the law would have to be fulfilled before the building was used. This would be a great advantage in the erection of new buildings, as proper conveniences, including accessible fire-escapes, guarded elevators, and other appointments would be required and easily furnished when new buildings were being erected or when old ones were being changed for manufacturing purposes. Nor does this involve any radical innovation. It is simply applying the recognized principle upon which boards of health now everywhere act in requiring that the plans for erecting new buildings or alterations of old ones must be submitted to the building and health departments and a certificate of approval granted, before the building can be erected, alterations made, or the premises occupied. Legitimate manufacturers will not object to this, because they are desirous of furnishing safe and wholesome appointments for their employees. Only those who desire to evade the law and disregard the common demands of sanitation, domestic decency, and wholesome industrial methods will object, and it is these the law desires to reach.

I submit this to the serious consideration of the legislature, and suggest that an amendment to the law embodying this idea be adopted, to the end that the uneconomic, unwholesome, and un-American sweat-shop system shall disappear from our industrial life.

The law requiring an eight-hour day and a prevailing rate of wages for State employees is not intrusted to any authority for enforcement. If this law is to remain on the statute-books, it should be enforced, and, therefore, the legislature should make it the particular business of somebody to enforce it.

A recent decision of the Court of Appeals has decided unconstitutional the law which provides that there shall be a mark on prison-made goods, indicating that they are such. This matter should receive the attention of the legislature in order that some means may be devised whereby the free mechanic shall not be brought into competition with prison labor.

The Bureau of Labor Statistics, the Board of Mediation and Arbitration, and the Factory Inspectors' Department must be brought to the highest standard of efficiency and usefulness. The work of these departments, to report the actual conditions of labor, to seek to establish harmonious relations between labor and capital, and to enforce such labor legislation as has met with the approval of the people of the State, is of supreme importance. The efficiency of their service concerns not only those immediately affected, but also the entire public, and they should receive our prompt and cordial co-operation in every attempt to fulfil their respective duties.

The Bureau of Labor Statistics in collecting the material for its reports has received valuable aid from manufacturers and officers of labor organizations. The reports of the department must be practical, strictly accurate in all statements of fact, and based on investigations conducted in accordance with modern scientific methods.

In various trades the relations between labor and capital have frequently been adjusted to the advantage of both by conferences between intelligent employers and reasonable working men. Such mutual understanding is in the highest degree desirable; it promotes industrial peace and general prosperity. Where disturbance exists, and before it has gone too far, the Board of Mediation and Arbitration should seek to secure a fair settlement of the difficulties and a re-establishment of harmonious relations. It should also constantly endeavor to promote the extension of intelligent methods of settlement of labor disputes so that, through the recognition by each party of the just rights of the other, strikes and lockouts may yield to wiser and more peaceful measures.

THE NATIONAL GUARD

The National Guard of this State requires especial attention. During the past year the guard was suddenly called upon to supply deficiencies in our scheme of national defense, due to the very small size of our Regular Army, which was, and is, totally inadequate to the necessities of the nation, admirable though the army itself is in quality. The emergency was so sudden as to necessitate the calling out of the men of the National Guard regiments, the time to raise and discipline ordinary volunteer regiments being lacking. It is much to be hoped that some well-thought-out plan may be adopted by the National Government for the use of the guard in any future war. It would probably prove wisest to order out the guard for use in the United States, thus freeing the Regular Army for any expedition, at the same time calling for volunteer regiments, into which those guardsmen who wish might go; then, when the volunteer force proper had been put in fair condition, the guard could be ordered home. In other words, the guard should be used as it was in the Civil War, and should not be called out for foreign service. The identity of each organization of the guard should be preserved.

This calling out of the guard to do the work which should have been done by the regulars, and by special volunteer organizations, caused great hardship, and has resulted in much temporary disorganization in the guard itself. The work which the National Guardsmen ought normally to perform, differs entirely from that expected from regulars. All men who are admitted to the National Guard should be physically and morally fit for any soldierly duty; but there are many men who do invaluable service in the guard who ought not to be called upon to serve in long campaigns, unless there is urgent need. For instance, a large number of our most useful guardsmen who gladly give their service to the State are men of small means, business men, mechanics, clerks, and laborers, with families who are dependent upon their exertions. Ordinary service does not interfere in the least with these men's work, and absence from their work for a few weeks to meet a special emergency does not cause any great hardship; but absence on a long campaign means the actual loss of the job, with delay in securing another after the return. This causes wide-spread suffering and hardship. It is right to ask them to perform a short term of duty, but not a long term; and the disinclination to enlist for a long term should not be held to in any way reflect on them. If the country needs the services even of men with families, then, whatever the individual suffering, the service should be freely given; but where the necessity can be met by enlisting some of the tens of thousands of young unmarried men who are eager to volunteer, it is a pity to employ men who can be ill spared. The guard gave conclusive proof of its patriotism by the quickness with which it sought the chance to go to the war. New York has a right to be proud of the way in which her citizen-soldiers sought opportunity to get to the front; and an equal meed of praise attaches to those who were fortunate enough to cross the seas, and those equally devoted and equally patriotic, but less fortunate, soldiers to whom fell the harder task of waiting in camps on American soil through the weary months for the call to action which never came. The volunteers, the National Guardsmen, not only of New York, but of all the United States, have won by their ready response to the country's call the right to full justice, to full recognition of their services, by National and State government alike.

Many of the troops who volunteered gladly for the emergency, now that the war is over are most anxious to return. That they are not all of them able to return is due to the utterly inadequate size of our Regular Army. If our Regular Army is, as it should be, increased to 100,000 men, the hard necessity of retaining in the service the volunteer organizations which should not be retained, will disappear.

A very wise act of the last legistlature has, for the first time, put the organization of the guard in this State on a proper footing. We now have a major-general who is in fact, and not merely in name, the head of the National Guard. The adjutant-general is to work in conjunction with him; he is not an independent officer, still less a superior officer. He can do no more than deliver the orders of the governor and act as his representative. The major-general has the power, and he should be given every possible facility for the exercise of this power. If he fails to do his duty, or fails to bring the guard up to the proper pitch of efficiency, he should be removed and another put in his place; but so long as he is in the office he must be given a free hand. In other words, he must be given full power, so that the responsibility can be settled upon him, and then he should be held responsible for the exercise of this power and responsibility.

I call your especial attention to the arms of the guard. The lamentable result of keeping the guard armed with archaic weapons, utterly unfit for modern warfare, was shown very conclusively in the late contest with Spain. It is an understatement of the case to say that a single first-class regiment, armed with the Krag-Jorgensen, is worth three regiments armed with a low-power, single-shot, black-powder piece like the Springfield. The National Guard should be armed with a small-caliber, high-power rifle, preferably that used by the Regular Army. In any event the cartridge should be the same. The last point is of the utmost importance. All the fighting forces of this country should use the same cartridge. It is a great mistake for the army and the navy to use different rifles, but it is an even greater mistake for the army and the National Guard to use different rifles. The Springfield musket as a modern arm has two drawbacks. First, owing to the limited range, it is of small value against a foe armed with high-power, repeating rifles. Second, owing to the black powder, it is a source of utmost danger to whoever uses it, as the smoke that it makes serves as a target, and the body of men using it immediately become the object of all the hostile fire from every part of the field within range. This was shown not merely by the experience of the National Guard in Cuba, but by the experience of the regular artillery, which also had black-powdered weapons, and which suffered in consequence exactly as the guard did. It has been proposed as a remedy to supply smokeless powder for the present weapon. It is doubtful whether or not this could be done, but if done it would merely render the weapon less dangerous to the user without rendering it much more formidable to the foe. Any such half-measure would be a failure. Our National Guardsmen are entitled to the best type of weapon. In a riot they could probably do the best work with shotguns; but we must have rifles, and these rifles should be of the highest type, and should take the same cartridge that is used by the United States regular troops.

The regimental hospital corps should be kept up, and encouraged. The war with Spain has demonstrated the necessity of the regimental hospital.

The Red Cross, and kindred organizations, have done admirable work for our soldiers during the summer just past. The Red Cross Society should be the right hand of the Medical Department of the army, in peace and war; for even the best medical department will always need volunteer aid in the case either of battles or of camp epidemics. In America the Red Cross should have a Federal organization, with, in every State, chapters which should be in close touch with the National Guard, attending the encampments and forming schools of instruction in military methods. We should then have in this State, for instance, "The Red Cross of the National Guard of New York"; which should be recognized by the National Government.

THE NAVAL MILITIA

The Naval Militia did admirable work in the late war, justifying their existence as completely as the National Guard did. The New York Naval Militia furnished practically the entire crew, and all but two of the highest officers, on board of the war-ship *Yankee*. They were fortunate in having in the person of Commander Bronson one of the most gallant and efficient captains in the United States navy; and they did their duty in first-class style. It would be difficult to parallel in the history of other naval nations what was done in this war by those Naval Militia organizations which, in addition to helping provide for our coast defense, actually furnished the entire crews of four large war-ships, thereby supplying a pressing need, due to the inadequate size of our splendid regular navy. The State should carefully preserve and build up this arm of the service. It must be remembered, however, that it is exactly what its name shows, namely, a Naval Militia, and not a naval reserve. It was called upon in the late war to do duty which should ordinarily be done by the regular navy, or by a proper naval reserve, one composed of seafaring men similar in type to those who actually man our war-ships. The Naval Militia ought normally to be used for coast-defense purposes.

In a war with a more formidable power than Spain it would be highly undesirable to put any part of our naval force to the use for which it is not best fitted, though it may always be necessary to do this if we do not greatly enlarge our regular navy, so that in number of ships and men it may more nearly than at present correspond to the greatness and the needs of the nation. Our Naval Militia should be kept up and built up, but it is to be earnestly hoped that they will be supplemented by a naval reserve proper, called into being by the action of the Federal Government.

THE CIVIL SERVICE

The methods of appointment to the civil service of the State are now in utter confusion, no less than three systems being in effect—one in the city of New York, one in other cities, and one in the State at large. I recommend that a law be passed introducing one uniform practice for the entire State, and providing, as required by the Constitution, for the enforcement of proper civil-service regulations in the State and its subdivisions. This law should be modelled in its essential provisions upon the old civil-service law which was repealed by the civil-service law now upon the statute-books. The inquiries I have made have satisfied me that the present law works badly from every standpoint, and the half-mark given upon the so-called fitness test represents not a competitive examination at all, but the individual preference of the appointing officer, or rather of the outsider who has requested the appointment. It would be much better to have it stated outright that this was the case and that the examination was merely a pass or non-competitive examination, instead of going through the farce of a nominally competitive examination which is not such in reality. Where there is a large list of eligibles, as is the case now on some registers, it is practically impossible for the appointing officer to examine the whole list, and if he tried, it would merely result in a great loss of time to him, and a loss of both time and money to the unfortunate candidates. For the head of a department to try to examine at Albany a list of 300 applicants for a $1,000 clerkship, these applicants coming from all over the State, would mean, if they all came, an expenditure of about $3,000 by them, and the loss of several days by the appointing power. Practically, in the great majority of cases, only the applicants from the neighborhood of Albany come, and in most cases the appointing officer has made up his mind before he examines a man; so that the result is in effect to work a fraud upon men who enter the examination trusting to their own merits and not to favoritism. Where competitive examinations are to be held, they should be competitive in fact and not in name only. Where it appears after trial, or after careful investigation, that competitive examinations will not work well, then the places should be exempted from examination, or pass examinations submitted, the reasons for excepting them being set forth in full. I do not make a fetich of written competitive examinations for admission to the civil service. There are situations where these written competitive examinations are not applicable at all. There are others where they can be used simply as makeshifts; that is, as being better than a system of appointment through political favoritism, but as being very far from perfect, and not as good as if the appointments were made by an unhampered official trying to get the best man without regard to political considerations. Physical examinations, and technical examinations into the capacity of the man to do the work sought, should, wherever advisable, be used to supplement or even to supplant the written examination proper, and this written examination itself should be of as practical a type as possible, and directed to the special needs of the position sought. There is no need of discussing the advantages of the methods which we have grown to group together when we speak of civil-service reform. They have by long experience been proved to work admirably. In the postal service, for instance, the examinations for clerks, letter-carriers, and railway-mail clerks are entirely practical, and the application of the reformed system to the postal service has produced a very great improvement in the character of the work done. In the navy-yards of the nation the benefit resultant upon taking the appointment and retention of navy-yard employees out of the hands of local politicians, and making them consequent upon fitness and good conduct only has resulted in an incredible improvement, not only in the character of the work done, but in saving of expense to the government. Our present navy would not have been able to do its duty in the war with Spain in the way that it actually did, had the government service in the navy-yard not been put upon a merit basis. What has succeeded in these great branches of the national service will surely succeed in the State service if given a proper trial. Let the clerks, stenographers, and the like be appointed as the result of written competitive examinations. Let other employees be appointed after written competitive examinations where possible, and where it is not possible, then let the places be subject to other kinds of competitive examinations, or of non-competitive examinations, or be excepted from examination, in accordance with the actual needs of the service.

The veteran of the Civil War should be legally guaranteed preference in appointment to, and in retention in, office; that is, he should be appointed to any vacancy when he can show his fitness to fill it, and he should not be removed without trial by the appointing officer, at which he can make his defense. There is no intention to condone corruption or pass over inefficiency in a veteran; but, if he is honest and efficient, he is entitled to preference.

OVERLEGISLATION AND BIENNIAL SESSIONS

I invite the attention of the legislature particularly to the evils of overlegislation. The tendency to pass laws which are utterly unnecessary, even when not pernicious or which are enacted purely to favor certain special private interests, seems to grow instead of diminish. It is difficult to devise an efficient check for it, but strenuous efforts should be made to find out and put into operation some such check. The State suffers very much more from overlegislation than it does from lack of legislation. One partial remedy for the evil would be to amend the Constitution so as to provide for biennial sessions of the legislature. The legislature has already passed this proposed amendment once. I recommend that it be passed again this year, in order that it may be submitted to the people next fall. I also advise that an investigation be made of the methods employed in other representative bodies for getting rid of the evil. I direct your attention to the custom of the British Parliament, which puts upon the would-be beneficiary the cost of all private and special legislation, and wisely makes it difficult to obtain at all, and impossible to obtain without full advertisement and discussion. No special law should be passed where passing a general law will serve the purpose.

SCHOOL SUFFRAGE

I call the attention of the legislature to the desirability of gradually extending the sphere in which the suffrage can be exercised by women.

GOOD ROADS

The legislature should see that the excellent movement to better our roads is continued, and that it is conducted primarily in the interests of the farmers and market gardeners.

THE FORESTS OF THE STATE

The forest reserve will be a monument to the wisdom of its founders. It is very important that in acquiring additional land we should not forget that it is even more necessary to preserve what we have already acquired and to protect it, not only against the depredations of man, but against the most serious of all enemies to forests—fire. One or two really great forest-fires might do damage which could not be repaired for a generation. The laws for the protection of the game and the fish of the wilderness seem to be working well, but they should be more rigidly enforced.

ECONOMY

Every effort should be made to reduce the expenses of the State government. Appropriations should be itemized and not, save in rare cases, made in lump sums. All needless offices should be abolished. For instance, the attorney-general's office should do the work now done by the special counsel for the different hospitals for the insane; and these special counsel should be abolished. Wherever possible commissions should be consolidated, and the number of commissioners and of their employees reduced. In the State's charitable work, which is now very expensive, especially as regards the care of the insane, care should be taken not needlessly to multiply institutions nor to erect buildings more costly than is absolutely necessary, and the salary list should be kept down. The economical and efficient administration of these institutions is interfered with by the custom which has grown up of treating each as if it existed for the benefit of the locality in which it exists, whereas of course this is an utterly improper view, as the administration should always be simply in the interest of the State at large. Great improvement has resulted from putting the care of the insane under the control of the State instead of the counties.

UNIVERSITY OF THE STATE OF NEW YORK

For more than a century New York has taken a leading position in fostering secondary and higher education. This work she accomplishes through the agency of her university. The growth of these interests has been specially marked since 1889. Within this decade, though the increase in attendance on our public elementary schools has been less than 20 per cent, there has been an increase of more than 100 per cent in those completing requirements for admission to the high school and of more than 200 per cent in high-school graduates. By setting the standard for graduation from the elementary schools and by providing teachers for these schools the university has been a potent factor in improving the whole school system. In comparison with results attained and with other expenditures the State appropriations for high schools are small. In 1898 the State expended about $150 for each convict in her prisons, and $185.31 for each lunatic in her asylums. The cost to the State of each student in her high schools was $4.45.

In the medical schools of New York are nearly one-fifth of all the medical students in the United States. In her law schools are fully one-quarter of all the law students. In other higher educational lines she is equally prominent. The standards for admission to the professions, which are recognized as the highest in the country, are determined by the university.

The reputation of the university has been increased by the valuable work of its museum, its paleontologist, botanist, and entomologist. Important original research in these fields has added to the knowledge of the natural history and of the resources of the State.

The New York State Library, another department of the university, has more than doubled its efficiency within the past ten years, and is an inspiration to intellectual life throughout the State. Through its local public libraries, its travelling libraries, its valuable photographic reproductions which are sent from school to school, and its other facilities for home education, it comes in direct contact with every class of the community.

The State owes loyal support to an organization which so guards and unites her most vital interests.

RAPID TRANSIT IN NEW YORK CITY

I call the attention of the legislature to the need of improved facilities for rapid transit in the city of New York. As the city extends, the need for the establishment of an improved system of rapid transit becomes more and more imperative, and the legislature should take every means to find out the best system to adopt.

ECONOMY IN NEW YORK'S MUNICIPAL GOVERNMENT

In New York City, even more than in the State, there is need of cutting down the salaries of certain officials, of forcing others to do more work, and of altogether getting rid of yet others. I suggest that you investigate carefully whether there is need to retain in existence such offices as those of the chamberlain of the city and the special commissioner of jurors; whether the fees given to the sheriffs of the county of New York and of the county of Kings, and the county clerk and register of Kings should not be turned into the counties, salaries being allowed the officials in their stead; and whether the judges of the municipal courts of the city should not be required to sit every day, so that working men who are the chief patrons of these courts, in such suits as those for the payment of wages, may not be compelled to lose day after day in attendance. Very many clerkships, inspectorships, and positions held by deputies could be abolished. The evils of the police system in New York have become very serious; I may find it necessary to communicate with you again on this matter.

SUGGESTION REGARDING SMALL CITIES

Of an interest and importance secondary only to that of the Greater New York are the cities of the second and third classes. Owing to their relative unimportance when taken singly, their needs have often been overlooked. While the condition of each of these cities differs from that of the others, all have substantially the same problems to solve, and the experience of each should be readily available for all. Practical students of municipal affairs, as represented by the city officials who form the League of American Municipalities and by the New York Senate committee on cities in the so-called Fassett Report, have urged as a matter of the greatest importance for good government in cities a uniform system of accounting. Foreign countries in which municipal government has been most successful have invariably provided some means to secure uniformity of accounting and a general interchange of information. The commissions on second and third class cities in 1896, recommended for this State an advisory board for cities of the second and third classes, and I venture to urge upon you the consideration of the establishment of an unsalaried State municipal board which shall have no coercive power in shaping the policy of any city, but which shall have for its duties the securing of uniformity of accounting systems in the cities of the second and third classes, the publishing of information regarding the work and conditions of these cities, besides also the duty of examining bills regarding them which are presented to the legislature, and of making recommendations concerning legislative action upon them. Probably no other measure could be of so great assistance to these cities in the way of stimulating local pride and securing active local self-government.

SECRETARY OF STATE

In the secretary of state's office 8,000 corporation papers have been filed during the past year, including certificates of incorporation, of which 414, exclusive of real-estate corporations, are stock corporations. This increase in the volume of business transacted, necessarily means a corresponding increase of the sums turned into the State treasury, for the organization tax on corporations. It is a curious fact that during the last fiscal year a large number of claims have been filed for gold and silver mines in this State.

COMPTROLLER

The report of the comptroller shows a very large increase in the revenue from indirect taxes during the last fiscal year. The amounts received from the organization and corporation tax for the fiscal year ending September 30, 1898, exceeded the amount received during the preceding fiscal year by the sum of $84,934.22. The amounts received from the tax on inheritances during the fiscal year ending September 30, 1898, exceeded the amount received during the preceding fiscal year by $167,268.41. The amounts received from the sale of liquors, under the excise law, exceeded the amount received during the preceding fiscal year by $212,922.71. These figures are of peculiar interest, because the amounts received represent a decrease in the burden of taxation upon those least able to contribute to the necessary revenues of the State.

STATE TREASURER

Notwithstanding the extraordinary expenditures, necessarily incurred by reason of the recent war with Spain, a large balance, to wit: the sum of $3,973,804.45, still remained in the State treasury at the end of the last fiscal year.

ATTORNEY-GENERAL

The report of the attorney-general shows the increased business conducted through his department. It is gratifying to note that claims against the State have been reduced by reason of judicious management.

SUPERINTENDENT OF PUBLIC INSTRUCTION

During the past year the sum of $29,515,935 has been expended for public schools under the jurisdiction of this department. Of this amount $4,027,615 was appropriated by the legislature and the $25,488,320 was raised by local taxation. These large expenditures for public education show that the people of the State fully appreciate the importance of their public-school system and do not hesitate to make liberal provision for its support.

The results of the compulsory-attendance law are surprising. The aggregate days' attendance for the school year was 56,000,000, or a gain of nearly 2,000,000 over the previous year, which, I am informed, can be almost directly shown to be the result of this law. It is suggested that, inasmuch as many of the statutes relating to public schools are conflicting and confusing, "the school law" should be revised and simplified.

DEPARTMENT OF BANKS

The report of the superintendent of banks shows an apparently healthy condition among our banks, savings-banks, trust companies, and other kindred institutions which are within the peculiar province of the Banking Department. The legislature will note with pleasure that there has been a very large increase during the last fiscal year in the number of depositors and in the amounts deposited in our savings institutions. This shows that business has revived throughout the State, and that thrift has correspondingly increased among our people.

SUPERINTENDENT OF STATE PRISONS

Satisfactory results appear to have succeeded the enactment of the law, relating to the products of prison industries, which went into effect January 1, 1897.

During the past year the health of the convicts has been generally good and the death-rate small; it would appear, however, that the condition of the cells in the several prisons is a matter to which the attention of the legislature should be directed. Auburn Prison was built in 1817, Sing Sing in 1825, and Clinton, although of later date, was built upon the same general plans as the other two, in relation to its cells. It would almost seem that the time had come when these cells should be renovated and placed in a more sanitary and healthful condition. This work could be done by the convicts, at small expense to the State for material.

RAILROAD COMMISSIONERS

The work of the board of railroad commissioners has more than doubled during the past year. The legislature of 1898 appropriated the sum of $100,000, for the purpose of defraying the State's share of the expense for the abolition of those crossings at which steam railroads cross public highways at grade. The importance of protecting the travelling public against accident at grade crossings is shown by the fact that during the year ending June 30, 1898, 102 persons were killed and 113 injured at such crossings. It would seem that an amount equal to that appropriated last year should be again appropriated this year.

DEPARTMENT OF AGRICULTURE

The work done by the commissioner of agriculture, in the matter of adulteration, shows that the enforcement of the provisions of law, relating to farm and dairy products, has greatly increased the volume and size of plants, and the aggregate value of productions. The beneficent result to the farmer of these laws is shown by the largely increased production of milk, and particularly of cheese, during the last year, an increase which is certainly in part due to wise legislation, although of course the chief credit must be given to the industry, energy, and shrewd foresight of the farmers themselves.

Upward of twenty-five per cent of our population till the soil as a means of livelihood; and they form the foundation and mainstay of the Commonwealth. They pay a large percentage of the taxes, in proportion to their means. Few of their number are found in penal or charitable institutions. They are intelligent, hard-working, and deeply patriotic. They do not look for aid from the State to carry on their ordinary avocations. Indeed, it is doubtful if they would approve any special legislation in their favor; all they ask is protection against improper competition and improper legislation. It is within the province of the legislature to see that the cost of transportation of farm and garden products is not excessive; that vitiated compounds and adulterations be not permitted; and that those public servants especially charged with caring for the health of the State be provided with all necessary appliances to prevent the spread of disease among cattle, or among fruit, vegetables, and cereals, and to inquire as to noxious insects, which so often overrun and destroy the results of the husbandsman's labor. It is especially on their behalf that every effort should be made to reduce taxation and to secure the utmost economy in administration.

THE EXCISE LAW

The present excise law has proved to be the best revenue-raising law on the statute-book. One of its gratifying features is the fact that, compared with the old law which it supplanted, it is administered by a very small number of officials, while bringing in so much more revenue.

GENERAL

The various heads of other departments, such as Public Works, Public Buildings, State Engineer and Surveyor, Fisheries, Forest and Game, State Board of Health, Civil Service Commission, State Tax Commission, Bureau of Labor Statistics, State Commission in Lunacy, State Hospitals for Insane, State Reformatories, and other penal and eleemosynary institutions, will in due time make their several detailed reports to the legislature, and I invite your careful attention to these reports, when they are received, to the end, that if defects are found in the systems of administration, there may be proper remedial legislation.

III

ANNUAL MESSAGE[1]

TO THE LEGISLATURE OF THE STATE OF NEW YORK:
It is a very genuine pleasure to congratulate the legislature upon the substantial sum of achievement in legislation and administration of the past year. Laws of the utmost usefulness to the community have been enacted, and there has been a steady betterment throughout the year in the methods and results of the administration of the government.

CANALS

The first matter which had to be dealt with on the incoming of the new administration was the question of the canals. New York State led the Union in the development of canal navigation. Of recent years the change in the methods of transportation, by immensely increasing the railroad competition with the canal, has greatly altered the conditions of successful administration of the latter. There were really two questions to be solved in reference to the canals. The first was as to their administration; the second as to the general canal policy of the State in the future. A very slight examination showed that as regards the latter there were not sufficient data to warrant the formulation of an intelligent policy. A commission appointed by my predecessor to examine into the conditions which make for the commercial supremacy of the State, was still sitting. This commission was continued. The subject with which it dealt was of so vast and of such vital importance that it has not yet been able to complete its labors; and it was evident it would not have time to consider the canal

[1] Dated, Executive Chamber, Albany, January 3, 1900.

30

problem in the way that was desirable. I accordingly appointed a committee consisting of General Francis V. Greene, of New York, Mr. Frank S. Witherbee, of Port Henry, Major Symons, of the U. S. army, Mr. John P. Scatchard, of Buffalo, and ex-Mayor George E. Green, of Binghamton, to examine the whole canal question. Their report will be ready in about a fortnight, and will be submitted to the legislature with a special message, probably submitting at the same time the report of the Commerce Commission. I wish to call attention to the fact that the gentlemen serving on these two bodies are business men, whose lives are filled with exacting duties; yet they have given, unpaid, months of their valuable time and their best thought and effort to the solution of these problems. Such disinterested expert service is of incalculable value to the State, and makes it greatly the debtor to the men rendering the service. The conduct of these two commissions, and of the Commission on the Educational Bill emphasizes one of the most pleasing features of our public life, viz.: the readiness with which able and high-minded private citizens will do special public work when they are convinced of its necessity from the public standpoint.

There remained the question of the proper administration of the canals. Very grave accusations had been made against the former canal management; accusations which varied from charges of mere inefficiency and bad judgment, to charges of wholesale personal corruption, criminal in its character.

Such being the conditions, there were two things to be done: first, to secure by the employment of the best counsel an investigation which would be final and complete, and determine whether it were possible to proceed criminally against any contractor or public employee; and, second, if there had been no criminal misconduct, but if there had been failure to manage the canals so as to secure the best results for the State then, to provide a thorough and radical change in the management. These were the only two lines on which action could be taken. On both of them action was taken. On the one hand, the investigation was so conducted as to leave no room for any further question as to criminal proceedings; and, on the other hand, the reformation in the methods of management has been so complete as to leave nothing to be done save to continue and perfect the new system.

As a result of the reports made to my predecessor in office by the commission appointed by him to make an investigation concerning the work of improving and enlarging the canals under the acts of 1895 and 1896, commonly known as the "Nine Million Dollar Acts," the accusation against the then existing canal management had been resolved into two categories.

In the first place it was asserted that there had been on the part of the outgoing State engineer and surveyor and of the former superintendent of public works, malfeasance and misfeasance in office which called for the criminal prosecution of themselves, of their subordinates, and of certain contractors. This was a legal question, for if guilty, their punishment could come only through the courts, inasmuch as they were out of office. The ordinary machinery of the law was set in motion by the attorney-general with the purpose of securing the punishment of any delinquent. In almost any other case, in view of the zeal with which the attorney-general was carrying on these prosecutions, I should not have deemed it necessary to take any extraordinary action. But the charges were so grave and had been given such wide-spread publicity that I felt warranted in asking the assistance of the legislature to enable me to take steps that would guarantee beyond all possibility of doubt the prosecution and punishment of any criminal who could be discovered by rigorous and searching investigation.

Accordingly, I appointed Mr. Austen G. Fox and Mr. Wallace Macfarlane, of New York, well-known members of the bar, of opposite political faith to the accused, and the latter United States district attorney in New York under President Cleveland, to assist the attorney-general in the institution and prosecution of such criminal proceedings as should be warranted by the testimony taken by the Investigating Commission and the reports made thereupon to my predecessor. The legislature appropriated $20,000 to pay the expenses of the investigation. After working for several months, counsel reported to me that, in their opinion, on the evidence obtainable by them, criminal prosecutions were inadvisable and impracticable. In the absence of evidence of fraudulent collusion between the State officers and the contractors, counsel concluded that the numerous instances of apparently unjustifiable favoritism to contractors, and of improvident agreements, reported by the commission, could not be said to be of a criminal character, though they did subject the State to a large pecuniary loss, and apparently showed grave deliquency on the part of those charged with the execution of the work. The delinquency shown justified public indignation; but it did not afford ground for criminal prosecution.

The special counsel stated at length their reasons for their conclusions, and the report is herewith transmitted to you.

There is probably no lawyer of high standing in the State who, after studying the report of counsel in this case and the testimony taken by the Investigating Commission, would disagree with them as to the impracticability of a successful prosecution. Under such circumstances the one remedy was a thorough change in the methods and management. This change has been made.

The new superintendent has managed the canals with the care and skill which would be expected in a private business enterprise. It is unnecessary to say that the highest standard of integrity has been demanded. There has been no toleration whatever of inefficiency, and no retention of any man who filled a needless position or who filled unworthily a necessary position. The season of 1899 was one of unusual activity on the canals; but the good effect of the new superintendent's administration was made strikingly evident when, at the close of the fiscal year on October 1st, the accounts were made up. For the last eight months of the fiscal year ending October

1, 1899, although more business was done, the canals were run at a cost of about $450,000 as against about $590,000 for the same eight months of the preceding year, a net saving of nearly $140,000, or about twenty-five per cent. No work has been entered upon or permitted for any cause whatsoever save the needs of the canals. No man has been appointed save when it appeared that there was actual need of his services and that he could ably and honestly perform the duties of the place sought. No man who did his duty well has been jeopardized in his position; and no man known to have failed in his duty has been retained. In short, the canals have been managed with an eye single to the public good.

THE CANAL BOARD

Under chapter 544, Laws of 1899, providing for the termination of certain of the outstanding contracts aggregating upward of $4,000,000, contractors representing contracts aggregating upward of $2,350,000 made application to the Canal Board for their termination. Before "finding and determining what amounts were properly due," a committee of the Canal Board consisting of the comptroller, the attorney-general, the State engineer, and the superintendent of public works was appointed to examine and report upon the status of the contracts for the termination of which application had been made. The conditions surrounding every contract were carefully examined. Reference was made to the report of the Canal Investigating Commission, to the report of the engineers to the commission, and to the original testimony upon which the report of the Investigating Commission was based; also to the reports of Messrs. Fox and Macfarlane, and Mr. Shove. The contracts, specifications, and agreements for extra work were carefully scrutinized, and all the attending circumstances were considered as they actually existed.

TAXATION

The whole problem of taxation is now, as it has been at almost all times and in almost all places, one of extreme difficulty. It has become more and more evident in recent years that existing methods of taxation, which worked well enough in a simpler state of society, are not adequate to secure justice when applied to the conditions of our complex and highly specialized modern industrial development. At present the real-estate owner is certainly bearing an excessive proportion of the tax burden. Men who have made a special study of the theory of taxation and men who have had long experience in its practical application are alike in conflict among themselves as to the best general system. Absolute equality, absolute justice in matters of taxation will probably never be realized; but we can approximate it much more closely than at present. The last legislature most wisely appointed a committee to consider the feasibility of a thorough and far-reaching change in our tax laws; and there is good reason to believe that their forthcoming report will present a scheme which will receive the support of substantially all classes of taxpayers, and which will be of such a character as to commend itself to the most careful consideration of your body upon broad lines.

The law must not only be correct in the abstract; it must work well in the concrete. Experience shows that certain classes or symbols of property which in theory ought to be taxed cannot under the present practice be reached. Some kinds of taxes are so fertile in tempting to perjury and sharp dealing that they amount to taxes on honesty—the last quality on which we should impose a needless burden. Moreover, where the conditions and complexity of life vary widely as between different communities, the desirability and possibility of certain taxes may seem or be so different that it is hard to devise a common system that will work. If possible the State tax should be levied on classes of property, and in a manner which will render it collectible with entire fairness in all sec-

tions of the community, as, for instance, the corporation or
collateral inheritance tax is now collected. So far as possible
we should divorce the State and municipal taxes, so as to
render unnecessary the annual equalization of values between
the several counties which has proved so fertile a source of
friction between the city and the country.

There is a constant influx into New York State of capital
ofttimes previously incorporated under the laws of other
States, and an increasing number of men of means from other
parts of the country, non-residents of New York, come into
this State to sojourn and to conduct and be at the head of
various business enterprises which are drawn to New York as
the financial centre of the whole country. This calls for legislation which shall provide, in a broad and fair spirit, for tax-
ing foreign capital in this State, whether in corporate or individual form, exactly as we tax domestic capital doing business
along the same lines.

I call your attention to the fact that the great burden of
taxation is local, not State. In the large cities the heavy local
charges are mainly due to the action of the local authorities
themselves. For this the local authorities are of course responsible. But sometimes taxation is added to by legislative enactment.

On certain points the failure of the tax laws has become so
evident that it is possible to provide more or less complete
remedies without waiting for a general scheme of reorganization. Again and again in recent years this has been recognized, and through legislative enactment certain species of
property which had escaped taxation have been made to pay
their proper share of the public burdens. The collateral inheritance tax offers a case in point. The corporation tax offers
another. In all these matters of taxation, however, it is necessary to proceed with extreme caution, the path never being so
simple and clear as the advocates of any particular measure
invariably believe. Every wealthy corporation that perpe-
trates or is allowed to perpetrate a wrong helps to produce or

inflame a condition of angry excitement against all corporations, which in its turn may in the end harm alike the honest and the dishonest agents of public service, and thereby do far-reaching damage to the whole body politic. Much of the outcry against wealth, against the men who acquire wealth, and against the means by which it is acquired, is blind, unreasoning, and unjust; but in too many cases it has a basis in real abuses; and we must remember that every act of misconduct which affords any justification for this clamor is not only bad because of the wrong done, but also because the justification thus given inevitably strengthens movements which are in reality profoundly antisocial and anticivic. Our laws should be so drawn as to protect and encourage corporations which do their honest duty by the public; and to discriminate sharply against those organized in a spirit of mere greed, or for improper speculative purposes.

There is plenty of misconduct, plenty of selfish disregard of the rights of others, and especially of the weak. There is also plenty of honorable and disinterested effort to prevent such misconduct or to minimize its effects. Any rational attempt to prevent or counteract the evils, by legislation or otherwise, is deserving of hearty support; but it cannot be too deeply impressed upon us that such attempts can result in permanent good only in proportion as they are made in a sane and wholesome spirit, as far removed as possible from whatever is hysterical or revolutionary. It is infinitely better when needed social and civic changes can be brought about as the result of natural and healthy growth than when they come with the violent dislocation and wide-spread wreck and damage inevitably attendant upon any movement which is revolutionary in its nature.

THE FRANCHISE TAX

At the same time a change should never be shirked on the ground of its being radical, when the abuse has become flagrant and no other remedy appears possible. This was the case with the taxation of local franchises in this State. For years most of these franchises escaped paying their proper share of the public burdens. The last legislature placed on the statute-book a law requiring them to be treated as real estate for the purposes of taxation, the tax to be assessed and collected by the State assessors for the benefit of the localities concerned. This marks an immense stride in advance. Of course, at first, serious difficulties are sure to arise in enforcing it. The means for carrying it into effect are very inadequate. There may be delay before we get from it the substantial additions to the revenue which will finally accrue, and there may be disappointment to the enthusiasts who are so apt to hope too much from such legislation. But it will undoubtedly add largely to the public revenues as soon as it is fairly in operation, and the amount thus added will increase steadily year by year. The principle which this law establishes has come to stay. There will doubtless have to be additional legislation from time to time to perfect the system as its shortcomings are made evident in actual practice. But the corporations owning valuable public franchises must pay their full and proper share of the public burdens.

The franchise tax law is framed with the intent of securing exact and equal justice, no more and no less. It is not in any way intended as a means for persecuting or oppressing corporations. It is not intended to cut down legitimate dividends; still less to cut down wages or to prevent a just return for the far-sighted business skill of some captain of industry who has been able to establish a public service greatly to the advantage of the localities concerned, where before his time men of less business capacity had failed. But it is intended that property which derives its value from the grant of a privilege by the public shall be taxed proportionately to the value of the privilege granted. In enforcing this law, much tact, patience, resolution, and judgment will be needed. All these qualities the State Board of Tax Commissioners have thus far shown. Their salaries are altogether inadequate, for the new law has immensely increased not only their responsibilities, but their work. They should be given not only the needed increase for themselves, but also an appropriation for an additional number of clerks and experts.

During the year 1899 not a single corporation has received at the hands of the State of New York one privilege of any kind, sort, or description, by law or otherwise, to which it was not entitled, and which was not in the public interest; nor has corporate influence availed against any measure which was in the public interest. At certain times, and in certain places, corporations have undoubtedly exerted a corrupting influence in political life; but in this State for this year it is absolutely true, as shown by the history of every measure that has come before the legislature from the franchise tax down, that no corporate influence has been able to prevail against the interests of the public.

THE STATE AND PUBLIC UTILITIES

It has become more and more evident of late years that the State will have to act in its collective capacity as regards certain subjects which we have been accustomed to treat as matters affecting the private citizen only, and that furthermore, it must exercise an increasing and more rigorous control over other matters which it is not desirable that it should directly manage. It is neither possible nor desirable to lay down a general hard-and-fast rule as to what this control should be in all cases. There is no possible reason in pure logic why a city, for instance, should supply its inhabitants with water, and allow private companies to supply them with gas, any more than there is why the general government should take charge of the delivery of letters but not of telegrams. On the other hand, pure logic has a very restricted application to actual social and civic life, and there is no possible reason for changing from one system to the other simply because the change would make our political system in theory more symmetrical. Obviously it is undesirable that the government should do anything that private individuals could do with better results to the community. Everything that tends to deaden individual initiative is to be avoided, and unless in a given case there is some very evident gain which will flow from State or municipal ownership, it should not be adopted. On the other hand, when private ownership entails grave abuses, and where the work is of a kind that can be performed with efficiency by the State or municipality acting in its collective capacity, no theory or tradition should interfere with our making the change. There is grave danger in attempting to establish invariable rules; indeed it may be that each case will have to be determined upon its own merits. In one instance a private corporation may be able to do the work best. In another the State or city may do it best. In yet a third, it may be to the advantage of everybody to give free scope to the power of some individual captain of industry.

On one point there must be no step backward. There is a consensus of opinion that New York must own its own water-supply. Any legislation permitting private ownership should be annulled.

MODERN INDUSTRIAL CONDITIONS

Nothing needs closer attention, nothing deserves to be treated with more courage, caution, and sanity, than the relations of the State to corporate wealth, and indeed to vast individual wealth. For almost every gain there is a penalty, and the great strides in the industrial upbuilding of the country, which have on the whole been attended with marked benefit, have also been attended by no little evil. Great fortunes are usually made under very complex conditions both of effort and of surrounding, and the mere fact of the complexity makes it difficult to deal with the new conditions thus created. The contrast offered in a highly specialized industrial community between the very rich and the very poor is exceedingly distressing, and while under normal conditions the acquirement of wealth by an individual is necessarily of great incidental benefit to the community as a whole, yet this is by no means always the case. In our great cities there is plainly in evidence much wealth contrasted with much poverty, and some of the wealth has been acquired, or is used, in a manner for which there is no moral justification.

A profound political and social thinker has recently written: "Wealth which is expended in multiplying and elaborating real comforts, or even in pleasures which produce enjoyment at all proportionate to their cost, will never excite serious indignation. It is the colossal waste of the means of human happiness in the most selfish and most vulgar forms of social advertisement and competition that gives a force to passions which menace the whole future of our civilization." But in continuance this writer points out that the only effectual check lies in the law of public opinion. Any attempt to interfere by statute in moral questions of this kind, by fettering the freedom of individual action, would be injurious to a degree far greater than is the evil aimed at. Probably the large majority of the fortunes that now exist in this country have been amassed, not by injuring mankind, but as an incident to the conferring of great benefits on the community—whatever the conscious purpose of those amassing them may have been. The occasional wrongs committed or injuries endured are on the whole far outweighed by the mass of good which has resulted. The true questions to be asked are: Has any given individual been injured by the acquisition of wealth by any man? Were the rights of that individual, if they have been violated, insufficiently protected by law? If so, these rights, and all similar rights, ought to be guaranteed by additional legislation. The point to be aimed at is the protection of the individual against wrong, not the attempt to limit and hamper the acquisition and output of wealth.

It is almost equally dangerous either to blink evils and refuse to acknowledge their existence, or to strike at them in a spirit of ignorant revenge, thereby doing far more harm than is remedied. The need can be met only by careful study of conditions, and by action which while taken boldly and without hesitation is neither heedless nor reckless. It is well to remember on the one hand that the adoption of what is reasonable in the demands of reformers is the surest way to prevent the adoption of what is unreasonable; and on the other hand that many of the worst and most dangerous laws which have been put upon statute-books have been put there by zealous reformers with excellent intentions.

TRUSTS

This problem has a hundred phases. The relation of the capitalist and the wage-worker makes one; the proper attitude of the State toward extreme poverty another; the proper attitude of the State toward the questions of the ownership and running of so-called "public utilities" a third. But among all these phases, the one which at this time has the greatest prominence, is the question of what are commonly termed "trusts," meaning by the name those vast combinations of capital, usually flourishing by virtue of some monopolistic element, which have become so startlingly common a feature in the industrial revolution which has progressed so rapidly during recent years.

Every new feature of this industrial revolution produces hardship because in its later stages it has been literally a revolution instead of an evolution. The new inventions and discoveries and the new methods of taking advantage of the business facilities afforded by the extraordinary development of our material civilization have caused the changes to proceed with such marvellous rapidity, that at each stage some body of workers finds itself unable to accommodate itself to the new conditions with sufficient speed to escape hardship. In the end the accommodation of the class takes place; at times too late for the well-being of many individuals. The change which would be unaccompanied by hardship if it came slowly may be fraught with severe suffering if it comes too fast, even when it is in the end beneficial. Occasionally, moreover, the change is positively deleterious, and very often, even when it is on the whole beneficial, it has features which are the reverse. In some cases, while recognizing the evil, it is impossible with our present knowledge to discover any remedy. In others, a remedy can be applied, but as yet only at a cost that would make it worse than the trouble itself. In yet others it is possible, by acting with wisdom, coolness, and fearlessness, to apply a remedy which will wholly or in great part remove the evil while leaving the good behind. We do not wish to discourage enterprise. We do not desire to destroy corporations; we do desire to put them fully at the service of the State and the people.

The machinery of modern business is so vast and complicated that great caution must be exercised in introducing radical changes for fear the unforeseen effects may take the shape of wide-spread disaster. Moreover, much that is complained about is not really the abuse so much as the inevitable development of our modern industrial life. We have moved far away from the old simple days when each community transacted almost all its work for itself and relied upon outsiders for but a fraction of the necessaries, and for not a very large portion even of the luxuries, of life. Very many of the anti-trust laws which have made their appearance on the statute-books of recent years have been almost or absolutely ineffective because they have blinked the all-important fact that much of what they thought to do away with was incidental to modern industrial conditions, and could not be eliminated unless we were willing to turn back the wheels of modern progress by also eliminating the forces which had brought about these industrial conditions. Not only trusts, but the immense importance of machinery, the congestion of city life, the capacity to make large fortunes by speculative enterprises, and many other features of modern existence could be thoroughly changed by doing away with steam and electricity; but the most ardent denouncer of trusts would hesitate to advocate so drastic a remedy. What remains for us to do, as practical men, is to look the conditions squarely in the face and not to permit the emotional side of the question, which has its proper place, to blind us to the fact that there are other sides. We must set about finding out what the real abuses are, with their causes, and to what extent remedies can be applied.

That abuses exist, and that they are of a very grave char-acter, it is worse than idle to deny. Just so long as in the business world unscrupulous cunning is allowed the free rein which, thanks to the growth of humanity during the past centuries, we now deny to unscrupulous physical force, then just so long there will be a field for the best effort of every honest social and civic reformer who is capable of feeling an impulse of generous indignation and who is far-sighted enough to appreciate where the real danger to the country lies. The effects are bad enough when the unscrupulous individual works by himself. They are much worse when he works in conjunction with his fellows through a giant corporation or trust. Law is largely crystallized custom, largely a mass of remedies which have been slowly evolved to meet the wrongs with which humanity has become thoroughly familiar. In a simple society only simple forms of wrong can be committed. There is neither the ability nor the opportunity to inflict others. A primitive people provides for the punishment of theft, assault, and murder, because the conditions of the ex-isting society allow the development of thieves and murderers and the commission of deeds of violence; but it does not pro-vide for the punishment of forgery because there is nothing to forge, and, therefore, no forgers. The gradual growth of humanitarian sentiment, often unconscious or but semicon-scious, combined with other causes, step by step emancipated the serf from bodily subjection to his overlord; he was then protected in his freedom by statute; but when he became a factory hand the conditions were new, and there were no laws which prevented the use of unguarded machinery in the fac-tories, or the abuses of child labor, forced upon the conscien-tious employers by the unscrupulous until legislation put them on an equality. When new evils appear there is always at first difficulty in finding the proper remedy; and as the evils grow more complex, the remedies become increasingly difficult of application. There is no use whatever in seeking to apply a remedy blindly; yet this is just what has been done in reference to trusts.

Much of the legislation not only proposed but enacted against trusts is not one whit more intelligent than the mediæval bull against the comet, and has not been one particle more effective. Yet there can and must be courageous and effective remedial legislation.

To say that the present system, of haphazard license and lack of supervision and regulation, is the best possible is absurd. The men who endeavor to prevent the remedying of real abuses, not only show callous disregard for the suffering of others, but also weaken those who are anxious to prevent the adoption of indiscriminate would-be remedies which would subvert our whole industrial fabric. The chicanery and the dishonest, even though not technically illegal, methods through which some great fortunes have been made, are scandals to our civilization. The man who by swindling or wrong-doing acquires great wealth for himself at the expense of his fellow, stands as low morally as any predatory mediæval nobleman and is a more dangerous member of society. Any law, and any method of construing the law which will enable the community to punish him, either by taking away his wealth or by imprisonment, should be welcomed. Of course, such laws are even more needed in dealing with great corporations or trusts than with individuals. They are needed quite as much for the sake of honest corporations as for the sake of the public. The corporation that manages its affairs honestly has a right to demand protection against the dishonest corporation. We do not wish to put any burden on honest corporations. Neither do we wish to put an unnecessary burden of responsibility on enterprising men for acts which are immaterial; they should be relieved from such burdens, but held to a rigid financial accountability for acts that mislead the upright investor or stockholder, or defraud the public.

The first essential is knowledge of the facts, publicity. Much can be done at once by amendment of the corporation laws so as to provide for such publicity as will not work injustice as between business rivals.

The chief abuses alleged to arise from trusts are probably the following: Misrepresentation or concealment regarding material facts connected with the organization of an enterprise; the evils connected with unscrupulous promotion; overcapitalization; unfair competition, resulting in the crushing out of competitors who themselves do not act improperly; raising of prices above fair competitive rates; the wielding of increased power over the wage-earners. Of course, none of these abuses may exist in a particular trust, but in many trusts, as well as in many corporations not ordinarily called trusts, one or more of them are evident. Some of these evils could be partially remedied by a modification of our corporation laws; here we can safely go along the lines of the more conservative New England States, and probably not a little farther. Such laws will themselves provide the needed publicity and the needed circumstantiality of statement. We should know authoritatively whether stock represents actual value of plants, or whether it represents brands or good-will; or if not, what it does represent, if anything. It is desirable to know how much was actually bought, how much was issued free, and to whom; and, if possible, for what reason. In the first place, this would be invaluable in preventing harm being done as among the stockholders, for many of the grossest wrongs that are perpetrated are those of promoters and organizers at the expense of the general public who are invited to take shares in business organizations. In the next place, this would enable us to see just what the public have a right to expect in the way of service and taxation. There is no reason whatever for refusing to tax a corporation because by its own acts it has created a burden of charges under which it staggers. The extravagant man who builds a needlessly large house nevertheless pays taxes on the house; and the corporation which has to pay great sums of interest owing to juggling transactions in the issue of stocks and bonds has just as little right to consideration. But very great hardship may result to innocent purchasers, and publicity by lessening the possibility of this would also serve the purpose of the State.

Where a trust becomes a monopoly the State has an immediate right to interfere. Care should be taken not to stifle enterprise or disclose any facts of a business that are essentially private; but the State for the protection of the public should exercise the right to inspect, to examine thoroughly all the workings of great corporations just as is now done with banks; and wherever the interests of the public demand it, it should publish the results of its examination. Then, if there are inordinate profits, competition or public sentiment will give the public the benefit in lowered prices; and if not, the power of taxation remains. It is therefore evident that publicity is the one sure and adequate remedy which we can now invoke. There may be other remedies, but what these others are we can only find out by publicity, as the result of investigation. The first requisite is knowledge, full and complete.

LABOR

I call the attention of the legislature to the reports of the State Board of Mediation and Arbitration, of the commissioner of labor statistics, and of the State factory inspector. During the past year very valuable labor measures have been enacted into laws, and they are well enforced. I am happy to say that in speaking of labor legislation I can talk mainly of performance—not of promise. Additional legislation will undoubtedly from time to time become necessary; but many vitally needed laws have already been put upon the statute-books. As experience shows their defects, these will be remedied. A stringent eight-hour labor law has been enacted. This is working well as a whole.

In nothing do we need to exercise cooler judgment than in labor legislation. Such legislation is absolutely necessary, alike from the humanitarian and the industrial standpoints, and it is as much our duty to protect the weaker wage-workers from oppression as to protect helpless investors from fraud. But we must beware above all things of that injudicious and ill-considered benevolence which usually in the long run defeats its own ends. To discourage industry and thrift ultimately amounts to putting a premium on poverty and shiftlessness. It is neither of benefit to the individual nor to society needlessly to handicap superior ability and energy, and to reduce their possessor to the level of work and gain suited for his less able and energetic rivals.

There have been a large number of strikes for increase of wages during the past year. The fact that these strikes were not against a reduction, but for an increase, is due to the prosperous condition of the country and State generally. The services of the present excellent Board of Mediation and Arbitration have been in almost constant demand, and they have been gratifyingly successful. The number of controversies amicably adjusted directly and indirectly through its influence has been greater than that during any year since its creation. The work of mediation—that is, of settling the dispute before it has reached an acute stage—is even more important and successful than that of arbitration proper, after the strike is once on. This being so, it would be well to enact legislation which would compel parties to labor disputes to notify the board of impending trouble, or of strikes and lockouts.

The experiment of publishing a quarterly bulletin by the Bureau of Labor Statistics has worked excellently, and the bulletin should be continued and improved. I suggest that it would be well to define by statute the questions that may legally be asked of manufacturers by this bureau. Abuses have occurred in connection with the employment officers in the larger cities, which are now allowed to violate the law with impunity, the power of punishment lying with the local authorities. It would be well to require the keeper of any employment office to procure a license from the State, as in Minnesota and other States. This license should be granted on the payment of a substantial fee, and the business would thus be restricted to responsible parties and kept under the control of the State administration.

The measures suggested in my message of last year and carried into effect by legislation, increasing the number of factory inspectors, and requiring a license for all shops and rooms where garments are made for general employers, have already greatly increased the efficiency of the Factory Inspectors' Department, and enlarged its service to the public. Too little time has elapsed since the sweat-shop law went into effect, in September, to give a full report of its benefits. As illustrating its efficiency in interfering with sweat-shops I may mention that so far under its provision 4,942 licenses have been granted and 918 refused. These 918 cases represent the sweat-shops which would now have been in operation save for this law and for the way it has been enforced.

I shall not ask for any increase of the number of salaried inspectors this year, but I recommend that the power be given to the governor and to the factory inspector to name, whenever necessary, unsalaried inspectors to undertake special investigation or aid the department at special times. Such assistance would increase the efficiency of the work of the department without imposing added burdens upon the State.

I urge that the legislature give particular attention to the need of reform in the laws governing the tenement-houses. The Tenement House Commission of 1894 declared that, in its opinion, the tenement-house laws needed to be revised as often as once in five years, and I am confident that the improvements in building materials and construction of tenements and the advance in sanitary legislation all demand further modification of existing laws. Probably the best course to follow would be to appoint a commission to present a revised code of tenement-house laws.

Owing to defects in the drug clerks' bill presented last year,

I was unable to sign it. I am, however, in hearty sympathy with the objects sought in the bill. I trust that a satisfactory bill may be presented this year, and shall be glad to give such a bill my approval.

The liability of employers to their employees is now recognized in the laws of most of the great industrial communities of the world. While employers ought not to be burdened to such an extent as to endanger ordinary business transactions, yet the State should, so far as possible, protect those employees engaged in dangerous occupations, and should see that every reasonable provision is taken to guard their rights.

NATIONAL GUARD AND NAVAL MILITIA

I call attention to the report of the adjutant-general on the National Guard and Naval Militia of the State. The new code has worked great improvement. In some matters of organization, notably in reference to the detail of line-officers to serve for a time in staff positions, the organization of the National Guard of New York is ahead of the organization of the United States army.

The Spanish War had resulted in great disorganization of the guard and an immense amount of work had to be done to re-establish it upon an efficient basis. This has been done and the guard has never been more efficient than at present. It is to be hoped that in a comparatively short time the National Government will be in a position to arm the guard with the rifle used in the Regular Army.

During the past year the guard has been called upon to furnish New York's quota of officers for service in the volunteer regiments of the army. All of the officers thus recommended were men who had served in the Spanish War. In making the recommendations the colonels of the fifteen volunteer regiments sent into the service by New York were directed to submit the nominations of the three best men in each of their regiments for the volunteer appointments, the recommendations being based upon youth, character, fitness, intelligence, and demonstrated ability to command. In addition recommendations were sought from other officers who had special knowledge of the personnel of the New York volunteers, and the records of the various candidates were critically examined. The report sent to the secretary of war was based solely upon the records of the officers, no attention being paid any other considerations whatsoever save those of military fitness. Most of those thus recommended were appointed by the President. The rank and file of the guard had within the year sent hundreds of men into the Regular and volunteer army gathered for service in the Philippines.

During the summer of 1899 the first steps have been taken to give the State troops practical work in the field. Regiments were sent to the State camp at Peekskill, and from that point were given marches in the neighborhood of several days' duration with field-equipment only. The State camp at Peekskill when originally constructed represented a great advance, for work in the camp was much better than work in the armory. It no longer stands as it did, for it is of special advantage only to armory-trained troops; but it can still be made of much use. Probably it could best be used for the annual instruction of all of the officers and non-commissioned officers; but it might be a hardship to impose such extra duty on men most of whom are actually engaged in earning their own living. At any rate, the regiments should receive practical instructions by actual marching, cooking, camping, sanitation, outpost duties, and field-exercises over rough country. Soldiers must be able to take care of themselves under the conditions of a campaign, and this they cannot learn unless they cook their own food, pitch their own tents, and perform for themselves all the other duties incident to their profession. The mortality in the Spanish War shows how infinitely less dangerous to the lives of the soldiers are the bullets of the enemy than diseases caused by bad sanitation and failure to understand how to cook, and live in the open.

Furthermore, it is very much to be wished that means could

be taken to provide the most ample facilities for rifle practice. The United States must depend upon its citizen soldiery in the event of a great war. If the men already know how to march, to take cover, to live in the open and to shoot, and always provided that they understand the absolutely vital importance of discipline and obedience to orders, then the technical training can be mastered with comparative ease by volunteers as intelligent, as brave, and as self-reliant as those who make up American armies. It would be a good thing if there were a rifle-range in every village of this State as there is in Switzerland. Moreover, it should be remembered that target practice proper is but the alphabet of the soldier's marksmanship. He should also practise assiduously under conditions as nearly as possible like those of actual warfare; "terrainschiessen," as it is called in the German army, is indispensable to effectiveness. In any event, every company of the National Guard should receive all possible encouragement in rifle practice. In a battle the only bullets that count are those that hit.

The Naval Militia make a particularly valuable branch of the service. They deserve the highest praise for the way they do their difficult work. The drill that the Naval Militia receives is most practical in character. It is greatly to be desired that the Second Naval Battalion should have an armory.

Every opportunity should be given to, and should be sought by, the officers and men of the National Guard and Naval Militia, seriously to study and master both the theory and practice of their temporary profession. One of the officers of the guard is going abroad with the special purpose of studying the relation of the regulars, volunteers, and militia in England; special studies of this kind have great value. In addition we should know the methods of administration and of field-practice which mark the most efficient modern armies.

FISHERIES, FOREST, AND GAME COMMISSION

Under this commission great progress has been made through the fish-hatcheries in the propagation of valuable food and sporting fish. The laws for the protection of deer have resulted in their increase. Nevertheless, as railroads tend to encroach on the wilderness, the temptation to illegal hunting becomes greater, and the danger from forest-fires increases. There is need of great improvement both in our laws and in their administration. The game-wardens have been too few in number. More should be provided. None save fit men must be appointed and their retention in office must depend purely upon the zeal, ability, and efficiency with which they perform their duties. The game-wardens in the forests must be woodsmen; and they should have no outside business. In short, there should be a thorough reorganization of the work of the commission. A careful study of the resources and condition of the forests on State land must be made. It is certainly not too much to expect that the State forests should be managed as efficiently as the forests on private lands in the same neighborhoods, and the measure of difference in efficiency of management must be the measure of condemnation or praise of the way the public forests have been managed.

The subject of forest preservation is of the utmost importance to the State. The Adirondacks and Catskills should be great parks kept in perpetuity for the benefit and enjoyment of our people. Much has been done of late years toward their preservation, but very much remains to be done. The provisions of law in reference to sawmills and wood-pulp mills are defective and should be changed so as to prohibit dumping dyestuff, sawdust, or tan-bark in any amount whatsoever into the streams. Reservoirs should be made; but not where they will tend to destroy large sections of the forest, and only after a careful and scientific study of the water resources of the region. The people of the forest regions are themselves growing more and more to realize the necessity of preserving both the trees and the game. A live deer in the woods will attract to the neighborhood ten times the money that could be obtained for the deer's dead carcass. Timber theft on the State lands is, of course, a grave offense against the whole public.

Hardy outdoor sports, like hunting, are in themselves of no small value to the national character, and should be encouraged in every way. Men who go into the wilderness, indeed men who take part in any field-sports with horse or rifle, receive a benefit which can hardly be given by even the most vigorous athletic games.

There is a further, and more immediate and practical, end in view. A primæval forest is a great sponge which absorbs and distils the rain-water; and when it is destroyed the result is apt to be an alternation of flood and drought. Forest-fires ultimately make the land a desert, and are a detriment to all that portion of the State tributary to the streams through the woods where they occur. Every effort should be made to minimize their destructive influence. We need to have our system of forestry gradually developed and conducted along scientific principles. When this has been done it will be possible to allow marketable lumber to be cut everywhere without damage to the forests—indeed, with positive advantage to them; but until lumbering is thus conducted, on strictly scientific principles no less than upon principles of the strictest honesty toward the State, we cannot afford to suffer it at all in the State forests. Unrestrained greed means the ruin of the great woods and the drying up of the sources of the rivers.

Ultimately the administration of the State lands must be so centralized as to enable us definitely to place responsibility in respect to everything concerning them, and to demand the highest degree of trained intelligence in their use.

The State should not permit within its limits factories to make bird-skins or bird-feathers into articles of ornament or wearing-apparel. Ordinarily birds, and especially song-birds, should be rigidly protected. Game-birds should never be shot to a greater extent than will offset the natural rate of increase. All spring shooting should be prohibited and efforts made by correspondence with the neighboring States to secure its prohibition within their borders. Care should be taken not to encourage the use of cold storage or other market systems which are a benefit to no one but the wealthy epicure who can afford to pay a heavy price for luxuries. These systems tend to the destruction of the game; which would bear most severely upon the very men whose rapacity has been appealed to in order to secure its extermination.

The open season for the different species of game and fish should be made uniform throughout the entire State, save that it should be shorter on Long Island for certain species which are not plentiful, and which are pursued by a greater number of people than in other game portions of the State.

BUILDING AND LOAN ASSOCIATIONS

Ample occasion exists for some modification of the statutes relating to the corporations popularly known as building and loan associations. A law which authorizes the formation of associations vested with extraordinary powers and possessing special exemptions, because they are designed to encourage thrift and to enable working men to provide homes for their families, urgently needs revision when under it there occur such instances of extravagance and mismanagement, if not of actual fraud, as have recently been brought to the public attention. If there can be degrees in fidelity, the highest should prevail in the discharge of those trusts in which the interests at stake are those of the poorer and more helpless members of society. Reckless real-estate speculations, arbitrary amendment of by-laws without the consent of shareholders, whereby the contracts between associations and their members are changed, and excessive expense accounts for salaries, luxurious offices, etc., not to charge practices which in some cases can be reconciled with no purpose except dishonesty, are among the abuses disclosed during the year by the work of the Banking Department. With this state of facts established, argument is not required to place upon the legislature the imperative obligation to revise the law governing these associations so as to make commission of wrongs by their management less easy, and to lodge with the superintendent of banks adequate power to deal promptly and effectively with associations whose directors may attempt to transcend the bounds of safety and honesty.

An evil of growing proportions is the incorporation of stock companies with titles suggestive of powers to which their certificates make no claim, and which they cannot possess under the general corporation law. Allied to it is the assumption of names similarly objectionable by partnerships or individuals operating as private bankers, and also the establishment of offices in this State by foreign corporations whose names indicate them to be moneyed corporations. The employment of such titles is certainly misleading, and it is readily conceivable that it might prove mischievous. It is plain that it should not be permitted to any person or firm or to any company having but an insignificant capital and organized to do merely an agency business, or to any foreign corporation maintaining an office in New York for the transaction of non-prohibited business, to have a name which conveys the idea that it is a banking institution; and the general corporation act should be amended to inhibit it. The matter is discussed more fully in the annual report of the superintendent of banks, to which I ask the attention of the legislature, with such action as will prevent a continuation of the evil.

BOXING

I call the attention of the legislature to the so-called Horton boxing law now on the statute-books, and recommend its repeal. If this law merely fulfilled the expectations of its original advocates, and if it were executed as it was executed during the first year it was enacted, there would be no need of this recommendation. Rough, vigorous pastimes are excellent things for the nation, for they promote manliness, being good in their effects not merely upon the body, but upon the character, which is far more important than the body. It is an admirable thing for any boy or young man whose work is of a sedentary character to take part in vigorous play, so long as it is not carried to excess, or allowed to interfere with his work. Every exercise that tends to develop bodily vigor, daring, endurance, resolution, and self-command should be encouraged. Boxing is a fine sport; but this affords no justification of prize-fighting, any more than the fact that a cross-country run or a ride on a wheel is healthy justifies such a demoralizing exhibition as a six-day race. When any sport is carried on primarily for money—that is, as a business—it is in danger of losing much that is valuable, and of acquiring some exceedingly undesirable characteristics. In the case of prize-fighting, not only do all the objections which apply to the abuse of other professional sports apply in aggravated form, but in addition the exhibition has a very demoralizing and brutalizing effect. There is no need to argue these points. They are expressly admitted in the Horton law itself. Moreover the evils are greatly aggravated by the fact that the fight is for a money prize, and is the occasion for unlimited gambling and betting. As the law is construed by the Police Department of New York at present, it permits prize-fights pure and simple. If as is alleged the police are technically justified in so construing the law, it only renders it the more necessary that the law should be repealed. However proper it may have been in its intent and as originally construed and administered, the gross abuses in its present administration make its existence on the statute-books of the Empire State an offense against decency.

Athletic sports are excellent when treated as what they should be, that is as healthy pastimes; they become harmful if indulged in to excess, and if their importance in relation to the serious work of life is misestimated; and still more harmful when twisted into adjuncts of brutality or gambling.

THE VAGRANCY LAW

Crime against a woman is peculiarly abhorrent, not only because she is weaker, but because she has no direct voice in the government. There should be no sentimentality about excusing a female criminal who is as guilty as a male criminal; but an even severer punishment should be meted out to those who commit crimes of brutal violence against women and children than to those who commit them against men. In the same way, it is greatly to be desired that our laws should be changed so as to provide for the punishment of men who profit by the commission of immoral acts by women. At present the wretched women are punished and the men who make their living by their infamy may go free. Such a condition of affairs is intolerable in the eyes of every right-thinking person. This kind of immoral conduct is punished under the vagrancy law, which should be amended as it has recently been amended in England, so as to do away with such unjust discrimination. In connection with this matter I call your attention to the desirability of completing the work of the New Bedford Reformatory which is specially designed for dealing with girls and women who have fallen, but whom there is a chance to redeem.

THE REVISION OF THE STATUTES

A commission to revise the statutes with a view of condensing, combining, and harmonizing the subjects of general legislation was created in 1889. Several general laws which were originally proposed have been rendered unnecessary by the reason of the changes of the Constitution of 1894, and several additional subjects of general legislation have been suggested. The revision of the Code of Civil Procedure was not originally contemplated, but has now become a part of the work of the commission. A large number of the bills advocated by the commission have become laws and some have been submitted but have not passed. During the winter it is intended that bills will be presented amending the general laws by incorporating them into various general statutes passed since those laws were enacted for the double purpose of bringing the plan of revision down to date and codifying under proper heads various independent statutes which can fairly be incorporated in an existing general law. It has been the custom heretofore to refer these bills either to the Committee on Judiciary or the Committee on Codes, but it is doubtful whether, if the numerous other bills which come from individual members are referred to these committees, such careful attention can be given to the bills of the Statutory Revision Commission as their importance warrants.

I beg leave to respectfully suggest the appointment of a special committee in each House, or a special joint committee, to take charge of these revision bills. Due attention to the various measures which the Statutory Revision Commission has prepared will greatly facilitate the work of closing up the commission, which ought to be done during the present year. I recommend that steps be taken to close the commission during the year.

DEPARTMENT OF THE COMPTROLLER

The office of the comptroller shows a balance on hand in the treasury on the first day of October, 1898, of $3,973,804.45. The receipts from all sources during the fiscal year ending September 30, 1899, were $25,837,136.19, making a total receipt, with the balance of last year, of $29,810,941.37. The payments for all purposes during the fiscal year were $25,306,-126.63, leaving a balance in the treasury of $4,505,814.74. The tax-rate for the fiscal year ending October 1, 1899, was 2.49 mills. The present valuation of the State is $5,076,396,824. The amount received for corporation and organization taxes was $2,741,318.05. The amount in 1898 was $2,497,247.05, showing an increase during the fiscal year of $244,071. The amount received for tax on inheritance during the fiscal year was $2,194,612.24, being an increase over the last fiscal year of $197,402. The amount received from the Excise Department was $4,231,278.55, an increase of $15,417.63 over the last preceding year.

Attention is called to the increasing payments from transfer-tax receipts by reason of special legislative enactments providing for the pay of assistants to surrogates and district attorneys, in addition to the fees allowed by the act itself to county treasurers and the comptroller of the city of New York for receiving this tax and remitting it to the State treasury. The counties of Erie, Kings, Monroe, New York, Oneida, Onondaga, Queens, Suffolk, Ulster, and Westchester have now these extra assistants at an aggregate cost for salaries and expenses each year of $36,940 payable from this tax. While admitting that this law has increased the labors of surrogates somewhat, it has not increased them to the extent of generally requiring assistants. I do not believe that any special provision should be made for additional help except in counties which have paid to the State for the past five years an average transfer tax of at least $50,000.

I recommend the repeal of all the acts giving district attorneys transfer-tax assistants, for the reason that the assistants do little or nothing to earn the compensation therein allowed, and that their employment is therefore a useless expenditure of public money.

The Transfer Tax Act provides that county treasurers and the comptroller of the city of New York shall receive a fee of 5 per cent on the first $50,000 collected; 3 per cent on the second $50,000, and 1 per cent upon all additional sums each year for receiving this tax and remitting it quarterly to the State treasury. Their only duty, in addition to this, consists in issuing duplicate receipts to the executors for the payment of this tax, and making a quarterly report to the State comptroller, and the payment of appraisers' fees and other legal disbursements. All the county treasurers retain this fee or commission for their own use and benefit, except in the county of Monroe, where it is turned into the county treasury. As a rule these officers take little or no interest in the enforcement of the law, and do practically nothing to warrant their receiving this large special compensation. In Erie County the fees formerly were paid into the county treasury, but the statute was amended recently restoring them to the treasurer. During the last fiscal year the amount of fees thus paid to county treasurers and the comptroller of New York City aggregated $67,425.06. Of this amount the comptroller of New York City received $15,975.83.

I believe that these fees should either go to the county, or that the aggregate amount allowed any official should be limited to a reasonable sum. At least $100,000 should be saved to the State annually by properly curtailing the expenditures payable from this tax.

SECRETARY OF STATE

Originally and in the early history of the State, corporations were created by special acts of the legislature. They were limited as to time, and as terms of existence would expire, legislative action was necessary to continue their existence.

General statutes were afterward enacted providing for the formation of corporations without resort to the legislature.

Notwithstanding these general laws, the legislature has continued to create corporations by special act, granting powers not given by the general laws.

Section 6 of the General Corporation Law prohibits the filing and recording in any office for the purpose of effecting incorporations of a certificate of incorporation of a proposed corporation having the same name as an existing domestic corporation, or a name so nearly resembling it as to be calculated to deceive.

By section 2411, Code of Civil Procedure, a petition to a court for the change of the corporate name of a domestic corporation must have annexed thereto a certificate of the secretary of state that the name proposed is not the name of any other domestic corporation or a name which the secretary of state deems so nearly resembling it as to be calculated to deceive.

To enable the secretary of state to comply with the above provisions, the names of all domestic corporations should be on file in his office, alphabetically arranged, just as the names of all corporations are, which are incorporated under the general statutes.

In all cases where a corporation is created by special act a clause should be contained in the act requiring the filing and recording in the secretary of state's office of a certified copy of such special act. The effect of this would be to bring the names of all domestic corporations, except banking and insurance corporations, upon our general index.

The secretary of state has paid to the State treasurer during the past fiscal year, for the benefit of the State, $557,460.25, and the number of new corporations, companies increasing their capital stock and amount of increased capital, have shown a large gain over preceding years.

ATTORNEY-GENERAL

I call your particular attention to the report of the attorney-general which will be handed you in a few days and the excellent showing it makes for that office. I cordially concur in what he will say as to the advisability of having all laws take effect at some definite time, say the 1st of September, so as to give opportunity to every one to know that they are on the statute-books. Of course, exceptions will be made in cases where emergencies exist.

SUPERINTENDENTS OF PRISONS

The superintendent calls attention to the excellent working of the principle of indeterminate sentence for maximum and minimum limits fixed by the court, the prison parole board being allowed to parole under supervision any prisoner at any time after the expiration of the minimum term. He recommends that all prisoners sentenced for a first offense for felony, save of course murder and arson, be sentenced to indeterminate terms. There should be a separate prison for the confinement and execution of condemned prisoners.

STATE COMMISSION OF PRISONS

Under the present laws none of the products of our own prisons are put upon the open market to compete with the products of free labor; but the products of convicts of other States and countries are brought into this State, and are in competition with the products of our free labor. As under the decisions of the courts the State is powerless to prevent this, it is to be wished that there could be national legislation on the subject. The present system is furnishing reasonable employment to our own convicts, and the heads of State institutions must see that there is full compliance with the laws requiring them to purchase from the prisons goods used by their departments and made in the prisons.

A very gratifying feature of the present prison laws of this State is the rapid diminution in the population of the prisons, the penitentiary population having shrunk from 4,600 in 1895 to but little over 2,200 in 1899.

STATE ENGINEER AND SURVEYOR

The work of the State engineer and surveyor has been executed with signal ability and fidelity during the past year.

There has been considerable duplication of work by the National and State Governments in surveys. It certainly does not seem worth while that the State should have two separate departments doing surveying work. The legislature last year declined to appropriate anything further for the State Land Survey, but did not abolish it. This creates a most undesirable state of affairs. It seems to me obvious that one department should do all the work, and I therefore recommend that the State Land Survey be put under the State engineer and surveyor, either as a separate bureau or otherwise, and that the work be done in his office, in which all the records of the State Land Survey should be placed.

PUBLIC INSTRUCTION

Under the Regents the institutions for higher education have continued to progress as in the past.

The superintendent of public instruction reports the public schools of the State in a prosperous condition. They have been liberally maintained, and results have been satisfactory. Public interest in education is steadily increasing. The total expenditures for public schools during the year, directly or indirectly, by the Department of Public Instruction, exceeded $29,000,000. What the State has done and is still doing along many lines to encourage professional training of teachers is bearing good fruit in the increasing number of professionally trained teachers in our schools, and in the development of a higher professional spirit. The superintendent will recommend the establishment of a pedagogical department in Cornell University, and will call attention to certain equities which exist in the relations between the State and this institution in connection with State scholarships. A reasonable appropriation will be asked to carry the proposed plan into execution.

It has for a long time been the well-nigh unanimous opinion of all those conversant with the history and practical working of the educational system of this State that the laws in reference to the official oversight and superintendence of education by the State Government ought to be revised and unified for the sake of greater general efficiency, economy, and entire harmony wherever there may be confusion and friction resulting from the needless overlapping of jurisdictions. That so vast a development as that which has come about in the work of instructing the children of this State should have been possible under the existing system is of itself a testimony to the wise and substantial way in which our predecessors laid the foundations of our educational organization.

The University of the State of New York, with its Board

of Regents, is an institution peculiar to this Commonwealth, and one now venerable with its 116 years of history. Its exercise of authority over higher education has been of very great public service, and its methods and standards have exercised a wide influence for good upon those of other States. These facts have led to the adoption by the people of an amendment to the constitution of the State whereby the university itself and its organization under a board of not less than nine Regents, has been provided and safeguarded in the organic law.

The Department of Public Instruction on the other hand, concerned chiefly with the supervision of all the free common schools of the State supported by public taxation, has grown to a vast importance; for the number of children of school age in the State has largely increased, and nine-tenths of them attend no other institution than the public school. The work done in both departments has been, in the main, excellent and needful to be done; they are amply worthy of the confidence and continued support of the people. But, that their work could be done better if the two systems were unified is a proposition hardly open to question. The problem has been not whether unification were desirable, but by what means this end was to be attained.

From the point of view of the public interests, it is neither desirable nor practicable merely to extend the jurisdiction of either department over the other. The University Convocation at its annual meeting in July, 1899, requested the governor to appoint a commission for the purpose of recommending a practicable plan of unification, and in accordance with this suggestion the following commission was appointed: Frederick W. Holls, Daniel H. McMillan, Judge Joseph T. Daly, William Kernan, Robt. F. Wilkinson, and the secretary of the Board of Regents and the assistant superintendent of public instruction. All were men of the highest standing, of trained capacity, and specially interested in the whole subject. I cannot too heartily thank them for their invaluable and wholly disinterested labor for the public welfare.

This commission, after careful consideration, has arrived at suggestions embodied in a report suggesting statutory changes which, if adopted by the legislature, will give effect to the system which they recommend. What they propose is the creation of a Department of Education, including both the university and the Department of Public Instruction, of which a single officer, known as the chancellor of the university, shall be the responsible executive and administrative head. The university is, of course, continued, and has its oversight extended to cover the entire field of education, so that its real authority and opportunity for public service will be much increased.

The plan proposed is simple, effective, and wholly free from political or partisan considerations. It deserves the cordial support of all friends of public education, and this means of every patriotic citizen of the State.

It is impossible to exaggerate the importance of the interests involved or the importance of considering them solely from the point of view of the general welfare of the State.

DEPARTMENT OF EXCISE

The Excise Department has apparently been most carefully and judicially managed, and the work of that department commends itself to the legislature.

The net balance for the fiscal year in this department is $12,582,248.72, of which $4,231,278.55 goes to the State, the balance being distributed among the cities and towns of the State. The expense of this department during the fiscal year was $274,862.10, and at the end of the fiscal year there was a balance on hand over and above expense of $91,723.92, showing that the most careful expenditure in the department has been the rule. There has been a decrease of between five and six thousand licensed places in the State, and each succeeding year shows a slight decrease in the number in force at the end of the fiscal year. The so-called slot-machine gambling nuisance has greatly decreased, and has been driven from places where liquor is sold.

STATE COMMISSION IN LUNACY

In this department progressive improvement shows that the State Care system was wisely founded and must remain the permanent policy of the State. The care of the insane has bettered and the cost has lessened. The accommodations have been increased and improved and the annual increment of permanent cases, the ultimate cost to the State of each of which is computed at $5,000, has been diminished. While the reduction of cost of maintenance the past year from the per capita of $185.20 in 1898 to $178.42, in the face of a general advance in prices, and contrasted with $216 before the State Care Act, is satisfactory, it is of far more importance that the annual increase of patients in hospitals is steadily decreasing; in 1899 it was 529, in 1898 it was 634, in 1897 it was 733. These figures allow but one conclusion—better care of the insane. That conclusion is supported by the fact that 1,009 patients have been discharged fully recovered, and 921 others have sufficiently improved to allow their return to their homes.

STATE CHARITABLE INSTITUTIONS

Great interests are involved in the administration of the State charitable institutions. During the past year a long stride forward has been taken in elevating the standard of supervision on the part of boards of managers. Wherever possible these boards of managers are now selected without reference to local demands or preferences and without reference to their politics. While there should be one or two representatives of the locality, the bulk should be men and women coming from other parts of the State, who realize that the institution is of State and not merely local consequence.

I call your attention to the desirability of repealing chapter 374 of the Laws of 1896, which permits courts to send female felons of mature age to "houses of refuge" for a period of less than one year. This is contrary to the purpose with which these institutions were founded, and to chapter 632 of the Laws of 1899, which provides for a sentence of three years, with power of prior discharge by the board of managers. Houses of refuge are not proper places for felons of mature age, and moreover, the managers of these houses should, like the trustees of the Elmira Reformatory, be given the privilege of transferring to the prison authorities, under proper conditions, inmates who are found to derive no benefit from the discipline employed.

COMMISSIONERS OF THE LAND OFFICE

I call your attention to the desirability of allowing the commissioners of the Land Office to grant leases with power of renewal for riparian lands. At present it is more than questionable whether such leases are valid, and unless the leases can be issued in this form, they are often useless. Where improvements of great value are made it seems probable that the land should be granted in fee; but where improvements are not made the State should certainly retain the fee.

CIVIL SERVICE COMMISSION

A very great advance was made last year by the action of the legislature in putting upon the books the present bill to secure recognition of merit in appointments to the civil service. Under this law the great bulk of the classified offices are taken out of the domain of politics. There is need of an increased appropriation for the Civil Service Commission. Their salaries should at least be made equal to those of other commissioners.

The civil-service rules framed under the provisions of chapter 370, Laws of 1899, were promulgated on June 8th last. While the law and rules have been in operation for a period too brief to demonstrate their benefits to their fullest extent or to detect their defects, enough has been shown to prove their efficiency in carrying out the constitutional provisions.

Examinations for all positions subject to them have been held in at least thirty cities so as to accommodate applicants in every part of the State. The increased attendance at these examinations indicates an appreciation of the relief from the double examinations under the previous law, which were costly and onerous to all, without any advantage to the public interests. The provisions of law requiring pay-rolls to be certified by the State or municipal commissions respectively have worked well, both in securing strict compliance with the law, and in obtaining accurate rosters of those in service. The same may be said of the larger powers of supervision of the work of municipal commissions given to the State Commission, securing uniformity in methods and procedure and the application of the merit system in all the cities of the State, a result never before reached. The State Commission should have larger means at its disposal for frequent inspection of the city service and concurrent advice and instruction to such inexperienced officials as may need it.

RAILROAD COMMISSION

Important progress has been made in the elimination of grade crossings, the commission exercising its powers with tact and judgment. I recommend that the legislature provide for the continuance of this work. Of recent years the legislature has given the board proper power, and in consequence it has been enabled to do excellent work.

HEALTH OFFICER AND QUARANTINE

The health officer of the port of New York and the quarantine commissioners find their work sadly handicapped for lack of funds. This branch of public service has in the past few years, by reason of the improved methods of sanitation, been of the greatest public benefit; but sufficient funds have not heretofore been placed at their disposal to acquire the best results. The port of New York is one which cannot be too carefully guarded, and the very scientific methods now used by those who have charge of this important branch of the State government require additional and increased appropriations. I trust this matter will receive your early and careful attention.

SELF-SUPPORTING OFFICES

The offices of Secretary of State, Railroad Commission, Banking and Insurance Departments are all self-supporting— more than paying their own expenses.

DEPARTMENT OF AGRICULTURE

The work of this department has steadily increased until it is now double what it was six years ago, while there has been but little increase in the appropriation. To some extent the work of this department is duplicated or clashes with that of the State Board of Health. The Assembly Committee appointed to consider the subject of tuberculosis in cattle will deal with this matter, at least in part, in their report to the legislature.

I call your attention to the special necessity of taking all possible steps to prevent the adulteration of food.

During the year 1899 the property of the State Agricultural Society at Syracuse, where the annual State Fair is held, was transferred to the State, and I recommend that the State now take under its own control the management of the State Fair.

The excellent educational work done by the Farmers' Institute deserves your cordial support; it has had a real and marked effect in bettering the condition of the farming communities where it has been most developed.

STATE ARCHITECT

Nowhere has the increased efficiency in the State service been more marked than in the office of the State architect. This office has carried on the work of preparing plans and specifications for the various new buildings and repairs and alterations to existing buildings for which appropriations have been made by the legislature. With a few unimportant exceptions all this work is now under contract notwithstanding the great increase in price of building materials during the current year and since the appropriations were made. It is recommended that the State architect be given an additional appropriation to increase the engineering force of his office so as to enable him to ascertain if it be practicable to secure greater economy in various directions, such as in the mechanical methods of using coal in State institutions, to inquire into the general subject of water-supply and sewerage of the various State institutions, and to formulate practical suggestions for the amelioration of existing defects, and to pay the salaries of building inspectors now paid out of the appropriations for buildings.

NEW YORK CITY CHARTER

I recommend that the governor be empowered to appoint a commission to deal with the question of remodelling the New York Charter in order to remedy the defects made evident by its workings during the last two years.

POLITICAL ASSESSMENTS AND THE JUDICIARY

I further recommend that legislation be passed at once prohibiting the payment by any candidate for judicial office, directly or indirectly, of assessments or contributions to political parties for campaign expenses.

GOOD ROADS

The movement to better the roads of the State should not be allowed to lag; it should be so directed as to be in the especial interest of the tiller of the soil.

PUBLIC PRINTING

It may well be considered by you whether by the passage of an act establishing a State printing bureau, equipped with every modern device, the cost to the State of its printing might not be reduced. This item has become a large one in the

State expenditure, and a trial of State ownership, if found to be economical, I would advise.

THE PALISADES

The State should sedulously preserve for its people the natural beauties within its limits. Great good has been done by the Niagara Falls Reservation, and its interests should be advanced in every way. I call the attention of the legislature to the report of the Palisades Commission, which has my hearty approval. The Palisades should be preserved. They form one of the most striking and beautiful features of nature in the entire country, and their marring and ruin should be a source not merely of regret, but of shame, to our people. New Jersey is in reality less interested in their preservation than we are, although they are in her territory, for their beauty can best be observed from ours.

There are two miles of the Palisades in the State of New York and ten in the State of New Jersey. No further riparian rights along their base should be granted, and I suggest that a commission to represent the State of New York be appointed, and that the governor be empowered to request the State of New Jersey to appoint a similar commission to serve with ours and endeavor to provide for joint action by the two States to secure the permanence of this splendid natural monument.

PAN-AMERICAN EXPOSITION

I particularly desire to call the attention of the legislature to the Pan-American Exposition. This exposition will be a source of the utmost pride to the whole State, and all our citizens should feel an active concern in making it a greater success than anything of its kind ever held on this continent— second only to the great national expositions.

My attention has been called to the desirability of having at this exposition a Department of Social Economy. Interesting and important as it is to exhibit the natural resources of the Americas and the products of their industries, it is no less important to present the life of the people themselves and to show their social institutions.

The industrial and social revolution, consequent upon the introduction of steam and electricity, has produced a new civilization, with many new problems yet unsolved, and new conditions to which we have only imperfectly adjusted ourselves. By providing for a Department of Social Economy at the Pan-American Exposition, much light may be thrown on these problems, and not a little may be done for the amelioration of social and industrial conditions.

The scope of this department should be broad enough to include, for the several countries and peoples, a comprehensive presentation of their industrial, agricultural, commercial, economic, social, and philanthropic conditions.

These subjects would be graphically represented by maps, charts, and photographs, which would constitute an important and attractive exhibit. Such a presentation of conditions in Cuba, Porto Rico, Hawaii, and the Philippines would be of special interest. These subjects might be further illustrated by a series of congresses, in which experts would discuss topics of popular interest and of practical value.

The beginning of a new century would seem to be a peculiarly fitting time to gather up the results of investigation and experience in the preceding century by which to help the peoples of North and South America up to a higher plane, physical, mental, and moral.

I am heartily in favor of the creation of such a department of the exposition, and recommend that a sufficient appropriation be made by the legislature to establish and successfully conduct it.

I commend the exposition to your special attention, and hope you will aid it in every way.

OVERLEGISLATION

Bills are continually passed providing for extraordinary repairs on the canals, for the erection of bridges and the like. It seems to me that there should be a blanket appropriation for all these repairs, and that the allotment of the money for the different places should be left to the discretion of the superintendent of public works. I believe that this will result in a considerable saving to the State.

I again call the attention of the legislature to the undesirability of cumbering our statute-books with a mass of needless legislation. Of course, any legislation that is slipped through so as to evade public notice is noxious; but aside from this the mere fact of having on the statute-books a large number of laws which, though not harmful, are of no particular benefit, is also undesirable. It is greatly to be desired that some plan for limiting private legislation should be adopted; a bill with this purpose was introduced last year.

I also again call the attention of the legislature to the need of economy. There are many objects excellent in themselves upon which the State could with advantage spend money, were it not for the steady tendency to increase expense beyond the limit that can be afforded by the taxpayers.

VICE-PRESIDENT OF THE
UNITED STATES

1901

INAUGURAL ADDRESS[1]

T HE history of free government is in large part the history of those representative legislative bodies in which,
from the earliest times, free government has found its
loftiest expression. They must ever hold a peculiar and ex-
alted position in the record which tells how the great nations
of the world have endeavored to achieve and preserve orderly
freedom. No man can render to his fellows greater service
than is rendered by him who, with fearlessness and honesty,
with sanity and disinterestedness, does his life-work as a member of such a body. Especially is this the case when the legislature in which the service is rendered is a vital part in the
governmental machinery of one of those world powers to
whose hands, in the course of the ages, is intrusted a leading
part in shaping the destinies of mankind. For weal or for
woe, for good or for evil, this is true of our own mighty nation. Great privileges and great powers are ours, and heavy
are the responsibilities that go with these privileges and these
powers. Accordingly as we do well or ill, so shall mankind
in the future be raised or cast down.

We belong to a young nation, already of giant strength,
yet whose political strength is but a forecast of the power that
is to come. We stand supreme in a continent, in a hemisphere.
East and west we look across the two great oceans toward
the larger world life in which, whether we will or not, we
must take an ever-increasing share. And as, keen-eyed, we
gaze into the coming years, duties, new and old, rise thick
and fast to confront us from within and from without. There
is every reason why we should face these duties with a sober

[1] Delivered in the Senate Chamber of the Capitol, Washington, D. C.,
March 4, 1901.

appreciation alike of their importance and of their difficulty. But there is also every reason for facing them with high-hearted resolution and eager and confident faith in our capacity to do them aright. A great work lies already to the hand of this generation; it should count itself happy, indeed, that to it is given the privilege of doing such a work. A leading part therein must be taken by this the august and powerful legislative body over which I have been called upon to preside. Most deeply do I appreciate the privilege of my position; for high, indeed, is the honor of presiding over the American Senate at the outset of the twentieth century.

PRESIDENT OF THE UNITED STATES

1901–1909

FIRST ANNUAL MESSAGE[1]

TO THE SENATE AND HOUSE OF REPRESENTATIVES:

The Congress assembles this year under the shadow of a great calamity. On the 6th of September, President McKinley was shot by an anarchist while attending the Pan-American Exposition at Buffalo, and died in that city on the 14th of that month.

Of the last seven elected Presidents, he is the third who has been murdered, and the bare recital of this fact is sufficient to justify grave alarm among all loyal American citizens. Moreover, the circumstances of this, the third assassination of an American President, have a peculiarly sinister significance. Both President Lincoln and President Garfield were killed by assassins of types unfortunately not uncommon in history; President Lincoln falling a victim to the terrible passions aroused by four years of Civil War, and President Garfield to the revengeful vanity of a disappointed office-seeker. President McKinley was killed by an utterly depraved criminal belonging to that body of criminals who object to all governments, good and bad alike, who are against any form of popular liberty if it is guaranteed by even the most just and liberal laws, and who are as hostile to the upright exponent of a free people's sober will as to the tyrannical and irresponsible despot.

PRESIDENT MCKINLEY

It is not too much to say that at the time of President McKinley's death he was the most widely loved man in all the United States; while we have never had any public man

[1] Dated, the White House, December 3, 1901.

of his position who has been so wholly free from the bitter animosities incident to public life. His political opponents were the first to bear the heartiest and most generous tribute to the broad kindliness of nature, the sweetness and gentleness of character which so endeared him to his close associates. To a standard of lofty integrity in public life he united the tender affections and home virtues which are all-important in the make-up of national character. A gallant soldier in the great war for the Union, he also shone as an example to all our people because of his conduct in the most sacred and intimate of home relations. There could be no personal hatred of him, for he never acted with aught but consideration for the welfare of others. No one could fail to respect him who knew him in public or private life. The defenders of those murderous criminals who seek to excuse their criminality by asserting that it is exercised for political ends, inveigh against wealth and irresponsible power. But for this assassination even this base apology cannot be urged.

President McKinley was a man of moderate means, a man whose stock sprang from the sturdy tillers of the soil, who had himself belonged among the wage-workers, who had entered the army as a private soldier. Wealth was not struck at when the President was assassinated, but the honest toil which is content with moderate gains after a lifetime of unremitting labor, largely in the service of the public. Still less was power struck at in the sense that power is irresponsible or centred in the hands of any one individual. The blow was not aimed at tyranny or wealth. It was aimed at one of the strongest champions the wage-worker has ever had; at one of the most faithful representatives of the system of public rights and representative government who has ever risen to public office. President McKinley filled that political office for which the entire people vote, and no president—not even Lincoln himself—was ever more earnestly anxious to represent the well-thought-out wishes of the people; his one anxiety in every crisis was to keep in closest touch with the people—to find out what they thought and to endeavor to give expression to their thought, after having endeavored to guide that thought aright. He had just been re-elected to the presidency because the majority of our citizens, the majority of our farmers and wage-workers, believed that he had faithfully upheld their interests for four years. They felt themselves in close and intimate touch with him. They felt that he represented so well and so honorably all their ideals and aspirations that they wished him to continue for another four years to represent them.

And this was the man at whom the assassin struck! That there might be nothing lacking to complete the Judas-like infamy of his act, he took advantage of an occasion when the President was meeting the people generally; and advancing as if to take the hand outstretched to him in kindly and brotherly fellowship, he turned the noble and generous confidence of the victim into an opportunity to strike the fatal blow. There is no baser deed in all the annals of crime.

The shock, the grief of the country, are bitter in the minds of all who saw the dark days, while the President yet hovered between life and death. At last the light was stilled in the kindly eyes and the breath went from the lips that even in mortal agony uttered no words save of forgiveness to his murderer, of love for his friends, and of unfaltering trust in the will of the Most High. Such a death, crowning the glory of such a life, leaves us with infinite sorrow, but with such pride in what he had accomplished and in his own personal character, that we feel the blow not as struck at him, but as struck at the nation. We mourn a good and great President who is dead; but while we mourn we are lifted up by the splendid achievements of his life and the grand heroism with which he met his death.

ANARCHISM

When we turn from the man to the nation, the harm done is so great as to excite our gravest apprehensions, and to demand our wisest and most resolute action. This criminal was a professed anarchist, inflamed by the teachings of professed anarchists, and probably also by the reckless utterances of those who, on the stump and in the public press, appeal to the dark and evil spirits of malice and greed, envy and sullen hatred. The wind is sowed by the men who preach such doctrines, and they cannot escape their share of responsibility for the whirlwind that is reaped. This applies alike to the deliberate demagogue, to the exploiter of sensationalism, and to the crude and foolish visionary who, for whatever reason, apologizes for crime or excites aimless discontent.

The blow was aimed not at this President, but at all Presidents; at every symbol of government. President McKinley was as emphatically the embodiment of the popular will of the nation expressed through the forms of law as a New England town meeting is in similar fashion the embodiment of the law-abiding purpose and practice of the people of the town. On no conceivable theory could the murder of the President be accepted as due to protest against "inequalities in the social order," save as the murder of all the freemen engaged in a town meeting could be accepted as a protest against that social inequality which puts a malefactor in jail. Anarchy is no more an expression of "social discontent" than picking pockets or wife-beating.

The anarchist, and especially the anarchist in the United States, is merely one type of criminal, more dangerous than any other because he represents the same depravity in a greater degree. The man who advocates anarchy directly or indirectly, in any shape or fashion, or the man who apologizes for anarchists and their deeds, makes himself morally accessory to murder before the fact. The anarchist is a criminal whose perverted instincts lead him to prefer confusion and chaos to the most beneficent form of social order. His protest of concern for working men is outrageous in its impudent falsity; for if the political institutions of this country do not afford opportunity to every honest and intelligent son of toil, then the door of hope is forever closed against him. The anarchist is everywhere not merely the enemy of system and of progress, but the deadly foe of liberty. If ever anarchy is triumphant, its triumph will last for but one red moment, to be succeeded for ages by the gloomy night of despotism.

For the anarchist himself, whether he preaches or practises his doctrines, we need not have one particle more concern than for any ordinary murderer. He is not the victim of social or political injustice. There are no wrongs to remedy in his case. The cause of his criminality is to be found in his own evil passions and in the evil conduct of those who urge him on, not in any failure by others or by the State to do justice to him or his. He is a malefactor and nothing else. He is in no sense, in no shape or way, a "product of social conditions," save as a highwayman is "produced" by the fact that an unarmed man happens to have a purse. It is a travesty upon the great and holy names of liberty and freedom to permit them to be invoked in such a cause. No man or body of men preaching anarchistic doctrines should be allowed at large any more than if preaching the murder of some specified private individual. Anarchistic speeches, writings, and meetings are essentially seditious and treasonable.

I earnestly recommend to the Congress that in the exercise of its wise discretion it should take into consideration the coming to this country of anarchists or persons professing principles hostile to all government and justifying the murder of those placed in authority. Such individuals as those who not long ago gathered in open meeting to glorify the murder of King Humbert of Italy perpetrate a crime, and the law should insure their rigorous punishment. They and those like them should be kept out of this country; and if found here they should be promptly deported to the country whence they came; and far-reaching provision should be made for the punishment of those who stay. No matter calls more urgently for the wisest thought of the Congress.

The Federal courts should be given jurisdiction over any man who kills or attempts to kill the President or any man who by the Constitution or by law is in line of succession for the presidency, while the punishment for an unsuccessful attempt should be proportioned to the enormity of the offense against our institutions.

Anarchy is a crime against the whole human race; and all mankind should band against the anarchist. His crime should be made an offense against the law of nations, like piracy and that form of man-stealing known as the slave-trade; for it is of far blacker infamy than either. It should be so declared by treaties among all civilized powers. Such treaties would give to the Federal Government the power of dealing with the crime.

A grim commentary upon the folly of the anarchist position was afforded by the attitude of the law toward this very criminal who had just taken the life of the President. The people would have torn him limb from limb if it had not been that the law he defied was at once invoked in his behalf. So far from his deed being committed on behalf of the people against the government, the government was obliged at once to exert its full police power to save him from instant death at the hands of the people. Moreover, his deed worked not the slightest dislocation in our governmental system, and the danger of a recurrence of such deeds, no matter how great it might grow, would work only in the direction of strengthening and giving harshness to the forces of order. No man will ever be restrained from becoming President by any fear as to his personal safety. If the risk to the President's life became great, it would mean that the office would more and more come to be filled by men of a spirit which would make them resolute and merciless in dealing with every friend of disorder. This great country will not fall into anarchy, and if anarchists should ever become a serious menace to its institutions, they would not merely be stamped out, but would involve in their own ruin every active or passive sympathizer with their doctrines. The American people are slow to wrath, but when their wrath is once kindled it burns like a consuming flame.

REGULATION OF CORPORATIONS

During the last five years business confidence has been restored, and the nation is to be congratulated because of its present abounding prosperity. Such prosperity can never be created by law alone, although it is easy enough to destroy it by mischievous laws. If the hand of the Lord is heavy upon any country, if flood or drought comes, human wisdom is powerless to avert the calamity. Moreover, no law can guard us against the consequences of our own folly. The men who are idle or credulous, the men who seek gains not by genuine work with head or hand but by gambling in any form, are always a source of menace not only to themselves but to others. If the business world loses its head, it loses what legislation cannot supply. Fundamentally, the welfare of each citizen, and therefore the welfare of the aggregate of citizens which makes the nation, must rest upon individual thrift and energy, resolution, and intelligence. Nothing can take the place of this individual capacity; but wise legislation and honest and intelligent administration can give it the fullest scope, the largest opportunity to work to good effect.

The tremendous and highly complex industrial development which went on with ever-accelerated rapidity during the latter half of the nineteenth century brings us face to face, at the beginning of the twentieth, with very serious social problems. The old laws, and the old customs which had almost the binding force of law, were once quite sufficient to regulate the accumulation and distribution of wealth. Since the industrial changes which have so enormously increased the productive power of mankind, they are no longer sufficient.

The growth of cities has gone on beyond comparison faster than the growth of the country, and the upbuilding of the great industrial centres has meant a startling increase, not merely in the aggregate of wealth, but in the number of very large individual, and especially of very large corporate, fortunes. The creation of these great corporate fortunes has not been due to the tariff nor to any other governmental action, but to natural causes in the business world, operating in other countries as they operate in our own.

The process has aroused much antagonism, a great part of which is wholly without warrant. It is not true that as the rich have grown richer the poor have grown poorer. On the contrary, never before has the average man, the wage-worker, the farmer, the small trader, been so well off as in this country and at the present time. There have been abuses connected with the accumulation of wealth; yet it remains true that a fortune accumulated in legitimate business can be accumulated by the person specially benefited only on condition of conferring immense incidental benefits upon others. Successful enterprise, of the type which benefits all mankind, can only exist if the conditions are such as to offer great prizes as the rewards of success.

The captains of industry who have driven the railway systems across this continent, who have built up our commerce, who have developed our manufactures, have on the whole done great good to our people. Without them the material development of which we are so justly proud could never have taken place. Moreover, we should recognize the immense importance of this material development of leaving as unhampered as is compatible with the public good the strong and forceful men upon whom the success of business operations inevitably rests. The slightest study of business conditions will satisfy any one capable of forming a judgment that the personal equation is the most important factor in a business operation; that the business ability of the man at the head of any business concern, big or little, is usually the factor which fixes the gulf between striking success and hopeless failure.

An additional reason for caution in dealing with corporations is to be found in the international commercial conditions of to-day. The same business conditions which have produced the great aggregations of corporate and individual wealth have made them very potent factors in international commercial competition. Business concerns which have the largest means at their disposal and are managed by the ablest men are naturally those which take the lead in the strife for commercial supremacy among the nations of the world. America has only just begun to assume that commanding position in the international business world which we believe will more and more be hers. It is of the utmost importance that this position be not jeopardized, especially at a time when the overflowing abundance of our own natural resources and the skill, business energy, and mechanical aptitude of our people make foreign markets essential. Under such conditions it would be most unwise to cramp or to fetter the youthful strength of our nation.

Moreover, it cannot too often be pointed out that to strike with ignorant violence at the interests of one set of men almost inevitably endangers the interests of all. The fundamental rule in our national life—the rule which underlies all others —is that, on the whole, and in the long run, we shall go up or down together. There are exceptions; and in times of prosperity some will prosper far more, and in times of adversity, some will suffer far more, than others; but speaking generally, a period of good times means that all share more or less in them, and in a period of hard times all feel the stress to a greater or less degree. It surely ought not to be necessary to enter into any proof of this statement; the memory of the lean years which began in 1893 is still vivid, and we can contrast them with the conditions in this very year which is now closing. Disaster to great business enterprises can never have its effects limited to the men at the top. It spreads throughout, and while it is bad for everybody, it is worst for those farthest down. The capitalist may be shorn of his luxuries; but the wage-worker may be deprived of even bare necessities.

The mechanism of modern business is so delicate that extreme care must be taken not to interfere with it in a spirit of rashness or ignorance. Many of those who have made it their vocation to denounce the great industrial combinations which are popularly, although with technical inaccuracy, known as "trusts," appeal especially to hatred and fear. These are precisely the two emotions, particularly when combined with ignorance, which unfit men for the exercise of cool and steady judgment. In facing new industrial conditions, the whole history of the world shows that legislation will generally be both unwise and ineffective unless undertaken after calm inquiry and with sober self-restraint. Much of the legislation directed at the trusts would have been exceedingly mischievous had it not also been entirely ineffective. In accordance with a well-known sociological law, the ignorant or reckless agitator has been the really effective friend of the evils which he has been nominally opposing. In dealing with business interests, for the government to undertake by crude and ill-considered legislation to do what may turn out to be bad, would be to incur the risk of such far-reaching national disaster that it would be preferable to undertake nothing at all. The men who demand the impossible or the undesirable serve as the allies of the forces with which they are nominally at war, for they hamper those who would endeavor to find out in rational fashion what the wrongs really are and to what extent and in what manner it is practicable to apply remedies.

All this is true; and yet it is also true that there are real and grave evils, one of the chief being overcapitalization because of its many baleful consequences; and a resolute and practical effort must be made to correct these evils.

There is a wide-spread conviction in the minds of the American people that the great corporations known as trusts are in certain of their features and tendencies hurtful to the general welfare. This springs from no spirit of envy or uncharitableness, nor lack of pride in the great industrial achievements that have placed this country at the head of the nations struggling for commercial supremacy. It does not rest upon a lack of intelligent appreciation of the necessity of meeting changing and changed conditions of trade with new methods, nor upon ignorance of the fact that combination of capital in the effort to accomplish great things is necessary when the world's progress demands that great things be done. It is based upon sincere conviction that combination and concentration should be, not prohibited, but supervised and within reasonable limits controlled; and in my judgment this conviction is right.

It is no limitation upon property rights or freedom of contract to require that when men receive from government the privilege of doing business under corporate form, which frees them from individual responsibility, and enables them to call into their enterprises the capital of the public, they shall do so upon absolutely truthful representations as to the value of the property in which the capital is to be invested. Corporations engaged in interstate commerce should be regulated if they are found to exercise a license working to the public injury. It should be as much the aim of those who seek for social betterment to rid the business world of crimes of cunning as to rid the entire body politic of crimes of violence. Great corporations exist only because they are created and safeguarded by our institutions; and it is therefore our right and our duty to see that they work in harmony with these institutions.

The first essential in determining how to deal with the great industrial combinations is knowledge of the facts—publicity. In the interest of the public, the government should have the right to inspect and examine the workings of the great corporations engaged in interstate business. Publicity is the only sure remedy which we can now invoke. What further remedies are needed in the way of governmental regulation, or taxation, can only be determined after publicity has been obtained, by process of law, and in the course of administration. The first requisite is knowledge, full and complete—knowledge which may be made public to the world.

Artificial bodies, such as corporations and joint-stock or other associations, depending upon any statutory law for their existence or privileges, should be subject to proper governmental supervision, and full and accurate information as to their operations should be made public regularly at reasonable intervals.

The large corporations, commonly called trusts, though organized in one State, always do business in many States, often doing very little business in the State where they are incorporated. There is utter lack of uniformity in the State laws about them; and as no State has any exclusive interest in or power over their acts, it has in practice proved impossible to get adequate regulation through State action. Therefore, in the interest of the whole people, the nation should, without interfering with the power of the States in the matter itself, also assume power of supervision and regulation over all corporations doing an interstate business. This is especially true where the corporation derives a portion of its wealth from the existence of some monopolistic element or tendency in its business. There would be no hardship in such supervision; banks are subject to it, and in their case it is now accepted as a simple matter of course. Indeed, it is probable that supervision of corporations by the National Government need not go so far as is now the case with the supervision exercised over them by so conservative a State as Massachusetts, in order to produce excellent results.

When the Constitution was adopted, at the end of the eighteenth century, no human wisdom could foretell the sweeping changes, alike in industrial and political conditions, which were to take place by the beginning of the twentieth century. At that time it was accepted as a matter of course that the several States were the proper authorities to regulate, so far as was then necessary, the comparatively insignificant and strictly localized corporate bodies of the day. The conditions are now wholly different and wholly different action is called for. I believe that a law can be framed which will enable the National Government to exercise control along the lines above indicated; profiting by the experience gained through the passage and administration of the Interstate Commerce Act. If, however, the judgment of the Congress is that it lacks the constitutional power to pass such an act, then a constitutional amendment should be submitted to confer the power.

DEPARTMENT OF COMMERCE AND INDUSTRIES

There should be created a Cabinet officer, to be known as secretary of commerce and industries, as provided in the bill introduced at the last session of the Congress. It should be his province to deal with commerce in its broadest sense; including among many other things whatever concerns labor and all matters affecting the great business corporations and our merchant marine.

The course proposed is one phase of what should be a comprehensive and far-reaching scheme of constructive statesmanship for the purpose of broadening our markets, securing our business interests on a safe basis, and making firm our new position in the international industrial world; while scrupulously safeguarding the rights of wage-worker and capitalist, or investor and private citizen, so as to secure equity as between man and man in this Republic.

LABOR

With the sole exception of the farming interest, no one matter is of such vital moment to our whole people as the welfare of the wage-workers. If the farmer and the wage-worker are well off, it is absolutely certain that all others will be well off too. It is therefore a matter for hearty congratulation that on the whole wages are higher to-day in the United States than ever before in our history, and far higher than in any other country. The standard of living is also higher than ever before. Every effort of legislator and administrator should be bent to secure the permanency of this condition of things and its improvement wherever possible. Not only must our labor be protected by the tariff, but it should also be protected so far as it is possible from the presence in this country of any laborers brought over by contract, or of those who, coming freely, yet represent a standard of living so depressed that they can undersell our men in the labor market and drag them to a lower level. I regard it as necessary, with this end in view, to re-enact immediately the law excluding Chinese laborers and to strengthen it wherever necessary in order to make its enforcement entirely effective.

The National Government should demand the highest quality of service from its employees; and in return it should be a good employer. If possible legislation should be passed, in connection with the Interstate Commerce Law, which will render effective the efforts of different States to do away with the competition of convict contract labor in the open labor market. So far as practicable under the conditions of government work, provision should be made to render the enforcement of the eight-hour law easy and certain. In all industries carried on directly or indirectly for the United States Government women and children should be protected from excessive hours of labor, from night-work, and from work under unsanitary conditions. The government should provide in its contracts that all work should be done under "fair" conditions, and in addition to setting a high standard should uphold it by proper inspection, extending if necessary to the subcontractors. The government should forbid all night-work for women and children, as well as excessive overtime. For the District of Columbia a good factory law should be passed; and, as a powerful indirect aid to such laws, provision should be made to turn the inhabited alleys, the existence of which is a reproach to our capital city, into minor streets, where the inhabitants can live under conditions favorable to health and morals.

American wage-workers work with their heads as well as their hands. Moreover, they take a keen pride in what they are doing; so that, independent of the reward, they wish to turn out a perfect job. This is the great secret of our success in competition with the labor of foreign countries.

The most vital problem with which this country, and for that matter the whole civilized world, has to deal, is the problem which has for one side the betterment of social conditions, moral and physical, in large cities, and for another side the effort to deal with that tangle of far-reaching questions which we group together when we speak of "labor." The chief factor in the success of each man—wage-worker, farmer, and capitalist alike—must ever be the sum total of his own individual qualities and abilities. Second only to this comes the power of acting in combination or association with others. Very great good has been and will be accomplished by associations or unions of wage-workers, when managed with forethought, and when they combine insistence upon their own rights with law-abiding respect for the rights of others. The display of these qualities in such bodies is a duty to the nation no less than to the associations themselves. Finally, there must also in many cases be action by the government in order to safeguard the rights and interests of all. Under our Constitution there is much more scope for such action by the State and the municipality than by the nation. But on points such as those touched on above the National Government can act.

When all is said and done, the rule of brotherhood remains as the indispensable prerequisite to success in the kind of national life for which we strive. Each man must work for himself, and unless he so works no outside help can avail him; but each man must remember also that he is indeed his brother's keeper, and that while no man who refuses to walk can be carried with advantage to himself or any one else, yet that each at times stumbles or halts, that each at times needs to have the helping hand outstretched to him. To be permanently effective, aid must always take the form of helping a man to help himself; and we can all best help ourselves by joining together in the work that is of common interest to all.

IMMIGRATION

Our present immigration laws are unsatisfactory. We need every honest and efficient immigrant fitted to become an American citizen, every immigrant who comes here to stay, who brings here a strong body, a stout heart, a good head, and a resolute purpose to do his duty well in every way and to bring up his children as law-abiding and God-fearing members of the community. But there should be a comprehensive law enacted with the object of working a threefold improvement over our present system. First, we should aim to exclude absolutely not only all persons who are known to be believers in anarchistic principles or members of anarchistic societies, but also all persons who are of a low moral tendency or of unsavory reputation. This means that we should require a more thorough system of inspection abroad and a more rigid system of examination at our immigration ports, the former being especially necessary.

The second object of a proper immigration law ought to be to secure by a careful and not merely perfunctory educational test some intelligent capacity to appreciate American institutions and act sanely as American citizens. This would not keep out all anarchists, for many of them belong to the intelligent criminal class. But it would do what is also in point, that is, tend to decrease the sum of ignorance, so potent in producing the envy, suspicion, malignant passion, and hatred of order, out of which anarchistic sentiment inevitably springs. Finally, all persons should be excluded who are below a certain standard of economic fitness to enter our industrial field as competitors with American labor. There should be proper proof of personal capacity to earn an American living and enough money to insure a decent start under American conditions. This would stop the influx of cheap labor, and the resulting competition which gives rise to so much of bitterness in American industrial life; and it would dry up the springs of the pestilential social conditions in our great cities, where anarchistic organizations have their greatest possibility of growth.

Both the educational and economic tests in a wise immigration law should be designated to protect and elevate the general body politic and social. A very close supervision should be exercised over the steamship companies which mainly bring over the immigrants, and they should be held to a strict accountability for any infraction of the law.

THE TARIFF AND RECIPROCITY

There is general acquiescence in our present tariff system as a national policy. The first requisite to our prosperity is the continuity and stability of this economic policy. Nothing could be more unwise than to disturb the business interests of the country by any general tariff change at this time. Doubt, apprehension, uncertainty are exactly what we most wish to avoid in the interest of our commercial and material well-being. Our experience in the past has shown that sweeping revisions of the tariff are apt to produce conditions closely approaching panic in the business world. Yet it is not only possible, but eminently desirable, to combine with the stability of our economic system a supplementary system of reciprocal benefit and obligation with other nations. Such reciprocity is an incident and result of the firm establishment and preservation of our present economic policy. It was specially provided for in the present tariff law.

Reciprocity must be treated as the handmaiden of protection. Our first duty is to see that the protection granted by the tariff in every case where it is needed is maintained, and that reciprocity be sought for so far as it can safely be done without injury to our home industries. Just how far this is must be determined according to the individual case, remembering always that every application of our tariff policy to meet our shifting national needs must be conditioned upon the cardinal fact that the duties must never be reduced below the point that will cover the difference between the labor cost here and abroad. The well-being of the wage-worker is a prime consideration of our entire policy of economic legislation.

Subject to this proviso of the proper protection necessary to our industrial well-being at home, the principle of reciprocity must command our hearty support. The phenomenal growth of our export trade emphasizes the urgency of the need for wider markets and for a liberal policy in dealing with foreign nations. Whatever is merely petty and vexatious in the way of trade restrictions should be avoided. The customers to whom we dispose of our surplus products in the long run, directly or indirectly, purchase those surplus products by giving us something in return. Their ability to purchase our products should as far as possible be secured by so arranging our tariff as to enable us to take from them those products which we can use without harm to our own industries and labor, or the use of which will be of marked benefit to us.

It is most important that we should maintain the high level of our present prosperity. We have now reached the point in the development of our interests where we are not only able to supply our own markets but to produce a constantly growing surplus for which we must find markets abroad. To secure these markets we can utilize existing duties in any case where they are no longer needed for the purpose of protection, or in any case where the article is not produced here and the duty is no longer necessary for revenue, as giving us something to offer in exchange for what we ask. The cordial relations with other nations which are so desirable will naturally be promoted by the course thus required by our own interests.

The natural line of development for a policy of reciprocity will be in connection with those of our productions which no longer require all of the support once needed to establish them upon a sound basis, and with those others where either because of natural or of economic causes we are beyond the reach of successful competition.

I ask the attention of the Senate to the reciprocity treaties laid before it by my predecessor.

MERCHANT MARINE

The condition of the American merchant marine is such as to call for immediate remedial action by the Congress. It is discreditable to us as a nation that our merchant marine should be utterly insignificant in comparison to that of other nations which we overtop in other forms of business. We should not longer submit to conditions under which only a trifling portion of our great commerce is carried in our own ships. To remedy this state of things would not merely serve to build up our shipping interests, but it would also result in benefit to all who are interested in the permanent establishment of a wider market for American products, and would provide an auxiliary force for the navy. Ships work for their own countries just as railroads work for their terminal points. Shipping lines, if established to the principal countries with which we have dealings, would be of political as well as commercial benefit. From every standpoint it is unwise for the United States to continue to rely upon the ships of competing nations for the distribution of our goods. It should be made advantageous to carry American goods in American-built ships.

At present American shipping is under certain great disadvantages when put in competition with the shipping of foreign countries. Many of the fast foreign steamships, at a speed of fourteen knots or above, are subsidized; and all our ships, sailing-vessels and steamers alike, cargo-carriers of slow speed and mail-carriers of high speed, have to meet the fact that the original cost of building American ships is greater than is the case abroad; that the wages paid American officers and seamen are very much higher than those paid the officers and seamen of foreign competing countries; and that the standard of living on our ships is far superior to the standard of living on the ships of our commercial rivals.

Our government should take such action as will remedy these inequalities. The American merchant marine should be restored to the ocean.

GOLD STANDARD

The Act of March 14, 1900, intended unequivocally to establish gold as the standard money and to maintain at a parity therewith all forms of money medium in use with us, has been shown to be timely and judicious. The price of our government bonds in the world's market, when compared with the price of similar obligations issued by other nations, is a flattering tribute to our public credit. This condition it is evidently desirable to maintain.

BANKING LAW

In many respects the National Banking law furnishes sufficient liberty for the proper exercise of the banking function; but there seems to be need of better safeguards against the deranging influence of commercial crises and financial panics. Moreover, the currency of the country should be made responsive to the demands of our domestic trade and commerce.

REDUCTION OF REVENUE

The collections from duties on imports and internal taxes continue to exceed the ordinary expenditures of the government, thanks mainly to the reduced army expenditures. The utmost care should be taken not to reduce the revenues so that there will be any possibility of a deficit; but, after providing against any such contingency, means should be adopted which will bring the revenues more nearly within the limit of our actual needs. In his report to the Congress the secretary of the treasury considers all these questions at length, and I ask your attention to the report and recommendations.

ECONOMY

I call special attention to the need of strict economy in expenditures. The fact that our national needs forbid us to be niggardly in providing whatever is actually necessary to our well-being, should make us doubly careful to husband our national resources, as each of us husbands his private resources, by scrupulous avoidance of anything like wasteful or reckless expenditure. Only by avoidance of spending money on what is needless or unjustifiable can we legitimately keep our income to the point required to meet our needs that are genuine.

RAILROAD LEGISLATION

In 1887 a measure was enacted for the regulation of interstate railways, commonly known as the Interstate Commerce Act. The cardinal provisions of that act were that railway rates should be just and reasonable and that all shippers, localities, and commodities should be accorded equal treatment. A commission was created and endowed with what were supposed to be the necessary powers to execute the provisions of this act.

That law was largely an experiment. Experience has shown the wisdom of its purposes, but has also shown, possibly that some of its requirements are wrong, certainly that the means devised for the enforcement of its provisions are defective. Those who complain of the management of the railways allege that established rates are not maintained; that rebates and similar devices are habitually resorted to; that these preferences are usually in favor of the large shipper; that they drive out of business the smaller competitor; that while many rates are too low, many others are excessive; and that gross preferences are made, affecting both localities and commodities. Upon the other hand, the railways assert that the law by its very terms tends to produce many of these illegal practices by depriving carriers of that right of concerted action which they claim is necessary to establish and maintain non-discriminating rates.

The act should be amended. The railway is a public servant. Its rates should be just to and open to all shippers alike. The government should see to it that within its jurisdiction this is so and should provide a speedy, inexpensive, and effective remedy to that end. At the same time it must not be forgotten that our railways are the arteries through which the commercial life-blood of this nation flows. Nothing could be more foolish than the enactment of legislation which would unnecessarily interfere with the development and operation of these commercial agencies. The subject is one of great importance and calls for the earnest attention of the Congress.

DEPARTMENT OF AGRICULTURE

The Department of Agriculture during the past fifteen years has steadily broadened its work on economic lines, and has accomplished results of real value in upbuilding domestic and foreign trade. It has gone into new fields until it is now in touch with all sections of our country and with two of the island groups that have lately come under our jurisdiction, whose people must look to agriculture as a livelihood. It is searching the world for grains, grasses, fruits, and vegetables specially fitted for introduction into localities in the several States and Territories where they may add materially to our resources. By scientific attention to soil survey and possible new crops, to breeding of new varieties of plants, to experimental shipments, to animal industry and applied chemistry, very practical aid has been given our farming and stock-growing interests. The products of the farm have taken an unprecedented place in our export trade during the year that has just closed.

FOREST CONSERVATION

Public opinion throughout the United States has moved steadily toward a just appreciation of the value of forests, whether planted or of natural growth. The great part played by them in the creation and maintenance of the national wealth is now more fully realized than ever before.

Wise forest protection does not mean the withdrawal of forest resources, whether of wood, water, or grass, from contributing their full share to the welfare of the people, but, on the contrary, gives the assurance of larger and more certain supplies. The fundamental idea of forestry is the perpetuation of forests by use. Forest protection is not an end of itself; it is a means to increase and sustain the resources of our country and the industries which depend upon them. The preservation of our forests is an imperative business necessity. We have come to see clearly that whatever destroys the forest, except to make way for agriculture threatens our well-being.

The practical usefulness of the national forest reserves to the mining, grazing, irrigation, and other interests of the regions in which the reserves lie has led to a wide-spread demand by the people of the West for their protection and extension. The forest reserves will inevitably be of still greater use in the future than in the past. Additions should be made to them whenever practicable, and their usefulness should be increased by a thoroughly businesslike management.

At present the protection of the forest reserves rests with the General Land Office, the mapping and description of their timber with the United States Geological Survey, and the preparation of plans for their conservative use with the Bureau of Forestry, which is also charged with the general advancement of practical forestry in the United States. These various functions should be united in the Bureau of Forestry, to which they properly belong. The present diffusion of responsibility is bad from every standpoint. It prevents that effective co-operation between the government and the men who utilize the resources of the reserves, without which the interests of both must suffer. The scientific bureaus generally should be put under the Department of Agriculture. The President should have by law the power of transferring lands for use as forest reserves to the Department of Agriculture. He already has such power in the case of lands needed by the Departments of War and the Navy.

The wise administration of the forest reserves will be not less helpful to the interests which depend on water than to those which depend on wood and grass. The water-supply itself depends upon the forest. In the arid region it is water, not land, which measures production. The western half of the United States would sustain a population greater than that of our whole country to-day if the waters that now run to waste were saved and used for irrigation. The forest and water problems are perhaps the most vital internal questions of the United States.

GAME PROTECTION

Certain of the forest reserves should also be made preserves for the wild forest creatures. All of the reserves should be better protected from fires. Many of them need special protection because of the great injury done by live stock, above all by sheep. The increase in deer, elk, and other animals in the Yellowstone Park shows what may be expected when other mountain forests are properly protected by law and properly guarded. Some of these areas have been so denuded of surface vegetation by overgrazing that the ground-breeding birds, including grouse and quail, and many mammals, including deer, have been exterminated or driven away. At the same time the water-storing capacity of the surface has been decreased or destroyed, thus promoting floods in times of rain and diminishing the flow of streams between rains.

In cases where natural conditions have been restored for a few years, vegetation has again carpeted the ground, birds and deer are coming back, and hundreds of persons, especially from the immediate neighborhood, come each summer to enjoy the privilege of camping. Some at least of the forest reserves should afford perpetual protection to the native fauna and flora, safe havens of refuge to our rapidly diminishing wild animals of the larger kinds, and free camping-grounds for the ever-increasing numbers of men and women who have learned to find rest, health, and recreation in the splendid forests and flower-clad meadows of our mountains. The forest reserves should be set apart forever for the use and benefit of our people as a whole and not sacrificed to the short-sighted greed of a few.

WATER CONSERVATION

The forests are natural reservoirs. By restraining the streams in flood and replenishing them in drought they make possible the use of waters otherwise wasted. They prevent the soil from washing, and so protect the storage reservoirs from filling up with silt. Forest conservation is therefore an essential condition of water conservation.

The forests alone cannot, however, fully regulate and conserve the waters of the arid region. Great storage works are necessary to equalize the flow of streams and to save the flood waters. Their construction has been conclusively shown to be an undertaking too vast for private effort. Nor can it be best accomplished by the individual States acting alone. Far-reaching interstate problems are involved; and the resources of single States would often be inadequate. It is properly a national function, at least in some of its features. It is as right for the National Government to make the streams and rivers of the arid region useful by engineering works for water storage as to make useful the rivers and harbors of the humid region by engineering works of another kind. The storing of the floods in reservoirs at the headwaters of our rivers is but an enlargement of our present policy of river control, under which levees are built on the lower reaches of the same streams.

The government should construct and maintain these reservoirs as it does other public works. Where their purpose is to regulate the flow of streams, the water should be turned freely into the channels in the dry season to take the same course under the same laws as the natural flow.

RECLAMATION AND IRRIGATION

The reclamation of the unsettled arid public lands presents a different problem. Here it is not enough to regulate the flow of streams. The object of the government is to dispose of the land to settlers who will build homes upon it. To accomplish this object water must be brought within their reach.

The pioneer settlers on the arid public domain chose their homes along streams from which they could themselves divert the water to reclaim their holdings. Such opportunities are practically gone. There remain, however, vast areas of public land which can be made available for homestead settlement, but only by reservoirs and main-line canals impracticable for private enterprise. These irrigation works should be built by the National Government. The lands reclaimed by them should be reserved by the government for actual settlers, and the cost of construction should so far as possible be repaid by the land reclaimed. The distribution of the water, the division of the streams among irrigators, should be left to the settlers themselves in conformity with State laws and without interference with those laws or with vested rights. The policy of the National Government should be to aid irrigation in the several States and Territories in such manner as will enable the people in the local communities to help themselves, and as will stimulate needed reforms in the State laws and regulations governing irrigation.

The reclamation and settlement of the arid lands will enrich every portion of our country, just as the settlement of the Ohio and Mississippi valleys brought prosperity to the Atlantic States. The increased demand for manufactured articles will stimulate industrial production, while wider home markets and the trade of Asia will consume the larger food-supplies and effectually prevent Western competition with Eastern agriculture. Indeed, the products of irrigation will be consumed chiefly in upbuilding local centres of mining and other industries, which would otherwise not come into existence at all. Our people as a whole will profit, for successful home-making is but another name for the upbuilding of the nation.

The necessary foundation has already been laid for the inauguration of the policy just described. It would be unwise to begin by doing too much, for a great deal will doubtless be learned, both as to what can and what cannot be safely attempted, by the early efforts, which must of necessity be partly experimental in character. At the very beginning the government should make clear, beyond shadow of doubt, its intention to pursue this policy on lines of the broadest public interest. No reservoir or canal should ever be built to satisfy selfish personal or local interests; but only in accordance with the advice of trained experts, after long investigation has shown the locality where all the conditions combine to make the work most needed and fraught with the greatest usefulness to the community as a whole. There should be no extravagance, and the believers in the need of irrigation will most benefit their cause by seeing to it that it is free from the least taint of excessive or reckless expenditure of the public moneys.

Whatever the nation does for the extension of irrigation should harmonize with, and tend to improve, the condition of those now living on irrigated land. We are not at the starting-point of this development. Over two hundred millions of private capital has already been expended in the construction of irrigation works, and many million acres of arid land reclaimed. A high degree of enterprise and ability has been shown in the work itself; but as much cannot be said in reference to the laws relating thereto. The security and value of the homes created depend largely on the stability of titles to water; but the majority of these rest on the uncertain foundation of court decisions rendered in ordinary suits at law. With a few creditable exceptions, the arid States have failed to provide for the certain and just division of streams in times of scarcity. Lax and uncertain laws have made it possible to establish rights to water in excess of actual uses or necessities, and many streams have already passed into private ownership, or a control equivalent to ownership.

Whoever controls a stream practically controls the land it renders productive, and the doctrine of private ownership of water apart from land cannot prevail without causing enduring wrong. The recognition of such ownership, which has been permitted to grow up in the arid regions, should give way to a more enlightened and larger recognition of the rights of the public in the control and disposal of the public water-supplies. Laws founded upon conditions obtaining in humid regions, where water is too abundant to justify hoarding it, have no proper application in a dry country.

In the arid States the only right to water which should be recognized is that of use. In irrigation this right should attach to the land reclaimed and be inseparable therefrom. Granting perpetual water-rights to others than users, without compensation to the public, is open to all the objections which apply to giving away perpetual franchises to the public utilities of cities. A few of the Western States have already recognized this, and have incorporated in their constitutions the doctrine of perpetual State ownership of water.

The benefits which have followed the unaided development of the past justify the nation's aid and co-operation in the more difficult and important work yet to be accomplished. Laws so vitally affecting homes as those which control the water-supply will only be effective when they have the sanction of the irrigators; reforms can only be final and satisfactory when they come through the enlightenment of the people most concerned. The larger development which national aid insures should, however, awaken in every arid State the determination to make its irrigation system equal in justice and effectiveness that of any country in the civilized world. Nothing could be more unwise than for isolated communities to continue to learn every thing experimentally, instead of profiting by what is already known elsewhere. We are dealing with a new and momentous question, in the pregnant years while institutions are forming, and what we do will affect not only the present but future generations.

Our aim should be not simply to reclaim the largest area of land and provide homes for the largest number of people, but to create for this new industry the best possible social and industrial conditions; and this requires that we not only understand the existing situation, but avail ourselves of the best experience of the time in the solution of its problems. A careful study should be made, both by the nation and the States, of the irrigation laws and conditions here and abroad. Ultimately it will probably be necessary for the nation to co-operate with the several arid States in proportion as these States by their legislation and administration show themselves fit to receive it.

HAWAII

In Hawaii our aim must be to develop the Territory on the traditional American lines. We do not wish a region of large estates tilled by cheap labor; we wish a healthy American community of men who themselves till the farms they own. All our legislation for the islands should be shaped with this end in view; the well-being of the average home-maker must afford the true test of the healthy development of the islands. The land policy should as nearly as possible be modelled on our homestead system.

PORTO RICO

It is a pleasure to say that it is hardly more necessary to report as to Porto Rico than as to any State or Territory within our continental limits. The island is thriving as never before, and it is being administered efficiently and honestly. Its people are now enjoying liberty and order under the protection of the United States, and upon this fact we congratulate them and ourselves. Their material welfare must be as carefully and jealously considered as the welfare of any other portion of our country. We have given them the great gift of free access for their products to the markets of the United States. I ask the attention of the Congress to the need of legislation concerning the public lands of Porto Rico.

CUBA

In Cuba such progress has been made toward putting the independent government of the island upon a firm footing that before the present session of Congress closes this will be an accomplished fact. Cuba will then start as her own mistress; and to the beautiful Queen of the Antilles, as she unfolds this new page of her destiny, we extend our heartiest greetings and good wishes. Elsewhere I have discussed the question of reciprocity. In the case of Cuba, however, there are weighty reasons of morality and of national interest why the policy should be held to have a peculiar application, and I most earnestly ask your attention to the wisdom, indeed to the vital need, of providing for a substantial reduction in the tariff duties on Cuban imports into the United States. Cuba has in her constitution affirmed what we desired, that she should stand, in international matters, in closer and more friendly relations with us than with any other power; and we are bound by every consideration of honor and expediency to pass commercial measures in the interest of her material well-being.

PHILIPPINES

In the Philippines our problem is larger. They are very rich tropical islands, inhabited by many varying tribes, representing widely different stages of progress toward civilization. Our earnest effort is to help these people upward along the stony and difficult path that leads to self-government. We hope to make our administration of the islands honorable to our nation by making it of the highest benefit to the Filipinos themselves; and as an earnest of what we intend to do, we point to what we have done. Already a greater measure of material prosperity and of governmental honesty and efficiency has been attained in the Philippines than ever before in their history.

It is no light task for a nation to achieve the temperamental qualities without which the institutions of free government are but an empty mockery. Our people are now successfully governing themselves, because for more than a thousand years they have been slowly fitting themselves, sometimes consciously, sometimes unconsciously, toward this end. What has taken us thirty generations to achieve, we cannot expect to see another race accomplish out of hand, especially when large portions of that race start very far behind the point which our ancestors had reached even thirty generations ago. In dealing with the Philippine people we must show both patience and strength, forbearance and steadfast resolution. Our aim is high. We do not desire to do for the islanders merely what has elsewhere been done for tropic peoples by even the best foreign governments. We hope to do for them what has never before been done for any people of the tropics—to make them fit for self-government after the fashion of the really free nations.

History may safely be challenged to show a single instance in which a masterful race such as ours, having been forced by the exigencies of war to take possession of an alien land, has behaved to its inhabitants with the disinterested zeal for their progress that our people have shown in the Philippines. To leave the islands at this time would mean that they would fall into a welter of murderous anarchy. Such desertion of duty on our part would be a crime against humanity. The character of Governor Taft and of his associates and subordinates is a proof, if such be needed, of the sincerity of our effort to give the islanders a constantly increasing measure of self-government, exactly as fast as they show themselves fit to exercise it. Since the civil government was established not an appointment has been made in the islands with any reference to considerations of political influence, or to aught else save the fitness of the man and the needs of the service.

In our anxiety for the welfare and progress of the Philippines, it may be that here and there we have gone too rapidly in giving them local self-government. It is on this side that our error, if any, has been committed. No competent observer, sincerely desirous of finding out the facts and influenced only by a desire for the welfare of the natives, can assert that we have not gone far enough. We have gone to the very verge of safety in hastening the process. To have taken a single step farther or faster in advance would have been folly and weakness, and might well have been crime. We are extremely anxious that the natives shall show the power of governing themselves. We are anxious, first for their sakes, and next, because it relieves us of a great burden. There need not be the slightest fear of our not continuing to give them all the liberty for which they are fit.

The only fear is lest in our overanxiety we give them a degree of independence for which they are unfit, thereby inviting reaction and disaster. As fast as there is any reasonable hope that in a given district the people can govern themselves, self-government has been given in that district. There is not a locality fitted for self-government which has not received it. But it may well be that in certain cases it will have to be withdrawn because the inhabitants show themselves unfit to exercise it; such instances have already occurred. In other words, there is not the slightest chance of our failing to show a sufficiently humanitarian spirit. The danger comes in the opposite direction.

There are still troubles ahead in the islands. The insurrection has become an affair of local banditti and marauders, who deserve no higher regard than the brigands of portions of the Old World. Encouragement, direct or indirect, to these insurrectos stands on the same footing as encouragement to hostile Indians in the days when we still had Indian wars. Exactly as our aim is to give to the Indian who remains peaceful the fullest and amplest consideration, but to have it understood that we will show no weakness if he goes on the war-path, so we must make it evident, unless we are false to our own traditions and to the demands of civilization and humanity, that while we will do everything in our power for the Filipino who is peaceful, we will take the sternest measures with the Filipino who follows the path of the insurrecto and the ladrone.

The heartiest praise is due to large numbers of the natives of the islands for their steadfast loyalty. The Macabebes have been conspicuous for their courage and devotion to the flag. I recommend that the secretary of war be empowered to take some systematic action in the way of aiding those of these men who are crippled in the service and the families of those who are killed.

The time has come when there should be additional legislation for the Philippines. Nothing better can be done for the islands than to introduce industrial enterprises. Nothing would benefit them so much as throwing them open to industrial development. The connection between idleness and mischief is proverbial, and the opportunity to do remunerative work is one of the surest preventatives of war. Of course no business man will go into the Philippines unless it is to his interest to do so, and it is immensely to the interest of the islands that he should go in. It is therefore necessary that the Congress should pass laws by which the resources of the islands can be developed; so that franchises (for limited terms of years) can be granted to companies doing business in them, and every encouragement be given to the incoming of business men of every kind.

Not to permit this is to do a wrong to the Philippines. The franchises must be granted and the business permitted only under regulations which will guarantee the islands against any kind of improper exploitation. But the vast natural wealth of the islands must be developed, and the capital willing to develop it must be given the opportunity. The field must be thrown open to individual enterprise, which has been the real factor in the development of every region over which our flag has flown. It is urgently necessary to enact suitable laws dealing with general transportation, mining, banking, currency, homesteads, and the use and ownership of the lands and timber. These laws will give free play to industrial enterprise;

and the commercial development which will surely follow will accord to the people of the islands the best proofs of the sincerity of our desire to aid them.

PACIFIC CABLES

I call your attention most earnestly to the crying need of a cable to Hawaii and the Philippines, to be continued from the Philippines to points in Asia. We should not defer a day longer than necessary the construction of such a cable. It is demanded not merely for commercial but for political and military considerations.

Either the Congress should immediately provide for the construction of a government cable, or else an arrangement should be made by which like advantages to those accruing from a government cable may be secured to the government by contract with a private cable company.

ISTHMIAN CANAL

No single great material work which remains to be undertaken on this continent is of such consequence to the American people as the building of a canal across the isthmus connecting North and South America. Its importance to the nation is by no means limited merely to its material effects upon our business prosperity; and yet with view to these effects alone it would be to the last degree important for us immediately to begin it. While its beneficial effects would perhaps be most marked upon the Pacific coast and the Gulf and South Atlantic States, it would also greatly benefit other sections. It is emphatically a work which it is for the interest of the entire country to begin and complete as soon as possible; it is one of those great works which only a great nation can undertake with prospects of success, and which when done are not only permanent assets in the nation's material interests, but standing monuments to its constructive ability.

I am glad to be able to announce to you that our negotiations on this subject with Great Britain, conducted on both sides in a spirit of friendliness and mutual good-will and respect, have resulted in my being able to lay before the Senate a treaty which if ratified will enable us to begin preparations for an isthmian canal at any time, and which guarantees to this nation every right that it has ever asked in connection with the canal. In this treaty, the old Clayton-Bulwer treaty, so long recognized as inadequate to supply the base for the construction and maintenance of a necessarily American ship canal, is abrogated. It specifically provides that the United States alone shall do the work of building and assume the responsibility of safeguarding the canal and shall regulate its neutral use by all nations on terms of equality without the guarantee or interference of any outside nation from any quarter. The signed treaty will at once be laid before the Senate, and if approved the Congress can then proceed to give effect to the advantages it secures us by providing for the building of the canal.

INTERNATIONAL PEACE

The true end of every great and free people should be self-respecting peace; and this nation most earnestly desires sincere and cordial friendship with all others. Over the entire world, of recent years, wars between the great civilized powers have become less and less frequent. Wars with barbarous or semi-barbarous peoples come in an entirely different category, being merely a most regrettable but necessary international police duty which must be performed for the sake of the welfare of mankind. Peace can only be kept with certainty where both sides wish to keep it; but more and more the civilized peoples are realizing the wicked folly of war and are attaining that condition of just and intelligent regard for the rights of others which will in the end, as we hope and believe, make world-wide peace possible. The peace conference at The Hague gave definite expression to this hope and belief and marked a stride toward their attainment.

MONROE DOCTRINE

This same peace conference acquiesced in our statement of the Monroe Doctrine as compatible with the purposes and aims of the conference.

The Monroe Doctrine should be the cardinal feature of the foreign policy of all the nations of the two Americas, as it is of the United States. Just seventy-eight years have passed since President Monroe in his Annual Message announced that "The American continents are henceforth not to be considered as subjects for future colonization by any European power." In other words, the Monroe Doctrine is a declaration that there must be no territorial aggrandizement by any non-American power at the expense of any American power on American soil. It is in nowise intended as hostile to any nation in the Old World. Still less is it intended to give cover to any aggression by one New World power at the expense of any other. It is simply a step, and a long step, toward assuring the universal peace of the world by securing the possibility of permanent peace on this hemisphere.

During the past century other influences have established the permanence and independence of the smaller states of Europe. Through the Monroe Doctrine we hope to be able to safeguard like independence and secure like permanence for the lesser among the New World nations.

This doctrine has nothing to do with the commercial relations of any American power, save that it in truth allows each of them to form such as it desires. In other words, it is really a guarantee of the commercial independence of the Americas. We do not ask under this doctrine for any exclusive commercial dealings with any other American State. We do not guarantee any State against punishment if it misconducts itself, provided that punishment does not take the form of the acquisition of territory by any non-American power.

Our attitude in Cuba is a sufficient guarantee of our own

good faith. We have not the slightest desire to secure any territory at the expense of any of our neighbors. We wish to work with them hand in hand, so that all of us may be uplifted together, and we rejoice over the good fortune of any of them, we gladly hail their material prosperity and political stability, and are concerned and alarmed if any of them fall into industrial or political chaos. We do not wish to see any Old World military power grow up on this continent, or to be compelled to become a military power ourselves. The peoples of the Americas can prosper best if left to work out their own salvation in their own way.

THE NAVY

The work of upbuilding the navy must be steadily continued. No one point of our policy, foreign or domestic, is more important than this to the honor and material welfare, and above all to the peace, of our nation in the future. Whether we desire it or not, we must henceforth recognize that we have international duties no less than international rights. Even if our flag were hauled down in the Philippines and Porto Rico, even if we decided not to build the Isthmian Canal, we should need a thoroughly trained navy of adequate size, or else be prepared definitely and for all time to abandon the idea that our nation is among those whose sons go down to the sea in ships. Unless our commerce is always to be carried in foreign bottoms, we must have war-craft to protect it.

Inasmuch, however, as the American people have no thought of abandoning the path upon which they have entered, and especially in view of the fact that the building of the Isthmian Canal is fast becoming one of the matters which the whole people are united in demanding, it is imperative that our navy should be put and kept in the highest state of efficiency, and should be made to answer to our growing needs. So far from being in any way a provocation to war, an adequate and highly trained navy is the best guarantee against war, the cheapest and most effective peace insurance. The cost of building and maintaining such a navy represents the very lightest premium for insuring peace which this nation can possibly pay.

Probably no other great nation in the world is so anxious for peace as we are. There is not a single civilized power which has anything whatever to fear from aggressiveness on our part. All we want is peace; and toward this end we wish to be able to secure the same respect for our rights from others which we are eager and anxious to extend to their rights in return, to insure fair treatment to us commercially, and to guarantee the safety of the American people.

Our people intend to abide by the Monroe Doctrine and to insist upon it as the one sure means of securing the peace of the western hemisphere. The navy offers us the only means of making our insistence upon the Monroe Doctrine anything but a subject of derision to whatever nation chooses to disregard it. We desire the peace which comes as of right to the just man armed; not the peace granted on terms of ignominy to the craven and the weakling.

It is not possible to improvise a navy after war breaks out. The ships must be built and the men trained long in advance. Some auxiliary vessels can be turned into makeshifts which will do in default of any better for the minor work, and a proportion of raw men can be mixed with the highly trained, their shortcomings being made good by the skill of their fellows; but the efficient fighting force of the navy when pitted against an equal opponent will be found almost exclusively in the warships that have been regularly built and in the officers and men who through years of faithful performance of sea duty have been trained to handle their formidable but complex and delicate weapons with the highest efficiency. In the late war with Spain the ships that dealt the decisive blows at Manila and Santiago had been launched from two to fourteen years, and they were able to do as they did because the men in the conning-towers, the gun-turrets, and, the engine-rooms had through long years of practice at sea learned how to do their duty.

Our present navy was begun in 1882. At that period our navy consisted of a collection of antiquated wooden ships, already almost as out of place against modern war-vessels as the galleys of Alcibiades and Hamilcar—certainly as the ships of Tromp and Blake. Nor at that time did we have men fit to handle a modern man-of-war. Under the wise legislation of the Congress and the successful administration of a succession of patriotic secretaries of the navy, belonging to both political parties, the work of upbuilding the navy went on, and ships equal to any in the world of their kind were continually added; and what was even more important, these ships were exercised at sea singly and in squadrons until the men aboard them were able to get the best possible service out of them. The result was seen in the short war with Spain, which was decided with such rapidity because of the infinitely greater preparedness of our navy than of the Spanish navy.

While awarding the fullest honor to the men who actually commanded and manned the ships which destroyed the Spanish sea forces in the Philippines and in Cuba, we must not forget that an equal meed of praise belongs to those without whom neither blow could have been struck. The congressmen who voted years in advance the money to lay down the ships, to build the guns, to buy the armor-plate; the department officials and the business men and wage-workers who furnished what the Congress had authorized; the secretaries of the navy who asked for and expended the appropriations; and finally the officers who, in fair weather and foul, on actual sea service, trained and disciplined the crews of the ships when there was no war in sight—all are entitled to a full share in the glory of Manila and Santiago, and the respect accorded by every true American to those who wrought such signal triumph for our country. It was forethought and preparation which secured us the overwhelming triumph of 1898. If we fail to show forethought and preparation now, there may come a time when disaster will befall us instead of triumph; and should this time come, the fault will rest primarily, not upon those whom the accident of events puts in supreme command at the moment, but upon those who have failed to prepare in advance.

There should be no cessation in the work of completing our navy. So far ingenuity has been wholly unable to devise a substitute for the great war-craft whose hammering guns beat out the mastery of the high seas. It is unsafe and unwise not to provide this year for several additional battleships and heavy armored cruisers, with auxiliary and lighter craft in proportion; for the exact numbers and character I refer you to the report of the secretary of the navy. But there is something we need even more than additional ships, and this is additional officers and men. To provide battleships and cruisers and then lay them up, with the expectation of leaving them unmanned until they are needed in actual war, would be worse than folly; it would be a crime against the nation.

To send any war-ship against a competent enemy unless those aboard it have been trained by years of actual sea service, including incessant gunnery practice, would be to invite not merely disaster, but the bitterest shame and humiliation. Four thousand additional seamen and 1,000 additional marines should be provided; and an increase in the officers should be provided by making a large addition to the classes at Annapolis. There is one small matter which should be mentioned in connection with Annapolis. The pretentious and unmeaning title of "naval cadet" should be abolished; the title of "midshipman," full of historic association, should be restored.

Even in time of peace a war-ship should be used until it wears out, for only so can it be kept fit to respond to any emergency. The officers and men alike should be kept as much as possible on blue water, for it is there only they can learn their duties as they should be learned. The big vessels should be manœuvred in squadrons containing not merely battleships, but the necessary proportion of cruisers and scouts. The torpedo-boats should be handled by the younger officers in such manner as will best fit the latter to take responsibility and meet the emergencies of actual warfare.

Every detail ashore which can be performed by a civilian should be so performed, the officer being kept for his special duty in the sea service. Above all, gunnery practice should be unceasing. It is important to have our navy of adequate size, but it is even more important that ship for ship it should equal in efficiency any navy in the world. This is possible only with highly drilled crews and officers, and this in turn imperatively demands continuous and progressive instruction in target practice, ship handling, squadron tactics, and general discipline. Our ships must be assembled in squadrons actively cruising away from harbors and never long at anchor. The resulting wear upon engines and hulls must be endured; a battleship worn out in long training of officers and men is well paid for by the results, while, on the other hand, no matter in how excellent condition, it is useless if the crew be not expert.

We now have seventeen battleships appropriated for, of which nine are completed and have been commissioned for actual service. The remaining eight will be ready in from two to four years, but it will take at least that time to recruit and train the men to fight them. It is of vast concern that we have trained crews ready for the vessels by the time they are commissioned. Good ships and good guns are simply good weapons, and the best weapons are useless save in the hands of men who know how to fight with them. The men must be trained and drilled under a thorough and well-planned system of progressive instruction, while the recruiting must be carried on with still greater vigor. Every effort must be made to exalt the main function of the officer—the command of men. The leading graduates of the Naval Academy should be assigned to the combatant branches, the line and marines.

Many of the essentials of success are already recognized by the general board, which, as the central office of a growing staff, is moving steadily toward a proper war efficiency and a proper efficiency of the whole navy, under the secretary. This general board, by fostering the creation of a general staff, is providing for the official and then the general recognition of our altered conditions as a nation and of the true meaning of a great war fleet, which meaning is, first, the best men, and, second, the best ships.

The Naval Militia forces are State organizations and are trained for coast service, and in event of war they will constitute the inner line of defense. They should receive hearty encouragement from the general government.

But in addition we should at once provide for a National Naval Reserve, organized and trained under the direction of the Navy Department, and subject to the call of the Chief Executive whenever war becomes imminent. It should be a real auxiliary to the naval seagoing peace establishment, and offer material to be drawn on at once for manning our ships in time of war. It should be composed of graduates of the Naval Academy, graduates of the Naval Militia, officers and crews of coast-line steamers, longshore schooners, fishing-vessels, and steam-yachts, together with the coast population about such centres as life-saving stations and lighthouses.

The American people must either build and maintain an adequate navy or else make up their minds definitely to accept a secondary position in international affairs, not merely in political, but in commercial, matters. It has been well said that there is no surer way of courting national disaster than to be "opulent, aggressive, and unarmed."

THE ARMY

It is not necessary to increase our army beyond its present size at this time. But it is necessary to keep it at the highest point of efficiency. The individual units who as officers and enlisted men compose this army, are, we have good reason to believe, at least as efficient as those of any other army in the entire world. It is our duty to see that their training is of a kind to insure the highest possible expression of power to these units when acting in combination.

The conditions of modern war are such as to make an infinitely heavier demand than ever before upon the individual character and capacity of the officer and the enlisted man, and to make it far more difficult for men to act together with effect. At present the fighting must be done in extended order, which means that each man must act for himself and at the same time act in combination with others with whom he is no longer in the old-fashioned elbow-to-elbow touch. Under such conditions a few men of the highest excellence are worth more than many men without the special skill which is only found as the result of special training applied to men of exceptional physique and morale. But nowadays the most valuable fighting man and the most difficult to perfect is the rifleman who is also a skilful and daring rider.

The proportion of our cavalry regiments has wisely been increased. The American cavalryman, trained to manœuvre and fight with equal facility on foot and on horseback, is the best type of soldier for general purposes now to be found in the world. The ideal cavalryman of the present day is a man who can fight on foot as effectively as the best infantryman, and who is in addition unsurpassed in the care and management of his horse and in his ability to fight on horseback.

A general staff should be created. As for the present staff and supply departments, they should be filled by details from the line, the men so detailed returning after a while to their line duties. It is very undesirable to have the senior grades of the army composed of men who have come to fill the positions by the mere fact of seniority. A system should be adopted by which there shall be an elimination grade by grade of those who seem unfit to render the best service in the next grade. Justice to the veterans of the Civil War who are still in the army would seem to require that in the matter of retirements they be given by law the same privileges accorded to their comrades in the navy.

The process of elimination of the least fit should be conducted in a manner that would render it practically impossible to apply political or social pressure on behalf of any candidate, so that each man may be judged purely on his own merits. Pressure for the promotion of civil officials for political reasons is bad enough, but it is tenfold worse where applied on behalf of officers of the army or navy. Every promotion and every detail under the War Department must be made solely with regard to the good of the service and to the capacity and merit of the man himself. No pressure, political, social, or personal, of any kind, will be permitted to exercise the least effect in any question of promotion or detail; and if there is reason to believe that such pressure is exercised at the instigation of the officer concerned, it will be held to militate against him. In our army we cannot afford to have rewards or duties distributed save on the simple ground that those who by their own merits are entitled to the rewards get them, and those who are peculiarly fit to do the duties are chosen to perform them.

Every effort should be made to bring the army to a constantly increasing state of efficiency. When on actual service no work save that directly in the line of such service should be required. The paper work in the army, as in the navy, should be greatly reduced. What is needed is proved power of command and capacity to work well in the field. Constant care is necessary to prevent dry rot in the transportation and commissary departments.

Our army is so small and so much scattered that it is very difficult to give the higher officers (as well as the lower officers and the enlisted men) a chance to practice manœuvres in mass and on a comparatively large scale. In time of need no amount of individual excellence would avail against the paralysis which would follow inability to work as a coherent whole, under skilful and daring leadership. The Congress should provide means whereby it will be possible to have field exercises by at least a division of regulars, and if possible also a division of national guardsmen, once a year. These exercises might take the form of field manœuvres; or, if on the Gulf Coast or the Pacific or Atlantic seaboard, or in the region of the Great

Lakes, the army corps when assembled could be marched from some inland point to some point on the water, there embarked, disembarked after a couple of days' journey at some other point, and again marched inland. Only by actual handling and providing for men in masses while they are marching, camping, embarking, and disembarking, will it be possible to train the higher officers to perform their duties well and smoothly.

A great debt is owing from the public to the men of the army and navy. They should be so treated as to enable them to reach the highest point of efficiency, so that they may be able to respond instantly to any demand made upon them to sustain the interests of the nation and the honor of the flag. The individual American enlisted man is probably on the whole a more formidable fighting man than the regular of any other army. Every consideration should be shown him, and in return the highest standard of usefulness should be exacted from him. It is well worth while for the Congress to consider whether the pay of enlisted men upon second and subsequent enlistments should not be increased to correspond with the increased value of the veteran soldier.

Much good has already come from the act reorganizing the army, passed early in the present year. The three prime reforms, all of them of literally inestimable value, are, first, the substitution of four-year details from the line for permanent appointments in the so-called staff divisions; second, the establishment of a corps of artillery with a chief at the head; third, the establishment of a maximum and minimum limit for the army. It would be difficult to overestimate the improvement in the efficiency of our army which these three reforms are making, and have in part already effected.

The reorganization provided for by the act has been substantially accomplished. The improved conditions in the Philippines have enabled the War Department materially to reduce the military charge upon our revenue and to arrange the number of soldiers so as to bring this number much nearer to the minimum than to the maximum limit established by law. There is, however, need of supplementary legislation. Thorough military education must be provided, and in addition to the regulars the advantages of this education should be given to the officers of the National Guard and others in civil life who desire intelligently to fit themselves for possible mlitary duty. The officers should be given the chance to perfect themselves by study in the higher branches of this art. At West Point the education should be of the kind most apt to turn out men who are good in actual field-service; too much stress should not be laid on mathematics, nor should proficiency therein be held to establish the right of entry to a *corps d'élite*. The typical American officer of the best kind need not be a good mathematician; but he must be able to master himself, to control others, and to show boldness and fertility of resource in every emergency.

Action should be taken in reference to the militia and to the raising of volunteer forces. Our militia law is obsolete and worthless. The organization and armament of the National Guard of the several States, which are treated as militia in the appropriations by the Congress, should be made identical with those provided for the regular forces. The obligations and duties of the guard in time of war should be carefully defined, and a system established by law under which the method of procedure of raising volunteer forces should be prescribed in advance. It is utterly impossible in the excitement and haste of impending war to do this satisfactorily if the arrangements have not been made long beforehand. Provision should be made for utilizing in the first volunteer organizations called out the training of those citizens who have already had experience under arms, and especially for the selection in advance of the officers of any force which may be raised; for careful selection of the kind necessary is impossible after the outbreak of war.

That the army is not at all a mere instrument of destruction has been shown during the last three years. In the Philippines, Cuba, and Porto Rico it has proved itself a great constructive force, a most potent implement for the upbuilding of a peaceful civilization.

VETERANS

No other citizens deserve so well of the Republic as the veterans, the survivors of those who saved the Union. They did the one deed which if left undone would have meant that all else in our history went for nothing. But for their steadfast prowess in the greatest crisis of our history, all our annals would be meaningless, and our great experiment in popular freedom and self-government a gloomy failure. Moreover, they not only left us a united nation, but they left us also as a heritage the memory of the mighty deeds by which the nation was kept united. We are now indeed one nation, one in fact as well as in name; we are united in our devotion to the flag which is the symbol of national greatness and unity; and the very completeness of our union enables us all, in every part of the country, to glory in the valor shown alike by the sons of the North and the sons of the South in the times that tried men's souls.

The men who in the last three years have done so well in the East and the West Indies and on the mainland of Asia have shown that this remembrance is not lost. In any serious crisis the United States must rely for the great mass of its fighting men upon the volunteer soldiery who do not make a permanent profession of the military career; and whenever such a crisis arises the deathless memories of the Civil War will give to Americans the lift of lofty purpose which comes to those whose fathers have stood valiantly in the forefront of the battle.

CIVIL SERVICE

The merit system of making appointments is in its essence as democratic and American as the common-school system itself. It simply means that in clerical and other positions where the duties are entirely non-political, all applicants should have a fair field and no favor, each standing on his merits as he is able to show them by practical test. Written competitive examinations offer the only available means in many cases for applying this system. In other cases, as where laborers are employed, a system of registration undoubtedly can be widely extended. There are, of course, places where the written competitive examination cannot be applied, and others where it offers by no means an ideal solution, but where under existing political conditions it is, though an imperfect means, yet the best present means of getting satisfactory results.

Whenever the conditions have permitted the application of the merit system in its fullest and widest sense, the gain to the government has been immense. The navy-yards and postal service illustrate, probably better than any other branches of the government, the great gain in economy, efficiency, and honesty due to the enforcement of this principle.

I recommend the passage of a law which will extend the classified service to the District of Columbia, or will at least enable the President thus to extend it. In my judgment all laws providing for the temporary employment of clerks should hereafter contain a provision that they be selected under the civil-service law.

It is important to have this system obtain at home, but it is even more important to have it applied rigidly in our insular possessions. Not an office should be filled in the Philippines or Porto Rico with any regard to the man's partisan affiliations or services, with any regard to the political, social, or personal influence which he may have at his command; in short, heed should be paid to absolutely nothing save the man's own character and capacity and the needs of the service.

The administration of these islands should be as wholly free from the suspicion of partisan politics as the administration of the army and navy. All that we ask from the public servant in the Philippines or Porto Rico is that he reflect honor on his country by the way in which he makes that country's rule a benefit to the peoples who have come under it. This is all that we should ask, and we cannot afford to be content with less.

The merit system is simply one method of securing honest and efficient administration of the government, and in the long run the sole justification of any type of government lies in its proving itself both honest and efficient.

CONSULAR SERVICE

The consular service is now organized under the provisions of a law passed in 1856, which is entirely inadequate to existing conditions. The interest shown by so many commercial bodies throughout the country in the reorganization of the service is heartily commended to your attention. Several bills providing for a new consular service have in recent years been submitted to the Congress. They are based upon the just principle that appointments to the service should be made only after a practical test of the applicant's fitness, that promotions should be governed by trustworthiness, adaptability, and zeal in the performance of duty, and that the tenure of office should be unaffected by partisan considerations.

The guardianship and fostering of our rapidly expanding foreign commerce, the protection of American citizens resorting to foreign countries in lawful pursuit of their affairs, and the maintenance of the dignity of the nation abroad, combine to make it essential that our consuls should be men of character, knowledge, and enterprise. It is true that the service is now, in the main, efficient, but a standard of excellence cannot be permanently maintained until the principles set forth in the bills heretofore submitted to the Congress on this subject are enacted into law.

THE INDIANS

In my judgment the time has arrived when we should definitely make up our minds to recognize the Indian as an individual and not as a member of a tribe. The General Allotment Act is a mighty pulverizing engine to break up the tribal mass. It acts directly upon the family and the individual. Under its provisions some 60,000 Indians have already become citizens of the United States. We should now break up the tribal funds, doing for them what allotment does for the tribal lands; that is, they should be divided into individual holdings. There will be a transition period during which the funds will in many cases have to be held in trust. This is the case also with the lands. A stop should be put upon the indiscriminate permission to Indians to lease their allotments. The effort should be steadily to make the Indian work like any other man on his own ground. The marriage laws of the Indians should be made the same as those of the whites.

In the schools the education should be elementary and largely industrial. The need of higher education among the Indians is very, very limited. On the reservations care should be taken to try to suit the teaching to the needs of the particular Indian. There is no use in attempting to induce agriculture in a country suited only for cattle-raising where the Indian should be made a stock-grower. The ration system, which is merely the corral and the reservation system, is highly detrimental to the Indians. It promotes beggary, perpetuates pauperism, and stifles industry. It is an effectual barrier to progress. It must continue to a greater or less degree as long as tribes are herded on reservations and have everything in common. The Indian should be treated as an individual—like the white man. During the change of treatment inevitable hardships will occur; every effort should be made to minimize these hardships; but we should not because of them hesitate to make the change. There should be a continuous reduction in the number of agencies.

In dealing with the aboriginal races few things are more important than to preserve them from the terrible physical and moral degradation resulting from the liquor traffic. We are doing all we can to save our own Indian tribes from this evil. Wherever by international agreement this same end can be attained as regards races where we do not possess exclusive control, every effort should be made to bring it about.

NATIONAL EXPOSITIONS

I bespeak the most cordial support from the Congress and the people for the St. Louis Exposition to commemorate the One Hundredth Anniversary of the Louisiana Purchase. This purchase was the greatest instance of expansion in our history. It definitely decided that we were to become a great continental republic, by far the foremost power in the western hemisphere. It is one of three or four great landmarks in our history—the great turning-points in our development. It is eminently fitting that all our people should join with heartiest good-will in commemorating it, and the citizens of St. Louis, of Missouri, of all the adjacent region, are entitled to every aid in making the celebration a noteworthy event in our annals. We earnestly hope that foreign nations will appreciate the deep interest our country takes in this exposition, and our view of its importance from every standpoint, and that they will participate in securing its success. The National Government should be represented by a full and complete set of exhibits.

The people of Charleston, with great energy and civic spirit, are carrying on an exposition which will continue throughout most of the present session of the Congress. I heartily commend this exposition to the good-will of the people. It deserves all the encouragement that can be given it. The managers of the Charleston Exposition have requested the Cabinet officers to place thereat the government exhibits which have been at Buffalo, promising to pay the necessary expenses. I have taken the responsibility of directing that this be done, for I feel that it is due to Charleston to help her in her praiseworthy effort. In my opinion the management should not be required to pay all these expenses. I earnestly recommend that the Congress appropriate at once the small sum necessary for this purpose.

The Pan-American Exposition at Buffalo has just closed. Both from the industrial and the artistic standpoint this exposition has been in a high degree creditable and useful, not

merely to Buffalo but to the United States. The terrible
tragedy of the President's assassination interfered materially
with its being a financial success. The exposition was peculiarly
in harmony with the trend of our public policy, because it
represented an effort to bring into closer touch all the peoples
of the western hemisphere, and give them an increasing sense
of unity. Such an effort was a genuine service to the entire
American public.

SMITHSONIAN INSTITUTION

The advancement of the highest interests of national science
and learning and the custody of objects of art and of the
valuable results of scientific expeditions conducted by the
United States have been committed to the Smithsonian Institution. In furtherance of its declared purpose—for the
"increase and diffusion of knowledge among men"—the Congress has from time to time given it other important functions.
Such trusts have been executed by the institution with notable
fidelity. There should be no halt in the work of the institution,
in accordance with the plans which its secretary has presented,
for the preservation of the vanishing races of great North
American animals in the National Zoological Park. The urgent
needs of the National Museum are recommended to the favorable consideration of the Congress.

LIBRARY OF CONGRESS

Perhaps the most characteristic educational movement of the
past fifty years is that which has created the modern public
library and developed it into broad and active service. There
are now over 5,000 public libraries in the United States, the
product of this period. In addition to accumulating material,
they are also striving by organization, by improvement in
method, and by co-operation, to give greater efficiency to the
material they hold, to make it more widely useful, and by
avoidance of unnecessary duplication in process to reduce the
cost of its administration.

In these efforts they naturally look for assistance to the Federal library, which, though still the Library of Congress, and so entitled, is the one national library of the United States. Already the largest single collection of books on the western hemisphere, and certain to increase more rapidly than any other through purchase, exchange, and the operations of the copyright law, this library has a unique opportunity to render to the libraries of this country—to American scholarship—service of the highest importance. It is housed in a building which is the largest and most magnificent yet erected for library uses. Resources are now being provided which will develop the collection properly, equip it with the apparatus and service necessary to its effective use, render its bibliographic work widely available, and enable it to become, not merely a centre of research, but the chief factor in great co-operative efforts for the diffusion of knowledge and the advancement of learning.

CENSUS OFFICE

For the sake of good administration, sound economy, and the advancement of science, the Census Office as now constituted should be made a permanent government bureau. This would insure better, cheaper, and more satisfactory work, in the interest not only of our business but of statistic, economic, and social science.

POSTAL SERVICE

The remarkable growth of the postal service is shown in the fact that its revenues have doubled and its expenditures have nearly doubled within twelve years. Its progressive development compels constantly increasing outlay, but in this period of business energy and prosperity its receipts grow so much faster than its expenses that the annual deficit has been steadily reduced from $11,411,779 in 1897 to $3,923,727 in 1901. Among recent postal advances the success of rural free delivery wherever established has been so marked, and actual experience has made its benefits so plain, that the demand for its extension is general and urgent.

It is just that the great agricultural population should share in the improvement of the service. The number of rural routes now in operation is 6,009, practically all established within three years, and there are 6,000 applications awaiting action. It is expected that the number in operation at the close of the current fiscal year will reach 8,600. The mail will then be daily carried to the doors of 5,700,000 of our people who have heretofore been dependent upon distant offices, and one-third of all that portion of the country which is adapted to it will be covered by this kind of service.

The full measure of postal progress which might be realized has long been hampered and obstructed by the heavy burden imposed on the government through the intrenched and well-understood abuses which have grown up in connection with second-class mail matter. The extent of this burden appears when it is stated that while the second-class matter makes nearly three-fifths of the weight of all the mail, it paid for the last fiscal year only $4,294,445 of the aggregate postal revenue of $111,631,193. If the pound rate of postage, which produces the large loss thus entailed, and which was fixed by the Congress with the purpose of encouraging the dissemination of public information, were limited to the legitimate newspapers and periodicals actually contemplated by the law, no just exception could be taken. That expense would be the recognized and accepted cost of a liberal public policy deliberately adopted for a justifiable end. But much of the matter which enjoys the privileged rate is wholly outside of the intent of the law, and has secured admission only through an evasion of its requirements or through lax construction. The proportion of such wrongly included matter is estimated by postal experts to be one-half of the whole volume of second-class mail. If it be only one-third or one-quarter, the magnitude of the burden is apparent. The Post-Office Department has now undertaken to remove the abuses so far as is possible by a stricter application of the law; and it should be sustained in its effort.

CHINA

Owing to the rapid growth of our power and our interests on the Pacific, whatever happens in China must be of the keenest national concern to us.

The general terms of the settlement of the questions growing out of the antiforeign uprisings in China of 1900, having been formulated in a joint note addressed to China by the representatives of the injured powers in December last, were promptly accepted by the Chinese Government. After protracted conferences the plenipotentiaries of the several powers were able to sign a final protocol with the Chinese plenipotentiaries on the 7th of last September, setting forth the measures taken by China in compliance with the demands of the joint note, and expressing their satisfaction therewith. It will be laid before the Congress, with a report of the plenipotentiary on behalf of the United States, Mr. William Woodville Rockhill, to whom high praise is due for the tact, good judgment, and energy he has displayed in performing an exceptionally difficult and delicate task.

The agreement reached disposes in a manner satisfactory to the powers of the various grounds of complaint, and will contribute materially to better future relations between China and the powers. Reparation has been made by China for the murder of foreigners during the uprising and punishment has been inflicted on the officials, however high in rank, recognized as responsible for or having participated in the outbreak. Official examinations have been forbidden for a period of five years in all cities in which foreigners have been murdered or cruelly treated, and edicts have been issued making all officials directly responsible for the future safety of foreigners and for the suppression of violence against them.

Provisions have been made for insuring the future safety of the foreign representatives in Peking by setting aside for their exclusive use a quarter of the city which the powers can make defensible and in which they can if necessary maintain permanent military guards; by dismantling the military works between the capital and the sea; and by allowing the temporary maintenance of foreign military posts along this line. An edict has been issued by the Emperor of China prohibiting for two years the importation of arms and ammunitions into China. China has agreed to pay adequate indemnities to the states, societies, and individuals for the losses sustained by them and for the expenses of the military expeditions sent by the various powers to protect life and restore order.

Under the provisions of the joint note of December, 1900, China has agreed to revise the treaties of commerce and navigation, and to take such other steps for the purpose of facilitating foreign trade as the foreign powers may decide to be needed.

The Chinese Government has agreed to participate financially in the work of bettering the water approaches to Shanghai and to Tientsin, the centres of foreign trade in central and northern China, and an international conservancy board, in which the Chinese Government is largely represented, has been provided for the improvement of the Shanghai River and the control of its navigation. In the same line of commercial advantages a revision of the present tariff on imports has been assented to for the purpose of substituting specific for *ad valorem* duties, and an expert has been sent abroad on the part of the United States to assist in this work. A list of articles to remain free of duty, including flour, cereals, and rice, gold and silver coin and bullion, has also been agreed upon in the settlement.

During these troubles our government has unswervingly advocated moderation, and has materially aided in bringing about an adjustment which tends to enhance the welfare of China and to lead to a more beneficial intercourse between the empire and the modern world; while in the critical period of revolt and massacre we did our full share in safeguarding life and property, restoring order, and vindicating the national interest and honor. It behooves us to continue in these paths, doing what lies in our power to foster feelings of good-will, and leaving no effort untried to work out the great policy of full and fair intercourse between China and the nations, on a footing of equal rights and advantages to all. We advocate the "open door" with all that it implies; not merely the procurement of enlarged commercial opportunities on the coasts, but access to the interior by the waterways with which China has been so extraordinarily favored. Only by bringing the people of China into peaceful and friendly community of trade with all the peoples of the earth can the work now auspiciously begun be carried to fruition. In the attainment of this purpose we necessarily claim parity of treatment, under the conventions, throughout the empire for our trade and our citizens with those of all other powers.

PAN-AMERICAN CONGRESS

We view with lively interest and keen hopes of beneficial results the proceedings of the Pan-American Congress, convoked at the invitation of Mexico, and now sitting at the Mexican capital. The delegates of the United States are under the most liberal instructions to co-operate with their colleagues in all matters promising advantage to the great family of America commonwealths, as well in their relations among themselves as in their domestic advancement and in their intercourse with the world at large.

MEXICO

My predecessor communicated to the Congress the fact that the Weil and La Abra awards against Mexico have been adjudged by the highest courts of our country to have been obtained through fraud and perjury on the part of the claimants, and that in accordance with the acts of the Congress the money remaining in the hands of the secretary of state on these awards has been returned to Mexico. A considerable portion of the money received from Mexico on these awards had been paid by this government to the claimants before the decision of the courts was rendered. My judgment is that the Congress should return to Mexico an amount equal to the sums thus already paid to the claimants.

INTERNATIONAL GOOD-WILL

The death of Queen Victoria caused the people of the United States deep and heartfelt sorrow, to which the government gave full expression. When President McKinley died, our nation in turn received from every quarter of the British Empire expressions of grief and sympathy no less sincere. The death of the Empress Dowager Frederick of Germany also aroused the genuine sympathy of the American people; and this sympathy was cordially reciprocated by Germany when the President was assassinated. Indeed, from every quarter of the civilized world we received, at the time of the President's death, assurances of such grief and regard as to touch the hearts of our people. In the midst of our affliction we reverently thank the Almighty that we are at peace with the nations of mankind; and we firmly intend that our policy shall be such as to continue unbroken these international relations of mutual respect and good-will.

II

SECOND ANNUAL MESSAGE[1]

TO THE SENATE AND HOUSE OF REPRESENTATIVES:
We still continue in a period of unbounded prosperity. This prosperity is not the creature of law, but undoubtedly the laws under which we work have been instrumental in creating the conditions which made it possible, and by unwise legislation it would be easy enough to destroy it. There will undoubtedly be periods of depression. The wave will recede; but the tide will advance. This nation is seated on a continent flanked by two great oceans. It is composed of men the descendants of pioneers, or, in a sense, pioneers themselves; of men winnowed out from among the nations of the Old World by the energy, boldness, and love of adventure found in their own eager hearts. Such a nation, so placed, will surely wrest success from fortune.

As a people we have played a large part in the world, and we are bent upon making our future even larger than the past. In particular, the events of the last four years have definitely decided that, for woe or for weal, our place must be great among the nations. We may either fail greatly or succeed greatly; but we cannot avoid the endeavor from which either great failure or great success must come. Even if we would, we cannot play a small part. If we should try, all that would follow would be that we should play a large part ignobly and shamefully.

But our people, the sons of the men of the Civil War, the sons of the men who had iron in their blood, rejoice in the present and face the future high of heart and resolute of will.

[1] Dated, the White House, December 2, 1902.

Ours is not the creed of the weakling and the coward; ours is the gospel of hope and of triumphant endeavor. We do not shrink from the struggle before us. There are many problems for us to face at the outset of the twentieth century—grave problems abroad and still graver at home; but we know that we can solve them and solve them well, provided only that we bring to the solution the qualities of head and heart which were shown by the men who, in the days of Washington, founded this government, and, in the days of Lincoln, preserved it.

REGULATION OF CORPORATIONS

No country has ever occupied a higher plane of material well-being than ours at the present moment. This well-being is due to no sudden or accidental causes, but to the play of the economic forces in this country for over a century; to our laws, our sustained and continuous policies; above all, to the high individual average of our citizenship. Great fortunes have been won by those who have taken the lead in this phenomenal industrial development, and most of these fortunes have been won not by doing evil, but as an incident to action which has benefited the community as a whole. Never before has material well-being been so widely diffused among our people. Great fortunes have been accumuated, and yet in the aggregate these fortunes are small indeed when compared to the wealth of the people as a whole. The plain people are better off than they have ever been before. The insurance companies, which are practically mutual benefit societies—especially helpful to men of moderate means—represent accumulations of capital which are among the largest in this country. There are more deposits in the savings-banks, more owners of farms, more well-paid wage-workers in this country now than ever before in our history. Of course, when the conditions have favored the growth of so much that was good, they have also favored somewhat the growth of what was evil. It is eminently necessary that we should endeavor to cut out this evil, but let us keep a due sense of proportion; let us not in fixing our gaze upon the lesser evil forget the greater good. The evils are real and some of them are menacing, but they are the outgrowth, not of misery or decadence, but of prosperity—of the progress of our gigantic industrial development. This industrial development must not be checked, but side by side with it should go such progressive regulation as will diminish the evils. We should fail in our duty if we did not try to remedy the evils, but we shall succeed only if we proceed patiently, with practical common sense as well as resolution, separating the good from the bad and holding on to the former while endeavoring to get rid of the latter.

In my message to the present Congress at its first session I discussed at length the question of the regulation of those big corporations commonly doing an interstate business, often with some tendency to monopoly, which are popularly known as trusts. The experience of the past year has emphasized, in my opinion, the desirability of the steps I then proposed. A fundamental requisite of social efficiency is a high standard of individual energy and excellence; but this is in nowise inconsistent with power to act in combination for aims which cannot so well be achieved by the individual acting alone. A fundamental base of civilization is the inviolability of property; but this is in nowise inconsistent with the right of society to regulate the exercise of the artificial powers which it confers upon the owners of property, under the name of corporate franchises, in such a way as to prevent the misuse of these powers. Corporations, and especially combinations of corporations, should be managed under public regulation. Experience has shown that under our system of government the necessary supervision cannot be obtained by State action. It must therefore be achieved by national action. Our aim is not to do away with corporations; on the contrary, these big aggregations are an inevitable development of modern industrialism, and the effort to destroy them would be futile unless accomplished in ways that would work the utmost mischief to the entire body politic. We can do nothing of good in the way of regulating and supervising these corporations until we fix clearly in our minds that we are not attacking the corporations, but endeavoring to do away with any evil in them. We are not hostile to them; we are merely determined that they shall be so handled as to subserve the public good. We draw the line against misconduct, not against wealth. The capitalist who, alone or in conjunction with his fellows, performs some great industrial feat by which he wins money is a well-doer, not a wrong-doer, provided only he works in proper and legitimate lines. We wish to favor such a man when he does well. We wish to supervise and control his actions only to prevent him from doing ill. Publicity can do no harm to the honest corporation; and we need not be overtender about sparing the dishonest corporation.

In curbing and regulating the combinations of capital which are, or may become, injurious to the public we must be careful not to stop the great enterprises which have legitimately reduced the cost of production, not to abandon the place which our country has won in the leadership of the international industrial world, not to strike down wealth with the result of closing factories and mines, of turning the wage-worker idle in the streets and leaving the farmer without a market for what he grows. Insistence upon the impossible means delay in achieving the possible, exactly as, on the other hand, the stubborn defense alike of what is good and what is bad in the existing system, the resolute effort to obstruct any attempt at betterment, betrays blindness to the historic truth that wise evolution is the sure safeguard against revolution.

No more important subject can come before the Congress than this of the regulation of interstate business. This country cannot afford to sit supine on the plea that under our peculiar system of government we are helpless in the presence of the new conditions, and unable to grapple with them or to cut out whatever of evil has arisen in connection with them. The power of the Congress to regulate interstate commerce is an absolute and unqualified grant, and without limitations other than those prescribed by the Constitution. The Congress has constitutional authority to make all laws necessary and proper for executing this power, and I am satisfied that this power has not been exhausted by any legislation now on the statute-books. It is evident, therefore, that evils restrictive of commercial freedom and entailing restraint upon national commerce fall within the regulative power of the Congress and that a wise and reasonable law would be a necessary and proper exercise of congressional authority to the end that such evils should be eradicated.

I believe that monopolies, unjust discriminations, which prevent or cripple competition, fradulent overcapitalization and other evils in trust organizations and practices which injuriously affect interstate trade can be prevented under the power of the Congress to "regulate commerce with foreign nations and among the several States" through regulations and requirements operating directly upon such commerce, the instrumentalities thereof, and those engaged therein.

I earnestly recommend this subject to the consideration of the Congress with a view to the passage of a law reasonable in its provisions and effective in its operations, upon which the questions can be finally adjudicated that now raise doubts as to the necessity of constitutional amendment. If it prove impossible to accomplish the purposes above set forth by such a law, then, assuredly, we should not shrink from amending the Constitution so as to secure beyond peradventure the power sought.

The Congress has not heretofore made any appropriation for the better enforcement of the antitrust law as it now stands. Very much has been done by the Department of Justice in securing the enforcement of this law, but much more could be done if the Congress would make a special appropriation for this purpose, to be expended under the direction of the attorney-general.

TARIFF

One proposition advocated has been the reduction of the tariff as a means of reaching the evils of the trusts which fall within the category I have described. Not merely would this be wholly ineffective, but the diversion of our efforts in such a direction would mean the abandonment of all intelligent attempt to do away with these evils. Many of the largest corporations, many of those which should certainly be included in any proper scheme of regulation, would not be affected in the slightest degree by a change in the tariff, save as such change interfered with the general prosperity of the country. The only relation of the tariff to big corporations as a whole is that the tariff makes manufactures profitable, and the tariff remedy proposed would be in effect simply to make manufactures unprofitable. To remove the tariff as a punitive measure directed against trusts would inevitably result in ruin to the weaker competitors who are struggling against them. Our aim should be not by unwise tariff changes to give foreign products the advantage over domestic products, but by proper regulation to give domestic competition a fair chance; and this end cannot be reached by any tariff changes which would affect unfavorably all domestic competitors, good and bad alike. The question of regulation of the trusts stands apart from the question of tariff revision.

Stability of economic policy must always be the prime economic need of this country. This stability should not be fossilization. The country has acquiesced in the wisdom of the protective-tariff principle. It is exceedingly undesirable that this system should be destroyed or that there should be violent and radical changes therein. Our past experience shows that great prosperity in this country has always come under a protective tariff; and that the country cannot prosper under fitful tariff changes at short intervals. Moreover, if the tariff laws as a whole work well, and if business has prospered under them and is prospering, it is better to endure for a time slight inconveniences and inequalities in some schedules than to upset business by too quick and too radical changes. It is most earnestly to be wished that we could treat the tariff from the standpoint solely of our business needs. It is, perhaps, too much to hope that partisanship may be entirely excluded from consideration of the subject, but at least it can be made secondary to the business interests of the country—that is, to the interests of our people as a whole. Unquestionably these business interests will best be served if together with fixity of principle as regards the tariff we combine a system which will permit us from time to time to make the necessary reapplication of the principle to the shifting national needs. We must take scrupulous care that the reapplication shall be made in such a way that it will not amount to a dislocation of our system, the mere threat of which (not to speak of the performance) would produce paralysis in the business energies of the community. The first consideration in making these changes would, of course, be to preserve the principle which underlies our whole tariff system—that is, the principle of putting American business interests at least on a full equality with interests abroad, and of always allowing a sufficient rate of duty to more than cover the difference between the labor cost here and abroad. The well-being of the wage-worker, like the well-being of the tiller of the soil, should be treated as an essential in shaping our whole economic policy. There must never be any change which will jeopardize the standard of comfort, the standard of wages of the American wage-worker.

One way in which the readjustment sought can be reached is by reciprocity treaties. It is greatly to be desired that such treaties may be adopted. They can be used to widen our markets and to give a greater field for the activities of our producers on the one hand, and on the other hand to secure in practical shape the lowering of duties when they are no longer needed for protection among our own people, or when the minimum of damage done may be disregarded for the sake of the maximum of good accomplished. If it prove impossible to ratify the pending treaties, and if there seem to be no warrant for the endeavor to execute others, or to amend the pending treaties so that they can be ratified, then the same end—to secure reciprocity—should be met by direct legislation.

Wherever the tariff conditions are such that a needed change cannot with advantage be made by the application of the reciprocity idea, then it can be made outright by a lowering of duties on a given product. If possible, such change should be made only after the fullest consideration by practical experts, who should approach the subject from a business standpoint, having in view both the particular interests affected and the commercial well-being of the people as a whole. The machinery for providing such careful investigation can readily be supplied. The Executive Department has already at its disposal methods of collecting facts and figures; and if the Congress desires additional consideration to that which will be given the subject by its own committees, then a commission of business experts can be appointed whose duty it should be to recommend action by the Congress after a deliberate and scientific examination of the various schedules as they are affected by the changed and changing conditions. The unhurried and unbiassed report of this commission would show what changes should be made in the various schedules, and how far these changes could go without also changing the great prosperity which this country is now enjoying, or upsetting its fixed economic policy.

The cases in which the tariff can produce a monopoly are so few as to constitute an inconsiderable factor in the question; but of course if in any case it be found that a given rate of duty does promote a monopoly which works ill, no protectionist would object to such reduction of the duty as would equalize competition.

In my judgment, the tariff on anthracite coal should be removed, and anthracite put actually, where it now is nominally, on the free list. This would have no effect at all save in crisis; but in crisis it might be of service to the people.

FINANCIAL LEGISLATION

Interest rates are a potent factor in business activity, and in order that these rates may be equalized to meet the varying needs of the seasons and of widely separated communities, and to prevent the recurrence of financial stringencies which injuriously affect legitimate business, it is necessary that there should be an element of elasticity in our monetary system. Banks are the natural servants of commerce, and upon them should be placed, as far as practicable, the burden of furnishing and maintaining a circulation adequate to supply the needs of our diversified industries and of our domestic and foreign commerce; and the issue of this should be so regulated that a sufficient supply should be always available for the business interests of the country.

It would be both unwise and unnecessary at this time to attempt to reconstruct our financial system, which has been the growth of a century; but some additional legislation is, I think, desirable. The mere outline of any plan sufficiently comprehensive to meet these requirements would transgress the appropriate limits of this communication. It is suggested, however, that all future legislation on the subject should be with the view of encouraging the use of such instrumentalities as will automatically supply every legitimate demand of productive industries and of commerce, not only in the amount, but in the character of circulation; and of making all kinds of money interchangeable, and, at the will of the holder, convertible into the established gold standard.

IMMIGRATION

I again call your attention to the need of passing a proper immigration law, covering the points outlined in my message to you at the first session of the present Congress; substantially such a bill has already passed the House.

CAPITAL AND LABOR

How to secure fair treatment alike for labor and for capital, how to hold in check the unscrupulous man, whether employer or employee, without weakening individual initiative, without hampering and cramping the industrial development of the country, is a problem fraught with great difficulties and one which it is of the highest importance to solve on lines of sanity and far-sighted common sense as well as of devotion to the right. This is an era of federation and combination. Exactly as business men find they must often work through corporations, and as it is a constant tendency of these corporations to grow larger, so it is often necessary for laboring men to work in federations, and these have become important factors of modern industrial life. Both kinds of federation, capitalistic and labor, can do much good, and as a necessary corollary they can both do evil. Opposition to each kind of organization should take the form of opposition to whatever is bad in the conduct of any given corporation or union—not of attacks upon corporations as such nor upon unions as such; for some of the most far-reaching beneficent work for our people has been accomplished through both corporations and unions. Each must refrain from arbitrary or tyrannous interference with the rights of others. Organized capital and organized labor alike should remember that in the long run the interest of each must be brought into harmony with the interest of the general public; and the conduct of each must conform to the fundamental rules of obedience to the law, of individual freedom, and of justice and fair dealing toward all. Each should remember that in addition to power it must strive after the realization of healthy, lofty, and generous ideals. Every employer, every wage-worker, must be guaranteed his liberty and his right to do as he likes with his property or his labor so long as he does not infringe upon the rights of others. It is of the highest importance that employer and employee alike should endeavor to appreciate each the view-point of the other and the sure disaster that will come upon both in the long run if either grows to take as habitual an attitude of sour hostility and distrust toward the other. Few people deserve better of the country than those representatives both of capital and labor—and there are many such—who work continually to bring about a good understanding of this kind, based upon wisdom and upon broad and kindly sympathy between employers and employed. Above all, we need to remember that any kind of class animosity in the political world is, if possible, even more wicked, even more destructive to national welfare, than sectional, race, or religious animosity. We can get good government only upon condition that we keep true to the principles upon which this nation was founded, and judge each man not as a part of a class, but upon his individual merits. All that we have a right to ask of any man, rich or poor, whatever his creed, his occupation, his birthplace, or his residence, is that he shall act well and honorably by his neighbor and by his country. We are neither for the rich man as such nor for the poor man as such; we are for the upright man, rich or poor. So far as the constitutional powers of the National Government touch these matters of general and vital moment to the nation, they should be exercised in conformity with the principles above set forth.

DEPARTMENT OF COMMERCE

It is earnestly hoped that a secretary of commerce may be created, with a seat in the Cabinet. The rapid multiplication of questions affecting labor and capital, the growth and complexity of the organizations through which both labor and capital now find expression, the steady tendency toward the employment of capital in huge corporations, and the wonderful strides of this country toward leadership in the international business world justify an urgent demand for the creation of such a position. Substantially all the leading commercial bodies in this country have united in requesting its creation. It is desirable that some such measure as that which has already passed the Senate be enacted into law. The creation of such a department would in itself be an advance toward dealing with and exercising supervision over the whole subject of the great corporations doing an interstate business; and with this end in view, the Congress should endow the department with large powers, which could be increased as experience might show the need.

CUBA

I hope soon to submit to the Senate a reciprocity treaty with Cuba. On May 20 last the United States kept its promise to the island by formally vacating Cuban soil and turning Cuba over to those whom her own people had chosen as the first officials of the new republic.

Cuba lies at our doors, and whatever affects her for good or for ill affects us also. So much have our people felt this that in the Platt amendment we definitely took the ground that Cuba must herefter have closer political relations with us than with any other power. Thus in a sense Cuba has become a part of our international political system. This makes it necessary that in return she should be given some of the benefits of becoming part of our economic system. It is, from our own standpoint, a short-sighted and mischievous policy to fail to recognize this need. Moreover, it is unworthy of a mighty and generous nation, itself the greatest and most successful republic in history, to refuse to stretch out a helping hand to a young and weak sister republic just entering upon its career of independence. We should always fearlessly insist upon our rights in the face of the strong, and we should with ungrudging hand do our generous duty by the weak. I urge the adoption of reciprocity with Cuba not only because it is eminently for our own interests to control the Cuban market and by every means to foster our supremacy in the tropical lands and waters south of us, but also because we, of the giant republic of the north, should make all our sister nations of the American continent feel that whenever they will permit it we desire to show ourselves disinterestedly and effectively their friend.

RECIPROCITY WITH NEWFOUNDLAND

A convention with Great Britain has been concluded, which will be at once laid before the Senate for ratification, providing for reciprocal trade arrangements between the United States and Newfoundland on substantially the lines of the convention formerly negotiated by the secretary of state, Mr. Blaine. I believe reciprocal trade relations will be greatly to the advantage of both countries.

THE HAGUE TRIBUNAL

As civilization grows warfare becomes less and less the normal condition of foreign relations. The last century has seen a marked diminution of wars between civilized powers; wars with uncivilized powers are largely mere matters of international police duty, essential for the welfare of the world. Wherever possible, arbitration or some similar method should be employed in lieu of war to settle difficulties between civilized nations, although as yet the world has not progressed sufficiently to render it possible, or necessarily desirable, to invoke arbitration in every case. The formation of the international tribunal which sits at The Hague is an event of good omen from which great consequences for the welfare of all mankind may flow. It is far better, where possible, to invoke such a permanent tribunal than to create special arbitrators for a given purpose.

It is a matter of sincere congratulation to our country that the United States and Mexico should have been the first to use the good offices of the Hague Court. This was done last summer with most satisfactory results in the case of a claim at issue between us and our sister republic. It is earnestly to be hoped that this first case will serve as a precedent for others, in which not only the United States but foreign nations may take advantage of the machinery already in existence at The Hague.

HAWAII

I commend to the favorable consideration of the Congress the Hawaiian fire claims, which were the subject of careful investigation during the last session.

ISTHMIAN CANAL

The Congress has wisely provided that we shall build at once an isthmian canal, if possible at Panama. The attorney-general reports that we can undoubtedly acquire good title from the French Panama Canal Company. Negotiations are now pending with Colombia to secure her assent to our building the canal. This canal will be one of the greatest engineering feats of the twentieth century; a greater engineering feat than has yet been accomplished during the history of mankind. The work should be carried out as a continuing policy without regard to change of administration; and it should be begun under circumstances which will make it a matter of pride for all administrations to continue the policy.

The canal will be of great benefit to America, and of importance to all the world. It will be of advantage to us industrially and also as improving our military position. It will be of advantage to the countries of tropical America. It is earnestly to be hoped that all of these countries will do as some of them have already done with signal success, and will invite to their shores commerce and improve their material conditions by recognizing that stability and order are the prerequisites of successful development. No independent nation in America need have the slightest fear of aggression from the United States. It behooves each one to maintain order within its own borders and to discharge its just obligations to foreigners. When this is done, they can rest assured that, be they strong or weak, they have nothing to dread from outside interference. More and more the increasing interdependence and complexity of international political and economic relations render it incumbent on all civilized and orderly powers to insist on the proper policing of the world.

PACIFIC CABLES

During the fall of 1901 a communication was addressed to the secretary of state, asking whether permission would be granted by the President to a corporation to lay a cable from a point on the California coast to the Philippine Islands by way of Hawaii. A statement of conditions or terms upon which such corporation would undertake to lay and operate a cable was volunteered.

Inasmuch as the Congress was shortly to convene, and Pacific-cable legislation had been the subject of consideration by the Congress for several years, it seemed to me wise to defer action upon the application until the Congress had first an opportunity to act. The Congress adjourned without taking any action, leaving the matter in exactly the same condition in which it stood when the Congress convened.

Meanwhile it appears that the Commercial Pacific Cable Company had promptly proceeded with preparations for laying its cable. It also made application to the President for access to and use of soundings taken by the U. S. S. *Nero* for the purpose of discovering a practicable route for a transpacific cable, the company urging that with access to these soundings it could complete its cable much sooner than if it were required to take soundings upon its own account. Pending consideration of this subject, it appeared important and desirable to attach certain conditions to the permission to examine and use the soundings, if it should be granted.

In consequence of this solicitation of the cable company, certain conditions were formulated, upon which the President was willing to allow access to these soundings and to consent to the landing and laying of the cable, subject to any alterations or additions thereto imposed by the Congress. This was deemed proper, especially as it was clear that a cable connection of some kind with China, a foreign country, was a part of the company's plan. This course was, moreover, in accordance with a line of precedents, including President Grant's action in the case of the first French cable, explained to the Congress in his annual message of December, 1875, and the instance occurring in 1879 of the second French cable from Brest to St. Pierre, with a branch to Cape Cod.

These conditions prescribed, among other things, a maximum rate for commercial messages and that the company should construct a line from the Philippine Islands to China, there being at present, as is well known, a British line from Manila to Hongkong.

The representatives of the cable company kept these conditions long under consideration, continuing, in the meantime, to prepare for laying the cable. They have, however, at length acceded to them, and an all-American line between our Pacific coast and the Chinese Empire, by way of Honolulu and the Philippine Islands, is thus provided for, and is expected within a few months to be ready for business.

Among the conditions is one reserving the power of the Congress to modify or repeal any or all of them. A copy of the conditions is herewith transmitted.

PORTO RICO

Of Porto Rico it is only necessary to say that the prosperity of the island and the wisdom with which it has been governed have been such as to make it serve as an example of all that is best in insular administration.

PHILIPPINES

On July 4 last, on the 126th anniversary of the declaration of our independence, peace and amnesty were promulgated in the Philippine Islands. Some trouble has since from time to time threatened with the Mohammedan Moros, but with the late insurrectionary Filipinos the war has entirely ceased. Civil government has now been introduced. Not only does each Filipino enjoy such rights to life, liberty, and the pursuit of happiness as he has never before known during the recorded history of the islands, but the people taken as a whole now enjoy a measure of self-government greater than that granted to any other Orientals by any foreign power and greater than that enjoyed by any other Orientals under their own governments, save the Japanese alone. We have not gone too far in granting these rights of liberty and self-government; but we have certainly gone to the limit that in the interests of the Philippine people themselves it was wise or just to go. To hurry matters, to go faster than we are now going, would entail calamity on the people of the islands. No policy ever entered into by the American people has vindicated itself in more signal manner than the policy of holding the Philippines. The triumph of our arms, above all the triumph of our laws and principles, has come sooner than we had any right to expect. Too much praise cannot be given to the army for what it has done in the Philippines both in warfare and from an administrative standpoint in preparing the way for civil government; and similar credit belongs to the civil authorities for the way in which they have planted the seeds of self-government in the ground thus made ready for them. The courage, the unflinching endurance, the high soldierly efficiency, and the general kind-heartedness and humanity of our troops have been strikingly manifested. There now remain only some 15,000 troops in the island. All told, over 100,000 have been sent there. Of course, there have been individual instances of wrong-doing among them. They warred under fearful difficulties of climate and surroundings; and under the strain of the terrible provocations which they continually received from their foes, occasional instances of cruel retaliation occurred. Every effort has been made to prevent such cruelties, and finally these efforts have been completely successful. Every effort has also been made to detect and punish the wrongdoers. After making all allowance for these misdeeds, it remains true that few indeed have been the instances in which war has been waged by a civilized power against semi-civilized or barbarous forces where there has been so little wrong-doing by the victors as in the Philippine Islands. On the other hand, the amount of difficult, important, and beneficent work which has been done is well-nigh incalculable.

Taking the work of the army and the civil authorities together, it may be questioned whether anywhere else in modern times the world has seen a better example of real constructive statesmanship than our people have given in the Philippine Islands. High praise should also be given those Filipinos, in the aggregate very numerous, who have accepted the new conditions and joined with our representatives to work with hearty good-will for the welfare of the islands.

THE ARMY

The army has been reduced to the minimum allowed by law. It is very small for the size of the nation, and most certainly should be kept at the highest point of efficiency. The senior officers are given scant chance under ordinary conditions to exercise commands commensurate with their rank, under circumstances which would fit them to do their duty in time of actual war. A system of manœuvring our army in bodies of some little size has been begun and should be steadily continued. Without such manœuvres it is folly to expect that in the event of hostilities with any serious foe even a small army corps could be handled to advantage. Both our officers and enlisted men are such that we can take hearty pride in them. No better material can be found. But they must be thoroughly trained, both as individuals and in the mass. The marksmanship of the men must receive special attention. In the circumstances of modern warfare the man must act far more on his own individual responsibility than ever before, and the high individual efficiency of the unit is of the utmost importance. Formerly this unit was the regiment; it is now not the regiment, not even the troop or company; it is the individual soldier. Every effort must be made to develop every workmanlike and soldierly quality in both the officer and the enlisted man. I urgently call your attention to the need of passing a bill providing for a general staff and for the reorganization of the supply departments on the lines of the bill proposed by the secretary of war last year. When the young officers enter the army from West Point they probably stand above their compeers in any other military service. Every effort should be made, by training, by reward of merit, by scrutiny into their careers and capacity, to keep them of the same high relative excellence throughout their careers.

The measure providing for the reorganization of the militia system and for securing the highest efficiency in the National Guard, which has already passed the House, should receive prompt attention and action. It is of great importance that the relation of the National Guard to the militia and volunteer forces of the United States should be defined, and that in place of our present obsolete laws a practical and efficient system should be adopted.

Provision should be made to enable the secretary of war to keep cavalry and artillery horses, worn out in long performance of duty. Such horses fetch but a trifle when sold; and rather than turn them out to the misery awaiting them when thus disposed of, it would be better to employ them at light work around the posts, and when necessary to put them painlessly to death.

THE NAVY

For the first time in our history naval manœuvres on a large scale are being held under the immediate command of the admiral of the navy. Constantly increasing attention is being paid to the gunnery of the navy, but it is yet far from what it should be. I earnestly urge that the increase asked for by the secretary of the navy in the appropriation for improving the marksmanship be granted. In battle the only shots that count are the shots that hit. It is necessary to provide ample funds for practice with the great guns in time of peace. These funds must provide not only for the purchase of projectiles, but for allowances for prizes to encourage the gun crews, and especially the gun pointers, and for perfecting an intelligent system under which alone it is possible to get good practice.

There should be no halt in the work of building up the navy, providing every year additional fighting craft. We are a very rich country, vast in extent of territory and great in population; a country, moreover, which has an army diminutive indeed when compared with that of any other first-class power. We have deliberately made our own certain foreign policies which demand the possession of a first-class navy. The Isthmian Canal will greatly increase the efficiency of our navy if the navy is of sufficient size; but if we have an inadequate navy, then the building of the Canal would be merely giving a hostage to any power of superior strength. The Monroe Doctrine should be treated as the cardinal feature of American foreign policy; but it would be worse than idle to assert it unless we intended to back it up, and it can be backed up only by a thoroughly good navy. A good navy is not a provocative of war. It is the surest guarantee of peace.

Each individual unit of our navy should be the most efficient of its kind as regards both material and personnel that is to be found in the world. I call your special attention to the need of providing for the manning of the ships. Serious trouble threatens us if we cannot do better than we are now doing as regards securing the services of a sufficient number of the highest type of sailormen, of sea mechanics. The veteran seamen of our war-ships are of as high a type as can be found in any navy which rides the waters of the world; they are unsurpassed in daring, in resolution, in readiness, in thorough knowledge of their profession. They deserve every consideration that can be shown them. But there are not enough of them. It is no more possible to improvise a crew than it is possible to improvise a war-ship. To build the finest ship, with the deadliest battery, and to send it afloat with a raw crew, no matter how brave they were individually, would be to insure disaster if a foe of average capacity were encountered. Neither ships nor men can be improvised when war has begun.

We need a thousand additional officers in order properly to man the ships now provided for and under construction. The classes at the Naval School at Annapolis should be greatly enlarged. At the same time that we thus add the officers where we need them, we should facilitate the retirement of those at the head of the list whose usefulness has become impaired. Promotion must be fostered if the service is to be kept efficient.

The lamentable scarcity of officers, and the large number of recruits and of unskilled men necessarily put aboard the new vessels as they have been commissioned, has thrown upon our officers, and especially on the lieutenants and junior grades, unusual labor and fatigue and has gravely strained their powers of endurance. Nor is there sign of any immediate let-up in this strain. It must continue for some time longer, until more officers are graduated from Annapolis, and until the recruits become trained and skilful in their duties. In these difficulties incident upon the development of our war fleet the conduct of all our officers has been creditable to the service, and the lieutenants and junior grades in particular have displayed an ability and a steadfast cheerfulness which entitle them to the ungrudging thanks of all who realize the disheartening trials and fatigues to which they are of necessity subjected.

There is not a cloud on the horizon at present. There seems not the slightest chance of trouble with a foreign power. We most earnestly hope that this state of things may continue; and the way to insure its continuance is to provide for a thoroughly efficient navy. The refusal to maintain such a navy would invite trouble, and if trouble came would insure disaster. Fatuous self-complacency or vanity, or short-sightedness in refusing to prepare for danger, is both foolish and wicked in such a nation as ours; and past experience has shown that such fatuity in refusing to recognize or prepare for any crisis in advance is usually succeeded by a mad panic of hysterical fear once the crisis has actually arrived.

POSTAL SERVICE

The striking increase in the revenues of the Post-Office Department shows clearly the prosperity of our people and the increasing activity of the business of the country.

The receipts of the Post-Office Department for the fiscal year ending June 30 last amounted to $121,848,047.26, an increase of $10,216,853.87 over the preceding year, the largest increase known in the history of the postal service. The magnitude of this increase will best appear from the fact that the entire postal receipts for the year 1860 amounted to but $8,518,-067.

Rural free-delivery service is no longer in the experimental stage; it has become a fixed policy. The results following its introduction have fully justified the Congress in the large appropriations made for its establishment and extension. The average yearly increase in post-office receipts in the rural districts of the country is about two per cent. We are now able, by actual results, to show that where rural free-delivery service has been established to such an extent as to enable us to make comparisons the yearly increase has been upward of ten per cent.

On November 1, 1902, 11,650 rural free-delivery routes had been established and were in operation, covering about one-third of the territory of the United States available for rural free-delivery service. There are now awaiting the action of the department petitions and applications for the establishment of 10,748 additional routes. This shows conclusively the want which the establishment of the service has met and the need of further extending it as rapidly as possible. It is justified both by the financial results and by the practical benefits to our rural population; it brings the men who live on the soil into close relations with the active business world; it keeps the farmer in daily touch with the markets; it is a potential educational force; it enhances the value of farm property, makes farm life far pleasanter and less isolated, and will do much to check the undesirable current from country to city.

It is to be hoped that the Congress will make liberal appropriations for the continuance of the service already established and for its further extension.

IRRIGATION

Few subjects of more importance have been taken up by the Congress in recent years than the inauguration of the system of nationally aided irrigation for the arid regions of the far West. A good beginning therein has been made. Now that this policy of national irrigation has been adopted, the need of thorough and scientific forest protection will grow more rapidly than ever throughout the public-land States.

PROTECTION OF GAME

Legislation should be provided for the protection of the game, and the wild creatures generally, on the forest reserves. The senseless slaughter of game, which can by judicious protection be permanently preserved on our national reserves for the people as a whole, should be stopped at once. It is, for instance, a serious count against our national good sense to permit the present practice of butchering off such a stately and beautiful creature as the elk for its antlers or tusks.

PUBLIC LANDS

So far as they are available for agriculture, and to whatever extent they may be reclaimed under the national irrigation law, the remaining public lands should be held rigidly for the home-builder, the settler who lives on his land, and for no one else. In their actual use the desert-land law, the timber and stone law, and the commutation clause of the homestead law have been so perverted from the intention with which they were enacted as to permit the acquisition of large areas of the public domain for other than actual settlers and the consequent prevention of settlement. Moreover, the approaching exhaustion of the public ranges has of late led to much discussion as to the best manner of using these public lands in the West which are suitable chiefly or only for grazing. The sound and steady development of the West depends upon the building up of homes therein. Much of our prosperity as a nation has been due to the operation of the homestead law. On the other hand, we should recognize the fact that in the grazing region the man who corresponds to the homesteader may be unable to settle permanently if only allowed to use the same amount of pastureland that his brother, the homesteader, is allowed to use of arable land. One hundred and sixty acres of fairly rich and well-watered soil, or a much smaller amount of irrigated land, may keep a family in plenty, whereas no one could get a living from 160 acres of dry pastureland capable of supporting at the outside only one head of cattle to every ten acres. In the past great tracts of the public domain have been fenced in by persons having no title thereto, in direct defiance of the law forbidding the maintenance or construction of any such unlawful inclosure of public land. For various reasons there has been little interference with such inclosures in the past, but ample notice has now been given the trespassers, and all the resources at the command of the government will hereafter be used to put a stop to such trespassing.

In view of the capital importance of these matters, I commend them to the earnest consideration of the Congress, and if the Congress finds difficulty in dealing with them from lack of thorough knowledge of the subject, I recommend that provision be made for a commission of experts specially to investigate and report upon the complicated questions involved.

ALASKA

I especially urge upon the Congress the need of wise legislation for Alaska. It is not to our credit as a nation that Alaska, which has been ours for thirty-five years, should still have as poor a system of laws as is the case. No country has a more valuable possession—in mineral wealth, in fisheries, furs, forests, and also in land available for certain kinds of farming and stock-growing. It is a territory of great size and varied resources, well fitted to support a large permanent population. Alaska needs a good land-law and such provisions for homesteads and pre-emptions as will encourage permanent settlement. We should shape legislation with a view not to the exploiting and abandoning of the territory, but to the building up of homes therein. The land-laws should be liberal in type, so as to hold out inducements to the actual settler whom we most desire to see take possession of the country. The forests of Alaska should be protected, and, as a secondary but still important matter, the game also, and at the same time it is imperative that the settlers should be allowed to cut timber, under proper regulations, for their own use. Laws should be enacted to protect the Alaskan salmon-fisheries against the greed which would destroy them. They should be preserved as a permanent industry and food-supply. Their management and control should be turned over to the Commission of Fish and Fisheries. Alaska should have a delegate in the Congress. It would be well if a congressional committee could visit Alaska and investigate its needs on the ground.

THE INDIANS

In dealing with the Indians our aim should be their ultimate absorption into the body of our people. But in many cases this absorption must and should be very slow. In portions of the Indian Territory the mixture of blood has gone on at the same time with progress in wealth and education, so that there are plenty of men with varying degrees of purity of Indian blood who are absolutely indistinguishable in point of social, political, and economic ability from their white associates. There are other tribes which have as yet made no perceptible advance toward such equality. To try to force such tribes too fast is to prevent their going forward at all. Moreover, the tribes live under widely different conditions. Where a tribe has made considerable advance and lives on fertile farming soil it is possible to allot the members lands in severalty much as is the case with white settlers. There are other tribes where such a course is not desirable. On the arid prairie-lands the effort should be to induce the Indians to lead pastoral rather than agricultural lives, and to permit them to settle in villages rather than to force them into isolation.

The large Indian schools situated remote from any Indian reservation do a special and peculiar work of great importance. But, excellent though these are, an immense amount of additional work must be done on the reservations themselves among the old, and above all among the young, Indians.

The first and most important step toward the absorption of the Indian is to teach him to earn his living; yet it is not necessarily to be assumed that in each community all Indians must become either tillers of the soil or stock-raisers. Their industries may properly be diversified, and those who show special desire or adaptability for industrial or even commercial pursuits should be encouraged so far as practicable to follow out each his own bent.

Every effort should be made to develop the Indian along the lines of natural aptitude, and to encourage the existing native industries peculiar to certain tribes, such as the various kinds of basket-weaving, canoe-building, smith work, and blanket work. Above all, the Indian boys and girls should be given confident command of colloquial English, and should ordinarily be prepared for a vigorous struggle with the conditions under which their people live, rather than for immediate absorption into some more highly developed community.

The officials who represent the government in dealing with the Indians work under hard conditions, and also under conditions which render it easy to do wrong and very difficult to detect wrong. Consequently they should be amply paid on the one hand, and on the other hand a particularly high standard of conduct should be demanded from them, and where misconduct can be proved the punishment should be exemplary.

AGRICULTURE

In no department of governmental work in recent years has there been greater success than in that of giving scientific aid to the farming population, thereby showing them how most efficiently to help themselves. There is no need of insisting upon its importance, for the welfare of the farmer is fundamentally necessary to the welfare of the republic as a whole. In addition to such work as quarantine against animal and vegetable plagues, and warring against them when here introduced, much efficient help has been rendered to the farmer by the introduction of new plants specially fitted for cultivation under the peculiar conditions existing in different portions of the country. New cereals have been established in the semiarid West. For instance, the practicability of producing the best types of macaroni wheats in regions of an annual rainfall of only ten inches or thereabouts has been conclusively demonstrated. Through the introduction of new rices in Louisiana and Texas the production of rice in this country has been made to about equal the home demand. In the Southwest the possibility of regrassing overstocked rangelands has been demonstrated; in the North many new forage crops have been introduced, while in the East it has been shown that some of our choicest fruits can be stored and shipped in such a way as to find a profitable market abroad.

SMITHSONIAN INSTITUTION

I again recommend to the favorable consideration of the Congress the plans of the Smithsonian Institution for making the museum under its charge worthy of the nation, and for preserving at the national capital not only records of the vanishing races of men but of the animals of this continent which, like the buffalo, will soon become extinct unless specimens from which their representatives may be renewed are sought in their native regions and maintained there in safety.

DISTRICT OF COLUMBIA

The District of Columbia is the only part of our territory in which the National Government exercises local or municipal functions, and where in consequence the government has a free hand in reference to certain types of social and economic legislation which must be essentially local or municipal in their character. The government should see to it, for instance, that the hygienic and sanitary legislation affecting Washington is of a high character. The evils of slum dwellings, whether in the shape of crowded and congested tenement-house districts or of the back-alley type, should never be permitted to grow up in Washington. The city should be a model in every respect for all the cities of the country. The charitable and correctional systems of the District should receive consideration at the hands of the Congress to the end that they may embody the results of the most advanced thought in these fields. Moreover, while Washington is not a great industrial city, there is some industrialism here, and our labor legislation, while it would not be important in itself, might be made a model for the rest of the nation. We should pass, for instance, a wise employers' liability act for the District of Columbia, and we need such an act in our navy-yards. Railroad companies in the District ought to be required by law to block their frogs.

SAFETY-APPLIANCE LAW

The safety-appliance law, for the better protection of the lives and limbs of railway employees, which was passed in 1893, went into full effect on August 1, 1901. It has resulted in averting thousands of casualties. Experience shows, however, the necessity of additional legislation to perfect this law. A bill to provide for this passed the Senate at the last session. It is to be hoped that some such measure may now be enacted into law.

GOVERNMENT PRINTING

There is a growing tendency to provide for the publication of masses of documents for which there is no public demand and for the printing of which there is no real necessity. Large numbers of volumes are turned out by the government printing-presses for which there is no justification. Nothing should be printed by any of the departments unless it contains something of permanent value, and the Congress could with advantage cut down very materially on all the printing which it has now become customary to provide. The excessive cost of government printing is a strong argument in support of the position of those who are inclined on abstract grounds to advocate the government's not doing any work which can with propriety be left in private hands.

CIVIL SERVICE

Gratifying progress has been made during the year in the extension of the merit system of making appointments in the government service. It should be extended by law to the District of Columbia. It is much to be desired that our consular system be established by law on a basis providing for appointment and promotion only in consequence of proved fitness.

RESTORATION OF THE WHITE HOUSE

Through a wise provision of the Congress at its last session the White House, which had become disfigured by incongruous additions and changes, has now been restored to what it was planned to be by Washington. In making the restorations the utmost care has been exercised to come as near as possible to the early plans and to supplement these plans by a careful study of such buildings as that of the University of Virginia, which was built by Jefferson. The White House is the property of the nation, and so far as is compatible with living therein it should be kept as it originally was, for the same reasons that we keep Mount Vernon as it originally was. The stately simplicity of its architecture is an expression of the character of the period in which it was built, and is in accord with the purposes it was designed to serve. It is a good thing to preserve such buildings as historic monuments which keep alive our sense of continuity with the nation's past.

The reports of the several executive departments are submitted to the Congress with this communication.

III

THIRD ANNUAL MESSAGE[1]

TO THE SENATE AND HOUSE OF REPRESENTATIVES:
The country is to be congratulated on the amount of substantial achievement which has marked the past year both as regards our foreign and as regards our domestic policy.

DOMESTIC ACHIEVEMENTS

With a nation as with a man the most important things are those of the household, and therefore the country is especially to be congratulated on what has been accomplished in the direction of providing for the exercise of supervision over the great corporations and combinations of corporations engaged in interstate commerce. The Congress has created the Department of Commerce and Labor, including the Bureau of Corporations, with for the first time authority to secure proper publicity of such proceedings of these great corporations as the public has the right to know. It has provided for the expediting of suits for the enforcement of the Federal antitrust law; and by another law it has secured equal treatment to all producers in the transportation of their goods, thus taking a long stride forward in making effective the work of the Interstate Commerce Commission.

DEPARTMENT OF COMMERCE AND LABOR

The establishment of the Department of Commerce and Labor, with the Bureau of Corporations thereunder, marks a real advance in the direction of doing all that is possible for the solution of the questions vitally affecting capitalists and

[1] Dated, the White House, December 7, 1903.

wage-workers. The act creating the department was approved on February 14, 1903, and two days later the head of the department was nominated and confirmed by the Senate. Since then the work of organization has been pushed as rapidly as the initial appropriations permitted, and with due regard to thoroughness and the broad purposes which the department is designed to serve. After the transfer of the various bureaus and branches to the department at the beginning of the current fiscal year, as provided for in the act, the personnel comprised 1,289 employees in Washington and 8,836 in the country at large. The scope of the department's duty and authority embraces the commercial and industrial interests of the nation. It is not designed to restrict or control the fullest liberty of legitimate business action, but to secure exact and authentic information which will aid the Executive in enforcing existing laws, and which will enable the Congress to enact additional legislation if any should be found necessary, in order to prevent the few from obtaining privileges at the expense of diminished opportunities for the many.

The preliminary work of the Bureau of Corporations in the department has shown the wisdom of its creation. Publicity in corporate affairs will tend to do away with ignorance, and will afford facts upon which intelligent action may be taken. Systematic, intelligent investigation is already developing facts the knowledge of which is essential to a right understanding of the needs and duties of the business world. The corporation which is honestly and fairly organized, whose managers in the conduct of its business recognize their obligation to deal squarely with their stockholders, their competitors, and the public, has nothing to fear from such supervision. The purpose of this bureau is not to embarrass or assail legitimate business, but to aid in bringing about a better industrial condition—a condition under which there shall be obedience to law and recognition of public obligation by all corporations, great or small. The Department of Commerce and Labor will be not only the clearing-house for information regarding the business transactions of the nation, but the executive arm of the government to aid in strengthening our domestic and foreign markets, in perfecting our transportation facilities, in building up our merchant marine, in preventing the entrance of undesirable immigrants, in improving commercial and industrial conditions, and in bringing together on common ground those necessary partners in industrial progress—capital and labor. Commerce between the nations is steadily growing in volume, and the tendency of the times is toward closer trade relations. Constant watchfulness is needed to secure to Americans the chance to participate to the best advantage in foreign trade; and we may confidently expect that the new department will justify the expectation of its creators by the exercise of this watchfulness, as well as by the businesslike administration of such laws relating to our internal affairs as are intrusted to its care.

In enacting the laws above enumerated the Congress proceeded on sane and conservative lines. Nothing revolutionary was attempted; but a common-sense and successful effort was made in the direction of seeing that corporations are so handled as to subserve the public good. The legislation was moderate. It was characterized throughout by the idea that we were not attacking corporations, but endeavoring to provide for doing away with any evil in them; that we drew the line against misconduct, not against wealth; gladly recognizing the great good done by the capitalist who alone, or in conjunction with his fellows, does his work along proper and legitimate lines. The purpose of the legislation, which purpose will undoubtedly be fulfilled, was to favor such a man when he does well, and to supervise his action only to prevent him from doing ill. Publicity can do no harm to the honest corporation. The only corporation that has cause to dread it is the corporation which shrinks from the light, and about the welfare of such corporations we need not be oversensitive. The work of the Department of Commerce and Labor has been conditioned upon this theory, of securing fair treatment alike for labor and for capital.

The consistent policy of the National Government, so far as it has the power, is to hold in check the unscrupulous man, whether employer or employee; but to refuse to weaken individual initiative or to hamper or cramp the industrial development of the country. We recognize that this is an era of federation and combination, in which great capitalistic corporations and labor-unions have become factors of tremendous importance in all industrial centres. Hearty recognition is given the far-reaching, beneficent work which has been accomplished through both corporations and unions, and the line as between different corporations, as between different unions, is drawn as it is between different individuals; that is, it is drawn on conduct, the effort being to treat both organized capital and organized labor alike; asking nothing save that the interest of each shall be brought into harmony with the interest of the general public, and that the conduct of each shall conform to the fundamental rules of obedience to law, of individual freedom, and of justice and fair dealing toward all. Whenever either corporation, labor-union, or individual disregards the law or acts in a spirit of arbitrary and tyrannous interference with the rights of others, whether corporations or individuals, then where the Federal Government has jurisdiction, it will see to it that the misconduct is stopped, paying not the slightest heed to the position or power of the corporation, the union, or the individual, but only to one vital fact—that is, the question whether or not the conduct of the individual or aggregate of individuals is in accordance with the law of the land. Every man must be guaranteed his liberty and his right to do as he likes with his property or his labor, so long as he does not infringe the rights of others. No man is above the law and no man is below it; nor do we ask any man's permission when we require him to obey it. Obedience to the law is demanded as a right; not asked as a favor.

We have cause as a nation to be thankful for the steps that

have been so successfully taken to put these principles into effect. The progress has been by evolution, not by revolution. Nothing radical has been done; the action has been both moderate and resolute. Therefore the work will stand. There shall be no backward step. If in the working of the laws it proves desirable that they shall at any point be expanded or amplified, the amendment can be made as its desirability is shown. Meanwhile they are being administered with judgment, but with insistence upon obedience to them, and their need has been emphasized in signal fashion by the events of the past year.

REVENUE

From all sources, exclusive of the postal service, the receipts of the government for the last fiscal year aggregated $560,396,674. The expenditures for the same period were $506,099,007, the surplus for the fiscal year being $54,297,667. The indications are that the surplus for the present fiscal year will be very small, if indeed there be any surplus. From July to November the receipts from customs were, approximately, $9,000,000 less than the receipts from the same source for a corresponding portion of last year. Should this decrease continue at the same ratio throughout the fiscal year, the surplus would be reduced by, approximately, $30,000,000. Should the revenue from customs suffer much further decrease during the fiscal year, the surplus would vanish. A large surplus is certainly undesirable. Two years ago the war taxes were taken off with the express intention of equalizing the governmental receipts and expenditures, and though the first year thereafter still showed a surplus, it now seems likely that a substantial equality of revenue and expenditure will be attained. Such being the case it is of great moment both to exercise care and economy in appropriations, and to scan sharply any change in our fiscal revenue system which may reduce our income. The need of strict economy in our expenditures is emphasized by the fact that we cannot afford to be parsimonious in providing for what is essential to our national well-being. Careful economy wherever possible will alone prevent our income from falling below the point required in order to meet our genuine needs.

FINANCIAL LEGISLATION

The integrity of our currency is beyond question, and under present conditions it would be unwise and unnecessary to attempt a reconstruction of our entire monetary system. The same liberty should be granted the secretary of the treasury to deposit customs receipts as is granted him in the deposit of receipts from other sources. In my message of December 2, 1902, I called attention to certain needs of the financial situation, and I again ask the consideration of the Congress for these questions.

During the last session of the Congress at the suggestion of a joint note from the republic of Mexico and the imperial government of China, and in harmony with an act of the Congress appropriating $25,000 to pay the expenses thereof, a commission was appointed to confer with the principal European countries in the hope that some plan might be devised whereby a fixed rate of exchange could be assured between the gold-standard countries and the silver-standard countries. This commission has filed its preliminary report, which has been made public. I deem it important that the commission be continued, and that a sum of money be appropriated sufficient to pay the expenses of its further labors.

MERCHANT MARINE

A majority of our people desire that steps be taken in the interests of American shipping, so that we may once more resume our former position in the ocean carrying trade. But hitherto the differences of opinion as to the proper method of reaching this end have been so wide that it has proved impossible to secure the adoption of any particular scheme. Having in view these facts, I recommended that the Congress direct the secretary of the navy, the postmaster-general, and the secretary of commerce and labor, associated with such a representation from the Senate and House of Representatives as the Congress in its wisdom may designate, to serve as a commission for the purpose of investigating and reporting to the Congress at its next session what legislation is desirable or necessary for the development of the American merchant marine and American commerce, and incidentally of a national ocean-mail service of adequate auxiliary naval cruisers and naval reserves. While such a measure is desirable in any event, it is especially desirable at this time, in view of the fact that our present governmental contract for ocean mail with the American Line will expire in 1905. Our ocean-mail act was passed in 1891. In 1895 our twenty-knot transatlantic mail line was equal to any foreign line. Since then the Germans have put on twenty-three-knot steamers, and the British have contracted for twenty-four-knot steamers. Our service should equal the best. If it does not, the commercial public will abandon it. If we are to stay in the business it ought to be with a full understanding of the advantages to the country on one hand, and on the other with exact knowledge of the cost and proper methods of carrying it on. Moreover, lines of cargo ships are of even more importance than fast mail lines; save so far as the latter can be depended upon to furnish swift auxiliary cruisers in time of war. The establishment of new lines of cargo ships to South America, to Asia, and elsewhere would be much in the interest of our commercial expansion.

IMMIGRATION

We cannot have too much immigration of the right kind, and we should have none at all of the wrong kind. The need is to devise some system by which undesirable immigrants shall be kept out entirely, while desirable immigrants are properly distributed throughout the country. At present some districts which need immigrants have none; and in others, where the population is already congested, immigrants come in such numbers as to depress the conditions of life for those already there. During the last two years the immigration service at New York has been greatly improved, and the corruption and inefficiency which formerly obtained there have been eradicated. This service has just been investigated by a committee of New York citizens of high standing, Messrs. Arthur V. Briesen, Lee K. Frankel, Eugene A. Philbin, Thomas W. Hynes, and Ralph Trautman. Their report deals with the whole situation at length, and concludes with certain recommendations for administrative and legislative action. It is now receiving the attention of the secretary of commerce and labor.

NATURALIZATION

The special investigation of the subject of naturalization under the direction of the attorney-general, and the consequent prosecutions reveal a condition of affairs calling for the immediate attention of the Congress. Forgeries and perjuries of shameless and flagrant character have been perpetrated, not only in the dense centres of population, but throughout the country; and it is established beyond doubt that very many so-called citizens of the United States have no title whatever to that right, and are asserting and enjoying the benefits of the same through the grossest frauds. It is never to be forgotten that citizenship is, to quote the words recently used by the Supreme Court of the United States, an "inestimable heritage," whether it proceeds from birth within the country or is obtained by naturalization; and we poison the sources of our national character and strength at the fountain, if the privilege is claimed and exercised without right, and by means of fraud and corruption. The body politic cannot be sound and healthy if many of its constituent members claim their standing through the prostitution of the high right and calling of citizenship. It should mean something to become a citizen of the United States, and in the process no loop-hole whatever should be left open to fraud.

The methods by which these frauds—now under full investigation with a view to meting out punishment and providing adequate remedies—are perpetrated, include many variations of procedure by which false certificates of citizenship are forged in their entirety; or genuine certificates fraudulently or collusively obtained in blank are filled in by the criminal conspirators; or certificates are obtained on fraudulent statements as to the time of arrival and residence in this country; or imposition and substitution of another party for the real petitioner occur in court; or certificates are made the subject of barter and sale and transferred from the rightful holder to those not entitled to them; or certificates are forged by erasure of the original names and the insertion of the names of other persons not entitled to the same.

It is not necessary for me to refer here at large to the causes leading to this state of affairs. The desire for naturalization is heartily to be commended where it springs from a sincere and permanent intention to become citizens, and a real appreciation of the privilege. But it is a source of untold evil and trouble where it is traceable to selfish and dishonest motives, such as the effort by artificial and improper means, in wholesale fashion to create voters who are ready-made tools of corrupt politicians, or the desire to evade certain labor laws creating discriminations against alien labor. All good citizens, whether naturalized or native-born, are equally interested in protecting our citizenship against fraud in any form, and, on the other hand, in affording every facility for naturalization to those who in good faith desire to share alike our privileges and our responsibilities.

The Federal grand jury lately in session in New York City dealt with this subject and made a presentment which states the situation briefly and forcibly and contains important suggestions for the consideration of the Congress. This presentment is included as an appendix to the report of the attorney-general.

APPROPRIATION FOR ENFORCEMENT OF LAWS

In my last annual message, in connection with the subject of the due regulation of combinations of capital which are or may become injurious to the public, I recommended a special appropriation for the better enforcement of the antitrust law as it now stands, to be extended under the direction of the attorney-general. Accordingly (by the legislative, executive, and judicial appropriation act of February 25, 1903, 32 Stat., 854, 904), the Congress appropriated, for the purpose of enforcing the various Federal trust and interstate commerce laws, the sum of $500,000, to be expended under the direction of the attorney-general in the employment of special counsel and agents in the Department of Justice to conduct proceedings and prosecutions under said laws in the courts of the United States. I now recommend, as a matter of the utmost importance and urgency, the extension of the purposes of this appropriation, so that it may be available, under the direction of the attorney-general, and until used, for the due enforcement of the laws of the United States in general and especially of the civil and criminal laws relating to public lands and the laws relating to postal crimes and offenses and the subject of naturalization. Recent investigations have shown a deplorable state of affairs in these three matters of vital concern. By various frauds and by forgeries and perjuries, thousands of acres of the public domain, embracing lands of different character and extending through various sections of the country, have been dishonestly acquired. It is hardly necessary to urge the importance of recovering these dishonest acquisitions, stolen from the people, and of promptly and duly punishing the offenders. I speak in another part of this message of the wide-spread crimes by which the sacred right of citizenship is falsely asserted and that "inestimable heritage" perverted to base ends. By similar means—that is, through frauds, forgeries, and perjuries, and by shameless briberies—the laws relating to the proper conduct of the public service in general and to the due administration of the Post-Office Department have been notoriously violated, and many indictments have been found, and the consequent prosecutions are in course of hearing or on the eve thereof. For the reasons thus indicated, and so that the government may be prepared to enforce promptly and with the greatest effect the due penalties for such violations of law, and to this end may be furnished with sufficient instrumentalities and competent legal assistance for the investigations and trials which will be necessary at many different points of the country, I urge upon the Congress the necessity of making the said appropriation available for immediate use for all such purposes, to be expended under the direction of the attorney-general.

EXTENSION OF EXTRADITION TREATIES

Steps have been taken by the State Department looking to the making of bribery an extraditable offense with foreign powers. The need of more effective treaties covering this crime is manifest. The exposures and prosecutions of official corruption in St. Louis, Mo., and other cities and States have resulted in a number of givers and takers of bribes becoming fugitives in foreign lands. Bribery has not been included in extradition treaties heretofore, as the necessity for it has not arisen. While there may have been as much official corruption in former years, there has been more developed and brought to light in the immediate past than in the preceding century of our country's history. It should be the policy of the United States to leave no place on earth where a corrupt man fleeing from this country can rest in peace. There is no reason why bribery should not be included in all treaties as extraditable. The recent amended treaty with Mexico, whereby this crime was put in the list of extraditable offenses, has established a salutary precedent in this regard. Under this treaty the State Department has asked, and Mexico has granted, the extradition of one of the St. Louis bribe-givers.

There can be no crime more serious than bribery. Other offenses violate one law while corruption strikes at the foundation of all law. Under our form of government all authority is vested in the people and by them delegated to those who represent them in official capacity. There can be no offense heavier than that of him in whom such a sacred trust has been reposed, who sells it for his own gain and enrichment; and no less heavy is the offense of the bribe-giver. He is worse than the thief, for the thief robs the individual, while the corrupt official plunders an entire city or State. He is as wicked as the murderer, for the murderer may only take one life against the law, while the corrupt official and the man who corrupts the official alike aim at the assassination of the Commonwealth itself. Government of the people, by the people, for the people, will perish from the face of the earth if bribery is tolerated. The givers and takers of bribes stand on an evil pre-eminence of infamy. The exposure and punishment of public corruption is an honor to a nation, not a disgrace. The shame lies in toleration, not in correction. No city or State, still less the nation, can be injured by the enforcement of law. As long as public plunderers when detected can find a haven of refuge in any foreign land and avoid punishment, just so long encouragement is given them to continue their practices. If we fail to do all that in us lies to stamp out corruption we cannot escape our share of responsibility for the guilt. The first requisite of successful self-government is unflinching enforcement of the law and the cutting out of corruption.

ALASKA BOUNDARY QUESTION

For several years past the rapid development of Alaska and the establishment of growing American interests in regions theretofore unsurveyed and imperfectly known brought into prominence the urgent necessity of a practical demarcation of the boundaries between the jurisdictions of the United States and Great Britain. Although the treaty of 1825 between Great Britain and Russia, the provisions of which were copied in the treaty of 1867, whereby Russia conveyed Alaska to the United States, was positive as to the control, first by Russia and later by the United States, of a strip of territory along the continental mainland from the western shore of Portland Canal to Mount St. Elias, following and surrounding the indentations of the coast and including the islands to the westward, its description of the landward margin of the strip was indefinite, resting on the supposed existence of a continuous ridge or range of mountains skirting the coast, as figured in the charts of the early navigators. It had at no time been possible for either party in interest to lay down, under the authority of the treaty, a line so obviously exact according to its provisions as to command the assent of the other. For nearly three-fourths of a century the absence of tangible local interests demanding the exercise of positive jurisdiction on either side of the border left the question dormant. In 1878 questions of revenue administration on the Stikine River led to the establishment of a provincial demarcation, crossing the channel between two high peaks on either side about twenty-four miles above the river mouth. In 1899 similar questions growing out of the extraordinary development of mining interests in the region about the head of Lynn Canal brought about a temporary *modus vivendi,* by which a convenient separation was made at the watershed divides of the White and Chilkoot Passes and to the north of Klukwan, on the Klehini River. These partial and tentative adjustments could not, in the very nature of things, be satisfactory or lasting. A permanent disposition of the matter became imperative.

After unavailing attempts to reach an understanding through a joint high commission, followed by prolonged negotiations, conducted in an amicable spirit, a convention between the United States and Great Britain was signed, January 24, 1903, providing for an examination of the subject by a mixed tribunal of six members, three on a side, with a view to its final disposition. Ratifications were exchanged on March 3 last, whereupon the two governments appointed their respective members. Those on behalf of the United States were Elihu Root, secretary of war, Henry Cabot Lodge, a senator of the United

States, and George Turner, an ex-senator of the United States, while Great Britain named the Right Honorable Lord Alverstone, Lord Chief Justice of England, Sir Louis Amable Jetté, K. C. M. G., retired judge of the Supreme Court of Quebec, and A. B. Aylesworth, K. C., of Toronto. This tribunal met in London on September 3, under the presidency of Lord Alverstone. The proceedings were expeditious, and marked by a friendly and conscientious spirit. The respective cases, counter-cases, and arguments presented the issues clearly and fully. On the 20th of October a majority of the tribunal reached and signed an agreement on all the questions submitted by the terms of the convention. By this award the right of the United States to the control of a continuous strip or border of the mainland shore, skirting all the tide-water inlets and sinuosities of the coast, is confirmed; the entrance to Portland Canal (concerning which legitimate doubt appeared) is defined as passing by Tongass Inlet and to the northwestward of Wales and Pearse Islands; a line is drawn from the head of Portland Canal to the fifty-sixth degree of north latitude; and the interior border-line of the strip is fixed by lines connecting certain mountain summits lying between Portland Canal and Mount St. Elias, and running along the crest of the divide separating the coast slope from the inland watershed at the only part of the frontier where the drainage ridge approaches the coast within the distance of ten marine leagues stipulated by the treaty as the extreme width of the strip around the heads of Lynn Canal and its branches.

While the line so traced follows the provisional demarcation of 1878 at the crossing of the Stikine River, and that of 1899 at the summits of the White and Chilkoot Passes, it runs much farther inland from the Klehini than the temporary line of the later *modus vivendi,* and leaves the entire mining district of the Porcupine River and Glacier Creek within the jurisdiction of the United States.

The result is satisfactory in every way. It is of great material advantage to our people in the far Northwest. It has removed from the field of discussion and possible danger a question liable to become more acutely accentuated with each passing year. Finally, it has furnished a signal proof of the fairness and good-will with which two friendly nations can approach and determine issues involving national sovereignty and by their nature incapable of submission to a third power for adjudication.

The award is self-executing on the vital points. To make it effective as regards the others it only remains for the two governments to appoint, each on its own behalf, one or more scientific experts, who shall, with all convenient speed, proceed together to lay down the boundary-line in accordance with the decision of the majority of the tribunal. I recommend that the Congress make adequate provision for the appointment, compensation, and expenses of the members to serve on this joint boundary commission on the part of the United States.

EFFORTS TOWARD INTERNATIONAL PEACE

It will be remembered that during the second session of the last Congress Great Britain, Germany, and Italy formed an alliance for the purpose of blockading the ports of Venezuela and using such other means of pressure as would secure a settlement of claims due, as they alleged, to certain of their subjects. Their employment of force for the collection of these claims was terminated by an agreement brought about through the offices of the diplomatic representatives of the United States at Caracas and the government at Washington, thereby ending a situation which was bound to cause increasing friction, and which jeoparded the peace of the continent. Under this agreement Venezuela agreed to set apart a certain percentage of the customs receipts of two of her ports to be applied to the payment of whatever obligations might be ascertained by mixed commissions appointed for that purpose to be due from her, not only to the three powers already mentioned, whose proceedings against her had resulted in a state of war, but also to the United States, France, Spain, Belgium, the Netherlands, Sweden and Norway, and Mexico, who had not employed force for the collection of the claims alleged to be due to certain of their citizens.

A demand was then made by the so-called blockading powers that the sums ascertained to be due to their citizens by such mixed commissions should be accorded payment in full before anything was paid upon the claims of any of the so-called peace powers. Venezuela, on the other hand, insisted that all her creditors should be paid upon a basis of exact equality. During the efforts to adjust this dispute it was suggested by the powers in interest that it should be referred to me for decision, but I was clearly of the opinion that a far wiser course would be to submit the question to the Permanent Court of Arbitration at The Hague. It seemed to me to offer an admirable opportunity to advance the practice of the peaceful settlement of disputes between nations and to secure for the Hague Tribunal a memorable increase of its practical importance. The nations interested in the controversy were so numerous and in many instances so powerful as to make it evident that beneficent results would follow from their appearance at the same time before the bar of that august tribunal of peace.

Our hopes in that regard have been realized. Russia and Australia are represented in the persons of the learned and distinguished jurists who compose the tribunal, while Great Britain, Germany, France, Spain, Italy, Belgium, the Netherlands, Sweden and Norway, Mexico, the United States, and Venezuela are represented by their respective agents and counsel. Such an imposing concourse of nations presenting their arguments to and invoking the decision of that high court of international justice and international peace can hardly fail to secure a like submission of many future controversies. The nations now appearing there will find it far easier to appear there a second time, while no nation can imagine its just pride will be lessened by following the example now presented. This triumph of the principle of international arbitration is a subject of warm congratulation and offers a happy augury for the peace of the world.

There seems good ground for the belief that there has been a real growth among the civilized nations of a sentiment which will permit a gradual substitution of other methods than the method of war in the settlement of disputes. It is not pretended that as yet we are near a position in which it will be possible wholly to prevent war, or that a just regard for national interest and honor will in all cases permit of the settlement of international disputes by arbitration; but by a mixture of prudence and firmness with wisdom we think it is possible to do away with much of the provocation and excuse for war, and at least in many cases to substitute some other and more rational method for the settlement of disputes. The Hague Court offers so good an example of what can be done in the direction of such settlement that it should be encouraged in every way.

Further steps should be taken. In President McKinley's annual message of December 5, 1898, he made the following recommendation:

"The experiences of the last year bring forcibly home to us a sense of the burdens and the waste of war. We desire in common with most civilized nations, to reduce to the lowest possible point the damage sustained in time of war by peaceable trade and commerce. It is true we may suffer in such cases less than other communities, but all nations are damaged more or less by the state of uneasiness and apprehension into which an outbreak of hostilities throws the entire commercial world. It should be our object, therefore, to minimize, so far as practicable, this inevitable loss and disturbance. This purpose can probably best be accomplished by an international agreement to regard all private property at sea as exempt from capture or destruction by the forces of belligerent powers. The United States Government has for many years advocated this humane and beneficent principle, and is now in a position to recommend it to other powers without the imputation of selfish motives. I therefore suggest for your consideration that the Executive be authorized to correspond with the governments of the principal maritime powers with a view of incorporating into the permanent law of civilized nations the principle of the exemption of all private property at sea, not contraband of war, from capture or destruction by belligerent powers."

I cordially renew this recommendation.

The Supreme Court, speaking on December 11, 1899, through Mr. Justice Peckham, said:

"It is, we think, historically accurate to say that this Government has always been, in its views, among the most advanced of the governments of the world in favor of mitigating, as to all non-combatants, the hardships and horrors of war. To accomplish that object it has always advocated those rules which would in most cases do away with the right to capture the private property of an enemy on the high seas."

I advocate this as a matter of humanity and morals. It is anachronistic when private property is respected on land that it should not be respected at sea. Moreover, it should be borne in mind that shipping represents, internationally speaking, a much more generalized species of private property than is the case with ordinary property on land—that is, property found at sea is much less apt than is the case with property found on land really to belong to any one nation. Under the modern system of corporate ownership the flag of a vessel often differs from the flag which would mark the nationality of the real ownership and money control of the vessel; and the cargo may belong to individuals of yet a different nationality. Much American capital is now invested in foreign ships; and among foreign nations it often happens that the capital of one is largely invested in the shipping of another. Furthermore, as a practical matter, it may be mentioned that while commerce-destroying may cause serious loss and great annoyance, it can never be more than a subsidiary factor in bringing to terms a resolute foe. This is now well recognized by all of our naval experts. The fighting ship, not the commerce-destroyer, is the vessel whose feats add renown to a nation's history, and establish her place among the great powers of the world.

Last year the Interparliamentary Union for International Arbitration met at Vienna, 600 members of the different legislatures of civilized countries attending. It was provided that the next meeting should be in 1904 at St. Louis, subject to our Congress extending an invitation. Like the Hague Tribunal, this Interparliamentary Union is one of the forces tending toward peace among the nations of the earth, and it is entitled to our support. I trust the invitation can be extended.

BEIRUT INCIDENT

Early in July, having received intelligence, which happily turned out to be erroneous, of the assassination of our vice-consul at Beirut, I despatched a small squadron to that port for such service as might be found necessary on arrival. Although the attempt on the life of our vice-consul had not been successful, yet the outrage was symptomatic of a state of excitement and disorder which demanded immediate attention. The arrival of the vessels had the happiest result. A feeling of security at once took the place of the former alarm and disquiet; our officers were cordially welcomed by the consular body and the leading merchants, and ordinary business resumed its activity. The government of the Sultan gave a considerate hearing to the representations of our minister; the official who was regarded as responsible for the disturbed condition of affairs was removed. Our relations with the Turkish Government remain friendly; our claims founded on inequitable treatment of some of our schools and missions appear to be in process of amicable adjustment.

CHINA

The signing of a new commercial treaty with China, which took place at Shanghai on the 8th of October, is a cause for satisfaction. This act, the result of long discussion and negotiation, places our commercial relations with the great Oriental empire on a more satisfactory footing than they have ever heretofore enjoyed. It provides not only for the ordinary rights and privileges of diplomatic and consular officers, but also for an important extension of our commerce by increased facility of access to Chinese ports, and for the relief of trade by the removal of some of the obstacles which have embarrassed it in the past. The Chinese Government engages, on fair and equitable conditions, which will probably be accepted by the principal commercial nations, to abandon the levy of "liken" and other transit dues throughout the empire, and to introduce other desirable administrative reforms. Larger facilities are to be given to our citizens who desire to carry on mining enterprises in China. We have secured for our missionaries a valuable privilege, the recognition of their right to rent and lease in perpetuity such property as their religious societies may need in all parts of the empire. And, what was an indispensable condition for the advance and development of our commerce in Manchuria, China, by treaty with us, has opened to foreign commerce the cities of Mukden, the capital of the province of Manchuria, and Antung, an important port on the Yalu River, on the road to Korea. The full measure of development which our commerce may rightfully expect can hardly be looked for until the settlement of the present abnormal state of things in the empire; but the foundation for such development has at last been laid.

CONSULAR SERVICE

I call your attention to the reduced cost in maintaining the consular service for the fiscal year ending June 30, 1903, as shown in the annual report of the auditor for the State and other departments, as compared with the year previous. For the year under consideration the excess of expenditures over receipts on account of the consular service amounted to $26,-125.12, as against $96,972.50 for the year ending June 30, 1902, and $147,040.16 for the year ending June 30, 1901. This is the best showing in this respect for the consular service for the past fourteen years, and the reduction in the cost of the service to the government has been made in spite of the fact that the expenditures for the year in question were more than $20,000 greater than for the previous year.

POSTAL SERVICE

The rural free-delivery service has been steadily extended. The attention of the Congress is asked to the question of the compensation of the letter-carriers and clerks engaged in the postal service, especially on the new rural free-delivery routes. More routes have been installed since the 1st of July last than in any like period in the department's history. While a due regard to economy must be kept in mind in the establishment of new routes, yet the extension of the rural free-delivery system must be continued, for reasons of sound public policy. No governmental movement of recent years has resulted in greater immediate benefit to the people of the country districts. Rural free delivery, taken in connection with the telephone, the bicycle, and the trolley, accomplishes much toward lessening the isolation of farm life and making it brighter and more attractive. In the immediate past the lack of just such facilities as these has driven many of the more active and restless young men and women from the farms to the cities; for they rebelled at loneliness and lack of mental companionship. It is unhealthy and undesirable for the cities to grow at the expense of the country; and rural free delivery is not only a good thing in itself, but is good because it is one of the causes which check this unwholesome tendency toward the urban concentration of our population at the expense of the country districts. It is for the same reason that we sympathize with and approve of the policy of building good roads. The movement for good roads is one fraught with the greatest benefit to the country districts.

LOUISIANA PURCHASE EXPOSITION

I trust that the Congress will continue to favor in all proper ways the Louisiana Purchase Exposition. This exposition commemorates the Louisiana purchase, which was the first great step in the expansion which made us a continental nation. The expedition of Lewis and Clark across the continent followed thereon, and marked the beginning of the process of exploration and colonization which thrust our national boundaries to the Pacific. The acquisition of the Oregon country, including the present States of Oregon and Washington, was a fact of immense importance in our history; first giving us our place on the Pacific seaboard, and making ready the way for our ascendancy in the commerce of the greatest of the oceans. The centennial of our establishment upon the Western coast by the expedition of Lewis and Clark is to be celebrated at Portland, Ore., by an exposition in the summer of 1905, and this event should receive recognition and support from the National Government.

ALASKA

I call your special attention to the Territory of Alaska. The country is developing rapidly, and it has an assured future. The mineral wealth is great and has as yet hardly been tapped. The fisheries, if wisely handled and kept under national control, will be a business as permanent as any other, and of the utmost importance to the people. The forests if properly guarded will form another great source of wealth. Portions of Alaska are fitted for farming and stock-raising, although the methods must be adapted to the peculiar conditions of the country. Alaska is situated in the far North; but so are Norway and Sweden and Finland; and Alaska can prosper and play its part in the New World just as those nations have prospered and played their parts in the Old World. Proper land-laws should be enacted, and the survey of the public lands immediately begun. Coal-land laws should be provided whereby the coal-land entryman may make his location and secure patent under methods kindred to those now prescribed for homestead and mineral entrymen. Salmon-hatcheries, exclusively under government control, should be established. The cable should be extended from Sitka westward. Wagon roads and trails should be built, and the building of railroads promoted in all legitimate ways. Lighthouses should be built along the coast. Attention should be paid to the needs of the Alaskan Indians; provision should be made for an officer, with deputies, to study their needs, relieve their immediate wants, and help them adapt themselves to the new conditions.

The commission appointed to investigate, during the season of 1903, the condition and needs of the Alaskan salmon-fisheries, has finished its work in the field, and is preparing a detailed report thereon. A preliminary report reciting the measures immediately required for the protection and preservation of the salmon industry has already been submitted to the secretary of commerce and labor for his attention and for the needed action.

HAWAII

I recommend that an appropriation be made for building lighthouses in Hawaii, and taking possession of those already built. The Territory should be reimbursed for whatever amounts it has already expended for lighthouses. The governor should be empowered to suspend or remove any official appointed by him, without submitting the matter to the legislature.

PORTO RICO AND THE PHILIPPINES

Of our insular possessions the Philippines and Porto Rico it is gratifying to say that their steady progress has been such as to make it unnecessary to spend much time in discussing them. Yet the Congress should ever keep in mind that a peculiar obligation rests upon us to further in every way the welfare of these communities. The Philippines should be knit closer to us by tariff arrangements. It would, of course, be impossible suddenly to raise the people of the islands to the high pitch of industrial prosperity and of governmental efficiency to which they will in the end by degrees attain; and the caution and moderation shown in developing them have been among the main reasons why this development has hitherto gone on so smoothly. Scrupulous care has been taken in the choice of governmental agents, and the entire elimination of partisan politics from the public service. The condition of the islanders is in material things far better than ever before, while their governmental, intellectual, and moral advance has kept pace with their material advance. No one people ever benefited another people more than we have benefited the Filipinos by taking possession of the islands.

PUBLIC LANDS

The cash receipts of the General Land Office for the last fiscal year were $11,024,743.65, an increase of $4,762,816.47 over the preceding year. Of this sum, approximately, $8,461,-493 will go to the credit of the fund for the reclamation of arid land, making the total of this fund, up to the 30th of June, 1903, approximately, $16,191,836.

A gratifying disposition has been evinced by those having unlawful inclosures of public land to remove their fences. Nearly 2,000,000 acres so inclosed have been thrown open on demand. In but comparatively few cases has it been necessary to go into court to accomplish this purpose. This work will be vigorously prosecuted until all unlawful inclosures have been removed.

Experience has shown that in the Western States themselves, as well as in the rest of the country, there is wide-spread conviction that certain of the public-land laws and the resulting administrative practice no longer meet the present needs. The character and uses of the remaining public lands differ widely from those of the public lands which Congress had especially in view when these laws were passed. The rapidly increasing rate of disposal of the public lands is not followed by a corresponding increase in home-building. There is a tendency to mass in large holdings public lands, especially timber and grazing lands, and thereby to retard settlement. I renew and emphasize my recommendation of last year that so far as they are available for agriculture in its broadest sense, and to whatever extent they may be reclaimed under the national irrigation law, the remaining public lands should be held rigidly for the home-builder. The attention of the Congress is especially directed to the timber and stone law, the desert-land law, and the commutation clause of the homestead law, which in their operation have in many respects conflicted with wise public-land policy. The discussions in the Congress and elsewhere have made it evident that there is a wide divergence of opinions between those holding opposite views on these subjects; and that the opposing sides have strong and convinced representatives of weight both within and without the Congress; the differences being not only as to matters of opinion but as to matters of fact. In order that definite information may be available for the use of the Congress, I have appointed a commission composed of W. A. Richards, commissioner of the General Land Office; Gifford Pinchot, chief of the Bureau of Forestry of the Department of Agriculture, and F. H. Newell, chief hydrographer of the Geological Survey, to report at the earliest practicable moment upon the condition, operation, and effect of the present land-laws and on the use, condition, disposal, and settlement of the public lands. The commission will report especially what changes in organization, laws, regulations, and practice affecting the public lands are needed to effect the largest practicable disposition of the public lands to actual settlers who will build permanent homes upon them, and to secure in permanence the fullest and most effective use of the resources of the public lands; and it will make such other reports and recommendations as its study of these questions may suggest. The commission is to report immediately upon those points concerning which its judgment is clear; on any point upon which it has doubt it will take the time necessary to make investigation and reach a final judgment.

RECLAMATION

The work of reclamation of the arid lands of the West is progressing steadily and satisfactorily under the terms of the law setting aside the proceeds from the disposal of public lands. The corps of engineers known as the Reclamation Service, which is conducting the surveys and examinations, has been thoroughly organized, especial pains being taken to secure under the civil-service rules a body of skilled, experienced, and efficient men. Surveys and examinations are progressing throughout the arid States and Territories, plans for reclaiming works being prepared and passed upon by boards of engineers before approval by the secretary of the interior. In Arizona and Nevada, in localities where such work is pre-eminently needed, construction has already been begun. In other parts of the arid West various projects are well advanced toward the drawing up of contracts, these being delayed in part by necessities of reaching agreements or understanding as regards rights of way or acquisition of real estate. Most of the works contemplated for construction are of national importance, involving interstate questions or the securing of stable, self-supporting communities in the midst of vast tracts of vacant land. The nation as a whole is of course the gainer by the creation of these homes, adding as they do to the wealth and stability of the country and furnishing a home market for the products of the East and South. The reclamation law, while perhaps not ideal, appears at present to answer the larger needs for which it is designed. Further legislation is not recommended until the necessities of change are more apparent.

The study of the opportunities of reclamation of the vast extent of arid land shows that whether this reclamation is done by individuals, corporations, or the State, the sources of water-supply must be effectively protected and the reservoirs guarded by the preservation of the forests at the headwaters of the streams. The engineers making the preliminary examinations continually emphasize this need and urge that the remaining public lands at the headwaters of the important streams of the West be reserved to insure permanency of water-supply for irrigation. Much progress in forestry has been made during the past year. The necessity for perpetuating our forest resources, whether in public or private hands, is recognized now as never before. The demand for forest reserves has become insistent in the West, because the West must use the water, wood, and summer range which only such reserves can supply. Progressive lumbermen are striving, through forestry, to give their business permanence. Other great business interests are awakening to the need of forest preservation as a business matter. The government's forest work should receive from the Congress hearty support, and especially support adequate for the protection of the forest reserves against fire. The forest-reserve policy of the government has passed beyond the experimental stage and has reached a condition where scientific methods are essential to its successful prosecution. The administrative features of forest reserves are at present unsatisfactory, being divided between three bureaus of two departments. It is therefore recommended that all matters pertaining to forest reserves, except those involving or pertaining to land titles, be consolidated in the Bureau of Forestry of the Department of Agriculture.

COTTON

The cotton-growing States have recently been invaded by a weevil that has done much damage and threatens the entire cotton industry. I suggest to the Congress the prompt enactment of such remedial legislation as its judgment may approve.

PATENTS

In granting patents to foreigners the proper course for this country to follow is to give the same advantages to foreigners here that the countries in which these foreigners dwell extend in return to our citizens; that is, to extend the benefits of our patent laws on inventions and the like where in return the articles would be patentable in the foreign countries concerned—where an American could get a corresponding patent in such countries.

THE INDIAN

The Indian agents should not be dependent for their appointment or tenure of office upon considerations of partisan politics; the practice of appointing, when possible, ex-army officers or bonded superintendents to the vacancies that occur is working well. Attention is invited to the wide-spread illiteracy due to lack of public schools in the Indian Territory. Prompt heed should be paid to the need of education for the children in this Territory.

SAFETY-APPLIANCE LAW

In my last annual message the attention of the Congress was called to the necessity of enlarging the safety-appliance law, and it is gratifying to note that this law was amended in important respects. With the increasing railway mileage of the country, the greater number of men employed, and the use of larger and heavier equipment, the urgency for renewed effort to prevent the loss of life and limb upon the railroads of the country, particularly to employees, is apparent. For the inspection of water-craft and the life-saving service upon the water the Congress has built up an elaborate body of protective legislation and a thorough method of inspection and is annually spending large sums of money. It is encouraging to observe that the Congress is alive to the interests of those who are employed upon our wonderful arteries of commerce—the railroads—who so safely transport millions of passengers and billions of tons of freight. The Federal inspection of safety appliances, for which the Congress is now making appropriations, is a service analogous to that which the government has upheld for generations in regard to vessels, and it is believed will prove of great practical benefit, both to railroad employees and the travelling public. As the greater part of commerce is interstate and exclusively under the control of the Congress the needed safety and uniformity must be secured by national legislation.

VETERANS

No other class of our citizens deserves so well of the nation as those to whom the nation owes its very being, the veterans of the Civil War. Special attention is asked to the excellent work of the Pension Bureau in expediting and disposing of pension claims. During the fiscal year ending July 1, 1903, the bureau settled 251,982 claims, an average of 825 claims for each working day of the year. The number of settlements since July 1, 1903, has been in excess of last year's average, approaching 1,000 claims for each working day, and it is believed that the work of the bureau will be current at the close of the present fiscal year.

CIVIL SERVICE

During the year ended June 30 last 25,566 persons were appointed through competitive examinations under the civil-service rules. This was 12,672 more than during the preceding year, and 40 per cent of those who passed the examinations. This abnormal growth was largely occasioned by the extension of classification to the rural free-delivery service and the appointment last year of over 9,000 rural carriers. A revision of the civil-service rules took effect on April 15 last, which has greatly improved their operation. The completion of the reform of the civil service is recognized by good citizens everywhere as a matter of the highest public importance, and the success of the merit system largely depends upon the effectiveness of the rules and the machinery provided for their enforcement. A very gratifying spirit of friendly co-operation exists in all the departments of the government in the enforcement and uniform observance of both the letter and spirit of the civil-service act. Executive orders of July 3, 1902, March 26, 1903, and July 8, 1903, require that appointments of all unclassified laborers, both in the departments at Washington and in the field-service, shall be made with the assistance of the United States Civil Service Commission, under a system of registration to test the relative fitness of applicants for appointment or employment. This system is competitive, and is open to all citizens of the United States qualified in respect to age, physical ability, moral character, industry, and adaptability for manual labor; except that in case of veterans of the Civil War the element of age is omitted. This system of appointment is distinct from the classified service and does not classify positions of mere laborer under the civil-service act and rules. Regulations in aid thereof have been put in operation in several of the departments and are being gradually extended in other parts of the service. The results have been very satisfactory, as extravagance has been checked by decreasing the number of unnecessary positions and by increasing the efficiency of the employees remaining.

DISTRICT OF COLUMBIA

The Congress, as the result of a thorough investigation of the charities and reformatory institutions in the District of Columbia, by a joint select committee of the two houses which made its report in March, 1898, created in the act approved June 6, 1900, a board of charities for the District of Columbia, to consist of five residents of the District, appointed by the President of the United States, by and with the advice and consent of the Senate, each for a term of three years, to serve without compensation. President McKinley appointed five men who had been active and prominent in the public charities in Washington, all of whom upon taking office July 1, 1900, resigned from the different charities with which they had been connected. The members of the board have been reappointed in successive years. The board serves under the commissioners of the District of Columbia. The board gave its first year to a careful and impartial study of the special problems before it, and has continued that study every year in the light of the best practice in public charities elsewhere. Its recommendations in its annual reports to the Congress through the commissioners of the District of Columbia "for the economical and efficient administration of the charities and reformatories of the District of Columbia," as required by the act creating it, have been based upon the principles commended by the joint select committee of the Congress in its report of March, 1898, and approved by the best administrators of public charities, and make for the desired systematization and improvement of the affairs under its supervision. They are worthy of favorable consideration by the Congress.

THE ARMY

The effect of the laws providing a general staff for the army and for the more effective use of the National Guard has been excellent. Great improvement has been made in the efficiency of our army in recent years. Such schools as those erected at Fort Leavenworth and Fort Riley and the institution of fall manœuvre work accomplish satisfactory results. The good effect of these manœuvres upon the National Guard is marked, and ample appropriation should be made to enable the guardsmen of the several States to share in the benefit. The government should as soon as possible secure suitable permanent camp sites for military manœuvres in the various sections of the country. The service thereby rendered not only to the Regular Army, but to the National Guard of the several States, will be so great as to repay many times over the relatively small expense. We should not rest satisfied with what has been done, however. The only people who are contented with a system of promotion by mere seniority are those who are contented with the triumph of mediocrity over excellence. On the other hand, a system which encouraged the exercise of social or political favoritism in promotions would be even worse. But it would surely be easy to devise a method of promotion from grade to grade in which the opinion of the higher officers of the service upon the candidates should be decisive upon the standing and promotion of the latter. Just such a system now obtains at West Point. The quality of each year's work determines the standing of that year's class, the man being dropped or graduated into the next class in the relative position which his military superiors decide to be warranted by his merit. In other words, ability, energy, fidelity, and all other similar qualities determine the rank of a man year after year in West Point, and his standing in the army when he graduates from West Point; but from that time on, all effort to find which man is best or worst, and reward or punish him accordingly, is abandoned; no brilliancy, no amount of hard work, no eagerness in the performance of duty, can advance him, and no slackness or indifference that falls short of a court-martial offense can retard him. Until this system is changed we cannot hope that our officers will be of as high grade as we have a right to expect, considering the material upon which we draw. Moreover, when a man renders such service as Captain Pershing rendered last spring in the Moro campaign, it ought to be possible to reward him without at once jumping him to the grade of brigadier-general.

THE NAVY

Shortly after the enunciation of that famous principle of American foreign policy now known as the "Monroe Doctrine," President Monroe, in a special message to Congress on January 30, 1824, spoke as follows: "The Navy is the arm from which our Government will always derive most aid in support of our . . . rights. Every power engaged in war will know the strength of our naval power, the number of our ships of each class, their condition, and the promptitude with which we may bring them into service, and will pay due consideration to that argument."

I heartily congratulate the Congress upon the steady progress in building up the American navy. We cannot afford a let-up in this great work. To stand still means to go back. There should be no cessation in adding to the effective units of the fighting strength of the fleet. Meanwhile the Navy Department and the officers of the navy are doing well their part by providing constant service at sea under conditions akin to those of actual warfare. Our officers and enlisted men are learning to handle the battleships, cruisers, and torpedo-boats with high efficiency in fleet and squadron formations, and the standard of marksmanship is being steadily raised. The best work ashore is indispensable, but the highest duty of a naval officer is to exercise command at sea.

The establishment of a naval base in the Philippines ought not to be longer postponed. Such a base is desirable in time of peace; in time of war it would be indispensable, and its lack would be ruinous. Without it our fleet would be helpless. Our naval experts are agreed that Subig Bay is the proper place for the purpose. The national interests require that the work of fortification and development of a naval station at Subig Bay be begun at an early date; for under the best conditions it is a work which will consume much time.

It is eminently desirable, however, that there should be provided a naval general staff on lines similar to those of the general staff lately created for the army. Within the Navy Department itself the needs of the service have brought about a system under which the duties of a general staff are partially performed; for the Bureau of Navigation has under its direction the War College, the Office of Naval Intelligence, and the Board of Inspection, and has been in close touch with the General Board of the Navy. But though under the excellent officers at their head, these boards and bureaus do good work, they have not the authority of a general staff, and have not sufficient scope to insure a proper readiness for emergencies. We need the establishment by law of a body of trained officers, who shall exercise a systematic control of the military affairs of the navy, and be authorized advisers of the secretary concerning it.

PANAMA CANAL

By the act of June 28, 1902, the Congress authorized the President to enter into treaty with Colombia for the building of the Canal across the Isthmus of Panama; it being provided that in the event of failure to secure such treaty after the lapse of a reasonable time, recourse should be had to building a canal through Nicaragua. It has not been necessary to consider this alternative, as I am enabled to lay before the Senate a treaty providing for the building of the Canal across the Isthmus of Panama. This was the route which commended itself to the deliberate judgment of the Congress, and we can now acquire by treaty the right to construct the Canal over this route. The question now, therefore, is not by which route the Isthmian Canal shall be built, for that question has been definitely and irrevocably decided. The question is simply whether or not we shall have an isthmian canal.

When the Congress directed that we should take the Panama route under treaty with Colombia, the essence of the condition, of course, referred not to the government which controlled that route, but to the route itself; to the territory across which the route lay, not to the name which for the moment the territory bore on the map. The purpose of the law was to authorize the President to make a treaty with the power in actual control of the Isthmus of Panama. This purpose has been fulfilled.

In the year 1846 this government entered into a treaty with New Granada, the predecessor upon the Isthmus of the republic of Colombia and of the present republic of Panama, by which treaty it was provided that the government and citizens of the United States should always have free and open right of way or transit across the Isthmus of Panama by any modes of communication that might be constructed, while in turn our government guaranteed the perfect neutrality of the above-mentioned Isthmus with the view that the free transit from the one to the other sea might not be interrupted or embarrassed. The treaty vested in the United States a substantial property right carved out of the rights of sovereignty and property which New Granada then had and possessed over the said territory. The name of New Granada has passed away and its territory has been divided. Its successor, the government of Colombia, has ceased to own any property in the Isthmus. A new republic, that of Panama, which was at one time a sovereign state, and at another time a mere department of the successive confederations known as New Granada and Colombia, has now succeeded to the rights which first one and then the other formerly exercised over the Isthmus. But as long as the Isthmus endures, the mere geographical fact of its existence, and the peculiar interest therein which is required by our position, perpetuate the solemn contract which binds the holders of the territory to respect our right to freedom of transit across it, and binds us in return to safeguard for the Isthmus and the world the exercise of that inestimable privilege. The true interpretation of the obligations upon which the United States entered in this treaty of 1846 has been given repeatedly in the utterances of Presidents and secretaries of state. Secretary Cass in 1858 officially stated the position of this government as follows:

"The progress of events has rendered the interoceanic route across the narrow portion of Central America vastly important to the commercial world, and especially to the United States, whose possessions extend along the Atlantic and Pacific coasts, and demand the speediest and easiest modes of communication. While the rights of sovereignty of the states occupying this region should always be respected, we shall expect that these rights be exercised in a spirit befitting the occasion and the wants and circumstances that have arisen. Sovereignty has its duties as well as its rights, and none of these local governments, even if administered with more regard to the just demands of other nations than they have been, would be permitted, in a spirit of Eastern isolation, to close the gates of intercourse on the great highways of the world, and justify the act by the pretension that these avenues of trade and travel belong to them and that they choose to shut them, or, what is almost equivalent, to encumber them with such unjust relations as would prevent their general use."

Seven years later, in 1865, Mr. Seward in different communications took the following position:

"The United States have taken and will take no interest in any question of internal revolution in the State of Panama, or any State of the United States of Colombia, but will maintain a perfect neutrality in connection with such domestic altercations. The United States will, nevertheless, hold themselves ready to protect the transit trade across the Isthmus against invasion of either domestic or foreign disturbers of the peace of the State of Panama. . . . Neither the text nor the spirit of the stipulation in that article by which the United States engages to preserve the neutrality of the Isthmus of Panama, imposes an obligation on this Government to comply with the requisition [of the President of the United States of Colombia for a force to protect the Isthmus of Panama from a body of insurgents of that country]. The purpose of the stipulation was to guarantee the Isthmus against seizure or invasion by a foreign power only."

Attorney-General Speed, under date of November 7, 1865, advised Secretary Seward as follows:

"From this treaty it cannot be supposed that New Granada invited the United States to become a party to the intestine troubles of that Government, nor did the United States become bound to take sides in the domestic broils of New Granada. The United States did guarantee New Granada in the sovereignty and property over the territory. This was as against other and foreign governments."

For 400 years, ever since shortly after the discovery of this hemisphere, the Canal across the Isthmus has been planned. For twoscore years it has been worked at. When made it is to last for the ages. It is to alter the geography of a continent and the trade routes of the world. We have shown by every treaty we have negotiated or attempted to negotiate with the peoples in control of the Isthmus and with foreign nations in reference thereto our consistent good faith in observing our obligations; on the one hand to the peoples of the Isthmus, and on the other hand to the civilized world whose commercial rights we are safeguarding and guaranteeing by our action. We have done our duty to others in letter and in spirit, and we have shown the utmost forbearance in exacting our own rights.

Last spring, under the act above referred to, a treaty concluded between the representatives of the republic of Colombia and of our government was ratified by the Senate. This treaty was entered into at the urgent solicitation of the people of Colombia and after a body of experts appointed by our government especially to go into the matter of the routes across the Isthmus had pronounced unanimously in favor of the Panama route. In drawing up this treaty every concession was made to the people and to the government of Colombia. We were more than just in dealing with them. Our generosity was such as to make it a serious question whether we had not gone too far in their interest at the expense of our own; for in our scrupulous desire to pay all possible heed, not merely to the real but even to the fancied rights of our weaker neighbor, who already owed so much to our protection and forbearance, we yielded in all possible ways to her desires in drawing up the treaty. Nevertheless, the government of Colombia not merely repudiated the treaty, but repudiated it in such manner as to make it evident by the time the Colombian Congress adjourned that not the scantiest hope remained of ever getting a satisfactory treaty from them. The government of Colombia made the treaty, and yet when the Colombian Congress was called to ratify it the vote against ratification was unanimous. It does not appear that the government made any real effort to secure ratification.

Immediately after the adjournment of the Congress a revolution broke out in Panama. The people of Panama had long been discontented with the republic of Colombia, and they had been kept quiet only by the prospect of the conclusion of the treaty, which was to them a matter of vital concern. When it became evident that the treaty was hopelessly lost, the people of Panama rose literally as one man. Not a shot was fired by a single man on the Isthmus in the interest of the Colombian Government. Not a life was lost in the accomplishment of the revolution. The Colombian troops stationed on the Isthmus, who had long been unpaid, made common cause with the people of Panama, and with astonishing unanimity the new republic was started. The duty of the United States in the premises was clear. In strict accordance with the principles laid down by Secretaries Cass and Seward in the official documents above quoted, the United States gave notice that it would permit the landing of no expeditionary force, the arrival of which would mean chaos and destruction along the line of the railroad and of the proposed canal, and an interruption of transit as an inevitable consequence. The de facto government of Panama was recognized in the following telegram to Mr. Ehrman:

"The people of Panama have, by apparently unanimous movement, dissolved their political connection with the Republic of Colombia and resumed their independence. When you are satisfied that a de facto government, Republican in form and without substantial opposition from its own people, has been established in the State of Panama, you will enter into relations with it as the responsible government of the territory and look to it for all due action to protect the persons and property of citizens of the United States and to keep open the isthmian transit, in accordance with the obligations of existing treaties governing the relations of the United States to that Territory."

The government of Colombia was notified of our action by the following telegram to Mr. Beaupre:

"The people of Panama having, by an apparently unanimous movement, dissolved their political connection with the Republic of Colombia and resumed their independence, and having adopted a Government of their own, Republican in form, with which the Government of the United States of America has entered into relations, the President of the United States, in accordance with the ties of friendship which have so long and so happily existed between the respective nations, most earnestly commends to the Governments of Colombia and of Panama the peaceful and equitable settlement of all questions at issue between them. He holds that he is bound not merely by treaty obligations, but by the interests of civilization, to see that the peaceful traffic of the world across the Isthmus of Panama shall not longer be disturbed by a constant succession of unnecessary and wasteful civil wars."

When these events happened, fifty-seven years had elapsed since the United States had entered into its treaty with New Granada. During that time the governments of New Granada and of its successor, Colombia, have been in a constant state of flux. The following is a partial list of the disturbances on the Isthmus of Panama during the period in question as reported to us by our consuls. It is not possible to give a complete list, and some of the reports that speak of "revolutions" must mean unsuccessful revolutions.

May 22, 1850.—Outbreak; two Americans killed. War-vessel demanded to quell outbreak.

October, 1850.—Revolutionary plot to bring about independence of the Isthmus.

July 22, 1851.—Revolution in four Southern provinces.

November 14, 1851.—Outbreak at Chagres. Man-of-war requested for Chagres.

June 27, 1853.—Insurrection at Bogota, and consequent disturbance on Isthmus. War-vessel demanded.

May 23, 1854.—Political disturbances; war-vessel requested.

June 28, 1854.—Attempted revolution.

October 24, 1854.—Independence of Isthmus demanded by provincial legislature.

April, 1856.—Riot, and massacre of Americans.

May 4, 1856.—Riot.

May 18, 1856.—Riot.

June 3, 1856.—Riot.

October 2, 1856.—Conflict between two native parties. United States forces landed.

December 18, 1858.—Attempted secession of Panama.

April, 1859.—Riots.

September, 1860.—Outbreak.

October 4, 1860.—Landing of United States forces in consequence.

May 23, 1861.—Intervention of the United States forces required by intendente.

October 2, 1861.—Insurrection and civil war.

April 4, 1862.—Measures to prevent rebels crossing Isthmus.

June 13, 1862.—Mosquera's troops refused admittance to Panama.

March, 1865.—Revolution, and United States troops landed.

August, 1865.—Riots; unsuccessful attempt to invade Panama.

March, 1866.—Unsuccessful revolution.

April, 1867.—Attempt to overthrow government.

August, 1867.—Attempt at revolution.

July 5, 1868.—Revolution; provisional government inaugurated.

August 29, 1868.—Revolution; provisional government overthrown.

April, 1871.—Revolution; followed apparently by counter-revolution.

April, 1873.—Revolution and civil war which lasted to October, 1875.

August, 1876.—Civil war which lasted until April, 1877.

July, 1878.—Rebellion.

December, 1878.—Revolt.

April, 1879.—Revolution.

June, 1879.—Revolution.

March, 1883.—Riot.

May, 1883.—Riot.

June, 1884.—Revolutionary attempt.

December, 1884.—Revolutionary attempt.

January, 1885.—Revolutionary disturbances.

March, 1885.—Revolution.

April, 1887.—Disturbance on Panama Railroad.

November, 1887.—Disturbance on line of Canal.

January, 1889.—Riot.

January, 1895.—Revolution which lasted until April.

March, 1895.—Incendiary attempt.

October, 1899.—Revolution.

February, 1900, to July, 1900.—Revolution.

January, 1901.—Revolution.

July, 1901.—Revolutionary disturbances.

September, 1901.—City of Colon taken by rebels.

March, 1902.—Revolutionary disturbances.

July, 1902.—Revolution.

The above is only a partial list of the revolutions, rebellions, insurrections, riots, and other outbreaks that have occurred during the period in question; yet they number fifty-three for the fifty-seven years. It will be noted that one of them lasted for nearly three years before it was quelled; another for nearly a year. In short, the experience of over half a century has shown Colombia to be utterly incapable of keeping order on the Isthmus. Only the active interference of the United States has enabled her to preserve so much as a semblance of sovereignty. Had it not been for the exercise by the United States of the police power in her interest, her connection with the Isthmus would have been sundered long ago. In 1856, in 1860, in 1873, in 1885, in 1901, and again in 1902, sailors and marines from United States war-ships were forced to land in order to patrol the Isthmus, to protect life and property, and to see that the transit across the Isthmus was kept open. In 1861, in 1862, in 1885, and in 1900, the Colombian Government asked that the United States Government would land troops to protect its interests and maintain order on the Isthmus. Perhaps the most extraordinary request is that which has just been received and which runs as follows:

"Knowing that revolution has already commenced in Panama [an eminent Colombian] says that if the Government of the United States will land troops to preserve Colombian sovereignty, and the transit, if requested by Colombian chargé d'affaires, this Government will declare martial law; and, by virtue of vested constitutional authority, when public order is disturbed, will approve by decree ratification of the canal treaty as signed; or, if the Government of the United States prefers, will call extra session of the Congress—with new and friendly members—next May to approve the treaty. [An eminent Colombian] has the perfect confidence of vice-president, he says, and if it become necessary will go to the Isthmus or send representatives there to adjust matters along above lines to the satisfaction of the people there."

This despatch is noteworthy from two standpoints. Its offer of immediately guaranteeing the treaty to us is in sharp contrast with the positive and contemptuous refusal of the Congress which has just closed its sessions to consider favorably such a treaty; it shows that the government which made the treaty really had absolute control over the situation, but did not choose to exercise this control. The despatch further calls on us to restore order and secure Colombian supremacy in the Isthmus from which the Colombian Government has just by its action decided to bar us by preventing the construction of the Canal.

The control, in the interest of the commerce and traffic of the whole civilized world, of the means of undisturbed transit across the Isthmus of Panama has become of transcendent importance to the United States. We have repeatedly exercised this control by intervening in the course of domestic dissension, and by protecting the territory from foreign invasion. In 1853 Mr. Everett assured the Peruvian minister that we should not hesitate to maintain the neutrality of the Isthmus in the case of war between Peru and Colombia. In

1864 Colombia, which has always been vigilant to avail itself of its privileges conferred by the treaty, expressed its expectation that in the event of war between Peru and Spain the United States would carry into effect the guarantee of neutrality. There have been few administrations of the State Department in which this treaty has not, either by the one side or the other, been used as a basis of more or less important demands. It was said by Mr. Fish in 1871 that the Department of State had reason to believe that an attack upon Colombian sovereignty on the Isthmus had, on several occasions, been averted by warning from this government. In 1886, when Colombia was under the menace of hostilities from Italy in the Cerruti case, Mr. Bayard expressed the serious concern that the United States could not but feel, that a European power should resort to force against a sister republic of this hemisphere, as to the sovereign and uninterrupted use of a part of whose territory we are guarantors under the solemn faith of a treaty.

The above recital of facts establishes beyond question: First, that the United States has for over half a century patiently and in good faith carried out its obligations under the treaty of 1846; second, that when for the first time it became possible for Colombia to do anything in requital of the services thus repeatedly rendered to it for fifty-seven years by the United States, the Colombian Government peremptorily and offensively refused thus to do its part, even though to do so would have been to its advantage and immeasurably to the advantage of the State of Panama, at that time under its jurisdiction; third, that throughout this period revolutions, riots, and factional disturbances of every kind have occurred one after the other in almost uninterrupted succession, some of them lasting for months and even for years, while the central government was unable to put them down or to make peace with the rebels; fourth, that these disturbances instead of showing any sign of abating have tended to grow more numerous and more serious in the immediate past; fifth, that the control of Colombia over the Isthmus of Panama could not be maintained without the armed intervention and assistance of the United States. In other words, the government of Colombia, though wholly unable to maintain order on the Isthmus, has nevertheless declined to ratify a treaty the conclusion of which opened the only chance to secure its own stability and to guarantee permanent peace on, and the construction of a canal across, the Isthmus.

Under such circumstances the government of the United States would have been guilty of folly and weakness, amounting in their sum to a crime against the nation, had it acted otherwise than it did when the revolution of November 3 last took place in Panama. This great enterprise of building the interoceanic canal cannot be held up to gratify the whims, or out of respect to the governmental impotence, or to the even more sinister and evil political peculiarities, of people who, though they dwell afar off, yet, against the wish of the actual dwellers on the Isthmus, assert an unreal supremacy over the territory. The possession of a territory fraught with such peculiar capacities as the Isthmus in question carries with it obligations to mankind. The course of events has shown that this canal cannot be built by private enterprise, or by any other nation than our own; therefore it must be built by the United States.

Every effort has been made by the government of the United States to persuade Colombia to follow a course which was essentially not only to our interests and to the interests of the world, but to the interests of Colombia itself. These efforts have failed; and Colombia, by her persistence in repulsing the advances that have been made, has forced us, for the sake of our own honor, and of the interest and well-being, not merely of our own people, but of the people of the Isthmus of Panama and the people of the civilized countries of the world, to take decisive steps to bring to an end a condition of affairs which had become intolerable. The new republic of Panama immediately offered to negotiate a treaty with us. This treaty I herewith submit. By it our interests are better safeguarded than in the treaty with Colombia which was ratified by the Senate at its last session. It is better in its terms than the treaties offered to us by the republics of Nicaragua and Costa Rica. At last the right to begin this great undertaking is made available. Panama has done her part. All that remains is for the American Congress to do its part, and forthwith this Republic will enter upon the execution of a project colossal in its size and of well-nigh incalculable possibilities for the good of this country and the nations of mankind.

By the provisions of the treaty the United States guarantees and will maintain the independence of the republic of Panama. There is granted to the United States in perpetuity the use, occupation, and control of a strip ten miles wide and extending three nautical miles into the sea at either terminal, with all lands lying outside of the zone necessary for the construction of the Canal or for its auxiliary works, and with the islands in the Bay of Panama. The cities of Panama and Colon are not embraced in the Canal zone, but the United States assumes their sanitation and, in case of need, the maintenance of order therein; the United States enjoys within the granted limits all the rights, power, and authority which it would possess were it the sovereign of the territory to the exclusion of the exercise of sovereign rights by the republic. All railway and Canal property rights belonging to Panama and needed for the Canal pass to the United States, including any property of the respective companies in the cities of Panama and Colon; the works, property, and personnel of the Canal and railways are exempted from taxation as well in the cities of Panama and Colon as in the Canal zone and its dependencies. Free immigration of the personnel and importation of supplies for the construction and operation of the Canal are granted. Provision is made for the use of military force and the building of fortifications by the United States for the protection of the transit. In other details, particularly as to the acquisition of the interests of the New Panama Canal Company and the

Panama Railway by the United States and the condemnation of private property for the uses of the Canal, the stipulations of the Hay-Herran treaty are closely followed, while the compensation to be given for these enlarged grants remains the same, being ten millions of dollars payable on exchange of ratifications; and, beginning nine years from that date, an annual payment of $250,000 during the life of the convention.

IV

FOURTH ANNUAL MESSAGE[1]

TO THE SENATE AND HOUSE OF REPRESENTATIVES:

The nation continues to enjoy noteworthy prosperity. Such prosperity is of course primarily due to the high individual average of our citizenship, taken together with our great natural resources; but an important factor therein is the working of our long-continued governmental policies. The people have emphatically expressed their approval of the principles underlying these policies, and their desire that these principles be kept substantially unchanged, although of course applied in a progressive spirit to meet changing conditions.

The enlargement of scope of the functions of the National Government required by our development as a nation involves, of course, increase of expense; and the period of prosperity through which the country is passing justifies expenditures for permanent improvements far greater than would be wise in hard times. Battleships and forts, public buildings, and improved waterways are investments which should be made when we have the money; but abundant revenues and a large surplus always invite extravagance, and constant care should be taken to guard against unnecessary increase of the ordinary expenses of government. The cost of doing government business should be regulated with the same rigid scrutiny as the cost of doing a private business.

CAPITAL AND LABOR

In the vast and complicated mechanism of our modern civilized life the dominant note is the note of industrialism; and

[1] Dated, the White House, December 6, 1904.

the relations of capital and labor, and especially of organized capital and organized labor, to each other and to the public at large come second in importance only to the intimate questions of family life. Our peculiar form of government, with its sharp division of authority between the nation and the several States, has been on the whole far more advantageous to our development than a more strongly centralized government. But it is undoubtedly responsible for much of the difficulty of meeting with adequate legislation the new problems presented by the total change in industrial conditions on this continent during the last half-century. In actual practice it has proved exceedingly difficult, and in many cases impossible, to get unanimity of wise action among the various States on these subjects. From the very nature of the case this is especially true of the laws affecting the employment of capital in huge masses.

With regard to labor the problem is no less important, but it is simpler. As long as the States retain the primary control of the police power the circumstances must be altogether extreme which require interference by the Federal authorities, whether in the way of safeguarding the rights of labor or in the way of seeing that wrong is not done by unruly persons who shield themselves behind the name of labor. If there is resistance to the Federal courts, interference with the mails, or interstate commerce, or molestation of Federal property, or if the State authorities in some crisis which they are unable to face call for help, then the Federal Government may interfere; but though such interference may be caused by a condition of things arising out of trouble connected with some question of labor, the interference itself simply takes the form of restoring order without regard to the questions which have caused the breach of order—for to keep order is a primary duty and in a time of disorder and violence all other questions sink into abeyance until order has been restored. In the District of Columbia and in the Territories the Federal law covers the entire field of government; but the labor question is only acute in populous centres of commerce, manufactures, or mining. Nevertheless, both in the enactment and in the enforcement of law the Federal Government within its restricted sphere should set an example to the State governments, especially in a matter so vital as this affecting labor. I believe that under modern industrial conditions it is often necessary, and even where not necessary it is yet often wise, that there should be organization of labor in order better to secure the rights of the individual wage-worker. All encouragement should be given to any such organization, so long as it is conducted with a due and decent regard for the rights of others. There are in this country some labor-unions which have habitually, and other labor-unions which have often, been among the most effective agents in working for good citizenship and for uplifting the condition of those whose welfare should be closest to our hearts. But when any labor-union seeks improper ends, or seeks to achieve proper ends by improper means, all good citizens and more especially all honorable public servants must oppose the wrong-doing as resolutely as they would oppose the wrong-doing of any great corporation. Of course any violence, brutality, or corruption, should not for one moment be tolerated. Wage-workers have an entire right to organize and by all peaceful and honorable means to endeavor to persuade their fellows to join with them in organizations. They have a legal right, which, according to circumstances, may or may not be a moral right, to refuse to work in company with men who decline to join their organizations. They have under no circumstances the right to commit violence upon those, whether capitalists or wage-workers, who refuse to support their organizations, or who side with those with whom they are at odds; for mob rule is intolerable in any form.

EMPLOYERS' LIABILITY LAW

The wage-workers are peculiarly entitled to the protection and the encouragement of the law. From the very nature of their occupation railroad men, for instance, are liable to be maimed in doing the legitimate work of their profession, unless the railroad companies are required by law to make ample provision for their safety. The Administration has been zealous in enforcing the existing law for this purpose. That law should be amended and strengthened. Wherever the National Government has power there should be a stringent employers' liability law, which should apply to the government itself where the government is an employer of labor.

In my message to the Fifty-seventh Congress, at its second session, I urged the passage of an employers' liability law for the District of Columbia. I now renew that recommendation, and further recommend that the Congress appoint a commission to make a comprehensive study of employers' liability with the view of extending the provisions of a great and constitutional law to all employments within the scope of Federal power.

RECOGNITION OF HEROISM

The government has recognized heroism upon the water, and bestows medals of honor upon those persons who by extreme and heroic daring have endangered their lives in saving, or endeavoring to save, lives from the perils of the sea in the waters over which the United States has jurisdiction, or upon an American vessel. This recognition should be extended to cover cases of conspicuous bravery and self-sacrifice in the saving of life in private employments under the jurisdiction of the United States, and particularly in the land commerce of the nation.

RAILROAD CASUALTIES

The ever-increasing casualty list upon our railroads is a matter of grave public concern, and urgently calls for action by the Congress. In the matter of speed and comfort of railway travel our railroads give at least as good service as those of any other nation, and there is no reason why this service should not also be as safe as human ingenuity can make it.

Many of our leading roads have been foremost in the adoption of the most approved safeguards for the protection of travellers and employees, yet the list of clearly avoidable accidents continues unduly large. The passage of a law requiring the adoption of a block-signal system has been proposed to the Congress. I earnestly concur in that recommendation, and would also point out to the Congress the urgent need of legislation in the interest of the public safety limiting the hours of labor for railroad employees in train service upon railroads engaged in interstate commerce, and providing that only trained and experienced persons be employed in positions of responsibility connected with the operation of trains. Of course nothing can ever prevent accidents caused by human weakness or misconduct; and there should be drastic punishment for any railroad employee, whether officer or man, who by issuance of wrong orders or by disobedience of orders causes disaster. The law of 1901, requiring interstate railroads to make monthly reports of all accidents to passengers and employees on duty, should also be amended so as to empower the government to make a personal investigation, through proper officers, of all accidents involving loss of life which seem to require investigation, with a requirement that the results of such investigation be made public.

The safety-appliance law, as amended by the act of March 2, 1903, has proved beneficial to railway employees, and in order that its provisions may be properly carried out, the force of inspectors provided for by appropriation should be largely increased. This service is analogous to the Steamboat-Inspection Service, and deals with even more important interests. It has passed the experimental stage and demonstrated its utility, and should receive generous recognition by the Congress.

GOVERNMENT EMPLOYEES

There is no objection to employees of the government forming or belonging to unions; but the government can neither discriminate for nor discriminate against non-union men who are in its employment, or who seek to be employed under it. Moreover, it is a very grave impropriety for government employees to band themselves together for the purpose of extorting improperly high salaries from the government. Especially is this true of those within the classified service. The letter-carriers, both municipal and rural, are as a whole an excellent body of public servants. They should be amply paid. But their payment must be obtained by arguing their claims fairly and honorably before the Congress, and not by banding together for the defeat of those congressmen who refuse to give promises which they cannot in conscience give. The Administration has already taken steps to prevent and punish abuses of this nature; but it will be wise for the Congress to supplement this action by legislation.

LABOR CONDITIONS

Much can be done by the government in labor matters merely by giving publicity to certain conditions. The Bureau of Labor has done excellent work of this kind in many different directions. I shall shortly lay before you in a special message the full report of the investigation of the Bureau of Labor into the Colorado mining strike, as this was a strike in which certain very evil forces, which are more or less at work everywhere under the conditions of modern industrialism, became startlingly prominent. It is greatly to be wished that the Department of Commerce and Labor, through the Labor Bureau, should compile and arrange for the Congress a list of the labor laws of the various States, and should be given the means to investigate and report to the Congress upon the labor conditions in the manufacturing and mining regions throughout the country, both as to wages, as to hours of labor, as to the labor of women and children, and as to the effect in the various labor centres of immigration from abroad. In this investigation especial attention should be paid to the conditions of child labor and child-labor legislation in the several States. Such an investigation must necessarily take into account many of the problems with which this question of child labor is connected. These problems can be actually met, in most cases, only by the States themselves; but the lack of proper legislation in one State in such a matter as child labor often renders it excessively difficult to establish protective restriction upon the work in another State having the same industries, so that the worst tends to drag down the better. For this reason, it would be well for the nation at least to endeavor to secure comprehensive information as to the conditions of labor of children in the different States. Such investigation and publication by the National Government would tend toward the securing of approximately uniform legislation of the proper character among the several States.

REGULATION OF CORPORATIONS

When we come to deal with great corporations the need for the government to act directly is far greater than in the case of labor, because great corporations can become such only by engaging in interstate commerce, and interstate commerce is peculiarly the field of the general government. It is an absurdity to expect to eliminate the abuses in great corporations by State action. It is difficult to be patient with an argument that such matters should be left to the States because more than one State pursues the policy of creating on easy terms corporations which are never operated within that State at all, but in other States whose laws they ignore. The National Government alone can deal adequately with these great corporations. To try to deal with them in an intemperate, destructive, or demagogic spirit would, in all probability, mean that nothing whatever would be accomplished, and, with absolute certainty, that if anything were accomplished it would be of a harmful nature. The American people need to continue to show the very qualities that they have shown—that is, moderation, good sense, the earnest desire to avoid doing any damage, and yet the quiet determination to proceed, step by step, without halt and without hurry, in eliminating or at least in minimizing whatever of mischief or evil there is to interstate commerce in the conduct of great corporations. They are acting in no spirit of hostility to wealth, either individual or corporate. They are not against the rich man any more than against the poor man. On the contrary, they are friendly alike toward rich man and toward poor man, provided only that each acts in a spirit of justice and decency toward his fellows. Great corporations are necessary, and only men of great and singular mental power can manage such corporations successfully, and such men must have great rewards. But these corporations should be managed with due regard to the interest of the public as a whole. Where this can be done under the present laws it must be done. Where these laws come short others should be enacted to supplement them.

Yet we must never forget the determining factor in every kind of work, of head or hand, must be the man's own good sense, courage, and kindliness. More important than any legislation is the gradual growth of a feeling of responsibility and forbearance among capitalists and wage-workers alike; a feeling of respect on the part of each man for the rights of others; a feeling of broad community of interest, not merely of capitalists among themselves, and of wage-workers among themselves, but of capitalists and wage-workers in their relations to each other, and of both in their relations to their fellows who with them make up the body politic. There are many captains of industry, many labor leaders, who realize this. A recent speech by the president of one of our great railroad systems to the employees of that system contains sound common sense. It runs in part as follows:

"It is my belief we can better serve each other, better understand the man as well as his business, when meeting face to face, exchanging views, and realizing from personal contact we serve but one interest, that of our mutual prosperity.

"Serious misunderstandings cannot occur where personal good-will exists and opportunity for personal explanation is present.

"In my early business life I had experience with men of affairs of a character to make me desire to avoid creating a like feeling of resentment to myself and the interests in my charge, should fortune ever place me in authority, and I am solicitous of a measure of confidence on the part of the public and our employees that I shall hope may be warranted by the fairness and good fellowship I intend shall prevail in our relationship.

"But do not feel I am disposed to grant unreasonable requests, spend the money of our company unnecessarily or without value received, nor expect the days of mistakes are disappearing, or that cause for complaint will not continually occur; simply to correct such abuses as may be discovered, to better conditions as fast as reasonably may be expected, constantly striving, with varying success, for that improvement we all desire, to convince you there is a force at work in the right direction, all the time making progress—is the disposition with which I have come among you, asking your good-will and encouragement.

"The day has gone by when a corporation can be handled successfully in defiance of the public will, even though that will be unreasonable and wrong. A public may be led, but not driven, and I prefer to go with it and shape or modify, in a measure, its opinion, rather than be swept from my bearings, with loss to myself and the interests in my charge.

"Violent prejudice exists toward corporate activity and capital to-day, much of it founded in reason, more in apprehension, and a large measure is due to the personal traits of arbitrary, unreasonable, incompetent, and offensive men in positions of authority. The accomplishment of results by indirection, the endeavor to thwart the intention, if not the expressed letter of the law (the will of the people), a disregard of the rights of others, a disposition to withhold what is due, to force by main strength or inactivity a result not justified, depending upon the weakness of the claimant and his indisposition to become involved in litigation, has created a sentiment harmful in the extreme and a disposition to consider anything fair that gives gain to the individual at the expense of the company.

"If corporations are to continue to do the world's work, as they are best fitted to, these qualities in their representatives that have resulted in the present prejudice against them must be relegated to the background. The corporations must come out into the open and see and be seen. They must take the public into their confidence and ask for what they want, and no more, and be prepared to explain satisfactorily what advantage will accrue to the public if they are given their desires; for they are permitted to exist not that they may make money solely, but that they may effectively serve those from whom they derive their power.

"Publicity, and not secrecy, will win hereafter, and laws be construed by their intent and not by their letter, otherwise public utilities will be owned and operated by the public which created them, even though the service be less efficient and the result less satisfactory from a financial standpoint."

The Bureau of Corporations has made careful preliminary investigation of many important corporations. It will make a special report on the beef industry.

The policy of the bureau is to accomplish the purposes of its creation by co-operation, not antagonism; by making constructive legislation, not destructive prosecution, the immediate object of its inquiries; by conservative investigation of law and fact, and by refusal to issue incomplete and hence necessarily inaccurate reports. Its policy being thus one of open inquiry into, and not attack upon, business, the bureau has been able to gain not only the confidence, but, better still, the co-operation of men engaged in legitimate business.

The bureau offers to the Congress the means of getting at the cost of production of our various great staples of commerce.

Of necessity the careful investigation of special corporations will afford the commissioner knowledge of certain business facts, the publication of which might be an improper infringement of private rights. The method of making public the results of these investigations affords, under the law, a means for the protection of private rights. The Congress will have all facts except such as would give to another corporation information which would injure the legitimate business of a competitor and destroy the incentive for individual superiority and thrift.

The bureau has also made exhaustive examinations into the legal condition under which corporate business is carried on in the various States; into all judicial decisions on the subject; and into the various systems of corporate taxation in use. I call special attention to the report of the chief of the bureau; and I earnestly ask that the Congress carefully consider the report and recommendations of the commissioner on this subject.

The business of insurance vitally affects the great mass of the people of the United States and is national and not local in its application. It involves a multitude of transactions among the people of the different States and between American companies and foreign governments. I urge that the Congress carefully consider whether the power of the Bureau of Corporations cannot constitutionally be extended to cover interstate transactions in insurance.

RAILROAD REBATES

Above all else, we must strive to keep the highways of commerce open to all on equal terms; and to do this it is necessary to put a complete stop to all rebates. Whether the shipper or the railroad is to blame makes no difference; the rebate must be stopped, the abuses of the private car and private terminal-track and side-track systems must be stopped, and the legislation of the Fifty-eighth Congress which declares it to be unlawful for any person or corporation to offer, grant, give, solicit, accept, or receive any rebate, concession, or discrimination in respect of the transportation of any property in interstate or foreign commerce whereby such property shall by any device whatever be transported at a less rate than that named in the tariffs published by the carrier must be enforced. For some time after the enactment of the Act to Regulate Commerce it remained a mooted question whether that act conferred upon the Interstate Commerce Commission the power, after it had found a challenged rate to be unreasonable, to declare what thereafter should, prima facie, be the reasonable maximum rate for the transportation in dispute. The Supreme Court finally resolved that question in the negative, so that as the law now stands the commission simply possess the bare power to denounce a particular rate as unreasonable. While I am of the opinion that at present it would be undesirable, if it were not impracticable, finally to clothe the commission with general authority to fix railroad rates, I do believe that, as a fair security to shippers, the commission should be vested with the power, where a given rate has been challenged and after full hearing found to be unreasonable, to decide, subject to judicial review, what shall be a reasonable rate to take its place; the ruling of the commission to take effect immediately, and to obtain unless and until it is reversed by the court of review. The government must in increasing degree supervise and regulate the workings of the railways engaged in interstate commerce; and such increased supervision is the only alternative to an increase of the present evils on the one hand or a still more radical policy on the other. In my judgment the most important legislative act now needed as regards the regulation of corporations is this act to confer on the Interstate Commerce Commission the power to revise rates and regulations, the revised rate to at once go into effect, and stay in effect unless and until the court of review reverses it.

STEAMSHIP COMPANIES

Steamship companies engaged in interstate commerce and protected in our coastwise trade should be held to a strict observance of the interstate commerce act.

DISTRICT OF COLUMBIA

In pursuing the set plan to make the city of Washington an example to other American municipalities several points should be kept in mind by the legislators. In the first place, the people of this country should clearly understand that no amount of industrial prosperity, and above all no leadership in international industrial competition, can in any way atone for the sapping of the vitality of those who are usually spoken of as the working classes. The farmers, the mechanics, the skilled and unskilled laborers, the small shopkeepers, make up the bulk of the population of any country; and upon their well-being, generation after generation, the well-being of the country and the race depends. Rapid development in wealth and industrial leadership is a good thing, but only if it goes hand in hand with improvement, and not deterioration, physical and moral. The overcrowding of cities and the draining of country districts are unhealthy and even dangerous symptoms in our modern life. We should not permit overcrowding in cities. In certain European cities it is provided by law that the population of towns shall not be allowed to exceed a very limited density for a given area, so that the increase in density must be continually pushed back into a broad zone around the centre of the town, this zone having great avenues or parks within it. The death-rate statistics show a terrible increase in mortality, and especially in infant mortality, in overcrowded tenements. The poorest families in tenement-houses live in one room, and it appears that in these one-room tenements the average death-rate for a number of given cities at home and abroad is about twice what it is in a two-room tenement, four times what it is in a three-room tenement, and eight times what it is in a tenement consisting of four rooms or over. These figures vary somewhat for different cities, but they approximate in each city those given above; and in all cases the increase of mortality, and especially of infant mortality, with the decrease in the number of rooms used by the family and with the consequent overcrowding is startling. The slum exacts a heavy total of death from those who dwell therein; and this is the case not merely in the great crowded slums of high buildings in New York and Chicago, but in the alley slums of Washington. In Washington people cannot afford to ignore the harm that this causes. No Christian and civilized community can afford to show a happy-go-lucky lack of concern for the youth of to-day; for, if so, the community will have to pay a terrible penalty of financial burden and social degradation in the to-morrow. There should be severe child-labor and factory-inspection laws. It is very desirable that married women should not work in factories. The prime duty of the man is to work, to be the breadwinner; the prime duty of the woman is to be the mother, the housewife. All questions of tariff and finance sink into utter insignificance when compared with the tremendous, the vital importance of trying to shape conditions so that these two duties of the man and of the woman can be fulfilled under reasonably favorable circumstances. If a race does not have plenty of children, or if the children do not grow up, or if when they grow up they are unhealthy in body and stunted or vicious in mind, then that race is decadent, and no heaping up of wealth, no splendor of momentary material prosperity, can avail in any degree as offsets.

The Congress has the same power of legislation for the District of Columbia which the State legislatures have for the various States. The problems incident to our highly complex modern industrial civilization, with its manifold and perplexing tendencies both for good and for evil, are far less sharply accentuated in the city of Washington than in most other cities. For this very reason it is easier to deal with the various phases of these problems in Washington, and the District of Columbia government should be a model for the other municipal governments of the nation, in all such matters as supervision of the housing of the poor, the creation of small parks in the districts inhabited by the poor, in laws affecting labor, in laws providing for the taking care of the children, in truant laws, and in providing schools.

In the vital matter of taking care of children, much advantage could be gained by a careful study of what has been accomplished in such States as Illinois and Colorado by the juvenile courts. The work of the juvenile court is really a work of character-building. It is now generally recognized that young boys and young girls who go wrong should not be treated as criminals, not even necessarily as needing reformation, but rather as needing to have their characters formed, and for this end to have them tested and developed by a system of probation. Much admirable work has been done in many of our commonwealths by earnest men and women who have made a special study of the needs of those classes of children which furnish the greatest number of juvenile offenders, and therefore the greatest number of adult offenders; and by their aid, and by profiting by the experiences of the different States and cities in these matters, it would be easy to provide a good code for the District of Columbia.

Several considerations suggest the need for a systematic investigation into and improvement of housing conditions in Washington. The hidden residential alleys are breeding-grounds of vice and disease, and should be opened into minor streets. For a number of years influential citizens have joined with the District commissioners in the vain endeavor to secure laws permitting the condemnation of insanitary dwellings. The local death-rates, especially from preventable diseases, are so unduly high as to suggest that the exceptional wholesomeness of Washington's better sections is offset by bad conditions in her poorer neighborhoods. A special "Commission on Housing and Health Conditions in the National Capital" would not only bring about the reformation of existing evils, but would also formulate an appropriate building code to protect the city from mammoth brick tenements and other evils which threaten to develop here as they have in other cities. That the nation's capital should be made a model for other municipalities is an ideal which appeals to all patriotic citizens everywhere, and such a special commission might map out and organize the city's future development in lines of civic social service, just as Major L'Enfant and the recent Park Commission planned the arrangement of her streets and parks.

It is mortifying to remember that Washington has no compulsory-school-attendance law, and that careful inquiries indicate the habitual absence from school of some twenty per cent of all children between the ages of eight and fourteen. It must be evident to all who consider the problems of neglected child life or the benefits of compulsory education in other cities that one of the most urgent needs of the national capital is a law requiring the school attendance of all children, this law to be enforced by attendance agents directed by the Board of Education.

Public playgrounds are necessary means for the development of wholesome citizenship in modern cities. It is important that the work inaugurated here through voluntary efforts should be taken up and extended through congressional appropriation of funds sufficient to equip and maintain numerous convenient small playgrounds upon land which can be secured without purchase or rental. It is also desirable that small vacant places be purchased and reserved as small-park playgrounds in densely settled sections of the city which now have no public open spaces and are destined soon to be built up solidly. All these needs should be met immediately. To meet them would entail expenses; but a corresponding saving could be made by stopping the building of streets and levelling of ground for purposes largely speculative in outlying parts of the city.

There are certain offenders, whose criminality takes the shape of brutality and cruelty toward the weak, who need a special type of punishment. The wife-beater, for example, is inadequately punished by imprisonment; for imprisonment may often mean nothing to him, while it may cause hunger and want to the wife and children who have been the victims of his brutality. Probably some form of corporal punishment would be the most adequate way of meeting this kind of crime.

The Department of Agriculture has grown into an educational institution with a faculty of 2,000 specialists making research into all the sciences of production. The Congress appropriates, directly and indirectly, six millions of dollars annually to carry on this work. It reaches every State and Territory in the Union and the islands of the sea lately come under our flag. Co-operation is had with the State experiment stations, and with many other institutions and individuals. The world is carefully searched for new varieties of grains, fruits, grasses, vegetables, trees, and shrubs, suitable to various localities in our country; and marked benefit to our producers has resulted.

The activities of our age in lines of research have reached the tillers of the soil and inspired them with ambition to know more of the principles that govern the forces of nature with which they have to deal. Nearly half of the people of this country devote their energies to growing things from the soil. Until a recent date little has been done to prepare these millions for their life-work. In most lines of human activity college-trained men are the leaders. The farmer had no opportunity for special training until the Congress made provision for it forty years ago. During these years progress has been made and teachers have been prepared. Over 5,000 students are in attendance at our State agricultural colleges. The Federal Government expends ten millions of dollars annually toward this education and for research in Washington and in the several States and Territories. The Department of Agriculture has given facilities for postgraduate work to 500 young men during the last seven years, preparing them for advance lines of work in the department and in the State institutions.

The facts concerning meteorology and its relations to plant and animal life are being systematically inquired into. Temperature and moisture are controlling factors in all agricultural operations. The seasons of the cyclones of the Caribbean Sea and their paths are being forecasted with increasing accuracy. The cold winds that come from the north are anticipated and their times and intensity told to farmers, gardeners, and fruiterers in all southern localities.

We sell $250,000,000 worth of animals and animal products to foreign countries every year, in addition to supplying our own people more cheaply and abundantly than any other nation is able to provide for its people. Successful manufacturing depends primarily on cheap food, which accounts to a considerable extent for our growth in this direction. The Department of Agriculture, by careful inspection of meats, guards the health of our people and gives clean bills of health to deserving exports; it is prepared to deal promptly with imported diseases of animals, and maintain the excellence of our flocks and herds in this respect. There should be an annual census of the live stock of the nation.

We sell abroad about $600,000,000 worth of plants and their products every year. Strenuous efforts are being made to import from foreign countries such grains as are suitable to our varying localities. Seven years ago we bought three-fourths of our rice; by helping the rice-growers on the Gulf coast to secure seeds from the Orient suited to their conditions, and by giving them adequate protection, they now supply home demand and export to the islands of the Caribbean Sea and to other rice-growing countries. Wheat and other grains have been imported from light-rainfall countries to our lands in the West and Southwest that have not grown crops because of light precipitation, resulting in an extensive addition to our cropping area and our home-making territory that cannot be irrigated. Ten million bushels of first-class macaroni wheat were grown from these experimental importations last year. Fruits suitable to our soils and climates are being imported from all the countries of the Old World—the fig from Turkey, the almond from Spain, the date from Algeria, the mango from India. We are helping our fruit-growers to get their crops into European markets by studying methods of preservation through refrigeration, packing, and handling, which have been quite successful. We are helping our hop-growers by importing varieties that ripen earlier and later than the kinds they have been raising, thereby lengthening the harvesting-season. The cotton-crop of the country is threatened with root rot, the boll-worm, and the boll-weevil. Our pathologists will find immune varieties that will resist the root disease, and the boll-worm can be dealt with, but the boll-weevil is a serious menace to the cotton-crop. It is a Central American insect that has become acclimated in Texas and has done great damage. A scientist of the Department of Agriculture has found the weevil at home in Guatemala being kept in check by an ant, which has been brought to our cotton-fields for observation. It is hoped that it may serve a good purpose.

The soils of the country are getting attention from the farmer's standpoint, and interesting results are following. We have duplicates of the soils that grow the wrapper tobacco in Sumatra and the filler tobacco in Cuba. It will be only a question of time when the large amounts paid to these countries will be paid to our own people. The reclamation of alkali lands is progressing, to give object-lessons to our people in methods by which worthless lands may be made productive.

The insect friends and enemies of the farmer are getting attention. The enemy of the San José scale was found near the Great Wall of China, and is now cleaning up all our orchards. The fig-fertilizing insect imported from Turkey has helped to establish an industry in California that amounts to from fifty to one hundred tons of dried figs annually, and is extending over the Pacific coast. A parasitic fly from South Africa is keeping in subjection the black scale, the worst pest of the orange and lemon industry in California.

Careful preliminary work is being done toward producing

our own silk. The mulberry is being distributed in large numbers, eggs are being imported and distributed, improved reels were imported from Europe last year, and two expert reelers were brought to Washington to reel the crop of cocoons and teach the art to our own people.

The crop-reporting system of the Department of Agriculture is being brought closer to accuracy every year. It has 250,000 reporters selected from people in eight vocations in life. It has arrangements with most European countries for interchange of estimates, so that our people may know as nearly as possible with what they must compete.

RECLAMATION

During the two and a half years that have elapsed since the passage of the reclamation act rapid progress has been made in the surveys and examinations of the opportunities for reclamation in the thirteen States and three Territories of the arid West. Construction has already been begun on the largest and most important of the irrigation works, and plans are being completed for works which will utilize the funds now available. The operations are being carried on by the Reclamation Service, a corps of engineers selected through competitive civil-service examinations. This corps includes experienced consulting and constructing engineers as well as various experts in mechanical and legal matters, and is composed largely of men who have spent most of their lives in practical affairs connected with irrigation. The larger problems have been solved and it now remains to execute with care, economy, and thoroughness the work which has been laid out. All important details are being carefully considered by boards of consulting engineers, selected for their thorough knowledge and practical experience. Each project is taken up on the ground by competent men and viewed from the standpoint of the creation of prosperous homes, and of promptly refunding to the Treasury the cost of construction. The reclamation act has been found to be remarkably complete and effective, and so broad in its provisions that a wide range of undertakings has been possible under it. At the same time, economy is guaranteed by the fact that the funds must ultimately be returned to be used over again.

FOREST CONSERVATION

It is the cardinal principle of the forest-reserve policy of this Administration that the reserves are for use. Whatever interferes with the use of their resources is to be avoided by every possible means. But these resources must be used in such a way as to make them permanent.

The forest policy of the government is just now a subject of vivid public interest throughout the West and to the people of the United States in general. The forest reserves themselves are of extreme value to the present as well as to the future of all the Western public-land States. They powerfully affect the use and disposal of the public lands. They are of special importance because they preserve the water-supply and the supply of timber for domestic purposes, and so promote settlement under the reclamation act. Indeed, they are essential to the welfare of every one of the great interests of the West.

Forest reserves are created for two principal purposes. The first is to preserve the water-supply. This is their most important use. The principal users of the water thus preserved are irrigation ranchers and settlers, cities and towns to whom their municipal water-supplies are of the very first importance, users and furnishers of water-power, and the users of water for domestic, manufacturing, mining, and other purposes. All these are directly dependent upon the forest reserves.

The second reason for which forest reserves are created is to preserve the timber-supply for various classes of wood users. Among the more important of these are settlers under the reclamation act and other acts, for whom a cheap and accessible supply of timber for domestic uses is absolutely necessary; miners and prospectors, who are in serious danger of losing their timber-supply by fire or through export by lumber companies when timber-lands adjacent to their mines pass into private ownership; lumbermen, transportation companies, builders, and commercial interests in general.

Although the wisdom of creating forest reserves is nearly everywhere heartily recognized, yet in a few localities there has been misunderstanding and complaint. The following statement is therefore desirable:

The forest-reserve policy can be successful only when it has the full support of the people of the West. It cannot safely, and should not in any case, be imposed upon them against their will. But neither can we accept the views of those whose only interest in the forest is temporary; who are anxious to reap what they have not sown and then move away, leaving desolation behind them. On the contrary, it is everywhere and always the interest of the permanent settler and the permanent business man, the man with a stake in the country, which must be considered and which must decide.

The making of forest reserves within railroad and wagon-road land-grant limits will hereafter, as for the past three years, be so managed as to prevent the issue, under the act of June 4, 1897, of base for exchange or lieu selection (usually called scrip). In all cases where forest reserves within areas covered by land grants appear to be essential to the prosperity of settlers, miners, or others, the government lands within such proposed forest reserves will, as in the recent past, be withdrawn from sale or entry pending the completion of such negotiations with the owners of the land grants as will prevent the creation of so-called scrip.

It was formerly the custom to make forest reserves without first getting definite and detailed information as to the character of land and timber within their boundaries. This method of action often resulted in badly chosen boundaries and consequent injustice to settlers and others. Therefore this Administration adopted the present method of first withdrawing the land from disposal, followed by careful examination on the ground and the preparation of detailed maps and descriptions, before any forest reserve is created.

I have repeatedly called attention to the confusion which exists in government forest matters because the work is scattered among three independent organizations. The United States is the only one of the great nations in which the forest work of the government is not concentrated under one department, in consonance with the plainest dictates of good administration and common sense. The present arrangement is bad from every point of view. Merely to mention it is to prove that it should be terminated at once. As I have repeatedly recommended, all the forest work of the government should be concentrated in the Department of Agriculture, where the larger part of that work is already done, where practically all of the trained foresters of the government are employed, where chiefly in Washington there is comprehensive first-class knowledge of the problems of the reserves acquired on the ground, where all problems relating to growth from the soil are already gathered, and where all the sciences auxiliary to forestry are at hand for prompt and effective co-operation. These reasons are decisive in themselves, but it should be added that the great organizations of citizens whose interests are affected by the forest reserves, such as the National Live Stock Association, the National Wool Growers' Association, the American Mining Congress, the National Irrigation Congress, and the National Board of Trade, have uniformly, emphatically, and most of them repeatedly, expressed themselves in favor of placing all government forest work in the Department of Agriculture because of the peculiar adaptation of that department for it. It is true, also, that the forest services of nearly all the great nations of the world are under the respective departments of agriculture, while in but two of the smaller nations and in one colony are they under the department of the interior. This is the result of long and varied experience and it agrees fully with the requirements of good administration in our own case.

The creation of a forest service in the Department of Agriculture will have for its important results:

First. A better handling of all forest work; because it will be under a single head, and because the vast and indispensable experience of the department in all matters pertaining to the forest reserves, to forestry in general, and to other forms of production from the soil, will be easily and rapidly accessible.

Second. The reserves themselves, being handled from the point of view of the man in the field, instead of the man in the office, will be more easily and more widely useful to the people of the West than has been the case hitherto.

Third. Within a comparatively short time the reserves will become self-supporting. This is important, because continually and rapidly increasing appropriations will be necessary for the proper care of this exceedingly important interest of the nation, and they can and should be offset by returns from the national forests. Under similar circumstances the forest possessions of other great nations form an important source of revenue to their governments.

Every administrative officer concerned is convinced of the necessity for the proposed consolidation of forest work in the Department of Agriculture, and I myself have urged it more than once in former messages. Again I commend it to the early and favorable consideration of the Congress. The interests of the nation at large and of the West in particular have suffered greatly because of the delay.

I call the attention of the Congress again to the report and recommendation of the Commission on the Public Lands forwarded by me to the second session of the present Congress. The commission has prosecuted its investigations actively during the past season, and a second report is now in an advanced stage of preparation.

GAME REFUGES

In connection with the work of the forest reserves I desire again to urge upon the Congress the importance of authorizing the President to set aside certain portions of these reserves or other public lands as game refuges for the preservation of the bison, the wapiti, and other large beasts once so abundant in our woods and mountains and on our great plains, and now tending toward extinction. Every support should be given to the authorities of the Yellowstone Park in their successful efforts at preserving the large creatures therein; and at very little expense portions of the public domain in other regions which are wholly unsuited to agricultural settlement could be similarly utilized. We owe it to future generations to keep alive the noble and beautiful creatures which by their presence add such distinctive character to the American wilderness. The limits of the Yellowstone Park should be extended southward. The Canyon of the Colorado should be made a national park; and the national-park system should include the Yosemite and as many as possible of the groves of giant trees in California.

VETERANS

The veterans of the Civil War have a claim upon the nation such as no other body of our citizens possess. The Pension Bureau has never in its history been managed in a more satisfactory manner than is now the case.

THE INDIANS

The progress of the Indians toward civilization, though not rapid, is perhaps all that could be hoped for in view of the circumstances. Within the past year many tribes have shown, in a degree greater than ever before, an appreciation of the necessity of work. This changed attitude is in part due to the policy recently pursued of reducing the amount of subsistence to the Indians, and thus forcing them, through sheer necessity, to work for a livelihood. The policy, though severe, is a useful one, but it is to be exercised only with judgment and with a full understanding of the conditions which exist in each community for which it is intended. On or near the Indian reservations there is usually very little demand for labor, and if the Indians are to earn their living and when work cannot be furnished from outside (which is always preferable), then it must be furnished by the government. Practical instruction of this kind would in a few years result in the forming of habits of regular industry, which would render the Indian a producer and would effect a great reduction in the cost of his maintenance.

It is commonly declared that the slow advance of the Indians is due to the unsatisfactory character of the men appointed to take immediate charge of them, and to some extent this is true. While the standard of the employees in the Indian Service shows great improvement over that of bygone years, and while actual corruption or flagrant dishonesty is now the rare exception, it is nevertheless the fact that the salaries paid Indian agents are not large enough to attract the best men to that field of work. To achieve satisfactory results the official in charge of an Indian tribe should possess the high qualifications which are required in the manager of a large business, but only in exceptional cases is it possible to secure men of such a type for these positions. Much better service, however, might be obtained from those now holding the places were it practicable to get out of them the best that is in them, and this should be done by bringing them constantly into closer touch with their superior officers. An agent who has been content to draw his salary, giving in return the least possible equivalent in effort and service, may, by proper treatment, by suggestion and encouragement, or persistent urging, be stimulated to greater effort and induced to take a more active personal interest in his work.

Under existing conditions an Indian agent in the distant West may be wholly out of touch with the office of the Indian

Bureau. He may very well feel that no one takes a personal interest in him or his efforts. Certain routine duties in the way of reports and accounts are required of him, but there is no one with whom he may intelligently consult on matters vital to his work, except after long delay. Such a man would be greatly encouraged and aided by personal contact with some one whose interest in Indian affairs and whose authority in the Indian Bureau were greater than his own, and such contact would be certain to arouse and constantly increase the interest he takes in his work.

The distance which separates the agents—the workers in the field—from the Indian Office in Washington is a chief obstacle to Indian progress. Whatever shall more closely unite these two branches of the Indian Service, and shall enable them to co-operate more heartily and more effectively, will be for the increased efficiency of the work and the betterment of the race for whose improvement the Indian Bureau was established. The appointment of a field assistant to the commissioner of Indian affairs would be certain to insure this good end. Such an official, if possessed of the requisite energy and deep interest in the work, would be a most efficient factor in bringing into closer relationship and a more direct union of effort the bureau in Washington and its agents in the field; and with the co-operation of its branches thus secured the Indian Bureau would, in measure fuller than ever before, lift up the savage toward that self-help and self-reliance which constitute the man.

JAMESTOWN EXPOSITION

In 1907 there will be held at Hampton Roads the tri-centennial celebration of the settlement of Jamestown, Virginia, with which the history of what has now become the United States really begins. I commend this to your favorable consideration. It is an event of prime historic significance, in which all the people of the United States should feel, and should show, great and general interest.

POSTAL SERVICE

In the Post-Office Department the service has increased in efficiency, and conditions as to revenue and expenditure continue satisfactory. The increase of revenue during the year was $9,358,181.10, or 6.9 per cent, the total receipts amounting to $143,382,624.34. The expenditures were $152,362,-116.70, an increase of about 9 per cent over the previous year, being thus $8,979,492.36 in excess of the current revenue. Included in these expenditures was a total appropriation of $12,-956,637.35 for the continuation and extension of the rural free-delivery service, which was an increase of $4,902,237.35 over the amount expended for this purpose in the preceding fiscal year. Large as this expenditure has been, the beneficent results attained in extending the free distribution of mails to the residents of rural districts have justified the wisdom of the outlay. Statistics brought down to the 1st of October, 1904, show that on that date there were 27,138 rural routes established, serving approximately 12,000,000 of people in rural districts remote from post-offices, and that there were pending at that time 3,859 petitions for the establishment of new rural routes. Unquestionably some part of the general increase in receipts is due to the increased postal facilities which the rural service has afforded. The revenues have also been aided greatly by amendments in the classification of mail matter, and the curtailment of abuses of the second-class mailing privilege. The average increase in the volume of mail matter for the period beginning with 1902 and ending June, 1905 (that portion for 1905 being estimated), is 40.47 per cent, as compared with 25.46 per cent for the period immediately preceding, and 15.92 for the four-year period immediately preceding that.

CONSULAR SERVICE

Our consular system needs improvement. Salaries should be substituted for fees, and the proper classification, grading, and transfer of consular officers should be provided. I am not prepared to say that a competitive system of examinations for appointment would work well; but it should be provided that consuls should be familiar, according to places for which they apply, with the French, German, or Spanish languages, and should possess acquaintance with the resources of the United States.

SMITHSONIAN INSTITUTION

The collection of objects of art contemplated in section 5,586 of the Revised Statutes should be designated and established as a National Gallery of Art; and the Smithsonian Institution should be authorized to accept any additions to said collection that may be received by gift, bequest, or devise.

QUARANTINE LAW

It is desirable to enact a proper national quarantine law. It is most undesirable that a State should on its own initiative enforce quarantine regulations which are in effect a restriction upon interstate and international commerce. The question should properly be assumed by the government alone. The surgeon-general of the National Public Health and Marine-Hospital Service has repeatedly and convincingly set forth the need for such legislation.

PUBLIC PRINTING

I call your attention to the great extravagance in printing and binding government publications, and especially to the fact that altogether too many of these publications are printed. There is a constant tendency to increase their number and their volume. It is an understatement to say that no appreciable harm would be caused by, and substantial benefit would accrue from, decreasing the amount of printing now done by at least one-half. Probably the great majority of the government reports and the like now printed are never read at all, and furthermore the printing of much of the material contained in many of the remaining ones serves no useful purpose whatever.

THE CURRENCY

The attention of the Congress should be especially given to the currency question, and that the standing committees on the matter in the two houses charged with the duty, take up the matter in our currency and see whether it is not possible to secure an agreement in the business world for bettering the system; the committees should consider the question of the retirement of the greenbacks and the problem of securing in our currency such elasticity as is consistent with safety. Every silver dollar should be made by law redeemable in gold at the option of the holder.

MERCHANT MARINE

I especially commend to your immediate attention the encouragement of our merchant marine by appropriate legislation.

ORIENTAL TRADE

The growing importance of the Orient as a field for American exports drew from my predecessor, President McKinley, an urgent request for its special consideration by the Congress. In his message of 1898 he stated:

"In this relation, as showing the peculiar volume and value of our trade with China and the peculiarly favorable conditions which exist for their expansion in the normal course of trade, I refer to the communication addressed to the Speaker of the House of Representatives by the Secretary of the Treasury on the 14th of last June, with its accompanying letter of the Secretary of State, recommending an appropriation for a commission to study the industrial and commercial conditions in the Chinese Empire and to report as to the opportunities for and the obstacles to the enlargement of markets in China for the raw products and manufactures of the United States. Action was not taken thereon during the last session. I cordially urge

that the recommendation receive at your hands the consideration which its importance and timeliness merit."

In his annual message of 1899 he again called attention to
this recommendation, quoting it, and stated further:

"I now renew this recommendation, as the importance of
the subject has steadily grown since it was first submitted to
you, and no time should be lost in studying for ourselves the
resources of this great field for American trade and enterprise."

The importance of securing proper information and data
with a view to the enlargement of our trade with Asia is undi-
minished. Our consular representatives in China have strongly
urged a place for permanent display of American products in
some prominent trade centre of that empire, under government control and management, as an effective means of advancing our export trade therein. I call the attention of the
Congress to the desirability of carrying out these suggestions.

IMMIGRATION AND NATURALIZATION

In dealing with the questions of immigration and naturalization it is indispensable to keep certain facts ever before the
minds of those who share in enacting the laws. First and
foremost, let us remember that the question of being a good
American has nothing whatever to do with a man's birthplace
any more than it has to do with his creed. In every generation from the time this government was founded men of foreign birth have stood in the very foremost rank of good citizenship, and that not merely in one but in every field of American activity; while to try to draw a distinction between the
man whose parents came to this country and the man whose
ancestors came to it several generations back is a mere absurdity. Good Americanism is a matter of heart, of conscience, of lofty aspiration, of sound common sense, but not
of birthplace or of creed. The medal of honor, the highest
prize to be won by those who serve in the army and the navy
of the United States decorates men born here, and it also deco-

rates men born in Great Britain and Ireland, in Germany, in Scandinavia, in France, and doubtless in other countries also. In the field of statesmanship, in the field of business, in the field of philanthropic endeavor, it is equally true that among the men of whom we are most proud as Americans no distinction whatever can be drawn between those who themselves or whose parents came over in sailing ship or steamer from across the water and those whose ancestors stepped ashore into the wooded wilderness at Plymouth or at the mouth of the Hudson, the Delaware, or the James nearly three centuries ago. No fellow citizen of ours is entitled to any peculiar regard because of the way in which he worships his Maker, or because of the birthplace of himself or his parents, nor should he be in any way discriminated against therefor. Each must stand on his worth as a man and each is entitled to be judged solely thereby.

There is no danger of having too many immigrants of the right kind. It makes no difference from what country they come. If they are sound in body and in mind, and, above all, if they are of good character, so that we can rest assured that their children and grandchildren will be worthy fellow citizens of our children and grandchildren, then we should welcome them with cordial hospitality.

But the citizenship of this country should not be debased. It is vital that we should keep high the standard of well-being among our wage-workers, and therefore we should not admit masses of men whose standards of living and whose personal customs and habits are such that they tend to lower the level of the American wage-worker; and above all we should not admit any man of an unworthy type, any man concerning whom we can say that he will himself be a bad citizen, or that his children and grandchildren will detract from instead of adding to the sum of the good citizenship of the country. Similarly we should take the greatest care about naturalization. Fraudulent naturalization, the naturalization of improper persons, is a curse to our government; and it is the affair of every honest voter, wherever born, to see that no fraudulent voting is allowed, that no fraud in connection with naturalization is permitted.

In the past year the cases of false, fraudulent, and improper naturalization of aliens coming to the attention of the executive branches of the government have increased to an alarming degree. Extensive sales of forged certificates of naturalization have been discovered, as well as many cases of naturalization secured by perjury and fraud; and in addition, instances have accumulated showing that many courts issue certificates of naturalization carelessly and upon insufficient evidence.

Under the Constitution it is the power of the Congress "to establish a uniform rule of naturalization," and numerous laws have from time to time been enacted for that purpose, which have been supplemented in a few States by State laws having special application. The Federal statutes permit naturalization by any court of record in the United States having common-law jurisdiction and a seal and clerk, except the police court of the District of Columbia, and nearly all these courts exercise this important function. It results that where so many courts of such varying grades have jurisdiction, there is lack of uniformity in the rules applied in conferring naturalization. Some courts are strict and others lax. An alien who may secure naturalization in one place might be denied it in another, and the intent of the constitutional provision is in fact defeated. Furthermore, the certificates of naturalization issued by the courts differ widely in wording and appearance, and when they are brought into use in foreign countries, are frequently subject to suspicion.

There should be a comprehensive revision of the naturalization laws. The courts having power to naturalize should be definitely named by national authority; the testimony upon which naturalization may be conferred should be definitely prescribed; publication of impending naturalization applications should be required in advance of their hearing in court;

the form and wording of all certificates issued should be uniform throughout the country, and the courts should be required to make returns to the secretary of state at stated periods of all naturalizations conferred.

Not only are the laws relating to naturalization now defective, but those relating to citizenship of the United States ought to be made the subject of scientific inquiry with a view to probable further legislation. By what acts expatriation may be assumed to have been accomplished, how long an American citizen may reside abroad and receive the protection of our passport, whether any degree of protection should be extended to one who has made the declaration of intention to become a citizen of the United States but has not secured naturalization, are questions of serious import, involving personal rights and often producing friction between this government and foreign governments. Yet upon these questions our laws are silent. I recommend that an examination be made into the subjects of citizenship, expatriation, and protection of Americans abroad, with a view to appropriate legislation.

FEDERAL ELECTIONS

The power of the government to protect the integrity of the elections of its own officials is inherent and has been recognized and affirmed by repeated declarations of the Supreme Court. There is no enemy of free government more dangerous and none so insidious as the corruption of the electorate. No one defends or excuses corruption, and it would seem to follow that none would oppose vigorous measures to eradicate it. I recommend the enactment of a law directed against bribery and corruption in Federal elections. The details of such a law may be safely left to the wise discretion of the Congress, but it should go as far as under the Constitution it is possible to go, and should include severe penalties against him who gives or receives a bribe intended to influence his act or opinion as an elector; and provisions for the publication not only of the expenditures for nominations and elections of all candidates but also of all contributions received and expenditures made by political committees.

THE LAW'S DELAY

No subject is better worthy the attention of the Congress than that portion of the report of the attorney-general dealing with the long delays and the great obstruction to justice experienced in the cases of Beavers, Green and Gaynor, and Benson. Were these isolated and special cases, I should not call your attention to them; but the difficulties encountered as regards these men who have been indicted for criminal practices are not exceptional; they are precisely similar in kind to what occurs again and again in the case of criminals who have sufficient means to enable them to take advantage of a system of procedure which has grown up in the Federal courts and which amounts in effect to making the law easy of enforcement against the man who has no money, and difficult of enforcement, even to the point of sometimes securing immunity, as regards the man who has money. In criminal cases the writ of the United States should run throughout its borders. The wheels of justice should not be clogged, as they have been clogged in the cases above mentioned, where it has proved absolutely impossible to bring the accused to the place appointed by the Constitution for his trial. Of recent years there has been grave and increasing complaint of the difficulty of bringing to justice those criminals whose criminality, instead of being against one person in the republic, is against all persons in the republic, because it is against the republic itself. Under any circumstance and from the very nature of the case it is often exceedingly difficult to secure proper punishment of those who have been guilty of wrong-doing against the government. By the time the offender can be brought into court the popular wrath against him has generally subsided; and there is in most instances very slight danger indeed of any prejudice existing in the minds of the jury against him. At present the interests of the innocent man are amply safeguarded; but the interests of the government, that is, the interests of honest administration, that is the interests of the people, are not recognized as they should be. No subject better warrants the attention of the Congress. Indeed, no subject better warrants the attention of the bench and the bar throughout the United States.

ALASKA

Alaska, like all our Territorial acquisitions, has proved resourceful beyond the expectations of those who made the purchase. It has become the home of many hardy, industrious, and thrifty American citizens. Towns of a permanent character have been built. The extent of its wealth in minerals, timber, fisheries, and agriculture, while great, is probably not comprehended yet in any just measure by our people. We do know, however, that from a very small beginning its products have grown until they are a steady and material contribution to the wealth of the nation. Owing to the immensity of Alaska and its location in the far North, it is a difficult matter to provide many things essential to its growth and to the happiness and comfort of its people by private enterprise alone. It should, therefore, receive reasonable aid from the government. The government has already done excellent work for Alaska in laying cables and building telegraph-lines. This work has been done in the most economical and efficient way by the Signal Corps of the army.

In some respects it has outgrown its present laws, while in others those laws have been found to be inadequate. In order to obtain information upon which I could rely I caused an official of the Department of Justice, in whose judgment I have confidence, to visit Alaska during the past summer for the purpose of ascertaining how government is administered there and what legislation is actually needed at present. A statement of the conditions found to exist, together with some recommendations and the reasons therefor, in which I strongly concur, will be found in the annual report of the attorney-general. In some instances I feel that the legislation suggested is so imperatively needed that I am moved briefly to emphasize the attorney-general's proposals.

Under the Code of Alaska as it now stands many purely administrative powers and duties, including by far the most important, devolve upon the district judges or upon the clerks of the district court acting under the direction of the judges, while the governor, upon whom these powers and duties should logically fall, has nothing specific to do except to make annual reports, issue Thanksgiving Day proclamations, and appoint Indian policemen and notaries public. I believe it essential to good government in Alaska, and therefore recommend, that the Congress divest the district judges and the clerks of their courts of the administrative or executive functions that they now exercise and cast them upon the governor. This would not be an innovation; it would simply conform the government of Alaska to fundamental principles, making the governorship a real instead of a merely nominal office, and leaving the judges free to give their entire attention to their judicial duties and at the same time removing them from a great deal of the strife that now embarrasses the judicial office in Alaska.

I also recommend that the salaries of the district judges and district attorneys in Alaska be increased so as to make them equal to those received by corresponding officers in the United States after deducting the difference in the cost of living; that the district attorneys should be prohibited from engaging in private practice; that United States commissioners be appointed by the governor of the Territory instead of by the district judges, and that a fixed salary be provided for them to take the place of the discredited "fee system," which should be abolished in all offices; that a mounted constabulary be created to police the territory outside the limits of incorporated towns —a vast section now wholly without police protection; and that some provision be made to at least lessen the oppressive delays and costs that now attend the prosecution of appeals from the district court of Alaska. There should be a division of the existing judicial districts, and an increase in the number of judges.

Alaska should have a delegate in the Congress. Where possible, the Congress should aid in the construction of needed wagon roads. Additional lighthouses should be provided. In my judgment, it is especially important to aid in such manner as seems just and feasible in the construction of a trunk line of railway to connect the Gulf of Alaska with the Yukon River through American territory. This would be most beneficial to the development of the resources of the Territory, and to the comfort and welfare of its people.

Salmon-hatcheries should be established in many different streams, so as to secure the preservation of this valuable food fish. Salmon fisheries and canneries should be prohibited on certain of the rivers where the mass of those Indians dwell who live almost exclusively on fish.

The Alaskan natives are kindly, intelligent, anxious to learn, and willing to work. Those who have come under the influence of civilization, even for a limited period, have proved their capability of becoming self-supporting, self-respecting citizens, and ask only for the just enforcement of law and intelligent instruction and supervision. Others, living in more remote regions, primitive, simple hunters and fisherfolk, who know only the life of the woods and the waters, are daily being confronted with twentieth-century civilization with all of its complexities. Their country is being overrun by strangers, the game slaughtered and driven away, the streams depleted of fish, and hitherto unknown and fatal diseases brought to them, all of which combine to produce a state of abject poverty and want which must result in their extinction. Action in their interest is demanded by every consideration of justice and humanity.

The needs of these people are:

The abolition of the present fee system, whereby the native is degraded, imposed upon, and taught the injustice of law.

The establishment of hospitals at central points, so that

contagious diseases that are brought to them continually by incoming whites may be localized and not allowed to become epidemic, to spread death and destitution over great areas.

The development of the educational system in the form of practical training in such industries as will assure the Indians self-support under the changed conditions in which they will have to live.

The duties of the office of the governor should be extended to include the supervision of Indian affairs, with necessary assistants in different districts. He should be provided with the means and the power to protect and advise the native people, to furnish medical treatment in time of epidemics, and to extend material relief in periods of famine and extreme destitution.

The Alaskan natives should be given the right to acquire, hold, and dispose of property upon the same conditions as given other inhabitants; and the privilege of citizenship should be given to such as may be able to meet certain definite requirements. In Hawaii Congress should give the governor power to remove all the officials appointed under him. The harbor of Honolulu should be dredged. The Marine-Hospital Service should be empowered to study leprosy in the islands. I ask special consideration for the report and recommendation of the governor of Porto Rico.

FOREIGN POLICY

In treating of our foreign policy and of the attitude that this great nation should assume in the world at large, it is absolutely necessary to consider the army and the navy, and the Congress, through which the thought of the nation finds its expression, should keep ever vividly in mind the fundamental fact that it is impossible to treat our foreign policy, whether this policy takes shape in the effort to secure justice for others or justice for ourselves, save as conditioned upon the attitude we are willing to take toward our army, and especially toward our navy. It is not merely unwise, it is contemptible, for a nation, as for an individual, to use high-sounding language to proclaim its purposes, or to take positions which are ridiculous if unsupported by potential force, and then to refuse to provide this force. If there is no intention of providing and of keeping the force necessary to back up a strong attitude, then it is far better not to assume such an attitude.

The steady aim of this nation, as of all enlightened nations, should be to strive to bring ever nearer the day when there shall prevail throughout the world the peace of justice. There are kinds of peace which are highly undesirable, which are in the long run as destructive as any war. Tyrants and oppressors have many times made a wilderness and called it peace. Many times peoples who were slothful or timid or short-sighted, who had been enervated by ease or by luxury, or misled by false teachings, have shrunk in unmanly fashion from doing duty that was stern and that needed self-sacrifice, and have sought to hide from their own minds their shortcomings, their ignoble motives, by calling them love of peace. The peace of tyrannous terror, the peace of craven weakness, the peace of injustice, all these should be shunned as we shun unrighteous war. The goal to set before us as a nation, the goal which should be set before all mankind, is the attainment of the peace of justice, of the peace which comes when each nation is not merely safeguarded in its own rights, but scrupulously recognizes and performs its duty toward others. Generally peace tells for righteousness; but if there is conflict between the two, then our fealty is due first to the cause of righteousness. Unrighteous wars are common, and unrighteous peace is rare; but both should be shunned. The right of freedom and the responsibility for the exercise of that right cannot be divorced. One of our great poets has well and finely said that freedom is not a gift that tarries long in the hands of cowards. Neither does it tarry long in the hands of those too slothful, too dishonest, or too unintelligent to exercise it. The eternal vigilance which is the price of liberty must be exercised, sometimes to guard against outside foes; although of course far more often to guard against our own selfish or thoughtless shortcomings.

If these self-evident truths are kept before us, and only if they are so kept before us, we shall have a clear idea of what our foreign policy in its larger aspects should be. It is our duty to remember that a nation has no more right to do injustice to another nation, strong or weak, than an individual has to do injustice to another individual; that the same moral law applies in one case as in the other. But we must also remember that it is as much the duty of the nation to guard its own rights and its own interests as it is the duty of the individual so to do. Within the nation the individual has now delegated this right to the State, that is, to the representative of all the individuals, and it is a maxim of the law that for every wrong there is a remedy. But in international law we have not advanced by any means as far as we have advanced in municipal law. There is as yet no judicial way of enforcing a right in international law. When one nation wrongs another or wrongs many others, there is no tribunal before which the wrong-doer can be brought. Either it is necessary supinely to acquiesce in the wrong, and thus put a premium upon brutality and aggression, or else it is necessary for the aggrieved nation valiantly to stand up for its rights. Until some method is devised by which there shall be a degree of international control over offending nations, it would be a wicked thing for the most civilized powers, for those with most sense of international obligations and with keenest and most generous appreciation of the difference between right and wrong, to disarm. If the great civilized nations of the present day should completely disarm, the result would mean an immediate recrudescence of barbarism in one form or another. Under any circumstances a sufficient armament would have to be kept up to serve the purposes of international police; and until international cohesion and the sense of international duties and rights are far more advanced than at present, a nation desirous both of securing respect for itself and of doing good to others must have a force adequate for the work which it feels is allotted to it as its part of the general world duty. Therefore it follows that a self-respecting, just, and far-seeing nation should on the one hand endeavor by every means to aid in the development of the various movements which tend to provide substitutes for war, which tend to render nations in their actions toward one another, and indeed toward their own peoples, more responsive to the general sentiment of humane and civilized mankind; and on the other hand that it should keep prepared, while scrupulously avoiding wrong-doing itself, to repel any wrong, and in exceptional cases to take action which in a more advanced stage of international relations would come under the head of the exercise of the international peace. A great free people owes it to itself and to all mankind not to sink into helplessness before the powers of evil.

We are in every way endeavoring to help on, with cordial good-will, every movement which will tend to bring us into more friendly relations with the rest of mankind. In pursuance of this policy I shall shortly lay before the Senate treaties of arbitration with all powers which are willing to enter into these treaties with us. It is not possible at this period of the world's development to agree to arbitrate all matters, but there are many matters of possible difference between us and other nations which can be thus arbitrated. Furthermore, at the request of the Interparliamentary Union, an eminent body composed of practical statesmen from all countries, I have asked the powers to join with this government in a second Hague conference, at which it is hoped that the work already so happily begun at The Hague may be carried some steps further toward completion. This carries out the desire expressed by the first Hague conference itself.

It is not true that the United States feels any land hunger or entertains any projects as regards the other nations of the western hemisphere save such as are for their welfare. All that this country desires is to see the neighboring countries stable, orderly, and prosperous. Any country whose people conduct themselves well can count upon our hearty friendship. If a nation shows that it knows how to act with reasonable efficiency and decency in social and political matters, if it keeps order and pays its obligations, it need fear no interference from the United States. Chronic wrong-doing, or an impotence which results in a general loosening of the ties of civilized society, may in America, as elsewhere, ultimately require intervention by some civilized nation, and in the western hemisphere the adherence of the United States to the Monroe Doctrine may force the United States, however reluctantly, in flagrant cases of such wrong-doing or impotence, to the exercise of an international police power. If every country washed by the Caribbean Sea would show the progress in stable and just civilization which with the aid of the Platt amendment Cuba has shown since our troops left the island, and which so many of the republics in both Americas are constantly and brilliantly showing, all question of interference by this nation with their affairs would be at an end. Our interests and those of our Southern neighbors are in reality identical. They have great natural riches, and if within their borders the reign of law and justice obtains, prosperity is sure to come to them. While they thus obey the primary laws of civilized society they may rest assured that they will be treated by us in a spirit of cordial and helpful sympathy. We would interfere with them only in the last resort, and then only if it became evident that their inability or unwillingness to do justice at home and abroad had violated the rights of the United States or had invited foreign aggression to the detriment of the entire body of American nations. It is a mere truism to say that every nation, whether in America or anywhere else, which desires to maintain its freedom, its independence, must ultimately realize that the right of such independence cannot be separated from the responsibility of making good use of it.

In asserting the Monroe Doctrine, in taking such steps as

we have taken in regard to Cuba, Venezuela, and Panama, and in endeavoring to circumscribe the theatre of war in the Far East, and to secure the open door in China, we have acted in our own interest as well as in the interest of humanity at large. There are, however, cases in which, while our own interests are not greatly involved, strong appeal is made to our sympathies. Ordinarily it is very much wiser and of more useful material betterment to concern ourselves here at home than with trying to better the condition of things in other nations. We have plenty of sins of our own to war against, and under ordinary circumstances we can do more for the general uplifting of humanity by striving with heart and soul to put a stop to civic corruption, to brutal lawlessness and violent race prejudices here at home than by passing resolutions about wrong-doing elsewhere. Nevertheless there are occasional crimes committed on so vast a scale and of such peculiar horror as to make us doubt whether it is not our manifest duty to endeavor at least to show our disapproval of the deed and our sympathy with those who have suffered by it. The cases must be extreme in which such a course is justifiable. There must be no effort made to remove the mote from our brother's eye if we refuse to remove the beam from our own. But in extreme cases action may be justifiable and proper. What form the action shall take must depend upon the circumstances of the case; that is, upon the degree of the atrocity and upon our power to remedy it. The cases in which we could interfere by force of arms as we interfered to put a stop to intolerable conditions in Cuba are necessarily very few. Yet it is not to be expected that a people like ours, which in spite of certain very obvious shortcomings, nevertheless as a whole shows by its consistent practice its belief in the principles of civil and religious liberty and of orderly freedom, a people among whom even the worst crime, like the crime of lynching, is never more than sporadic, so that individuals and not classes are molested in their fundamental rights—it is inevitable that such a nation should desire eagerly to give expression to its horror on an occasion like that of the massacre of the Jews in Kishenef, or when it witnesses such systematic and long-extended cruelty and oppression as the cruelty and oppression of which the Armenians have been the victims, and which have won for them the indignant pity of the civilized world.

Even where it is not possible to secure in other nations the observance of the principles which we accept as axiomatic, it is necessary for us firmly to insist upon the rights of our own citizens without regard to their creed or race; without regard to whether they were born here or born abroad. It has proved very difficult to secure from Russia the right for our Jewish fellow citizens to receive passports and travel through Russian territory. Such conduct is not only unjust and irritating toward us, but it is difficult to see its wisdom from Russia's standpoint. No conceivable good is accomplished by it. If an American Jew or an American Christian misbehaves himself in Russia he can at once be driven out; but the ordinary American Jew, like the ordinary American Christian, would behave just about as he behaves here, that is, behave as any good citizen ought to behave; and where this is the case it is a wrong against which we are entitled to protest to refuse him his passport without regard to his conduct and character, merely on racial and religious grounds. In Turkey our difficulties arise less from the way in which our citizens are sometimes treated than from the indignation inevitably excited in seeing such fearful misrule as has been witnessed both in Armenia and Macedonia.

THE NAVY

The strong arm of the government in enforcing respect for its just rights in international matters is the navy of the United States. I most earnestly recommend that there be no halt in the work of upbuilding the American navy. There is no more patriotic duty before us as a people than to keep the navy adequate to the needs of this country's position. We have undertaken to build the Isthmian Canal. We have undertaken to secure for ourselves our just share in the trade of the Orient. We have undertaken to protect our citizens from improper treatment in foreign lands. We continue steadily to insist on the application of the Monroe Doctrine to the western hemisphere. Unless our attitude in these and all similar matters is to be a mere boastful sham we cannot afford to abandon our naval programme. Our voice is now potent for peace, and is so potent because we are not afraid of war. But our protestations upon behalf of peace would neither receive nor deserve the slightest attention if we were impotent to make them good.

The war which now unfortunately rages in the Far East has emphasized in striking fashion the new possibilities of naval warfare. The lessons taught are both strategic and tactical, and are political as well as military. The experiences of the war have shown in conclusive fashion that while sea-going and sea-keeping torpedo destroyers are indispensable, and fast lightly armed and armored cruisers very useful, yet that the main reliance, the main standby, in any navy worthy the name must be the great battleships, heavily armored and heavily gunned. Not a Russian or Japanese battleship has been sunk by a torpedo-boat, or by gunfire, while among the less protected ships, cruiser after cruiser has been destroyed whenever the hostile squadrons have gotten within range of one another's weapons. There will always be a large field of usefulness for cruisers, especially of the more formidable type. We need to increase the number of torpedo-boat destroyers, paying less heed to their having a knot or two extra speed than to their capacity to keep the seas for weeks, and, if necessary, for months at a time. It is wise to build submarine torpedo-boats, as under certain circumstances they might be very useful. But most of all we need to continue building our fleet of battleships, or ships so powerfully armed that they can inflict the maximum of damage upon our opponents, and so well protected that they can suffer a severe hammering in return without fatal impairment of their ability to fight and manœuvre. Of course, ample means must be provided for enabling the personnel of the navy to be brought to the highest point of efficiency. Our great fighting ships and torpedo-boats must be ceaselessly trained and manœuvred in squadrons. The officers and men can only learn their trade thoroughly by ceaseless practice on the high seas. In the event of war it would be far better to have no ships at all than to have ships of a poor and ineffective type, or ships which, however good, were yet manned by untrained and unskilful crews. The best officers and men in a poor ship could do nothing against fairly good opponents; and on the other hand a modern war-ship is useless unless the officers and men aboard her have become adepts in their duties. The marksmanship in our navy has improved in an extraordinary degree during the last three years, and on the whole the types of our battleships are improving; but much remains to be done. Sooner or later we shall have to provide for some method by which there will be promotions for merit as well as for seniority, or else retirement of all those who after a certain age have not advanced beyond a certain grade; while no effort must be spared to make the service attractive to the enlisted men in order that they may be kept as long as possible in it. Reservation public schools should be provided wherever there are navy-yards.

THE ARMY

Within the last three years the United States has set an example in disarmament where disarmament was proper. By law our army is fixed at a maximum of 100,000 and a minimum of 60,000 men. When there was insurrection in the Philippines we kept the army at the maximum. Peace came in the Philippines, and now our army has been reduced to the minimum at which it is possible to keep it with due regard to its efficiency. The guns now mounted require 28,000 men, if the coast fortifications are to be adequately manned. Relatively to the nation, it is not now so large as the police force of New York or Chicago relatively to the population of either city. We need more officers; there are not enough to perform the regular army work. It is very important that the officers of the army should be accustomed to handle their men in masses, as it is also important that the National Guard of the several States should be accustomed to actual field manœuvring, especially in connection with the Regulars. For this reason we are to be congratulated upon the success of the field manœuvres at Manassas last fall, manœuvres in which a larger number of Regulars and National Guard took part than was ever before assembled together in time of peace. No other civilized nation has, relatively to its population, such a diminutive army as ours; and while the army is so small we are not to be excused if we fail to keep it at a very high grade of proficiency. It must be incessantly practised; the standard for the enlisted men should be kept very high, while at the same time the service should be made as attractive as possible; and the standard for the officers should be kept even higher—which, as regards the upper ranks, can best be done by introducing some system of selection and rejection into the promotions. We should be able, in the event of some sudden emergency, to put into the field one first-class army corps, which should be, as a whole, at least the equal of any body of troops of like number belonging to any other nation.

COAST DEFENSE

Great progress has been made in protecting our coasts by adequate fortifications with sufficient guns. We should, however, pay much more heed than at present to the development of an extensive system of floating mines for use in all our more important harbors. These mines have been proved to be a most formidable safeguard against hostile fleets.

THE CONGRESSIONAL MEDAL

I earnestly call the attention of the Congress to the need of amending the existing law relating to the award of Congressional medals of honor in the navy so as to provide that they may be awarded to commissioned officers and warrant officers as well as to enlisted men. These justly prized medals are given in the army alike to the officers and the enlisted men, and it is most unjust that the commissioned officers and warrant officers of the navy should not in this respect have the same rights as their brethren in the army and as the enlisted men of the navy.

THE PHILIPPINES

In the Philippine Islands there has been during the past year a continuation of the steady progress which has obtained ever since our troops definitely got the upper hand of the insurgents. The Philippine people, or, to speak more accurately, the many tribes, and even races, sundered from one another more or less sharply, who go to make up the people of the Philippine Islands, contain many elements of good, and some elements which we have a right to hope stand for progress. At present they are utterly incapable of existing in independence at all or of building up a civilization of their own. I firmly believe that we can help them to rise higher and higher in the scale of civilization and of capacity for self-government, and I most earnestly hope that in the end they will be able to stand, if not entirely alone, yet in some such relation to the United States as Cuba now stands. This end is not yet in sight, and it may be indefinitely postponed if our people are foolish enough to turn the attention of the Filipinos away from the problems of achieving moral and material prosperity, of working for a stable, orderly, and just government, and toward foolish and dangerous intrigues for a complete independence for which they are as yet totally unfit.

On the other hand, our people must keep steadily before their minds the fact that the justification for our stay in the Philippines must ultimately rest chiefly upon the good we are able to do in the islands. I do not overlook the fact that in the development of our interests in the Pacific Ocean and along its coasts, the Philippines have played and will play an important part; and that our interests have been served in more than one way by the possession of the islands. But our chief reason for continuing to hold them must be that we ought in good faith to try to do our share of the world's work, and this particular piece of work has been imposed upon us by the results of the war with Spain. The problem presented to us in the Philippine Islands is akin to, but not exactly like, the problems presented to the other great civilized powers which have possessions in the Orient. There are points of resemblance in our work to the work which is being done by the British in India and Egypt, by the French in Algiers, by the Dutch in Java, by the Russians in Turkestan, by the Japanese in Formosa; but more distinctly than any of these powers we are endeavoring to develop the natives themselves so that they shall take an ever-increasing share in their own government, and as far as is prudent we are already admitting their representatives to a governmental equality with our own. There are commissioners, judges, and governors in the islands who are Filipinos and who have exactly the same share in the government of the islands as have their colleagues who are Americans, while in the lower ranks, of course, the great majority of the public servants are Filipinos. Within two years we shall be trying the experiment of an elective lower house in the Philippine legislature. It may be that the Filipinos will misuse it if they are misled by foolish persons here at home into starting an agitation for their own independence or into any factious or improper action. In such case they will do themselves no good and will stop for the time being all further effort to advance them and give them a greater share in their own government. But if they act with wisdom and self-restraint, if they show that they are capable of electing a legislature which in its turn is capable of taking a sane and efficient part in the actual work of government, they can rest assured that a full and increasing measure of recognition will be given them. Above all they should remember that their prime needs are moral and industrial, not political. It is a good thing to try the experiment of giving them a legislature; but it is a far better thing to give them schools, good roads, railroads which will enable them to get their products to market, honest courts, an honest and efficient constabulary, and all that tends to produce order, peace, fair dealing as between man and man, and habits of intelligent industry and thrift. If they are safeguarded against oppression, and if their real wants, material and spiritual, are studied intelligently and in a spirit of friendly sympathy, much more good will be done them than by any effort to give them political power, though this effort may in its own proper time and place be proper enough.

Meanwhile our own people should remember that there is need for the highest standard of conduct among the Americans sent to the Philippine Islands, not only among the public servants but among the private individuals who go to them. It is because I feel this so deeply that in the administration of these islands I have positively refused to permit any discrimination whatsoever for political reasons and have insisted that in choosing the public servants consideration should be paid solely to the worth of the men chosen and to the needs of the islands. There is no higher body of men in our public service than we have in the Philippine Islands under Governor Wright and his associates. So far as possible these men should be given a free hand, and their suggestions should receive the hearty backing both of the Executive and of the Congress. There is need of a vigilant and disinterested support of our public servants in the Philippines by good citizens here in the United States. Unfortunately, hitherto those of our people here at home who have specially claimed to be the champions of the Filipinos have in reality been their worst enemies. This will continue to be the case as long as they strive to make the Filipinos independent, and stop all industrial development of the islands by crying out against the laws which would bring it on the ground that capitalists must not "exploit" the islands. Such proceedings are not only unwise, but are most harmful to the Filipinos, who do not need independence at all, but who do need good laws, good public servants, and the industrial development that can only come if the investment of American and foreign capital in the islands is favored in all legitimate ways.

Every measure taken concerning the islands should be taken primarily with a view to their advantage. We should certainly give them lower tariff rates on their exports to the United States; if this is not done it will be a wrong to extend our shipping laws to them. I earnestly hope for the immediate enactment into law of the legislation now pending to encourage American capital to seek investment in the islands in railroads, in factories, in plantations, and in lumbering and mining.

INAUGURAL ADDRESS[1]

MY fellow citizens, no people on earth have more cause to be thankful than ours, and this is said reverently, in no spirit of boastfulness in our own strength, but with gratitude to the Giver of Good who has blessed us with the conditions which have enabled us to achieve so large a measure of well-being and of happiness. To us as a people it has been granted to lay the foundations of our national life in a new continent. We are the heirs of the ages, and yet we have had to pay few of the penalties which in old countries are exacted by the dead hand of a bygone civilization. We have not been obliged to fight for our existence against any alien race; and yet our life has called for the vigor and effort without which the manlier and hardier virtues wither away. Under such conditions it would be our own fault if we failed; and the success which we have had in the past, the success which we confidently believe the future will bring, should cause in us no feeling of vainglory, but rather a deep and abiding realization of all which life has offered us; a full acknowledgment of the responsibility which is ours; and a fixed determination to show that under a free government a mighty people can thrive best, alike as regards the things of the body and the things of the soul.

Much has been given us, and much will rightfully be expected from us. We have duties to others and duties to ourselves; and we can shirk neither. We have become a great nation, forced by the fact of its greatness into relations with the other nations of the earth, and we must behave as beseems a people with such responsibilities. Toward all other nations,

[1] Delivered from the portico of the Capitol at Washington, March 4, 1905.

267

large and small, our attitude must be one of cordial and sincere friendship. We must show not only in our words, but in our deeds, that we are earnestly desirous of securing their goodwill by acting toward them in a spirit of just and generous recognition of all their rights. But justice and generosity in a nation, as in an individual, count most when shown not by the weak but by the strong. While ever careful to refrain from wronging others, we must be no less insistent that we are not wronged ourselves. We wish peace, but we wish the peace of justice, the peace of righteousness. We wish it because we think it is right and not because we are afraid. No weak nation that acts manfully and justly should ever have cause to fear us, and no strong power should ever be able to single us out as a subject for insolent aggression.

Our relations with the other powers of the world are important; but still more important are our relations among ourselves. Such growth in wealth, in population, and in power as this nation has seen during the century and a quarter of its national life is inevitably accompanied by a like growth in the problems which are ever before every nation that rises to greatness. Power invariably means both responsibility and danger. Our forefathers faced certain perils which we have outgrown. We now face other perils, the very existence of which it was impossible that they should foresee. Modern life is both complex and intense, and the tremendous changes wrought by the extraordinary industrial development of the last half-century are felt in every fibre of our social and political being. Never before have men tried so vast and formidable an experiment as that of administering the affairs of a continent under the forms of a Democratic republic. The conditions which have told for our marvellous material well-being, which have developed to a very high degree our energy, self-reliance, and individual initiative, have also brought the care and anxiety inseparable from the accumulation of great wealth in industrial centres. Upon the success of our experiment much depends, not only as regards our own welfare, but as regards the welfare of mankind. If we fail, the cause of free self-government throughout the world will rock to its foundations, and therefore our responsibility is heavy, to ourselves, to the world as it is to-day, and to the generations yet unborn. There is no good reason why we should fear the future, but there is every reason why we should face it seriously, neither hiding from ourselves the gravity of the problems before us nor fearing to approach these problems with the unbending, unflinching purpose to solve them aright.

Yet, after all, though the problems are new, though the tasks set before us differ from the tasks set before our fathers who founded and preserved this Republic, the spirit in which these tasks must be undertaken and these problems faced, if our duty is to be well done, remains essentially unchanged. We know that self-government is difficult. We know that no people needs such high traits of character as that people which seeks to govern its affairs aright through the freely expressed will of the freemen who compose it. But we have faith that we shall not prove false to the memories of the men of the mighty past. They did their work, they left us the splendid heritage we now enjoy. We in our turn have an assured confidence that we shall be able to leave this heritage unwasted and enlarged to our children and our children's children. To do so we must show, not merely in great crises, but in the everyday affairs of life, the qualities of practical intelligence, of courage, of hardihood, and endurance, and above all the power of devotion to a lofty ideal, which made great the men who founded this Republic in the days of Washington, which made great the men who preserved this Republic in the days of Abraham Lincoln.

VI

FIFTH ANNUAL MESSAGE[1]

TO THE SENATE AND HOUSE OF REPRESENTATIVES:

The people of this country continue to enjoy great prosperity. Undoubtedly there will be ebb and flow in such prosperity, and this ebb and flow will be felt more or less by all members of the community, both by the deserving and the undeserving. Against the wrath of the Lord the wisdom of man cannot avail; in time of flood or drought human ingenuity can but partially repair the disaster. A general failure of crops would hurt all of us. Again, if the folly of man mars the general well-being, then those who are innocent of the folly will have to pay part of the penalty incurred by those who are guilty of the folly. A panic brought on by the speculative folly of part of the business community would hurt the whole business community. But such stoppage of welfare, though it might be severe, would not be lasting. In the long run the one vital factor in the permanent prosperity of the country is the high individual character of the average American worker, the average American citizen, no matter whether his work be mental or manual, whether he be farmer or wage-worker, business man or professional man.

CONTROL OF CORPORATIONS

In our industrial and social system the interests of all men are so closely intertwined that in the immense majority of cases a straight-dealing man who by his efficiency, by his ingenuity and industry, benefits himself must also benefit others. Normally the man of great productive capacity who becomes

[1] Dated, the White House, December 5, 1905.

rich by guiding the labor of many other men does so by enabling them to produce more than they could produce without his guidance; and both he and they share in the benefit, which comes also to the public at large. The superficial fact that the sharing may be unequal must never blind us to the underlying fact that there is this sharing, and that the benefit comes in some degree to each man concerned. Normally the wageworker, the man of small means, and the average consumer, as well as the average producer, are all alike helped by making conditions such that the man of exceptional business ability receives an exceptional reward for his ability. Something can be done by legislation to help the general prosperity; but no such help of a permanently beneficial character can be given to the less able and less fortunate, save as the results of a policy which shall inure to the advantage of all industrious and efficient people who act decently; and this is only another way of saying that any benefit which comes to the less able and less fortunate must of necessity come even more to the more able and more fortunate. If, therefore, the less fortunate man is moved by envy of his more fortunate brother to strike at the conditions under which they have both, though unequally, prospered, the result will assuredly be that while danger may come to the one struck at, it will visit with an even heavier load the one who strikes the blow. Taken as a whole we must all go up or down together.

Yet, while not merely admitting, but insisting upon this, it is also true that where there is no governmental restraint or supervision some of the exceptional men use their energies not in ways that are for the common good, but in ways which tell against this common good. The fortunes amassed through corporate organization are now so large, and vest such power in those that wield them, as to make it a matter of necessity to give to the sovereign—that is, to the government, which represents the people as a whole—some effective power of supervision over their corporate use. In order to insure a healthy social and industrial life, every big corporation should be held responsible by, and be accountable to, some sovereign strong enough to control its conduct. I am in no sense hostile to corporations. This is an age of combination, and any effort to prevent all combination will be not only useless, but in the end vicious, because of the contempt for law which the failure to enforce law inevitably produces. We should, moreover, recognize in cordial and ample fashion the immense good effected by corporate agencies in a country such as ours, and the wealth of intellect, energy, and fidelity devoted to their service, and therefore normally to the service of the public, by their officers and directors. The corporation has come to stay, just as the trade-union has come to stay. Each can do and has done great good. Each should be favored so long as it does good. But each should be sharply checked where it acts against law and justice.

So long as the finances of the nation are kept upon an honest basis no other question of internal economy with which the Congress has the power to deal begins to approach in importance the matter of endeavoring to secure proper industrial conditions under which the individuals—and especially the great corporations—doing an interstate business are to act. The makers of our National Constitution provided especially that the regulation of interstate commerce should come within the sphere of the general government. The arguments in favor of their taking this stand were even then overwhelming. But they are far stronger to-day, in view of the enormous development of great business agencies, usually corporate in form. Experience has shown conclusively that it is useless to try to get any adequate regulation and supervision of these great corporations by State action. Such regulation and supervision can only be effectively exercised by a sovereign whose jurisdiction is coextensive with the field of work of the corporations —that is, by the National Government. I believe that this regulation and supervision can be obtained by the enactment of law by the Congress. If this proves impossible, it will certainly be necessary ultimately to confer in fullest form such power upon the National Government by a proper amendment of the Constitution. It would obviously be unwise to endeavor to secure such an amendment until it is certain that the result cannot be obtained under the Constitution as it now is. The laws of the Congress and of the several States hitherto, as passed upon by the courts, have resulted more often in showing that the States have no power in the matter than that the National Government has power; so that there at present exists a very unfortunate condition of things, under which these great corporations doing an interstate business occupy the position of subjects without a sovereign, neither any State government nor the National Government having effective control over them. Our steady aim should be by legislation, cautiously and carefully undertaken, but resolutely persevered in, to assert the sovereignty of the National Government by affirmative action.

This is only in form an innovation. In substance it is merely a restoration; for from the earliest time such regulation of industrial activities has been recognized in the action of the law-making bodies; and all that I propose is to meet the changed conditions in such a manner as will prevent the commonwealth abdicating the power it has always possessed not only in this country, but also in England before and since this country became a separate nation.

It has been a misfortune that the national laws on this subject have hitherto been of a negative or prohibitive rather than an affirmative kind, and still more that they have in part sought to prohibit what could not be effectively prohibited, and have in part in their prohibitions confounded what should be allowed and what should not be allowed. It is generally useless to try to prohibit all restraint on competition, whether this restraint be reasonable or unreasonable; and where it is not useless it is generally hurtful. Events have shown that it is not possible adequately to secure the enforcement of any law of this kind by incessant appeal to the courts. The Department of Justice has for the last four years devoted more attention to the enforcement of the antitrust legislation than to anything else.

Much has been accomplished, particularly marked has been the moral effect of the prosecutions; but it is increasingly evident that there will be a very insufficient beneficial result in the way of economic change. The successful prosecution of one device to evade the law immediately develops another device to accomplish the same purpose. What is needed is not sweeping prohibition of every arrangement, good or bad, which may tend to restrict competition, but such adequate supervision and regulation as will prevent any restriction of competition from being to the detriment of the public—as well as such supervision and regulation as will prevent other abuses in no way connected with restriction of competition. Of these abuses, perhaps the chief, although by no means the only one, is overcapitalization—generally itself the result of dishonest promotion—because of the myriad evils it brings in its train; for such overcapitalization often means an inflation that invites business panic; it always conceals the true relation of the profit earned to the capital actually invested, and it creates a burden of interest payments which is a fertile cause of improper reduction in or limitation of wages; it damages the small investor, discourages thrift, and encourages gambling and speculation; while perhaps worst of all is the trickiness and dishonesty which it implies—for harm to morals is worse than any possible harm to material interests, and the debauchery of politics and business by great dishonest corporations is far worse than any actual material evil they do the public. Until the National Government obtains, in some manner which the wisdom of the Congress may suggest, proper control over the big corporations engaged in interstate commerce—that is, over the great majority of the big corporations—it will be impossible to deal adequately with these evils.

RAILROAD LEGISLATION

I am well aware of the difficulties of the legislation that I am suggesting, and of the need of temperate and cautious action in securing it. I should emphatically protest against improperly radical or hasty action. The first thing to do is to deal with the great corporations engaged in the business of interstate transportation. As I said in my message of December 6 last, the immediate and most pressing need, so far as legislation is concerned, is the enactment into law of some scheme to secure to the agents of the government such supervision and regulation of the rates charged by the railroads of the country engaged in interstate traffic as shall summarily and effectively prevent the imposition of unjust or unreasonable rates. It must include putting a complete stop to rebates in every shape and form. This power to regulate rates, like all similar powers over the business world, should be exercised with moderation, caution, and self-restraint; but it should exist, so that it can be effectively exercised when the need arises.

The first consideration to be kept in mind is that the power should be affirmative and should be given to some administrative body created by the Congress. If given to the present Interstate Commerce Commission, or to a reorganized Interstate Commerce Commission, such commission should be made unequivocally administrative. I do not believe in the government interfering with private business more than is necessary. I do not believe in the government undertaking any work which can with propriety be left in private hands. But neither do I believe in the government flinching from overseeing any work when it becomes evident that abuses are sure to obtain therein unless there is governmental supervision. It is not my province to indicate the exact terms of the law which should be enacted; but I call the attention of the Congress to certain existing conditions with which it is desirable to deal. In my judgment the most important provision which such law should contain is that conferring upon some competent administrative body the power to decide, upon the case being brought before it, whether a given rate prescribed by a railroad is reasonable and just, and if it is found to be unreasonable and unjust, then, after full investigation of the complaint, to prescribe the limit of rate beyond which it shall not be lawful to go—the maximum reasonable rate, as it is commonly called—this decision to go into effect within a reasonable time and to obtain from thence onward, subject to review by the courts. It sometimes happens at present not that a rate is too high but that a favored shipper is given too low a rate. In such cases the commission would have the right to fix this already established minimum rate as the maximum; and it would need only one or two such decisions by the commision to cure railroad companies of the practice of giving improper minimum rates. I call your attention to the fact that my proposal is not to give the commission power to initiate or originate rates generally, but to regulate a rate already fixed or originated by the roads, upon complaint and after investigation. A heavy penalty should be exacted from any corporation which fails to respect an order of the commission. I regard this power to establish a maximum rate as being essential to any scheme of real reform in the matter of railway regulation. The first necessity is to secure it; and unless it is granted to the commission there is little use in touching the subject at all.

Illegal transactions often occur under the forms of law. It has often occurred that a shipper has been told by a traffic officer to buy a large quantity of some commodity and then after it has been bought an open reduction is made in the rate to take effect immediately, the arrangement resulting to the profit of one shipper and the one railroad and to the damage of all their competitors; for it must not be forgotten that the big shippers are at least as much to blame as any railroad in the matter of rebates. The law should make it clear so that nobody can fail to understand that any kind of commission paid on freight shipments, whether in this form or in the form of fictitious damages, or of a concession, a free pass, reduced passenger-rate, or payment of brokerage, is illegal. It is worth while considering whether it would not be wise to confer on the government the right of civil action against the beneficiary of a rebate for at least twice the value of the rebate; this would help stop what is really blackmail. Elevator allowances should be stopped, for they have now grown to such an extent that they are demoralizing and are used as rebates.

The best possible regulation of rates would, of course, be that regulation secured by an honest agreement among the railroads themselves to carry out the law. Such a general agreement would, for instance, at once put a stop to the efforts of any one big shipper or big railroad to discriminate against or secure advantages over some rival; and such agreement would make the railroads themselves agents for enforcing the law. The power vested in the government to put a stop to agreements to the detriment of the public should, in my judgment, be accompanied by power to permit, under specified conditions and careful supervision, agreements clearly in the interest of the public. But, in my judgment, the necessity for giving this further power is by no means as great as the necessity for giving the commission or administrative body the other powers I have enumerated above; and it may well be inadvisable to attempt to vest this particular power in the commission or other administrative body until it already possesses and is exercising what I regard as by far the most important of all the powers I recommend—as indeed the vitally important power—that to fix a given maximum rate, which rate, after the lapse of a reasonable time, goes into full effect, subject to review by the courts.

All private-car lines, industrial roads, refrigerator charges, and the like should be expressly put under the supervision of the Interstate Commerce Commission or some similar body so far as rates, and agreements practically affecting rates, are concerned. The private-car owners and the owners of industrial railroads are entitled to a fair and reasonable compensation on their investment, but neither private cars nor industrial railroads nor spur-tracks should be utilized as devices for securing preferential rates. A rebate in icing charges, or in mileage, or in a division of the rate for refrigerating charges is just as pernicious as a rebate in any other way. No lower rate should apply on goods imported than actually obtains on domestic goods from the American seaboard to destination except in cases where water competition is the controlling influence. There should be publicity of the accounts of common carriers; no common carrier engaged in interstate business should keep any books or memoranda other than those reported pursuant to law or regulation, and these books or memoranda should be open to the inspection of the government. Only in this way can violations or evasions of the law be surely detected. A system of examination of railroad accounts should be provided similar to that now conducted into the national banks by the bank examiners; a few first-class railroad accountants, if they had proper direction and proper authority to inspect books and papers, could accomplish much in preventing wilful violations of the law. It would not be necessary for them to examine into the accounts of any railroad unless for good reasons they were directed to do so by the Interstate Commerce Commission. It is greatly to be desired that some way might be found by which an agreement as to transportation within a State intended to operate as a fraud upon the Federal interstate commerce laws could be brought under the jurisdiction of the Federal authorities. At present it occurs that large shipments of interstate traffic are controlled by concessions on purely State business, which of course amounts to an evasion of the law. The commission should have power to enforce fair treatment by the great trunk lines of lateral and branch lines.

I urge upon the Congress the need of providing for expeditious action by the Interstate Commerce Commission in all these matters, whether in regulating rates for transportation or for storing or for handling property or commodities in transit. The history of the cases litigated under the present commerce act shows that its efficacy has been to a great degree destroyed by the weapon of delay, almost the most formidable weapon in the hands of those whose purpose it is to violate the law.

Let me most earnestly say that these recommendations are

not made in any spirit of hostility to the railroads. On ethical grounds, on grounds of right, such hostility would be intolerable; and on grounds of mere national self-interest we must remember that such hostility would tell against the welfare not merely of some few rich men, but of a multitude of small investors, a multitude of railway employees, wage-workers, and most severely against the interest of the public as a whole. I believe that on the whole our railroads have done well and not ill; but the railroad men who wish to do well should not be exposed to competition with those who have no such desire, and the only way to secure this end is to give to some government tribunal the power to see that justice is done by the unwilling exactly as it is gladly done by the willing. Moreover, if some government body is given increased power the effect will be to furnish authoritative answer on behalf of the railroad whenever irrational clamor against it is raised, or whenever charges made against it are disproved. I ask this legislation not only in the interest of the public but in the interest of the honest railroad man and the honest shipper alike, for it is they who are chiefly jeoparded by the practices of their dishonest competitors. This legislation should be enacted in a spirit as remote as possible from hysteria and rancor. If we of the American body politic are true to the traditions we have inherited we shall always scorn any effort to make us hate any man because he is rich, just as much as we should scorn any effort to make us look down upon or treat contemptuously any man because he is poor. We judge a man by his conduct— that is, by his character—and not by his wealth or intellect. If he makes his fortune honestly, there is no just cause of quarrel with him. Indeed, we have nothing but the kindliest feelings of admiration for the successful business man who behaves decently, whether he has made his success by building or managing a railroad or by shipping goods over that railroad. The big railroad men and big shippers are simply Americans of the ordinary type who have developed to an extraordinary degree certain great business qualities. They are neither better nor worse than their fellow citizens of smaller means. They are merely more able in certain lines and therefore exposed to certain peculiarly strong temptations. These temptations have not sprung newly into being; the exceptionally successful among mankind have always been exposed to them; but they have grown amazingly in power as a result of the extraordinary development of industrialism along new lines, and under these new conditions, which the lawmakers of old could not foresee and therefore could not provide against, they have become so serious and menacing as to demand entirely new remedies. It is in the interest of the best type of railroad man and the best type of shipper no less than of the public that there should be governmental supervision and regulation of these great business operations, for the same reason that it is in the interest of the corporation which wishes to treat its employees aright that there should be an effective employers' liability act, or an effective system of factory laws to prevent the abuse of women and children. All such legislation frees the corporation that wishes to do well from being driven into doing ill, in order to compete with its rival, which prefers to do ill. We desire to set up a moral standard. There can be no delusion more fatal to the nation, than the delusion that the standard of profits, of business prosperity, is sufficient in judging any business or political question—from rate legislation to municipal government. Business success, whether for the individual or for the nation, is a good thing only so far as it is accompanied by and develops a high standard of conduct—honor, integrity, civic courage. The kind of business prosperity that blunts the standard of honor, that puts an inordinate value on mere wealth, that makes a man ruthless and conscienceless in trade, and weak and cowardly in citizenship, is not a good thing at all, but a very bad thing for the nation. This government stands for manhood first and for business only as an adjunct of manhood.

The question of transportation lies at the root of all industrial success, and the revolution in transportation which has taken place during the last half-century has been the most important factor in the growth of the new industrial conditions. Most emphatically we do not wish to see the man of great talents refused the reward for his talents. Still less do we wish to see him penalized; but we do desire to see the system of railroad transportation so handled that the strong man shall be given no advantage over the weak man. We wish to insure as fair treatment for the small town as for the big city; for the small shipper as for the big shipper. In the old days the highway of commerce, whether by water or by a road on land, was open to all; it belonged to the public and the traffic along it was free. At present the railway is this highway, and we must do our best to see that it is kept open to all on equal terms. Unlike the old highway it is a very difficult and complex thing to manage, and it is far better that it should be managed by private individuals than by the government. But it can only be so managed on condition that justice is done the public. It is because, in my judgment, public ownership of railroads is highly undesirable and would probably in this country entail far-reaching disaster, that I wish to see such supervision and regulation of them in the interest of the public as will make it evident that there is no need for public ownership. The opponents of government regulation dwell upon the difficulties to be encountered and the intricate and involved nature of the problem. Their contention is true. It is a complicated and delicate problem, and all kinds of difficulties are sure to arise in connection with any plan of solution, while no plan will bring all the benefits hoped for by its more optimistic adherents. Moreover, under any healthy plan the benefits will develop gradually and not rapidly. Finally, we must clearly understand that the public servants who are to do this peculiarly responsible and delicate work must themselves be of the highest type both as regards integrity and efficiency. They must be well paid, for otherwise able men cannot in the long run be secured; and they must possess a lofty probity which will revolt as quickly at the thought of pandering to any gust of popular prejudice against rich men as at the thought of anything even remotely resembling subserviency to rich men. But while I fully admit the difficulties in the way, I do not for a moment admit that these difficulties warrant us in stopping in our effort to secure a wise and just system. They should have no other effect than to spur us on to the exercise of the resolution, the even-handed justice, and the fertility of resource, which we like to think of as typically American, and which will in the end achieve good results in this as in other fields of activity. The task is a great one and underlies the task of dealing with the whole industrial problem. But the fact that it is a great problem does not warrant us in shrinking from the attempt to solve it. At present we face such utter lack of supervision, such freedom from the restraints of law, that excellent men have often been literally forced into doing what they deplored because otherwise they were left at the mercy of unscrupulous competitors. To rail at and assail the men who have done as they best could under such conditions accomplishes little. What we need to do is to develop an orderly system, and such a system can only come through the gradually increased exercise of the right of efficient government control.

SAFETY-APPLIANCE LAWS

In my annual message to the Fifty-eighth Congress, at its third session, I called attention to the necessity for legislation requiring the use of block-signals upon railroads engaged in interstate commerce. The number of serious collisions upon unblocked roads that have occurred within the past year adds force to the recommendation then made. The Congress should provide, by appropriate legislation, for the introduction of block-signals upon all railroads engaged in interstate commerce at the earliest practicable date, as a measure of increased safety to the travelling public.

Through decisions of the Supreme Court of the United States and the lower Federal courts in cases brought before them for adjudication the safety-appliance law has been materially strengthened, and the government has been enabled to secure its effective enforcement in almost all cases, with the result that the condition of railroad equipment throughout the country is much improved and railroad employees perform their duties under safer conditions than heretofore. The government's most effective aid in arriving at this result has been its inspection service, and that these improved conditions are not more general is due to the insufficient number of inspectors employed. The inspection service has fully demonstrated its usefulness, and in appropriating for its maintenance the Congress should make provision for an increase in the number of inspectors.

The excessive hours of labor to which railroad employees in train service are in many cases subjected is also a matter which may well engage the serious attention of the Congress. The strain, both mental and physical, upon those who are engaged in the movement and operation of railroad trains under modern conditions is perhaps greater than that which exists in any other industry, and if there are any reasons for limiting by law the hours of labor in any employment, they certainly apply with peculiar force to the employment of those upon whose vigilance and alertness in the performance of their duties the safety of all who travel by rail depends.

EMPLOYERS' LIABILITY LAW

In my annual message to the Fifty-seventh Congress, at its second session, I recommended the passage of an employers' liability law for the District of Columbia and in our navy-yards. I renewed that recommendation in my message to the Fifty-eighth Congress, at its second session, and further suggested the appointment of a commission to make a comprehensive study of employers' liability, with a view to the enactment of a wise and constitutional law covering the subject, applicable to all industries within the scope of the Federal power. I hope that such a law will be prepared and enacted as speedily as possible.

LABOR

The National Government has, as a rule, but little occasion to deal with the formidable group of problems connected more or less directly with what is known as the labor question, for in the great majority of cases these problems must be dealt with by the State and municipal authorities, and not by the National Government. The National Government has control of the District of Columbia, however, and it should see to it that the city of Washington is made a model city in all respects, both as regards parks, public playgrounds, proper regulation of the system of housing, so as to do away with the evils of alley tenements, a proper system of education, a proper system of dealing with truancy and juvenile offenders, a proper handling of the charitable work of the district. Moreover, there should be proper factory laws to prevent all abuses in the employment of women and children in the district. These will be useful chiefly as object-lessons, but even this limited amount of usefulness would be of real national value.

There has been demand for depriving courts of the power to issue injunctions in labor disputes. Such special limitation of the equity powers of our courts would be most unwise. It is true that some judges have misused this power; but this does not justify a denial of the power any more than an improper exercise of the power to call a strike by a labor leader would justify the denial of the right to strike. The remedy is to regulate the procedure by requiring the judge to give due notice to the adverse parties before granting the writ, the hearing to be ex parte if the adverse party does not appear at the time and place ordered. What is due notice must depend upon the facts of the case; it should not be used as a pretext to permit violation of law or the jeopardizing of life or property. Of course, this would not authorize the issuing of a restraining order or injunction in any case in which it is not already authorized by existing law.

I renew the recommendation I made in my last annual message for an investigation by the Department of Commerce and Labor of general labor conditions, especial attention to be paid to the conditions of child labor and child-labor legislation in the several States. Such an investigation should take into account the various problems with which the question of child labor is connected. It is true that these problems can be actually met in most cases only by the States themselves, but it would be well for the nation to endeavor to secure and publish comprehensive information as to the conditions of the labor of children in the different States, so as to spur up those that are behindhand and to secure approximately uniform legislation of a high character among the several States. In such a Republic as ours the one thing that we cannot afford to neglect is the problem of turning out decent citizens. The future of the nation depends upon the citizenship of the generations to come; the children of to-day are those who to-morrow will shape the destiny of our land, and we cannot afford to neglect them. The legislature of Colorado has recommended that the National Government provide some general measure for the protection from abuse of children and dumb animals throughout the United States. I lay the matter before you for what I trust will be your favorable consideration.

The Department of Commerce and Labor should also make a thorough investigation of the conditions of women in industry. Over 5,000,000 American women are now engaged in gainful occupations; yet there is an almost complete dearth of data upon which to base any trustworthy conclusions as regards a subject as important as it is vast and complicated. There is need of full knowledge on which to base action looking toward State and municipal legislation for the protection of working women. The introduction of women into industry is working change and disturbance in the domestic and social life of the nation. The decrease in marriage, and especially in the birth-rate, has been coincident with it. We must face accomplished facts, and the adjustment of factory conditions must be made, but surely it can be made with less friction and less harmful effects on family life than is now the case. This whole matter in reality forms one of the greatest sociological phenomena of our time; it is a social question of the first importance, of far greater importance than any merely political or economic question can be, and to solve it we need ample data, gathered in a sane and scientific spirit in the course of an exhaustive investigation.

In any great labor disturbance not only are employer and employee interested, but a third party—the general public. Every considerable labor difficulty in which interstate commerce is involved should be investigated by the government and the facts officially reported to the public.

RELATIONS OF CAPITAL AND LABOR

The question of securing a healthy, self-respecting, and mutually sympathetic attitude as between employer and employee, capitalist and wage-worker, is a difficult one. All phases of the labor problem prove difficult when approached. But the underlying principles, the root principles, in accordance with which the problem must be solved are entirely simple. We can get justice and right dealing only if we put as of paramount importance the principle of treating a man on his worth as a man rather than with reference to his social position, his occupation, or the class to which he belongs. There are selfish and brutal men in all ranks of life. If they are capitalists their selfishness and brutality may take the form of hard indifference to suffering, greedy disregard of every moral restraint which interferes with the accumulation of wealth, and cold-blooded exploitation of the weak; or, if they are laborers, the form of laziness, of sullen envy of the more fortunate, and of willingness to perform deeds of murderous violence. Such conduct is just as reprehensible in one case as in the other, and all honest and far-seeing men should join in warring against it wherever it becomes manifest. Individual capitalist and individual wage-worker, corporation and union, are alike entitled to the protection of the law, and must alike obey the law. Moreover, in addition to mere obedience to the law, each man, if he be really a good citizen, must show broad sympathy for his neighbor and genuine desire to look at any question arising between them from the standpoint of that neighbor no less than from his own, and to this end it is essential that capitalist and wage-worker should consult freely one with the other, should each strive to bring closer the day when both shall realize that they are properly partners and not enemies. To approach the questions which inevitably arise between them solely from the standpoint which treats each side in the mass as the enemy of the other side in the mass is both wicked and foolish. In the past the most direful among the influences which have brought about the downfall of republics has ever been the growth of the class spirit, the growth of the spirit which tends to make a man subordinate the welfare of the public as a whole to the welfare of the particular class to which he belongs, the substitution of loyalty to a class for loyalty to the nation. This inevitably brings about a tendency to treat each man not on his merits as an individual, but on his position as belonging to a certain class in the community. If such a spirit grows up in this Republic it will ultimately prove fatal to us, as in the past it has proved fatal to every community in which it has become dominant. Unless we continue to keep a quick and lively sense of the great fundamental truth that our concern is with the individual worth of the individual man, this government cannot permanently hold the place which it has achieved among the nations. The vital lines of cleavage among our people do not correspond, and indeed run at right angles to, the lines of cleavage which divide occupation from occupation, which divide wage-workers from capitalists, farmers from bankers, men of small means from men of large means, men who live in the towns from men who live in the country; for the vital line of cleavage is the line which divides the honest man who tries to do well by his neighbor from the dishonest man who does ill by his neighbor. In other words, the standard we should establish is the standard of conduct, not the standard of occupation, of means, or of social position. It is the man's moral quality, his attitude toward the great questions which concern all humanity, his cleanliness of life, his power to do his duty toward himself and toward others, which really count; and if we substitute for the standard of personal judgment which treats each man according to his merits, another standard in accordance with which all men of one class are favored and all men of another class discriminated against, we shall do irreparable damage to the body politic. I believe that our people are too sane, too self-respecting, too fit for self-government, ever to adopt such an attitude. This government is not and never shall be government by a plutocracy. This government is not and never shall be government by a mob. It shall continue to be in the future what it has been in the past, a government based on the theory that each man, rich or poor, is to be treated simply and solely on his worth as a man, that all his personal and property rights are to be safeguarded, and that he is neither to wrong others nor to suffer wrong from others.

The noblest of all forms of government is self-government; but it is also the most difficult. We who possess this priceless boon, and who desire to hand it on to our children and our children's children, should ever bear in mind the thought so finely expressed by Burke: "Men are qualified for civil liberty in exact proportion to their disposition to put moral chains upon their own appetites; in proportion as they are disposed to listen to the counsels of the wise and good in preference to the flattery of knaves. Society cannot exist unless a controlling power upon will and appetite be placed somewhere, and the less of it there be within the more there must be without. It is ordained in the eternal constitution of things that men of intemperate minds cannot be free. Their passions forge their fetters."

INSURANCE COMPANIES

The great insurance companies afford striking examples of corporations whose business has extended so far beyond the jurisdiction of the States which created them as to preclude strict enforcement of supervision and regulation by the parent States. In my last annual message I recommended "that the Congress carefully consider whether the power of the Bureau of Corporations cannot constitutionally be extended to cover interstate transactions in insurance."

Recent events have emphasized the importance of an early and exhaustive consideration of this question, to see whether it is not possible to furnish better safeguards than the several States have been able to furnish against corruption of the flagrant kind which has been exposed. It has been only too clearly shown that certain of the men at the head of these large corporations take but small note of the ethical distinction between honesty and dishonesty; they draw the line only this side of what may be called law-honesty, the kind of honesty necessary in order to avoid falling into the clutches of the law. Of course the only complete remedy for this condition must be found in an aroused public conscience, a higher sense of ethical conduct in the community at large, and especially among business men and in the great profession of the law, and in the growth of a spirit which condemns all dishonesty, whether in rich man or in poor man, whether it takes the shape of bribery or of blackmail. But much can be done by legislation which is not only drastic but practical. There is need of a far stricter and more uniform regulation of the vast insurance interests of this country. The United States should in this respect follow the policy of other nations by providing adequate national supervision of commercial interests which are clearly national in character. My predecessors have repeatedly recognized that the foreign business of these companies is an important part of our foreign commercial relations. During the administrations of Presidents Cleveland, Harrison, and McKinley the

State Department exercised its influence, through diplomatic channels, to prevent unjust discrimination by foreign countries against American insurance companies. These negotiations illustrated the propriety of the Congress recognizing the national character of insurance, for in the absence of Federal legislation the State Department could only give expression to the wishes of the authorities of the several States, whose policy was ineffective through want of uniformity.

I repeat my previous recommendation that the Congress should also consider whether the Federal Government has any power or owes any duty with respect to domestic transactions in insurance of an interstate character. That State supervision has proved inadequate is generally conceded. The burden upon insurance companies, and therefore their policyholders, of conflicting regulations of many States, is unquestioned, while but little effective check is imposed upon any able and unscrupulous man who desires to exploit the company in his own interest at the expense of the policy-holders and of the public. The inability of a State to regulate effectively insurance corporations created under the laws of other States and transacting the larger part of their business elsewhere is also clear. As a remedy for this evil of conflicting, ineffective, and yet burdensome regulations there has been for many years a wide-spread demand for Federal supervision. The Congress has already recognized that interstate insurance may be a proper subject for Federal legislation, for in creating the Bureau of Corporations it authorized it to publish and supply useful information concerning interstate corporations, "including corporations engaged in insurance." It is obvious that if the compilation of statistics be the limit of the Federal power it is wholly ineffective to regulate this form of commercial intercourse between the States, and as the insurance business has outgrown in magnitude the possibility of adequate State supervision, the Congress should carefully consider whether further legislation can be had. What is said above applies with equal force to fraternal and benevolent organizations which contract for life insurance.

REVENUE AND TARIFF

There is more need of stability than of the attempt to attain an ideal perfection in the methods of raising revenue; and the shock and strain to the business world certain to attend any serious change in these methods render such change inadvisable unless for grave reason. It is not possible to lay down any general rule by which to determine the moment when the reasons for will outweigh the reasons against such a change. Much must depend, not merely on the needs, but on the desires, of the people as a whole; for needs and desires are not necessarily identical. Of course, no change can be made on lines beneficial to, or desired by, one section or one State only. There must be something like a general agreement among the citizens of the several States, as represented in the Congress, that the change is needed and desired in the interest of the people, as a whole; and there should then be a sincere, intelligent, and disinterested effort to make it in such shape as will combine, so far as possible, the maximum of good to the people at large with the minimum of necessary disregard for the special interests of localities or classes. But in time of peace the revenue must on the average, taking a series of years together, equal the expenditures or else the revenues must be increased. Last year there was a deficit. Unless our expenditures can be kept within the revenues then our revenue laws must be readjusted. It is as yet too early to attempt to outline what shape such a readjustment should take, for it is as yet too early to say whether there will be need for it. It should be considered whether it is not desirable that the tariff laws should provide for applying as against or in favor of any other nation maximum and minimum tariff rates established by the Congress, so as to secure a certain reciprocity of treatment between other nations and ourselves. Having in view even larger considerations of policy than those of a purely economic nature, it would, in my judgment, be well to endeavor to bring about closer commercial connections with the other peoples of this continent. I am happy to be able to announce to you that Russia now treats us on the most-favored-nation basis.

ECONOMY

I earnestly recommend to Congress the need of economy and to this end of a rigid scrutiny of appropriations. As examples merely, I call your attention to one or two specific matters. All unnecessary offices should be abolished. The commissioner of the General Land Office recommends the abolishment of the office of Receiver of Public Moneys for the United States Land Office. This will effect a saving of about a quarter of a million dollars a year. As the business of the nation grows, it is inevitable that there should be from time to time a legitimate increase in the number of officials, and this fact renders it all the more important that when offices become unnecessary they should be abolished. In the public printing also a large saving of public money can be made. There is a constantly growing tendency to publish masses of unimportant information. It is probably not unfair to say that many tens of thousands of volumes are published at which no human being ever looks and for which there is no real demand whatever.

Yet, in speaking of economy, I must in nowise be understood as advocating the false economy which is in the end the worst extravagance. To cut down on the navy, for instance, would be a crime against the nation. To fail to push forward all work on the Panama Canal would be as great a folly.

THE CURRENCY

In my message of December 2, 1902, to the Congress I said:

"Interest rates are a potent factor in business activity, and in order that these rates may be equalized to meet the varying needs of the seasons and of widely separated communities, and to prevent the recurrence of financial stringencies, which injuriously affect legitimate business, it is necessary that there should be an element of elasticity in our monetary system. Banks are the natural servants of commerce, and, upon them should be placed, as far as practicable, the burden of furnishing and maintaining a circulation adequate to supply the needs of our diversified industries and of our domestic and foreign commerce; and the issue of this should be so regulated that a sufficient supply should be always available for the business interests of the country."

Every consideration of prudence demands the addition of the element of elasticity to our currency system. The evil does not consist in an inadequate volume of money, but in the rigidity of this volume, which does not respond as it should to the varying needs of communities and of seasons. Inflation must be avoided; but some provision should be made that will insure a larger volume of money during the fall and winter months than in the less active seasons of the year; so that the currency will contract against speculation, and will expand for the needs of legitimate business. At present the Treasury Department is at irregularly recurring intervals obliged, in the interest of the business world—that is, in the interests of the American public—to try to avert financial crisis by providing a remedy which should be provided by congressional action.

REORGANIZATION OF GOVERNMENT DEPARTMENTS

At various times I have instituted investigations into the organization and conduct of the business of the executive departments. While none of these inquiries have yet progressed far enough to warrant final conclusions, they have already confirmed and emphasized the general impression that the organization of the departments is often faulty in principle and wasteful in results, while many of their business methods are antiquated and inefficient. There is every reason why our executive governmental machinery should be at least as well planned, economical, and efficient as the best machinery of the great business organizations, which at present is not the case. To make it so is a task of complex detail and essentially executive in its nature; probably no legislative body, no matter how wise and able, could undertake it with reasonable prospect of success. I recommend that the Congress consider this subject with a view to provide by legislation for the transfer, distribution, consolidation, and assignment of duties and executive organizations or part of organizations, and for the changes in business methods, within or between the several departments, that will best promote the economy, efficiency, and high character of the government work.

FEDERAL ELECTIONS

In my last annual message I said:

"The power of the government to protect the integrity of the elections of its own officials is inherent and has been recognized and affirmed by repeated declarations of the Supreme Court. There is no enemy of free government more dangerous and none so insidious as the corruption of the electorate. No one defends or excuses corruption, and it would seem to follow that none would oppose vigorous measures to eradicate it. I recommend the enactment of a law directed against bribery and corruption in Federal elections. The details of such a law may be safely left to the wise discretion of the Congress, but it should go as far as under the Constitution it is possible to go, and should include severe penalties against him who gives or receives a bribe intended to influence his act or opinion as an elector; and provisions for the publication not only of the expenditures for nominations and elections of all candidates, but also of all contributions received and expenditures made by political committees."

I desire to repeat this recommendation. In political campaigns in a country as large and populous as ours it is inevitable that there should be much expense of an entirely legitimate kind. This, of course, means that many contributions, and some of them of large size, must be made, and, as a matter of fact, in any big political contest such contributions are always made to both sides. It is entirely proper both to give and receive them, unless there is an improper motive connected with either gift or reception. If they are extorted by any kind of pressure or promise, express or implied, direct or indirect, in the way of favor or immunity, then the giving or receiving becomes not only improper but criminal. It will undoubtedly be difficult, as a matter of practical detail, to shape an act which shall guard with reasonable certainty against such misconduct; but if it is possible to secure by law the full and verified publication in detail of all the sums contributed to and expended by the candidates or committees of any political parties, the result cannot but be wholesome. All contributions by corporations to any political committee or for any political purpose should be forbidden by law; directors should not be permitted to use stockholders' money for such purposes; and, moreover, a prohibition of this kind would be, as far as it went, an effective method of stopping the evils aimed at in corrupt practices acts. Not only should both the national and the several State legislatures forbid any officer of a corporation from using the money of the corporation in or about any election, but they should also forbid such use of money in connection with any legislation save by the employment of counsel in public manner for distinctly legal services.

INTERNATIONAL PEACE

The first conference of nations held at The Hague in 1899, being unable to dispose of all the business before it, recommended the consideration and settlement of a number of important questions by another conference to be called subsequently and at an early date. These questions were the following: (1) The rights and duties of neutrals; (2) the limitation of the armed forces on land and sea, and of military budgets; (3) the use of new types and calibers of military and naval guns; (4) the inviolability of private property at sea in times of war; (5) the bombardment of ports, cities, and villages by naval forces. In October, 1904, at the instance of the Interparliamentary Union, which, at a conference held in the United States, and attended by the lawmakers of fifteen different nations, had reiterated the demand for a second conference of nations, I issued invitations to all the powers signatory to the Hague Convention to send delegates to such a conference, and suggested that it be again held at The Hague. In its note of December 16, 1904, the United States Government communicated to the representatives of foreign governments its belief that the conference could be best arranged under the provisions of the present Hague treaty.

From all the powers acceptance was received, coupled in some cases with the condition that we should wait until the end of the war then waging between Russia and Japan. The Emperor of Russia, immediately after the treaty of peace which so happily terminated this war, in a note presented to the President on September 13, through Ambassador Rosen, took the initiative in recommending that the conference be now called. The United States Government in response expressed its cordial acquiescence, and stated that it would, as a matter of course, take part in the new conference and endeavor to further its aims. We assume that all civilized governments will support the movement, and that the conference is now an assured fact. This government will do everything in its power to secure the success of the conference, to the end that substantial progress may be made in the cause of international peace, justice, and good-will.

This renders it proper at this time to say something as to the general attitude of this government toward peace. More and more war is coming to be looked upon as in itself a lamentable and evil thing. A wanton or useless war, or a war of mere aggression—in short, any war begun or carried on in a conscienceless spirit, is to be condemned as a peculiarly atrocious crime against all humanity. We can, however, do nothing of permanent value for peace unless we keep ever clearly in mind the ethical element which lies at the root of the problem. Our aim is righteousness. Peace is normally the handmaiden of righteousness; but when peace and righteousness conflict then a great and upright people can never for a moment hesitate to follow the path which leads toward righteousness, even though that path also leads to war. There are persons who advocate peace at any price; there are others who, following a false analogy, think that because it is no longer necessary in civilized countries for individuals to protect their rights with a strong hand, it is therefore unnecessary for nations to be ready to defend their rights. These persons would do irreparable harm to any nation that adopted their principles, and even as it is they seriously hamper the cause which they advocate by tending to render it absurd in the eyes of sensible and patriotic men. There can be no worse foe of mankind in general, and of his own country in particular, than the demagogue of war, the man who in mere folly or to serve his own selfish ends continually rails at and abuses others nations, who seeks to excite his countrymen against foreigners on insufficient pretexts, who excites and inflames a perverse and aggressive national vanity, and who may on occasions wantonly bring on conflict between his nation and some other nation. But there are demagogues of peace just as there are demagogues of war, and in any such movement as this for the Hague Conference it is essential not to be misled by one set of extremists any more than by the other. Whenever it is possible for a nation or an individual to work for real peace, assuredly it is failure of duty not so to strive, but if war is necessary and righteous then either the man or the nation shrinking from it forfeits all title to self-respect. We have scant sympathy with the sentimentalist who dreads oppression less than physical suffering, who would prefer a shameful peace to the pain and toil sometimes lamentably necessary in order to secure a righteous peace. As yet there is only a partial and imperfect analogy between international law and internal or municipal law, because there is no sanction of force for executing the former, while there is in the case of the latter. The private citizen is protected in his rights by the law, because the law rests in the last resort upon force exercised through the forms of law. A man does not have to defend his rights with his own hand, because he can call upon the police, upon the sheriff's posse, upon the militia, or in certain extreme cases upon the army, to defend him. But there is no such sanction of force for international law. At present there could be no greater calamity than for the free peoples, the enlightened, independent, and peace-loving peoples, to disarm while yet leaving it open to any barbarism or despotism to remain armed. So long as the world is as unorganized as now the armies and navies of those peoples who on the whole stand for justice, offer not only the best, but the only possible, security for a just peace. For instance, if the United States alone, or in company only with the other nations that on the whole tend to act justly, disarmed, we might sometimes avoid bloodshed, but we would cease to be of weight in securing the peace of justice—the real peace for which the most law-abiding and high-minded men must at times be willing to fight. As the world is now, only that nation is equipped for peace that knows how to fight, and that will not shrink from fighting if ever the conditions become such that war is demanded in the name of the highest morality.

So much it is emphatically necessary to say in order both that the position of the United States may not be misunderstood, and that a genuine effort to bring nearer the day of the peace of justice among the nations may not be hampered by a folly which, in striving to achieve the impossible, would render it hopeless to attempt the achievement of the practical. But, while recognizing most clearly all above set forth, it remains our clear duty to strive in every practicable way to bring nearer the time when the sword shall not be the arbiter among nations. At present the practical thing to do is to try to minimize the number of cases in which it must be the arbiter, and to offer, at least to all civilized powers, some substitute for war which will be available in at least a considerable number of instances. Very much can be done through another Hague conference in this direction, and I most earnestly urge that this nation do all in its power to try to further the movement and to make the result of the decisions of the Hague Conference effective. I earnestly hope that the conference may be able to devise some way to make arbitration between nations the customary way of settling international disputes in all save a few classes of cases, which should themselves be as sharply defined and rigidly limited as the present governmental and social development of the world will permit. If possible, there should be a general arbitration treaty negotiated among all the nations represented at the conference. Neutral rights and property should be protected at sea as they are protected on land. There should be an international agreement to this purpose and a similar agreement defining contraband of war.

During the last century there has been a distinct diminution in the number of wars between the most civilized nations. International relations have become closer and the development of The Hague tribunal is not only a symptom of this growing closeness of relationship, but is a means by which the growth can be furthered. Our aim should be from time to time to take such steps as may be possible toward creating something like an organization of the civilized nations, because as the world becomes more highly organized the need for navies and armies will diminish. It is not possible to secure anything like an immediate disarmament, because it would first be necessary to settle what peoples are on the whole a menace to the rest of mankind, and to provide against the disarmament of the rest being turned into a movement which would really chiefly benefit these obnoxious peoples; but it may be possible to exercise some check upon the tendency to swell indefinitely the budgets for military expenditure. Of course such an effort could succeed only if it did not attempt to do too much; and if it were undertaken in a spirit of sanity as far removed as possible from a merely hysterical pseudo-philanthropy. It is worth while pointing out that since the end of the insurrection in the Philippines this nation has shown its practical faith in the policy of disarmament by reducing its little army one-third.

But disarmament can never be of prime importance; there is more need to get rid of the causes of war than of the implements of war.

I have dwelt much on the dangers to be avoided by steering clear of any mere foolish sentimentality because my wish for peace is so genuine and earnest; because I have a real and great desire that this second Hague conference may mark a long stride forward in the direction of securing the peace of justice throughout the world. No object is better worthy the attention of enlightened statesmanship than the establishment of a surer method than now exists of securing justice as between nations, both for the protection of the little nations and for the prevention of war between the big nations. To this aim we should endeavor not only to avert bloodshed, but, above all, effectively to strengthen the forces of right. The Golden Rule should be, and as the world grows in morality it will be, the guiding rule of conduct among nations as among individuals; though the Golden Rule must not be construed, in fantastic manner, as forbidding the exercise of the police power. This mighty and free Republic should ever deal with all other States, great or small, on a basis of high honor, respecting their rights as jealously as it safeguards its own.

THE MONROE DOCTRINE

One of the most effective instruments for peace is the Monroe Doctrine as it has been and is being gradually developed by this nation and accepted by other nations. No other policy could have been as efficient in promoting peace in the western hemisphere and in giving to each nation thereon the chance to develop along its own lines. If we had refused to apply the doctrine to changing conditions it would now be completely outworn, would not meet any of the needs of the present day, and, indeed, would probably by this time have sunk into complete oblivion. It is useful at home, and is meeting with recognition abroad because we have adapted our application of it to meet the growing and changing needs of the hemisphere.

When we announce a policy such as the Monroe Doctrine we thereby commit ourselves to the consequences of the policy, and those consequences from time to time alter. It is out of the question to claim a right and yet shirk the responsibility for its exercise. Not only we, but all American republics who are benefited by the existence of the doctrine, must recognize the obligations each nation is under as regards foreign peoples no less than its duty to insist upon its own rights.

That our rights and interests are deeply concerned in the maintenance of the doctrine is so clear as hardly to need argument. This is especially true in view of the construction of the Panama Canal. As a mere matter of self-defense we must exercise a close watch over the approaches to this canal; and this means that we must be thoroughly alive to our interests in the Caribbean Sea.

There are certain essential points which must never be forgotten as regards the Monroe Doctrine. In the first place we must as a nation make it evident that we do not intend to treat it in any shape or way as an excuse for aggrandizement on our part at the expense of the republics to the south. We must recognize the fact that in some South American countries there has been much suspicion lest we should interpret the Monroe Doctrine as in some way inimical to their interests, and we must try to convince all the other nations of this continent once and for all that no just and orderly government has anything to fear from us. There are certain republics to the south of us which have already reached such a point of stability, order, and prosperity that they themselves, though as yet hardly consciously, are among the guarantors of this doctrine. These republics we now meet not only on a basis of entire equality, but in a spirit of frank and respectful friendship, which we hope is mutual. If all of the republics to the south of us will only grow as those to which I allude have already grown, all need for us to be the especial champion of the doctrine will disappear, for no stable and growing American republic wishes to see some great non-American military power acquire territory in its neighborhood. All that this country desires is that the other republics on this continent shall be happy and prosperous; and they cannot be happy and prosperous unless they maintain order within their boundaries and behave with a just regard for their obligations toward outsiders. It must be understood that under no circumstances will the United States use the Monroe Doctrine as a cloak for territorial aggression. We desire peace with all the world, but perhaps most of all with the other peoples of the American continent. There are, of course, limits to the wrongs which any self-respecting nation can endure. It is always possible that wrong actions toward this nation, or toward citizens of this nation, in some state unable to keep order among its own people, unable to secure justice from outsiders, and unwilling to do justice to those outsiders who treat it well, may result in our having to take action to protect our rights; but such action will not be taken with a view to territorial aggression, and it will be taken at all only with extreme reluctance and when it has become evident that every other resource has been exhausted.

Moreover, we must make it evident that we do not intend to permit the Monroe Doctrine to be used by any nation on this continent as a shield to protect it from the consequences of its own misdeeds against foreign nations. If a republic to the south of us commits a tort against a foreign nation, such as an outrage against a citizen of that nation, then the Monroe Doctrine does not force us to interfere to prevent punishment of the tort, save to see that the punishment does not assume the form of territorial occupation in any shape. The case is more difficult when it refers to a contractual obligation. Our own government has always refused to enforce such contractual obligations on behalf of its citizens by an appeal to arms. It is much to be wished that all foreign governments would take the same view. But they do not; and in consequence we are liable at any time to be brought face to face with disagreeable alternatives. On the one hand, this country would certainly decline to go to war to prevent a foreign government from collecting a just debt; on the other hand, it is very inadvisable to permit any foreign power to take possession, even temporarily, of the custom-houses of an American republic in order to enforce the payment of its obligations; for such temporary occupation might turn into a permanent occupation. The only escape from these alternatives may at any time be that we must ourselves undertake to bring about some arrangement by which so much as possible of a just obligation shall be paid. It is far better that this country should put through such an arrangement, rather than allow any foreign country to undertake it. To do so insures the defaulting republic from having to pay debt of an improper character under duress, while it also insures honest creditors of the republic from being passed by in the interest of dishonest or grasping creditors. Moreover, for the United States to take such a position offers the only possible way of insuring us against a clash with some foreign power. The position is, therefore, in the interest of peace as well as in the interest of justice. It is of benefit to our people; it is of benefit to foreign peoples; and most of all it is really of benefit to the people of the country concerned.

This brings me to what should be one of the fundamental objects of the Monroe Doctrine. We must ourselves in good faith try to help upward toward peace and order those of our sister republics which need such help. Just as there has been a gradual growth of the ethical element in the relations of one individual to another, so we are, even though slowly, more and more coming to recognize the duty of bearing one another's burdens, not only as among individuals, but also as among nations.

SANTO DOMINGO

Santo Domingo, in her turn, has now made an appeal to us to help her, and not only every principle of wisdom but every generous instinct within us bids us respond to the appeal. It is not of the slightest consequence whether we grant the aid needed by Santo Domingo as an incident to the wise development of the Monroe Doctrine or because we regard the case of Santo Domingo as standing wholly by itself, and to be treated as such, and not on general principles or with any reference to the Monroe Doctrine. The important point is to give the needed aid, and the case is certainly sufficiently peculiar to deserve to be judged purely on its own merits. The conditions in Santo Domingo have for a number of years grown from bad to worse until a year ago all society was on the verge of dissolution. Fortunately, just at this time a ruler sprang up in Santo Domingo, who, with his colleagues, saw the dangers threatening their country and appealed to the friendship of the only great and powerful neighbor who possessed the power, and as they hoped also the will to help them. There was imminent danger of foreign intervention. The previous rulers of Santo Domingo had recklessly incurred debts, and owing to her internal disorders she had ceased to be able to provide means of paying the debts. The patience of her foreign creditors had become exhausted, and at least two foreign nations were on the point of intervention, and were only prevented from intervening by the unofficial assurance of this government that it would itself strive to help Santo Domingo in her hour of need. In the case of one of these nations, only the actual opening of negotiations to this end by our government prevented the seizure of territory in Santo Domingo by a European power. Of the debts incurred some were just, while some were not of a character which really renders it obligatory on or proper for Santo Domingo to pay them in full. But she could not pay any of them unless some stability was assured her government and people.

Accordingly, the Executive Department of our government negotiated a treaty under which we are to try to help the Dominican people to straighten out their finances. This treaty is pending before the Senate. In the meantime a temporary arrangement has been made which will last until the Senate has had time to take action upon the treaty. Under this arrangement the Dominican Government has appointed Americans to all the important positions in the customs service, and they are seeing to the honest collection of the revenues, turning over forty-five per cent to the government for running expenses and putting the other fifty-five per cent into a safe depository for equitable division in case the treaty shall be ratified, among the various creditors, whether European or American.

The custom-houses offer well-nigh the only sources of revenue in Santo Domingo, and the different revolutions usually have as their real aim the obtaining of these custom-houses. The mere fact that the collectors of customs are Americans, that they are performing their duties with efficiency and honesty, and that the treaty is pending in the Senate gives a certain moral power to the government of Santo Domingo which it has not had before. This has completely discouraged all revolutionary movement, while it has already produced such an increase in the revenues that the government is actually getting more from the forty-five per cent that the American collectors turn over to it than it got formerly when it took the entire revenue. It is enabling the poor, harassed people of Santo Domingo once more to turn their attention to industry and to be free from the cure of interminable revolutionary disturbance. It offers to all bona-fide creditors, American and European, the only really good chance to obtain that to which they are justly entitled, while it in return gives to Santo Domingo the only opportunity of defense against claims which it ought not to pay, for now if it meets the views of the Senate we shall ourselves thoroughly examine all these claims, whether American or foreign, and see that none that are improper are paid. There is, of course, opposition to the treaty from dishonest creditors, foreign and American, and from the professional revolutionists of the island itself. We have already reason to believe that some of the creditors who do not dare expose their claims to honest scrutiny are endeavoring to stir up sedition in the island and opposition to the treaty. In the meantime, I have exercised the authority vested in me by the joint resolution of the Congress to prevent the introduction of arms into the island for revolutionary purposes.

Under the course taken, stability and order and all the benefits of peace are at last coming to Santo Domingo, danger of foreign intervention has been suspended, and there is at last a prospect that all creditors will get justice, no more and no less. If the arrangement is terminated by the failure of the treaty chaos will follow; and if chaos follows, sooner or later this government may be involved in serious difficulties with foreign governments over the island, or else may be forced itself to intervene in the island in some unpleasant fashion. Under the proposed treaty the independence of the island is scrupulously respected, the danger of violation of the Monroe Doctrine by the intervention of foreign powers vanishes, and the interference of our government is minimized, so that we shall only act in conjunction with the Santo Domingo authorities to secure the proper administration of the customs, and therefore to secure the payment of just debts and to secure the Dominican Government against demands for unjust debts. The proposed method will give the people of Santo Domingo the same chance to move onward and upward which we have already given to the people of Cuba. It will be doubly to our discredit as a nation if we fail to take advantage of this chance; for it will be of damage to ourselves, and it will be of incalculable damage to Santo Domingo. Every consideration of wise policy, and, above all, every consideration of large generosity, bids us meet the request of Santo Domingo as we are now trying to meet it.

THE ARMY

We cannot consider the question of our foreign policy without at the same time treating of the army and the navy. We now have a very small army indeed, one well-nigh infinitesimal when compared with the army of any other large nation. Of course the army we do have should be as nearly perfect of its kind and for its size as is possible. I do not believe that any army in the world has a better average of enlisted men or a better type of junior officer; but the army should be trained to act effectively in a mass. Provision should be made by sufficient appropriations for manœuvres of a practical kind, so that the troops may learn how to take care of themselves under actual service conditions; every march, for instance, being made with the soldier loaded exactly as he would be in active campaign. The generals and colonels would thereby have opportunity of handling regiments, brigades, and divisions, and the commissary and medical departments would be tested in the field. Provision should be made for the exercise at least of a brigade and by preference of a division in marching and embarking at some point on our coast and disembarking at some other point and continuing its march. The number of posts in which the army is kept in time of peace should be materially diminished and the posts that are left made correspondingly larger. No local interests should be allowed to stand in the way of assembling the greater part of the troops which would at need form our field armies in stations of such size as will permit the best training to be given to the personnel of all grades, including the high officers and staff officers. To accomplish this end we must have not company or regimental garrisons, but brigade and division garrisons. Promotion by mere seniority can never result in a thoroughly efficient corps of officers in the higher ranks unless there accompanies it a vigorous weeding-out process. Such a weeding-out process —that is, such a process of selection—is a chief feature of the four years' course of the young officer at West Point. There is no good reason why it should stop immediately upon his graduation. While at West Point he is dropped unless he comes up to a certain standard of excellence, and when he graduates he takes rank in the army according to his rank of graduation. The results are good at West Point; and there should be in the army itself something that will achieve the same end. After a certain age has been reached the average officer is unfit to do good work below a certain grade. Provision should be made for the promotion of exceptionally meritorious men over the heads of their comrades and for the retirement of all men who have reached a given age without getting beyond a given rank; this age of retirement of course changing from rank to rank. In both the army and the navy there should be some principle of selection, that is, of promotion for merit, and there should be a resolute effort to eliminate the aged officers of reputable character who possess no special efficiency.

There should be an increase in the coast-artillery force, so that our coast fortifications can be in some degree adequately manned. There is special need for an increase and reorganization of the Medical Department of the army. In both the army and navy there must be the same thorough training for duty in the staff corps as in the fighting line. Only by such training in advance can we be sure that in actual war field operations and those at sea will be carried on successfully. The importance of this was shown conclusively in the Spanish-American and the Russo-Japanese wars. The work of the medical departments in the Japanese army and navy is especially worthy of study. I renew my recommendation of January 9, 1905, as to the Medical Department of the army and call attention to the equal importance of the needs of the staff corps of the navy. In the Medical Department of the navy the first in importance is the reorganization of the Hospital Corps, on the lines of the Gallinger bill (S. 3,984, February 1, 1904), and the reappointment of the different grades of the medical officers to meet service requirements. It seems advisable also that medical officers of the army and navy should have similar rank and pay in their respective grades, so that their duties can be carried on without friction when they are brought together. The base hospitals of the navy should be put in condition to meet modern requirements and hospital ships be provided. Unless we now provide with ample forethought for the medical needs of the army and navy appalling suffering of a preventable kind is sure to occur if ever the country goes to war. It is not reasonable to expect successful administration in time of war of a department which lacks a third of the number of officers necessary to perform the medical service in time of peace. We need men who are not merely doctors; they must be trained in the administration of military medical service.

THE NAVY

Our navy must, relatively to the navies of other nations, always be of greater size than our army. We have most wisely continued for a number of years to build up our navy, and it has now reached a fairly high standard of efficiency. This standard of efficiency must not only be maintained, but increased. It does not seem to be necessary, however, that the navy should—at least in the immediate future—be increased beyond the present number of units. What is now clearly necessary is to substitute efficient for inefficient units as the latter become worn out or as it becomes apparent that they are useless. Probably the result would be attained by adding a single battleship to our navy each year, the superseded or outworn vessels being laid up or broken up as they are thus replaced. The four single-turret monitors built immediately after the close of the Spanish War, for instance, are vessels which would be of but little use in the event of war. The money spent upon them could have been more usefully spent in other ways. Thus it would have been far better never to have built a single one of these monitors and to have put the money into an ample supply of reserve guns. Most of the smaller cruisers and gunboats, though they serve a useful purpose so far as they are needed for international police work, would not add to the strength of our navy in a conflict with a serious foe. There is urgent need of providing a large increase in the number of officers, and especially in the number of enlisted men.

Recent naval history has emphasized certain lessons which ought not to, but which do, need emphasis. Sea-going torpedo-boats or destroyers are indispensable, not only for making night attacks by surprise upon an enemy, but even in battle for finishing already crippled ships. Under exceptional circumstances submarine boats would doubtless be of use. Fast scouts are needed. The main strength of the navy, however, lies, and can only lie, in the great battleships, the heavily armored, heavily gunned vessels which decide the mastery of the seas. Heavy-armed cruisers also play a most useful part, and unarmed cruisers, if swift enough, are very useful as scouts. Between antagonists of approximately equal prowess the comparative perfection of the instruments of war will ordinarily determine the fight. But it is, of course, true that the man behind the gun, the man in the engine-room, and the man in the conning-tower, considered not only individually, but especially with regard to the way in which they work together, are even more important than the weapons with which they work. The most formidable battleship is, of course, helpless against even a light cruiser if the men aboard it are unable to hit anything with their guns, and thoroughly well-handled cruisers may count seriously in an engagement with much superior vessels, if the men aboard the latter are ineffective, whether from lack of training or from any other cause. Modern war-ships are most formidable mechanisms when well handled, but they are utterly useless when not well handled, and they cannot be handled at all without long and careful training. This training can under no circumstance be given when once war has broken out. No fighting ship of the first class should ever be laid up save for necessary repairs, and her crew should be kept constantly exercised on the high seas, so that she may stand at the highest point of perfection. To put a new and untrained crew upon the most powerful battleship and send it out to meet a formidable enemy is not only to invite, but to insure, disaster and disgrace. To improvise crews at the outbreak of a war, so far as the serious fighting craft are concerned, is absolutely hopeless. If the officers and men are not thoroughly skilled in, and have not been thoroughly trained to, their duties, it would be far better to keep the ships in port during hostilities than to send them against a formidable opponent, for the result could only be that they would be either sunk or captured. The marksmanship of our navy is now on the whole in a gratifying condition, and there has been a great improvement in fleet practice. We need additional seamen; we need a large store of reserve guns; we need sufficient money for ample target practice, ample practice of every kind at sea. We should substitute for comparatively inefficient types—the old third-class battleship *Texas*, the single turreted monitors above mentioned, and, indeed, all the monitors and some of the old cruisers—efficient, modern seagoing vessels. Seagoing torpedo-boat destroyers should be substituted for some of the smaller torpedo-boats. During the present Congress there need be no additions to the aggregate number of units of the navy. Our navy, though very small relatively to the navies of other nations, is for the present sufficient in point of numbers for our needs, and while we must constantly strive to make its efficiency higher, there need be no additions to the total of ships now built and building, save in the way of substitution as above outlined. I recommend the report of the secretary of the navy to the careful consideration of the Congress, especially with a view to the legislation therein advocated.

NATURALIZATION

During the past year evidence has accumulated to confirm the expressions contained in my last two annual messages as to the importance of revising by appropriate legislation our system of naturalizing aliens. I appointed last March a commission to make a careful examination of our naturalization laws, and to suggest appropriate measures to avoid the notorious abuses resulting from the improvident or unlawful granting of citizenship. This commission, composed of an officer of the Department of State, of the Department of Justice, and of the Department of Commerce and Labor, has discharged the duty imposed upon it, and has submitted a report, which will be transmitted to the Congress for its consideration, and, I hope, for its favorable action.

The distinguishing recommendations of the commission are:

First—A Federal Bureau of Naturalization, to be established in the Department of Commerce and Labor, to supervise the administration of the naturalization laws and to receive returns of naturalizations pending and accomplished.

Second—Uniformity of naturalization certificates, fees to be charged, and procedure.

Third—More exacting qualifications for citizenship.

Fourth—The preliminary declaration of intention to be abolished and no alien to be naturalized until at least ninety days after the filing of his petition.

Fifth—Jurisdiction to naturalize aliens to be confined to United States district courts and to such State courts as have jurisdiction in civil actions in which the amount in controversy is unlimited; in cities of over 100,000 inhabitants the United States district courts to have exclusive jurisdiction in the naturalization of the alien residents of such cities.

THE CRIMINAL LAW

In my last message I asked the attention of the Congress to the urgent need of action to make our criminal law more effective; and I most earnestly request that you pay heed to the report of the attorney-general on this subject. Centuries ago it was especially needful to throw every safeguard round the accused. The danger then was lest he should be wronged by the State. The danger is now exactly the reverse. Our laws and customs tell immensely in favor of the criminal and against the interests of the public he has wronged. Some antiquated and outworn rules which once safeguarded the threatened rights of private citizens, now merely work harm to the general body politic. The criminal law of the United States stands in urgent need of revision. The criminal process of any court of the United States should run throughout the entire territorial extent of our country. The delays of the criminal law, no less than of the civil, now amount to a very great evil.

There seems to be no statute of the United States which provides for the punishment of a United States attorney or other officer of the government who corruptly agrees to wrongfully do or wrongfully refrain from doing any act when the consideration for such corrupt agreement is other than one possessing money value. This ought to be remedied by appropriate legislation. Legislation should also be enacted to cover explicitly, unequivocally, and beyond question breach of trust in the shape of prematurely divulging official secrets by an officer or employee of the United States, and to provide a suitable penalty therefor. Such officer or employee owes the duty to the United States to guard carefully and not to divulge or in any manner use, prematurely, information which is accessible to the officer or employee by reason of his official position. Most breaches of public trust are already covered by the law, and this one should be. It is impossible, no matter how much care is used, to prevent the occasional appointment to the public service of a man who when tempted proves unfaithful; but every means should be provided to detect and every effort made to punish the wrongdoer. So far as in my power lies each and every such wrong-doer shall be relentlessly hunted down; in no instance in the past has he been spared; in no instance in the future shall he be spared. His crime is a crime against every honest man in the nation, for it is a crime against the whole body politic. Yet in dwelling on such misdeeds it is unjust not to add that they are altogether exceptional, and that on the whole the employees of the government render upright and faithful service to the people. There are exceptions, notably in one or two branches of the service, but at no time in the nation's history has the public service of the nation taken as a whole stood on a higher plane than now, alike as regards honesty and as regards efficiency.

PUBLIC LANDS

Once again I call your attention to the condition of the public-land laws. Recent developments have given new urgency to the need for such changes as will fit these laws to actual present conditions. The honest disposal and right use of the remaining public land is of fundamental importance. The iniquitous methods by which the monopolizing of the public lands is being brought about under the present laws are becoming more generally known, but the existing laws do not furnish effective remedies. The recommendations of the Public Lands Commission upon this subject are wise and should be given effect.

The creation of small irrigated farms under the Reclamation Act is a powerful offset to the tendency of certain other laws to foster or permit monopoly of the land. Under that act the construction of great irrigation works has been proceeding rapidly and successfully, the lands reclaimed are eagerly taken up, and the prospect that the policy of national irrigation will accomplish all that was expected of it is bright. The act should be extended to include the State of Texas.

The Reclamation Act derives much of its value from the fact that it tends to secure the greatest possible number of homes on the land, and to create communities of freeholders, in part by settlement on public lands, in part by forcing the subdivision of large private holdings before they can get water from government irrigation works. The law requires that no right to the use of water for land in private ownership shall be sold for a tract exceeding 160 acres to any one landowner. This provision has excited active and powerful hostility, but the success of the law itself depends on the wise and firm enforcement of it. We cannot afford to substitute tenants for freeholders on the public domain.

The greater part of the remaining public lands cannot be irrigated. They are at present and will probably always be of greater value for grazing than for any other purpose. This fact has led to the grazing homestead of 640 acres in Nebraska and to the proposed extension of it to other States. It is argued that a family cannot be supported on 160 acres of arid grazing-land. This is obviously true, but neither can a family be supported on 640 acres of much of the land to which it is proposed to apply the grazing homestead. To establish universally any such arbitrary limit would be unwise at the present time. It would probably result on the one hand in enlarging the holdings of some of the great landowners, and on the other in needless suffering and failure on the part of a very considerable proportion of the bona-fide settlers who give faith to the implied assurance of the government that such an area is sufficient. The best use of the public grazing-lands requires the careful examination and classification of these lands in order to give each settler land enough to support his family and no more. While this work is being done, and until the lands are settled, the government should take control of the open range, under reasonable regulations suited to local needs, following the general policy already in successful operation on the forest reserves. It is probable that the present grazing value of the open public range is scarcely more than half what it once was or what it might easily be again under careful regulation.

FOREST POLICY

The forest policy of the Administration appears to enjoy the unbroken support of the people. The great users of timber are themselves forwarding the movement for forest preservation. All organized opposition to the forest preserves in the West has disappeared. Since the consolidation of all government forest work in the National Forest Service there has been a rapid and notable gain in the usefulness of the forest reserves to the people and in public appreciation of their value. The national parks within or adjacent to forest reserves should be transferred to the charge of the Forest Service also.

CONTROL OF THE MISSISSIPPI

The National Government already does something in connection with the construction and maintenance of the great system of levees along the lower course of the Mississippi; in my judgment it should do much more.

MERCHANT MARINE

To the spread of our trade in peace and the defense of our flag in war a great and prosperous merchant marine is indispensable. We should have ships of our own and seamen of our own to convey our goods to neutral markets, and in case of need to reinforce our battle-line. It cannot but be a source of regret and uneasiness to us that the lines of communication with our sister republics of South America should be chiefly under foreign control. It is not a good thing that American merchants and manufacturers should have to send their goods and letters to South America via Europe if they wish security and despatch. Even on the Pacific, where our ships have held their own better than on the Atlantic, our merchant flag is now threatened through the liberal aid bestowed by other governments on their own steamlines. I ask your earnest consideration of the report with which the Merchant Marine Commission has followed its long and careful inquiry.

JAMESTOWN EXPOSITION

I again heartily commend to your favorable consideration the tercentennial celebration at Jamestown, Va. Appreciating the desirability of this commemoration, the Congress passed an act, March 3, 1905, authorizing in the year 1907, on and near the waters of Hampton Roads, in the State of Virginia, an international naval, marine, and military celebration in honor of this event. By the authority vested in me by this act, I have made proclamation of said celebration, and have issued, in conformity with its instructions, invitations to all the nations of the earth to participate, by sending their naval vessels and such military organizations as may be practicable. This celebration would fail of its full purpose unless it were enduring in its results and commensurate with the importance of the event to be celebrated, the event from which our nation dates its birth. I earnestly hope that this celebration, already indorsed by the Congress of the United States, and by the legislatures of sixteen States since the action of the Congress, will receive such additional aid at your hands as will make it worthy of the great event it is intended to celebrate, and thereby enable the government of the United States to make provision for the exhibition of its own resources, and likewise enable our people who have undertaken the work of such a celebration to provide suitable and proper entertainment and instruction in the historic events of our country for all who may visit the exposition and to whom we have tendered our hospitality.

VETERANS

It is a matter of unmixed satisfaction once more to call attention to the excellent work of the Pension Bureau; for the veterans of the Civil War have a greater claim upon us than any other class of our citizens. To them, first of all among our people, honor is due.

CONFEDERATE GRAVES

Seven years ago my lamented predecessor, President McKinley, stated that the time had come for the nation to care for the graves of the Confederate dead. I recommend that the Congress take action toward this end. The first need is to take charge of the graves of the Confederate dead who died in Northern prisons.

IMMIGRATION

The question of immigration is of vital interest to this country. In the year ending June 30, 1905, there came to the United States 1,026,000 alien immigrants. In other words, in the single year that has just elapsed there came to this country a greater number of people than came here during the 169 years of our colonial life which intervened between the first landing at Jamestown and the Declaration of Independence. It is clearly shown in the report of the commissioner-general of immigration that while much of this enormous immigration is undoubtedly healthy and natural, a considerable proportion is undesirable from one reason or another; moreover, a considerable proportion of it, probably a very large proportion, including most of the undesirable class, does not come here of its own initiative, but because of the activity of the agents of the great transportation companies. These agents are distributed throughout Europe, and by the offer of all kinds of inducements they wheedle and cajole many immigrants, often against their best interest, to come here. The most serious obstacle we have to encounter in the effort to secure a proper regulation of the immigration to these shores arises from the determined opposition of the foreign steamship-lines who have no interest whatever in the matter save to increase the returns on their capital by carrying masses of immigrants hither in the steerage quarters of their ships.

As I said in my last message to the Congress, we cannot have too much immigration of the right sort and we should have none whatever of the wrong sort. Of course, it is desirable that even the right kind of immigration should be properly distributed in this country. We need more of such immigration for the South; and special effort should be made to secure it. Perhaps it would be possible to limit the number of immigrants allowed to come in any one year to New York and other Northern cities, while leaving unlimited the number allowed to come to the South; always provided, however, that a stricter effort is made to see that only immigrants of the right kind come to our country anywhere. In actual practice it has proved so difficult to enforce the immigration laws where long stretches of frontier marked by an imaginary line alone intervene between us and our neighbors that I recommend that no immigrants be allowed to come in from Canada and Mexico save natives of the two countries themselves. As much as possible should be done to distribute the immigrants upon the land and keep them away from the congested tenement-house districts of the great cities. But distribution is a palliative, not a cure. The prime need is to keep out all immigrants who will not make good American citizens. The laws now existing for the exclusion of undesirable immigrants should be strengthened. Adequate means should be adopted, enforced by sufficient penalties, to compel steamship companies engaged in the passenger business to observe in good faith the law which forbids them to encourage or solicit immigration to the United States. Moreover, there should be a sharp limitation imposed upon all vessels coming to our ports as to the number of immigrants in ratio to the tonnage which each vessel can carry. This ratio should be high enough to insure the coming hither of as good a class of aliens as possible. Provision should be made for the surer punishment of those who induce aliens to come to this country under promise or assurance of employment. It should be made possible to inflict a sufficiently heavy penalty on any employer violating this law to deter him from taking the risk. It seems to me wise that there should be an international conference held to deal with this question of immigration, which has more than a merely national significance; such a conference could, among other things, enter at length into the methods for securing a thorough inspection of would-be immigrants at the ports from which they desire to embark before permitting them to embark.

In dealing with this question it is unwise to depart from the old American tradition and to discriminate for or against any man who desires to come here and become a citizen, save on the ground of that man's fitness for citizenship. It is our right and duty to consider his moral and social quality. His standard of living should be such that he will not, by pressure of competition, lower the standard of living of our own wage-workers; for it must ever be a prime object of our legislation to keep high their standard of living. If the man who seeks to come here is from the moral and social standpoint of such a character as to bid fair to add value to the community he should be heartily welcomed. We cannot afford to pay heed to whether he is of one creed or another, of one nation or another. We cannot afford to consider whether he is Catholic or Protestant, Jew or Gentile; whether he is Englishman or Irishman, Frenchman or German, Japanese, Italian, Scandinavian, Slav, or Magyar. What we should desire to find out is the individual quality of the individual man. In my judgment, with this end in view, we shall have to prepare through our own agents a far more rigid inspection in the countries from which the immigrants come. It will be a great deal better to have fewer immigrants, but all of the right kind, than a great number of immigrants, many of whom are necessarily of the wrong kind. As far as possible we wish to limit the imigration to this country to persons who propose to become citizens of this country, and we can well afford to insist upon adequate scrutiny of the character of those who are thus proposed for future citizenship. There should be an increase in the stringency of the laws to keep out insane, idiotic, epileptic, and pauper immigrants. But this is by no means enough. Not merely the anarchist, but every man of anarchistic tendencies, all violent and disorderly people, all people of bad character, the incompetent, the lazy, the vicious, the physically unfit, defective, or degenerate should be kept out. The stocks out of which American citizenship is to be built should be strong and healthy, sound in body, mind, and character. If it be objected that the government agents would not always select well, the answer is that they would certainly select better than do the agents and brokers of foreign steamship companies, the people who now do whatever selection is done.

CHINA

The questions arising in connection with Chinese immigration stand by themselves. The conditions in China are such that the entire Chinese coolie class, that is, the class of Chinese laborers, skilled and unskilled, legitimately come under the head of undesirable immigrants to this country, because of their numbers, the low wages for which they work, and their low standard of living. Not only is it to the interest of this country to keep them out, but the Chinese authorities do not desire that they should be admitted. At present their entrance is prohibited by laws amply adequate to accomplish this purpose. These laws have been, are being, and will be, thoroughly enforced. The violations of them are so few in number as to be infinitesimal and can be entirely disregarded. There is no serious proposal to alter the immigration law as regards the Chinese laborer, skilled or unskilled, and there is no excuse for any man feeling or affecting to feel the slightest alarm on the subject.

But in the effort to carry out the policy of excluding Chinese laborers, Chinese coolies, grave injustice and wrong have been done by this nation to the people of China, and therefore ultimately to this nation itself. Chinese students, business and professional men of all kinds—not only merchants, but bankers, doctors, manufacturers, professors, travellers, and the like—should be encouraged to come here, and treated on precisely the same footing that we treat students, business men, travellers, and the like of other nations. Our laws and treaties should be framed, not so as to put these people in the excepted classes, but to state that we will admit all Chinese, except Chinese of the coolie class, Chinese skilled or unskilled laborers. There would not be the least danger that any such provision would result in any relaxation of the law about laborers. These will, under all conditions, be kept out absolutely. But it will be more easy to see that both justice and courtesy are shown, as they ought to be shown, to other Chinese, if the law or treaty is framed as above suggested. Examinations should be completed at the port of departure from China. For this purpose there should be provided a more adequate Consular Service in China than we now have. The appropriations both for the offices of the consuls and for the office forces in the consulates should be increased.

As a people we have talked much of the open door in China, and we expect, and quite rightly intend to insist upon, justice being shown us by the Chinese. But we cannot expect to receive equity unless we do equity. We cannot ask the Chinese to do to us what we are unwilling to do to them. They would have a perfect right to exclude our laboring men if our laboring men threatened to come into their country in such numbers as to jeopardize the well-being of the Chinese population; and as, *mutatis mutandis,* these were the conditions with which Chinese immigration actually brought this people face to face, we had and have a perfect right, which the Chinese Government in no way contests, to act as we have acted in the matter of restricting coolie immigration. That this right exists for each country was explicitly acknowledged in the last treaty between the two countries. But we must treat the Chinese student, traveller, and business man in a spirit of the broadest justice and courtesy if we expect similar treatment to be accorded to our own people of similar rank who go to China. Much trouble has come during the past summer from the organized boycott against American goods which has been started in China. The main factor in producing this boycott has been the resentment felt by the students and business people of China, by all the Chinese leaders, against the harshness of our law toward educated Chinamen of the professional and business classes.

This government has the friendliest feeling for China and desires China's well-being. We cordially sympathize with the announced purpose of Japan to stand for the integrity of China. Such an attitude tends to the peace of the world.

CIVIL SERVICE

The civil-service law has been on the statute-books for twenty-two years. Every President and a vast majority of heads of departments who have been in office during that period have favored a gradual extension of the merit system.

The more thoroughly its principles have been understood, the greater has been the favor with which the law has been regarded by administration officers. Any attempt to carry on the great executive departments of the government without this law would inevitably result in chaos. The civil-service commissioners are doing excellent work, and their compensation is inadequate considering the service they perform.

The statement that the examinations are not practical in character is based on a misapprehension of the practice of the commission. The departments are invariably consulted as to the requirements desired and as to the character of questions that shall be asked. General invitations are frequently sent out to all heads of departments asking whether any changes in the scope or character of examinations are required. In other words, the departments prescribe the requirements and qualifications desired, and the Civil Service Commission co-operates with them in securing persons with these qualifications and insuring open and impartial competition. In a large number of examinations (as, for example, those for trades positions), there are no educational requirements whatever, and a person who can neither read nor write may pass with a high average. Vacancies in the service are filled with reasonable expedition, and the machinery of the commission, which reaches every part of the country, is the best agency that has yet been devised for finding people with the most suitable qualifications for the various offices to be filled. Written competitive examinations do not make an ideal method for filling positions, but they do represent an immeasurable advance upon the "spoils" method, under which outside politicians really make the appointments nominally made by the executive officers, the appointees being chosen by the politicians in question, in the great majority of cases, for reasons totally unconnected with the needs of the service or of the public.

Statistics gathered by the Census Bureau show that the tenure of office in the government service does not differ materially from that enjoyed by employees of large business corporations. Heads of executive departments and members of the commission have called my attention to the fact that the rule requiring a filing of charges and three days' notice before an employee could be separated from the service for inefficiency has served no good purpose whatever, because that is not a matter upon which a hearing of the employee found to be inefficient can be of any value, and in practice the rule providing for such notice and hearing has merely resulted in keeping in a certain number of incompetents, because of the reluctance of the heads of departments and bureau chiefs to go through the required procedure. Experience has shown that this rule is wholly ineffective to save any man, if a superior for improper reasons wishes to remove him, and is mischievous because it sometimes serves to keep in the service incompetent men not guilty of specific wrong-doing. Having these facts in view the rule has been amended by providing that where the inefficiency or incapacity comes within the personal knowledge of the head of a department the removal may be made without notice, the reasons therefor being filed and made a record of the department. The absolute right of the removal rests where it always has rested, with the head of a department; any limitation of this absolute right results in grave injury to the public service. The change is merely one of procedure; it was much needed, and it is producing good results.

The civil-service law is being energetically and impartially enforced, and in the large majority of cases complaints of violations of either the law or rules are discovered to be unfounded. In this respect this law compares very favorably with any other Federal statute. The question of politics in the appointment and retention of the men engaged in merely ministerial work has been practically eliminated in almost the entire field of government employment covered by the civil-service law. The action of the Congress in providing the commission with its own force instead of requiring it to rely on detailed clerks has been justified by the increased work done at a smaller cost to the government. I urge upon the Congress a careful consideration of the recommendations contained in the annual report of the commission.

COPYRIGHT LAWS

Our copyright laws urgently need revision. They are imperfect in definition, confused and inconsistent in expression; they omit provision for many articles which, under modern reproductive processes, are entitled to protection; they impose hardships upon the copyright proprietor which are not essential to the fair protection of the public; they are difficult for the courts to interpret and impossible for the Copyright Office to administer with satisfaction to the public. Attempts to improve them by amendment have been frequent, no less than twelve acts for the purpose having been passed since the Revised Statutes. To perfect them by further amendment seems impracticable. A complete revision of them is essential. Such a revision, to meet modern conditions, has been found necessary in Germany, Austria, Sweden, and other foreign countries, and bills embodying it are pending in England and the Australian colonies. It has been urged here, and proposals for a commission to undertake it have, from time to time, been pressed upon the Congress. The inconveniences of the present conditions being so great, an attempt to frame appropriate legislation has been made by the Copyright Office, which has called conferences of the various interests especially and practically concerned with the operation of the copyright laws. It has secured from them suggestions as to the changes necessary; it has added from its own experience and investigations, and it has drafted a bill which embodies such of these changes and additions as, after full discussion and expert criticism, appeared to be sound and safe. In form this bill would replace the existing insufficient and inconsistent laws by one general copyright statute. It will be presented to the Congress at the coming session. It deserves prompt consideration.

PURE-FOOD LAW

I recommend that a law be enacted to regulate interstate commerce in misbranded and adulterated foods, drinks, and drugs. Such law would protect legitimate manufacture and commerce, and would tend to secure the health and welfare of the consuming public. Traffic in foodstuffs which have been debased or adulterated so as to injure health or to deceive purchasers should be forbidden.

THE SMOKE NUISANCE

The law forbidding the emission of dense black or gray smoke in the city of Washington has been sustained by the courts. Something has been accomplished under it, but much remains to be done if we would preserve the capital city from defacement by the smoke nuisance. Repeated prosecutions under the law have not had the desired effect. I recommend that it be made more stringent by increasing both the minimum and maximum fine; by providing for imprisonment in cases of repeated violation, and by affording the remedy of injunction against the continuation of the operation of plants which are persistent offenders. I recommend, also, an increase in the number of inspectors, whose duty it shall be to detect violations of the act.

NATIONAL PARKS

I call your attention to the generous act of the State of California in conferring upon the United States Government the ownership of the Yosemite Valley and the Mariposa Big Tree Grove. There should be no delay in accepting the gift, and appropriations should be made for the including thereof in the Yosemite National Park, and for the care and policing of the park. California has acted most wisely, as well as with great magnanimity, in the matter. There are certain mighty natural features of our land which should be preserved in perpetuity for our children and our children's children. In my judgment, the Grand Canyon of the Colorado should be made into a national park. It is greatly to be wished that the State of New York should copy as regards Niagara what the State of California has done as regards the Yosemite. Nothing should be allowed to interfere with the preservation of Niagara Falls in all their beauty and majesty. If the State cannot see to this, then it is earnestly to be wished that she should be willing to turn it over to the National Government, which should in such case (if possible, in conjunction with the Canadian Government) assume the burden and responsibility of preserving unharmed Niagara Falls; just as it should gladly assume a similar burden and responsibility for the Yosemite National Park, and as it has already assumed them for the Yellowstone National Park. Adequate provision should be made by the Congress for the proper care and supervision of all these national parks. The boundaries of the Yellowstone National Park should be extended to the south and east, to take in such portions of the abutting forest reservations as will enable the government to protect the elk on their winter range.

The most characteristic animal of the Western plains was the great, shaggy-maned wild ox, the bison, commonly known as buffalo. Small fragments of herds exist in a domesticated state here and there, a few of them in the Yellowstone Park. Such a herd as that on the Flathead Reservation should not be allowed to go out of existence. Either on some reservation or on some forest reserve like the Wichita reserve and game refuge provision should be made for the preservation of such a herd. I believe that the scheme would be of economic advantage, for the robe of the buffalo is of high market value, and the same is true of the robe of the crossbred animals.

LIFE-SAVING SERVICE PENSIONS

I call your especial attention to the desirability of giving to the members of the Life-Saving Service pensions such as are given to firemen and policemen in all our great cities. The men in the Life-Saving Service continually and in the most matter-of-fact way do deeds such as make Americans proud of their country. They have no political influence, and they live in such remote places that the really heroic services they continually render receive the scantiest recognition from the public. It is unjust for a great nation like this to permit these men to become totally disabled or to meet death in the performance of their hazardous duty and yet to give them no sort of reward. If one of them serves thirty years of his life in such a position he should surely be entitled to retire on half-pay, as a fireman or policeman does, and if he becomes totally incapacitated through accident or sickness, or loses his health in the discharge of his duty, he or his family should receive a pension just as any soldier should. I call your attention with especial earnestness to this matter because it appeals not only to our judgment but to our sympathy; for the people on whose behalf I ask it are comparatively few in number, render incalculable service of a particularly dangerous kind, and have no one to speak for them.

THE INDIANS

During the year just past, the phase of the Indian question which has been most sharply brought to public attention is the larger legal significance of the Indian's induction into citizenship. This has made itself manifest not only in a great access of litigation in which the citizen Indian figures as a party defendant and in a more wide-spread disposition to levy local taxation upon his personality, but in a decision of the United States Supreme Court which struck away the main prop on which has hitherto rested the government's benevolent effort to protect him against the evils of intemperance. The court holds, in effect, that when an Indian becomes, by virtue of an allotment of land to him, a citizen of the State in which his land is situated, he passes from under Federal control in such matters as this, and the acts of the Congress prohibiting the sale or gift to him of intoxicants become substantially inoperative. It is gratifying to note that the States and municipalities of the

West which have most at stake in the welfare of the Indians are taking up this subject and are trying to supply, in a measure at least, the abdication of its trusteeship forced upon the Federal Government. Nevertheless, I would urgently press upon the attention of the Congress the question whether some amendment of the internal-revenue laws might not be of aid in prosecuting those malefactors, known in the Indian country as "bootleggers," who are engaged at once in defrauding the United States Treasury of taxes and, what is far more important, in debauching the Indians by carrying liquors illicitly into territory still completely under Federal jurisdiction.

Among the crying present needs of the Indians are more day-schools situated in the midst of their settlements, more effective instruction in the industries pursued on their own farms, and a more liberal extension of the field-matron service, which means the education of the Indian women in the arts of home-making. Until the mothers are well started in the right direction we cannot reasonably expect much from the children who are soon to form an integral part of our American citizenship. Moreover the excuse continually advanced by male adult Indians for refusing offers of remunerative employment at a distance from their homes is that they dare not leave their families too long out of their sight. One effectual remedy for this state of things is to employ the minds and strengthen the moral fibre of the Indian women—the end to which the work of the field matron is especially directed. I trust that the Congress will make its appropriations for Indian day-schools and field matrons as generous as may consist with the other pressing demands upon its providence.

THE PHILIPPINES

During the last year the Philippine Islands have been slowly recovering from the series of disasters which, since American occupation, have greatly reduced the amount of agricultural products below what was produced in Spanish times. The war, the rinderpest, the locusts, the drought, and the cholera have been united as causes to prevent a return of the prosperity much needed in the islands. The most serious is the destruction by the rinderpest of more than seventy-five per cent of the draft cattle, because it will take several years of breeding to restore the necessary number of these indispensable aids to agriculture. The commission attempted to supply by purchase from adjoining countries the needed cattle, but the experiments made were unsuccessful. Most of the cattle imported were unable to withstand the change of climate and the rigors of the voyage and died from other diseases than rinderpest.

The income of the Philippine Government has necessarily been reduced by reason of the business and agricultural depression in the islands, and the government has been obliged to exercise great economy to cut down its expenses, to reduce salaries, and in every way to avoid a deficit. It has adopted an internal-revenue law, imposing taxes on cigars, cigarettes, and distilled liquors, and abolishing the old Spanish industrial taxes. The law has not operated as smoothly as was hoped, and although its principle is undoubtedly correct, it may need amendments for the purpose of reconciling the people to its provisions. The income derived from it has partly made up for the reduction in customs revenue.

There has been a marked increase in the number of Filipinos employed in the civil service, and a corresponding decrease in the number of Americans. The government in every one of its departments has been rendered more efficient by elimination of undesirable material and the promotion of deserving public servants.

Improvements of harbors, roads, and bridges continue, although the cutting down of the revenue forbids the expenditure of any great amount from current income for these purposes. Steps are being taken, by advertisement for competitive bids, to secure the construction and maintenance of 1,000 miles of railway by private corporations under the recent enabling legislation of the Congress. The transfer of the friar lands, in accordance with the contract made some two years ago, has been completely effected, and the purchase-money paid. Provision has just been made by statute for the speedy settlement in a special proceeding in the Supreme Court of controversies over the possession and title of church buildings and rectories arising between the Roman Catholic Church and schismatics claiming under ancient municipalities. Negotiations and hearings for the settlement of the amount due to the Roman Catholic Church for rent and occupation of churches and rectories by the army of the United States are in progress, and it is hoped a satisfactory conclusion may be submitted to the Congress before the end of the session.

Tranquility has existed during the past year throughout the archipelago, except in the Province of Cavite, the Province of Batangas, and the Province of Samar, and in the Island of Jolo among the Moros. The Jolo disturbance was put an end to by several sharp and short engagements, and now peace prevails in the Moro Province. Cavite, the mother of ladrones in the Spanish times, is so permeated with the traditional sympathy of the people for ladronism as to make it difficult to stamp out the disease. Batangas was only disturbed by reason of the fugitive ladrones from Cavite, Samar was thrown into disturbance by the uneducated and partly savage peoples living in the mountains, who, having been given by the municipal code more power than they were able to exercise discreetly, elected municipal officers who abused their trusts, compelled the people raising hemp to sell it at a much less price than it was worth, and by their abuses drove their people into resistance to constituted authority. Cavite and Samar are instances of reposing too much confidence in the self-governing power of a people. The disturbances have all now been suppressed, and it is hoped that with these lessons local governments can be formed which will secure quiet and peace to the deserving inhabitants. The incident is another proof of the fact that if there has been any error as regards giving self-government in the Philippines it has been in the direction of giving it too quickly, not too slowly. A year from next April the first legislative assembly for the islands will be held. On the sanity and self-restraint of this body much will depend so far as the future self-government of the islands is concerned.

The most encouraging feature of the whole situation has been the very great interest taken by the common people in education and the great increase in the number of enrolled students in the public schools. The increase was from 300,000 to half a million pupils. The average attendance is about 70 per cent. The only limit upon the number of pupils seems to be the capacity of the government to furnish teachers and school-houses.

The agricultural conditions of the islands enforce more strongly than ever the argument in favor of reducing the tariff on the products of the Philippine Islands entering the United States. I earnestly recommend that the tariff now imposed by the Dingley bill upon the products of the Philippine Islands be entirely removed, except the tariff on sugar and tobacco, and that that tariff be reduced to twenty-five per cent of the present rates under the Dingley Act; that after July 1, 1909, the tariff upon tobacco and sugar produced in the Philippine Islands must be entirely removed, and that free trade between the islands and the United States in the products of each country then be provided for by law.

A statute in force, enacted April 15, 1904, suspends the operation of the coastwise laws of the United States upon the trade between the Philippine Islands and the United States until July 1, 1906. I earnestly recommend that this suspension be postponed until July 1, 1909. I think it of doubtful utility to apply the coastwise laws to the trade between the United States and the Philippines under any circumstances, because I am convinced that it will do no good whatever to American bottoms, and will only interfere and be an obstacle to the trade between the Philippines and the United States, but if the coastwise law must be thus applied, certainly it ought not to have effect until free trade is enjoyed between the people of the United States and the people of the Philippine Islands in their respective products.

I do not anticipate that free trade between the islands and the United States will produce a revolution in the sugar and tobacco production of the Philippine Islands. So primitive are the methods of agriculture in the Philippine Islands, so slow is capital in going to the islands, so many difficulties surround a large agricultural enterprise in the islands, that it will be many, many years before the products of those islands will have any effect whatever upon the markets of the United States. The problem of labor is also a formidable one with the sugar and tobacco producers in the islands. The best friends of the Filipino people and the people themselves are utterly opposed to the admission of Chinese coolie labor. Hence the only solution is the training of Filipino labor, and this will take a long time. The enactment of a law by the Congress of the United States making provision for free trade between the islands and the United States, however, will be of great importance from a political and sentimental standpoint; and, while its actual benefit has doubtless been exaggerated by the people of the islands, they will accept this measure of justice as an indication that the people of the United States are anxious to aid the people of the Philippine Islands in every way, and especially in the agricultural development of their archipelago. It will aid the Filipinos without injuring interests in America.

HAWAII

In my judgment immediate steps should be taken for the fortification of Hawaii. This is the most important point in the Pacific to fortify in order to conserve the interests of this country. It would be hard to overstate the importance of this need. Hawaii is too heavily taxed. Laws should be enacted setting aside for a period of, say, twenty years seventy-five per cent of the internal-revenue and customs receipts from Hawaii as a special fund to be expended in the islands for educational and public buildings, and for harbor improvements and military and naval defenses. It cannot be too often repeated that our aim must be to develop the Territory of Hawaii on traditional American lines. That Territory has serious commercial and industrial problems to reckon with; but no measure of relief can be considered which looks to legislation admitting Chinese and restricting them by statute to field labor and domestic service. The status of servility can never again be tolerated on American soil. We cannot concede that the proper solution of its problems is special legislation admitting to Hawaii a class of laborers denied admission to the other States and Territories. There are obstacles, and great obstacles, in the way of building up a representative American community in the Hawaiian Islands; but it is not in the American character to give up in the face of difficulty. Many an American commonwealth has been built up against odds equal to those that now confront Hawaii.

No merely half-hearted effort to meet its problems as other American communities have met theirs can be accepted as final. Hawaii shall never become a Territory in which a governing class of rich planters exists by means of coolie labor. Even if the rate of growth of the Territory is thereby rendered slower, the growth must only take place by the admission of immigrants fit in the end to assume the duties and burdens of full American citizenship. Our aim must be to develop the Territory on the same basis of stable citizenship as exists on this continent.

PORTO RICO

I earnestly advocate the adoption of legislation which will explicitly confer American citizenship on all citizens of Porto Rico. There is, in my judgment, no excuse for failure to do this. The harbor of San Juan should be dredged and improved. The expenses of the Federal Court of Porto Rico should be met from the Federal Treasury and not from the Porto Rican treasury. The elections in Porto Rico should take place every four years, and the legislature should meet in session every two years. The present form of government in Porto Rico, which provides for the appointment by the President of the members of the Executive Council or Upper House of the legislature, has proved satisfactory and has inspired confidence in property-owners and investors. I do not deem it advisable at the present time to change this form in any material feature. The problems and needs of the island are industrial and commercial rather than political.

I wish to call the attention of the Congress to one question which affects our insular possessions generally; namely, the need of an increased liberality in the treatment of the whole franchise question in these islands. In the proper desire to prevent the islands being exploited by speculators and to have them develop in the interests of their own people an error has been made in refusing to grant sufficiently liberal terms to induce the investment of American capital in the Philippines and in Porto Rico. Elsewhere in this message I have spoken strongly against the jealousy of mere wealth, and especially of corporate wealth as such. But it is particularly regrettable to allow any such jealousy to be developed when we are dealing either with our insular or with foreign affairs. The big corporation has achieved its present position in the business world simply because it is the most effective instrument in business competition. In foreign affairs we cannot afford to put our people at a disadvantage with their competitors by in any way discriminating against the efficiency of our business organizations. In the same way we cannot afford to allow our insular possessions to lag behind in industrial development from any twisted jealousy of business success. It is, of course, a mere truism to say that the business interest of the islands will only be developed if it becomes the financial interest of somebody to develop them. Yet this development is one of the things most earnestly to be wished for in the interest of the islands themselves. We have been paying all possible heed to the political and educational interests of the islands, but, important though these objects are, it is not less important that we should favor their industrial development. The government can in certain ways help this directly, as by building good roads; but the fundamental and vital help must be given through the development of the industries of the islands, and a most efficient means to this end is to encourage big American corporations to start industries in them, and this means to make it advantageous for them to do so. To limit the ownership of mining claims, as has been done in the Philippines, is absurd. In both the Philippines and Porto Rico the limit of holdings of land should be largely raised.

ALASKA

I earnestly ask that Alaska be given an elective delegate. Some person should be chosen who can speak with authority of the needs of the Territory. The government should aid in the construction of a railroad from the Gulf of Alaska to the Yukon River, in American territory. In my last two messages I advocated certain additional action on behalf of Alaska. I shall not now repeat those recommendations, but I shall lay all my stress upon the one recommendation of giving to Alaska some one authorized to speak for it. I should prefer that the delegate was made elective, but if this is not deemed wise, then make him appointive. At any rate, give Alaska some person whose business it shall be to speak with authority on her behalf to the Congress. The natural resources of Alaska are great. Some of the chief needs of the peculiarly energetic, self-reliant, and typically American white population of Alaska were set forth in my last message. I also earnestly ask your attention to the needs of the Alaskan Indians. All Indians who are competent should receive the full rights of American citizenship. It is, for instance, a gross and indefensible wrong to deny to such hard-working, decent-living Indians as the Metlakahtlas the right to obtain licenses as captains, pilots, and engineers; the right to enter mining claims, and to profit by the homestead law. These particular Indians are civilized and are competent and entitled to be put on the same basis with the white men roundabout them.

NEW STATES

I recommend that Indian Territory and Oklahoma be admitted as one State and that New Mexico and Arizona be admitted as one State. There is no obligation upon us to treat territorial subdivisions, which are matters of convenience only, as binding us on the question of admission to statehood. Nothing has taken up more time in the Congress during the past few years than the question as to the statehood to be granted to the four Territories above mentioned, and after careful consideration of all that has been developed in the discussions of the question, I recommend that they be immediately admitted as two States. There is no justification for further delay; and the advisability of making the four Territories into two States has been clearly established.

GAMBLING

In some of the Territories the legislative assemblies issue licenses for gambling. The Congress should by law forbid this practice, the harmful results of which are obvious at a glance.

PANAMA CANAL

The treaty between the United States and the republic of Panama, under which the construction of the Panama Canal was made possible, went into effect with its ratification by the United States Senate on February 23, 1904. The canal properties of the French Canal Company were transferred to the United States on April 23, 1904, on payment of $40,000,000 to that company. On April 1, 1905, the commission was reorganized, and it now consists of Theodore P. Shonts, chairman; Charles E. Magoon, Benjamin M. Harrod, Rear-Admiral Mordecai T. Endicott, Brigadier-General Peter C. Hains, and Colonel Oswald H. Ernst. John F. Stevens was appointed chief engineer on July 1 last. Active work in canal construction, mainly preparatory, has been in progress for less than a year and a half. During that period two points about the Canal have ceased to be open to debate: First, the question of route; the Canal will be built on the Isthmus of Panama. Second, the question of feasibility; there are no physical obstacles on this route that American engineering skill will not be able to overcome without serious difficulty, or that will prevent the completion of the Canal within a reasonable time and at a reasonable cost. This is virtually the unanimous testimony of the engineers who have investigated the matter for the government.

The point which remains unsettled is the question of type, whether the Canal shall be one of several locks above sea-level, or at sea-level with a single tide lock. On this point I hope to lay before the Congress at an early day the findings of the Advisory Board of American and European Engineers, that at my invitation have been considering the subject, together with the report of the commission thereon, and such comments thereon or recommendations in reference thereto as may seem necessary.

The American people is pledged to the speediest possible construction of a canal adequate to meet the demands which the commerce of the world will make upon it, and I appeal most earnestly to the Congress to aid in the fulfilment of the pledge. Gratifying progress has been made during the past year, and especially during the past four months. The greater part of the necessary preliminary work has been done. Actual work of excavation could be begun only on a limited scale till the Canal Zone was made a healthful place to live in and to work in. The Isthmus had to be sanitated first. This task has been so thoroughly accomplished that yellow fever has been virtually extirpated from the Isthmus and general health conditions vastly improved. The same methods which converted the island of Cuba from a pest-hole, which menaced the health of the world, into a healthful place of abode, have been applied on the Isthmus with satisfactory results. There is no reason to doubt that when the plans for water-supply, paving, and sewerage of Panama and Colon and the large labor camps have been fully carried out, the Isthmus will be, for the tropics, an unusually healthy place of abode. The work is so far advanced now that the health of all those employed in canal work is as well guarded as it is on similar work in this country and elsewhere.

In addition to sanitating the Isthmus, satisfactory quarters are being provided for employees and an adequate system of supplying them with wholesome food at reasonable prices has been created. Hospitals have been established and equipped that of their kind are without their superiors anywhere. The country has thus been made fit to work in, and provision has been made for the welfare and comfort of those who are to do the work. During the past year a large portion of the plant with which the work is to be done has been ordered. It is confidently believed that by the middle of the approaching year a sufficient proportion of this plant will have been installed to enable us to resume the work of excavation on a large scale.

What is needed now and without delay is an appropriation by the Congress to meet the current and accruing expenses of the commission. The first appropriation of $10,000,000, out of the $135,000,000 authorized by the Spooner Act, was made three years ago. It is nearly exhausted. There is barely enough of it remaining to carry the commission to the end of the year. Unless the Congress shall appropriate before that time all work must cease. To arrest progress for any length of time now, when matters are advancing so satisfactorily, would be deplorable. There will be no money with which to meet pay-roll obligations and none with which to meet bills coming due for materials and supplies; and there will be demoralization of the forces, here and on the Isthmus, now working so harmoniously and effectively, if there is delay in granting an emergency appropriation. Estimates of the amount necessary will be found in the accompanying reports of the secretary of war and the commission.

DEPARTMENT OF STATE

I recommend more adequate provision than has been made heretofore for the work of the Department of State. Within a few years there has been a very great increase in the amount and importance of the work to be done by that department, both in Washington and abroad. This has been caused by the great increase of our foreign trade, the increase of wealth among our people, which enables them to travel more generally than heretofore, the increase of American capital which is seeking investment in foreign countries, and the growth of our power and weight in the councils of the civilized world. There has been no corresponding increase of facilities for doing the work afforded to the department having charge of our foreign relations.

Neither at home nor abroad is there a sufficient working force to do the business properly. In many respects the system which was adequate to the work of twenty-five years or even ten years ago, is inadequate now, and should be changed. Our consular force should be classified, and appointments should be made to the several classes, with authority to the Executive to assign the members of each class to duty at such posts as the interests of the service require, instead of the appointments being made as at present to specified posts. There should be an adequate inspection service, so that the department may be able to inform itself how the business of each consulate is being done, instead of depending upon casual private information or rumor. The fee system should be entirely abolished, and a due equivalent made in salary to the officers who now eke out their subsistence by means of fees. Sufficient provision should be made for a clerical force in every consulate, composed entirely of Americans, instead of the insufficient provision now made, which compels the employment of great numbers of citizens of foreign countries whose services can be obtained for less money. At a large part of our consulates the office quarters and the clerical force are inadequate to the performance of the onerous duties imposed by the recent provisions of our immigration laws as well as by our increasing trade. In many parts of the world the lack of suitable quarters for our embassies, legations, and consulates detracts from the respect in which our officers ought to be held, and seriously impairs their weight and influence.

Suitable provision should be made for the expense of keeping our diplomatic officers more fully informed of what is being done from day to day in the progress of our diplomatic affairs with other countries. The lack of such information, caused by insufficient appropriations available for cable tolls and for clerical and messenger service, frequently puts our officers at a great disadvantage and detracts from their usefulness. The salary list should be readjusted. It does not now correspond either to the importance of the service to be rendered and the degrees of ability and experience required in the different positions, or to the differences in the cost of living. In many cases the salaries are quite inadequate.

VII

SIXTH ANNUAL MESSAGE [1]

To the Senate and House of Representatives:

As a nation we still continue to enjoy a literally unprecedented prosperity; and it is probable that only reckless speculation and disregard of legitimate business methods on the part of the business world can materially mar this prosperity.

No Congress in our time has done more good work of importance than the present Congress. There were several matters left unfinished at your last session, however, which I most earnestly hope you will complete before your adjournment.

CAMPAIGN CONTRIBUTIONS

I again recommend a law prohibiting all corporations from contributing to the campaign expenses of any party. Such a bill has already passed one House of Congress. Let individuals contribute as they desire; but let us prohibit in effective fashion all corporations from making contributions for any political purpose, directly or indirectly.

THE GOVERNMENT'S RIGHT OF APPEAL

Another bill which has just passed one House of the Congress and which it is urgently necessary should be enacted into law is that conferring upon the government the right of appeal in criminal cases on questions of law. This right exists in many of the States; it exists in the District of Columbia by act of the Congress. It is of course not proposed that in any case a verdict for the defendant on the merits should be set aside. Recently in one district where the government had in-

[1] Dated, the White House, December 3, 1906.

dicted certain persons for conspiracy in connection with rebates, the court sustained the defendant's demurrer; while in another jurisdiction an indictment for conspiracy to obtain rebates has been sustained by the court, convictions obtained under it, and two defendants sentenced to imprisonment. The two cases referred to may not be in real conflict with each other, but it is unfortunate that there should even be an apparent conflict. At present there is no way by which the government can cause such a conflict, when it occurs, to be solved by an appeal to a higher court; and the wheels of justice are blocked without any real decision of the question. I cannot too strongly urge the passage of the bill in question. A failure to pass it will result in seriously hampering the government in its effort to obtain justice, especially against wealthy individuals or corporations who do wrong; and may also prevent the government from obtaining justice for wage-workers who are not themselves able effectively to contest a case where the judgment of an inferior court has been against them. I have specifically in view a recent decision by a district judge leaving railway employees without remedy for violation of a certain so-called labor statute. It seems an absurdity to permit a single district judge, against what may be the judgment of the immense majority of his colleagues on the bench, to declare a law solemnly enacted by the Congress to be "unconstitutional," and then to deny to the government the right to have the Supreme Court definitely decide the question.

It is well to recollect that the real efficiency of the law often depends not upon the passage of acts as to which there is great public excitement, but upon the passage of acts of this nature as to which there is not much public excitement, because there is little public understanding of their importance, while the interested parties are keenly alive to the desirability of defeating them. The importance of enacting into law the particular bill in question is further increased by the fact that the government has now definitely begun a policy of resorting to the criminal law in those trust and interstate commerce cases where such a course offers a reasonable chance of success. At first, as was proper, every effort was made to enforce these laws by civil proceedings; but it has become increasingly evident that the action of the government in finally deciding, in certain cases, to undertake criminal proceedings was justifiable; and though there have been some conspicuous failures ni these cases, we have had many successes, which have undoubtedly had a deterrent effect upon evil-doers, whether the penalty inflicted was in the shape of fine or imprisonment—and penalties of both kinds have already been inflicted by the courts. Of course, where the judge can see his way to inflict the penalty of imprisonment the deterrent effect of the punishment on other offenders is increased; but sufficiently heavy fines accomplish much. Judge Holt, of the New York district court, in a recent decision admirably stated the need for treating with just severity offenders of this kind. His opinion runs in part as follows:

"The Government's evidence to establish the defendant's guilt was clear, conclusive, and undisputed. The case was a flagrant one. The transactions which took place under this illegal contract were very large; the amounts of rebates returned were considerable; and the amount of the rebate itself was large, amounting to more than one-fifth of the entire tariff charge for the transportation of merchandise from this city to Detroit. It is not too much to say, in my opinion, that if this business was carried on for a considerable time on that basis —that is, if this discrimination in favor of this particular shipper was made with an 18 instead.of a 23 cent rate and the tariff rate was maintained as against their competitors—the result might be and not improbably would be that their competitors would be driven out of business. This crime is one which in its nature is deliberate and premeditated. I think over a fortnight elapsed between the date of Palmer's letter requesting the reduced rate and the answer of the railroad company deciding to grant it, and then for months afterward this business was carried on and these claims for rebates submitted month after month and checks in payment of them drawn month after month. Such a violation of the law, in my opinion, in its essential nature, is a very much more heinous act than the ordinary common, vulgar crimes which come before criminal courts constantly for punishment and which arise from sudden passion or temptation. This crime in this case was committed by men of education and of large business experience, whose standing in the community was such that they might have been expected to set an example of obedience to law, upon the maintenance of which alone in this country the security of their property depends. It was committeed on behalf of a great railroad corporation, which, like other railroad corporations, has received gratuitously from the State large and valuable privileges for the public's convenience and its own, which performs quasi-public functions and which is charged with the highest obligation in the transaction of its business to treat the citizens of this country alike, and not to carry on its business with unjust discriminations between different citizens or different classes of citizens. This crime in its nature is one usually done with secrecy, and proof of which it is very difficult to obtain. The Interstate Commerce Act was passed in 1887, nearly twenty years ago. Ever since that time complaints of the granting of rebates by railroads have been common, urgent, and insistent, and although the Congress has repeatedly passed legislation endeavoring to put a stop to this evil, the difficulty of obtaining proof upon which to bring prosecution in these cases is so great that this is the first case that has ever been brought in this court, and, as I am informed, this case and one recently brought in Philadelphia are the only cases that have ever been brought in the eastern part of this country. In fact, but few cases of this kind have ever been brought in this country, East or West. Now, under these circumstances, I am forced to the conclusion, in a case in which the proof is so clear and the facts are so flagrant, it is the duty of the court to fix a penalty which shall in some degree be commensurate with the gravity of the offense. As between the two defendants, in my opinion, the principal penalty should be imposed on the corporation. The traffic manager in this case, presumably, acted without any advantage to himself and without any interest in the transaction, either by the direct authority or in accordance with what he understood to be the policy or the wishes of his employer.

"The sentence of this court in this case is, that the defendant Pomeroy, for each of the six offenses upon which he has been convicted, be fined the sum of $1,000, making six fines, amounting in all to the sum of $6,000; and the defendant, The New York Central and Hudson River Railroad Company, for each of the six crimes of which it has been convicted, be fined the sum of $18,000, making six fines amounting in the aggregate to the sum of $108,000, and judgment to that effect will be entered in this case."

In connection with this matter, I would like to call attention to the very unsatisfactory state of our criminal law, resulting in large part from the habit of setting aside the judgments of inferior courts on technicalities absolutely unconnected with the merits of the case, and where there is no attempt to show that there has been any failure of substantial justice. It would be well to enact a law providing something to the effect that:

No judgment shall be set aside or new trial granted in any cause, civil or criminal, on the ground of misdirection of the jury or the improper admission or rejection of evidence, or for error as to any matter of pleading or procedure unless, in the opinion of the court to which the application is made, after an examination of the entire cause, it shall affirmatively appear that the error complained of has resulted in a miscarriage of justice.

INJUNCTIONS

In my last message I suggested the enactment of a law in connection with the issuance of injunctions, attention having been sharply drawn to the matter by the demand that the right of applying injunctions in labor cases should be wholly abolished. It is at least doubtful whether a law abolishing altogether the use of injunctions in such cases would stand the test of the courts; in which case of course the legislation would be ineffective. Moreover, I believe it would be wrong altogether to prohibit the use of injunctions. It is criminal to permit sympathy for criminals to weaken our hands in upholding the law; and if men seek to destroy life or property by mob violence there should be no impairment of the power of the courts to deal with them in the most summary and effective way possible. But so far as possible the abuse of the power should be provided against by some such law as I advocated last year.

In this matter of injunctions there is lodged in the hands of the judiciary a necessary power which is nevertheless subject to the possibility of grave abuse. It is a power that should be exercised with extreme care and should be subject to the jealous scrutiny of all men, and condemnation should be meted out as much to the judge who fails to use it boldly when necessary as to the judge who uses it wantonly or oppressively. Of course a judge strong enough to be fit for his office will enjoin any resort to violence or intimidation, especially by conspiracy, no matter what his opinion may be of the rights of the original quarrel. There must be no hesitation in dealing with disorder. But there must likewise be no such abuse of the injunctive power as is implied in forbidding laboring men to strive for their own betterment in peaceful and lawful ways; nor must the injunction be used merely to aid some big corporation in carrying out schemes for its own aggrandizement. It must be remembered that a preliminary injunction in a labor case, if granted without adequate proof (even when authority can be found to support the conclusions of law on which it is founded), may often settle the dispute between the parties; and therefore if improperly granted may do irreparable wrong. Yet there are many judges who assume a matter-of-course granting of a preliminary injunction to be the ordinary and proper judicial disposition of such cases; and there have undoubtedly been flagrant wrongs committed by judges in connection with labor disputes even within the last few years, although I think much less often than in former years. Such judges by their unwise action immensely strengthen the hands of those who are striving entirely to do away with the power of injunction; and therefore such careless use of the injunctive process tends to threaten its very existence, for if the American people ever become convinced that this process is habitually abused, whether in matters affecting labor or in matters affecting corporations, it will be well-nigh impossible to prevent its abolition.

CRITICISM OF THE JUDICIARY

It may be the highest duty of a judge at any given moment to disregard, not merely the wishes of individuals of great political or financial power, but the overwhelming tide of public sentiment; and the judge who does thus disregard public sentiment when it is wrong, who brushes aside the plea of any special interest when the pleading is not founded on righteousness, performs the highest service to the country. Such a judge is deserving of all honor; and all honor cannot be paid to this wise and fearless judge if we permit the growth of an absurd convention which would forbid any criticism of the judge of another type, who shows himself timid in the presence of arrogant disorder, or who on insufficient grounds grants an injunction that does grave injustice, or who in his capacity as a construer, and therefore in part a maker, of the law, in flagrant fashion thwarts the cause of decent government. The judge has a power over which no review can be exercised; he himself sits in review upon the acts of both the executive and legislative branches of the government; save in the most extraordinary cases he is amenable only at the bar of public opinion; and it is unwise to maintain that public opinion in reference to a man with such power shall neither be expressed nor led.

The best judges have ever been foremost to disclaim any immunity from criticism. This has been true since the days of the great English Lord Chancellor Parker, who said: "Let all people be at liberty to know what I found my judgment upon; that, so when I have given it in any cause, others may be at liberty to judge of *me*." The proprieties of the case were set forth with singular clearness and good temper by Judge W. H. Taft, when a United States circuit judge, eleven years ago, in 1895:

"The opportunity freely and publicly to criticise judicial action is of vastly more importance to the body politic than the immunity of courts and judges from unjust aspersions and attack. Nothing tends more to render judges careful in their decisions and anxiously solicitous to do exact justice than the consciousness that every act of theirs is to be subjected to the intelligent scrutiny and candid criticism of their fellow men. Such criticism is beneficial in proportion as it is fair, dispassionate, discriminating, and based on a knowledge of sound legal principles. The comments made by learned text writers and by the acute editors of the various law reviews upon judicial decisions are therefore highly useful. Such critics constitute more or less impartial tribunals of professional opinion before which each judgment is made to stand or fall on its merits, and thus exert a strong influence to secure uniformity of decision. But non-professional criticism also is by no means without its uses, even if accompanied, as it often is, by a direct attack upon the judicial fairness and motives of the occupants of the bench; for if the law is but the essence of common sense, the protest of many average men may evidence a defect in a judicial conclusion, though based on the nicest legal reasoning and profoundest learning. The two important elements of moral character in a judge are an earnest desire to reach a just conclusion and courage to enforce it. In so far as fear of public comment does not affect the courage of a judge, but only spurs him on to search his conscience and to reach the result which approves itself to his inmost heart such comment serves a useful purpose. There are few men, whether they are judges for life or for a shorter term, who do not prefer to earn and hold the respect of all, and who cannot be reached and made to pause and deliberate by hostile public criticism. In the case of judges having a life tenure, indeed, their very independence makes the right freely to comment on their decisions of greater importance, because it is the only practical and available instrument in the hands of a free people to keep such judges alive to the reasonable demands of those they serve.

"On the other hand, the danger of destroying the proper influence of judicial decisions by creating unfounded prejudices against the courts justifies and requires that unjust attacks shall be met and answered. Courts must ultimately rest their defense upon the inherent strength of the opinions they deliver as the ground for their conclusions and must trust to the calm and deliberate judgment of all the people as their best vindication."

There is one consideration which should be taken into account by the good people who carry a sound proposition to an excess in objecting to any criticism of a judge's decision. The instinct of the American people as a whole is sound in this matter. They will not subscribe to the doctrine that any public servant is to be above all criticism. If the best citizens, those most competent to express their judgment in such matters, and above all those belonging to the great and honorable profession of the bar, so profoundly influential in American life, take the position that there shall be no criticism of a judge under any circumstances, their view will not be accepted by the American people as a whole. In such event the people will turn to, and tend to accept as justifiable, the intemperate and improper criticism uttered by unworthy agitators. Surely it is a misfortune to leave to such critics a function, right, in itself, which they are certain to abuse. Just and temperate criticism, when necessary, is a safeguard against the acceptance by the people as a whole of that intemperate antagonism toward the judiciary which must be combated by every right-thinking man, and which, if it became wide-spread among the people at large, would constitute a dire menace to the Republic.

LYNCHING AND MOB VIOLENCE

In connection with the delays of the law, I call your attention and the attention of the nation to the prevalence of crime among us, and above all to the epidemic of lynching and mob violence that springs up, now in one part of our country, now in another. Each section, North, South, East, or West, has its own faults; no section can with wisdom spend its time jeering at the faults of another section; it should be busy trying to amend its own shortcomings. To deal with the crime of corruption it is necessary to have an awakened public conscience, and to supplement this by whatever legislation will add speed and certainty in the execution of the law. When we deal with lynching even more is necessary. A great many white men are lynched, but the crime is peculiarly frequent in respect to black men. The greatest existing cause of lynching is the perpetration, especially by black men, of the hideous crime of rape—the most abominable in all the category of crimes, even worse than murder. Mobs frequently avenge the commission of this crime by themselves torturing to death the man committing it; thus avenging in bestial fashion a bestial deed, and reducing themselves to a level with the criminal.

Lawlessness grows by what it feeds upon; and when mobs begin to lynch for rape they speedily extend the sphere of their operations and lynch for many other kinds of crimes, so that two-thirds of the lynchings are not for rape at all; while a considerable proportion of the individuals lynched are innocent of all crime. Governor Candler, of Georgia, stated on one occasion some years ago: "I can say of a verity that I have, within the last month, saved the lives of half a dozen innocent negroes who were pursued by the mob, and brought them to trial in a court of law in which they were acquitted." As Bishop Galloway, of Mississippi, has finely said: "When the rule of a mob obtains, that which distinguishes a high civilization is surrendered. The mob which lynches a negro charged with rape will in a little while lynch a white man suspected of crime. Every Christian patriot in America needs to lift up his voice in loud and eternal protest against the mob spirit that is threatening the integrity of this Republic." Governor Jelks, of Alabama, has recently spoken as follows: "The lynching of any person for whatever crime is inexcusable anywhere —it is a defiance of orderly government; but the killing of innocent people under any provocation is infinitely more horrible; and yet innocent people are likely to die when a mob's terrible lust is once aroused. The lesson is this: No good citizen can afford to countenance a defiance of the statutes, no matter what the provocation. The innocent frequently suffer, and, it is my observation, more usually suffer than the guilty. The white people of the South indict the whole colored race on the ground that even the better elements lend no assistance whatever in ferreting out criminals of their own color. The respectable colored people must learn not to harbor their criminals, but to assist the officers in bringing them to justice. This is the larger crime, and it provokes such atrocious offenses as the one at Atlanta. The two races can never get on until there is an understanding on the part of both to make common cause with the law-abiding against criminals of any color."

Moreover, where any crime committed by a member of one race against a member of another race is avenged in such fashion that it seems as if not the individual criminal, but the whole race, is attacked, the result is to exasperate to the highest degree race feeling. There is but one safe rule in dealing with black men as with white men; it is the same rule that must be applied in dealing with rich men and poor men; that is, to treat each man, whatever his color, his creed, or his social position, with even-handed justice on his real worth as a man. White people owe it quite as much to themselves as to the colored race to treat well the colored man who shows by his life that he deserves such treatment; for it is surely the highest wisdom to encourage in the colored race all those individuals who are honest, industrious, law-abiding, and who therefore make good and safe neighbors and citizens. Reward or punish the individual on his merits as an individual. Evil will surely come in the end to both races if we substitute for this just rule the habit of treating all the members of the race, good and bad, alike. There is no question of "social equality" or "negro domination" involved; only the question of relentlessly punishing bad men, and of securing to the good man the right to his life, his liberty, and the pursuit of his happiness as his own qualities of heart, head, and hand enable him to achieve it.

Every colored man should realize that the worst enemy of his race is the negro criminal, and above all the negro criminal who commits the dreadful crime of rape; and it should be felt as in the highest degree an offense against the whole country, and against the colored race in particular, for a colored man to fail to help the officers of the law in hunting down with all possible earnestness and zeal every such infamous offender. Moreover, in my judgment, the crime of rape should always be punished with death, as is the case with murder; assault with intent to commit rape should be made a capital crime, at least in the discretion of the court; and provision should be made by which the punishment may follow immediately upon the heels of the offense; while the trial should be so conducted that the victim need not be wantonly shamed while giving testimony, and that the least possible publicity shall be given to the details.

The members of the white race on the other hand should understand that every lynching represents by just so much a loosening of the bands of civilization; that the spirit of lynching inevitably throws into prominence in the community all the foul and evil creatures who dwell therein. No man can take part in the torture of a human being without having his own moral nature permanently lowered. Every lynching means just so much moral deterioration in all the children who have any knowledge of it, and therefore just so much additional trouble for the next generation of Americans.

Let justice be both sure and swift; but let it be justice under the law, and not the wild and crooked savagery of a mob.

EDUCATION OF THE NEGRO

There is another matter which has a direct bearing upon this matter of lynching and of the brutal crime which sometimes calls it forth and at other times merely furnishes the excuse for its existence. It is out of the question for our people as a whole permanently to rise by treading down any of their own number. Even those who themselves for the moment profit by such maltreatment of their fellows will in the long run also suffer. No more short-sighted policy can be imagined than, in the fancied interest of one class, to prevent the education of another class. The free public school, the chance for each boy or girl to get a good elementary education, lies at the foundation of our whole political situation. In every community the poorest citizens, those who need the schools most, would be deprived of them if they only received school facilities proportioned to the taxes they paid. This is as true of one portion of our country as of another. It is as true for the negro as for the white man. The white man, if he is wise, will decline to allow the negroes in a mass to grow to manhood and womanhood without education. Unquestionably education such as is obtained in our public schools does not do everything toward making a man a good citizen; but it does much. The lowest and most brutal criminals, those for instance who commit the crime of rape, are in the great majority men who have had either no education or very little; just as they are almost invariably men who own no property; for the man who puts money by out of his earnings, like the man who acquires education, is usually lifted above mere brutal criminality. Of course the best type of education for the colored man, taken as a whole, is such education as is conferred in schools like Hampton and Tuskegee; where the boys and girls, the young men and young women, are trained industrially as well as in the ordinary public-school branches. The graduates of these schools turn out well in the great majority of cases, and hardly any of them become criminals, while what little criminality there is never takes the form of that brutal violence which invites lynch-law. Every graduate of these schools—and for the matter of that every other colored man or woman—who leads a life so useful and honorable as to win the good-will and respect of those whites whose neighbor he or she is, thereby helps the whole colored race as it can be helped in no other way; for next to the negro himself, the man who can do most to help the negro is his white neighbor who lives near him; and our steady effort should be to better the relations between the two. Great though the benefit of these schools has been to their colored pupils and to the colored people, it may well be questioned whether the benefit has not been at least as great to the white people among whom these colored pupils live after they graduate.

Be it remembered, furthermore, that the individuals who, whether from folly, from evil temper, from greed for office, or in a spirit of mere base demagogy, indulge in the inflammatory and incendiary speeches and writings which tend to arouse mobs and to bring about lynching, not only thus excite the mob, but also tend by what criminologists call "suggestion," greatly to increase the likelihood of a repetition of the very crime against which they are inveighing. When the mob is composed of the people of one race and the man lynched is of another race, the men who in their speeches and writings either excite or justify the action tend, of course, to excite a bitter race feeling and to cause the people of the opposite race to lose sight of the abominable act of the criminal himself; and in addition, by the prominence they give to the hideous deed they undoubtedly tend to excite in other brutal and depraved natures thoughts of committing it. Swift, relentless, and orderly punishment under the law is the only way by which criminality of this type can permanently be suppressed.

CLASS HATRED

In dealing with both labor and capital, with the questions affecting both corporations and trades-unions, there is one matter more important to remember than aught else, and that is the infinite harm done by preachers of mere discontent. These are the men who seek to excite a violent class hatred against all men of wealth. They seek to turn wise and proper movements for the better control of corporations and for doing away with the abuses connected with wealth, into a campaign of hysterical excitement and falsehood in which the aim is to inflame to madness the brutal passions of mankind. The sinister demagogues and foolish visionaries who are always eager to undertake such a campaign of destruction sometimes seek to associate themselves with those working for a genuine reform in governmental and social methods, and sometimes masquerade as such reformers. In reality they are the worst enemies of the cause they profess to advocate, just as the purveyors of sensational slander in newspaper or magazine are the worst enemies of all men who are engaged in an honest effort to better what is bad in our social and governmental conditions. To preach hatred of the rich man as such, to carry on a campaign of slander and invective against him, to seek to mislead and inflame to madness honest men whose lives are hard and who have not the kind of mental training which will permit them to appreciate the danger in the doctrines preached—all this is to commit a crime against the body politic and to be false to every worthy principle and tradition of American national life. Moreover, while such preaching and such agitation may give a livelihood and a certain notoriety to some of those who take part in it, and may result in the temporary political success of others, in the long run every such movement will either fail or else will provoke a violent reaction, which will itself result not merely in undoing the mischief wrought by the demagogue and the agitator, but also in undoing the good that the honest reformer, the true upholder of popular rights, has painfully and laboriously achieved. Corruption is never so rife as in communities where the demagogue and the agitator bear full sway, because in such communities all moral bands become loosened, and hysteria and sensationalism replace the spirit of sound judgment and fair dealing as between man and man. In sheer revolt against the squalid anarchy thus produced men are sure in the end to turn toward any leader who can restore order, and then their relief at being free from the intolerable burdens of class hatred, violence, and demagogy is such that they cannot for some time be aroused to indignation against misdeeds by men of wealth; so that they permit a new growth of the very abuses which were in part responsible for the original outbreak. The one hope for success for our people lies in a resolute and fearless, but sane and cool-headed, advance along the path marked out last year by this very Congress. There must be a stern refusal to be misled into following either that base creature who appeals and panders to the lowest instincts and passions in order to arouse one set of Americans against their fellows, or that other creature, equally base but no baser, who in a spirit of greed, or to accumulate or add to an already huge fortune, seeks to exploit his fellow Americans with callous disregard to their welfare of soul and body. The man who debauches others in order to obtain a high office stands on an evil equality of corruption with the man who debauches others for financial profit; and when hatred is sown the crop which springs up can only be evil.

The plain people who think—the mechanics, farmers, merchants, workers with head or hand, the men to whom American traditions are dear, who love their country and try to act decently by their neighbors, owe it to themselves to remember that the most damaging blow that can be given popular government is to elect an unworthy and sinister agitator on a platform of violence and hypocrisy. Whenever such an issue is raised in this country nothing can be gained by flinching from it, for in such case democracy is itself on trial, popular self-government under Republican forms is itself on trial. The triumph of the mob is just as evil a thing as the triumph of the plutocracy, and to have escaped one danger avails nothing whatever if we succumb to the other. In the end the honest man, whether rich or poor, who earns his own living and tries to deal justly by his fellows, has as much to fear from the insincere and unworthy demagogue, promising much and performing nothing or else performing nothing but evil, who would set on the mob to plunder the rich, as from the crafty corruptionist, who, for his own ends, would permit the common people to be exploited by the very wealthy. If we ever let this government fall into the hands of men of either of these two classes, we shall show ourselves false to America's past. Moreover, the demagogue and the corruptionist often work hand in hand. There are at this moment wealthy reactionaries of such obtuse morality that they regard the public servant who prosecutes them when they violate the law, or who seeks to make them bear their proper share of the public burdens, as being even more objectionable than the violent agitator who hounds on the mob to plunder the rich. There is nothing to choose between such a reactionary and such an agitator; fundamentally they are alike in their selfish disregard of the rights of others; and it is natural that they should join in opposition to any movement of which the aim is fearlessly to do exact and even justice to all.

CONDITIONS OF LABOR

I call your attention to the need of passing the bill limiting the number of hours of employment of railroad employees. The measure is a very moderate one and I can conceive of no serious objection to it. Indeed, so far as it is in our power, it should be our aim steadily to reduce the number of hours of labor, with as a goal the general introduction of an eight-hour day. There are industries in which it is not possible that the hours of labor should be reduced; just as there are communities not far enough advanced for such a movement to be for their good, or, if in the tropics, so situated that there is no analogy between their needs and ours in this matter. On the Isthmus of Panama, for instance, the conditions are in every way so different from what they are here that an eight-hour day would be absurd; just as it is absurd, so far as the Isthmus is concerned, where white labor cannot be employed, to bother as to whether the necessary work is done by alien black men or by alien yellow men. But the wage-workers of the United States are of so high a grade that alike from the merely industrial standpoint and from the civic standpoint it should be our object to do what we can in the direction of securing the general observance of an eight-hour day. Until recently the eight-hour law on our Federal statute-books has been very scantily observed. Now, however, largely through the instrumentality of the Bureau of Labor, it is being rigidly enforced, and I shall speedily be able to say whether or not there is need of further legislation in reference thereto; for our purpose is to see it obeyed in spirit no less than in letter. Half-holidays during summer should be established for government employees; it is as desirable for wage-workers who toil with their hands as for salaried officials whose labor is mental that there should be a reasonable amount of holiday.

The Congress at its last session wisely provided for a truant court for the District of Columbia; a marked step in advance on the path of properly caring for the children. Let me again urge that the Congress provide for a thorough investigation of the conditions of child labor and of the labor of women in the United States. More and more our people are growing to recognize the fact that the questions which are not merely of industrial but of social importance outweigh all others; and these two questions most emphatically come in the category of those which affect in the most far-reaching way the home life of the nation. The horrors incident to the employment of young children in factories or at work anywhere are a blot on our civilization. It is true that each State must ultimately settle the question in its own way; but a thorough official investigation of the matter, with the results published broadcast, would greatly help toward arousing the public conscience and securing unity of State action in the matter. There is, however, one law on the subject which should be enacted immediately, because there is no need for an investigation in reference thereto, and the failure to enact it is discreditable to the National Government. A drastic and thoroughgoing child-labor law should be enacted for the District of Columbia and the Territories.

EMPLOYERS' LIABILITY LAW

Among the excellent laws which the Congress passed at the last session was an employers' liability law. It was a marked step in advance to get the recognition of employers' liability on the statute-books; but the law did not go far enough. In spite of all precautions exercised by employers there are unavoidable accidents and even deaths involved in nearly every line of business connected with the mechanic arts. This inevitable sacrifice of life may be reduced to a minimum, but it cannot be completely eliminated. It is a great social injustice to compel the employee, or rather the family of the killed or disabled victim, to bear the entire burden of such an inevitable sacrifice. In other words, society shirks its duty by laying the whole cost on the victim, whereas the injury comes from what may be called the legitimate risks of the trade. Compensation for accidents or deaths due in any line of industry to the actual conditions under which that industry is carried on, should be paid by that portion of the community for the benefit of which the industry is carried on—that is, by those who profit by the industry. If the entire trade risk is placed upon the employer he will promptly and properly add it to the legitimate cost of production and assess it proportionately upon the consumers of his commodity. It is therefore clear to my mind that the law should place this entire "risk of a trade" upon the employer. Neither the Federal law, nor, as far as I am informed, the State laws dealing with the question of employers' liability are sufficiently thoroughgoing. The Federal law should of course include employees in navy-yards, arsenals, and the like.

ARBITRATION OF LABOR DISPUTES

The commission appointed by the President October 16, 1902, at the request of both the anthracite-coal operators and miners, to inquire into, consider, and pass upon the questions in controversy in connection with the strike in the anthracite regions of Pennsylvania and the causes out of which the controversy arose, in their report, findings, and award expressed the belief "that the State and Federal governments should provide the machinery for what may be called the compulsory investigation of controversies between employers and employees when they arise." This expression of belief is deserving of the favorable consideration of the Congress and the enactment of its provisions into law. A bill has already been introduced to this end.

Records show that during the twenty years from January 1, 1881, to December 31, 1900, there were strikes affecting 117,-509 establishments, and 6,105,694 employees were thrown out of employment. During the same period there were 1,005 lockouts, involving nearly 10,000 establishments, throwing over one million people out of employment. These strikes and lockouts involved an estimated loss to employees of $307,000,000 and to employers of $143,000,000, a total of $450,000,000. The public suffered directly and indirectly probably as great additional loss. But the money loss, great as it was, did not measure the anguish and suffering endured by the wives and children of employees whose pay stopped when their work stopped, or the disastrous effect of the strike or lockout upon the business of employers, or the increase in the cost of products and the inconvenience and loss to the public.

Many of these strikes and lockouts would not have occurred had the parties to the dispute been required to appear before an unprejudiced body representing the nation and, face to face, state the reasons for their contention. In most instances the dispute would doubtless be found to be due to a misunderstanding by each of the other's rights, aggravated by an unwillingness of either party to accept as true the statements of the other as to the justice or injustice of the matters in dispute. The exercise of a judicial spirit by a disinterested body representing the Federal Government, such as would be provided by a commission on conciliation and arbitration, would tend to create an atmosphere of friendliness and conciliation between contending parties; and the giving each side an equal opportunity to present fully its case in the presence of the other would prevent many disputes from developing into serious strikes or lockouts, and, in other cases, would enable the commission to persuade the opposing parties to come to terms.

In this age of great corporate and labor combinations, neither employers nor employees should be left completely at the mercy of the stronger party to a dispute, regardless of the righteousness of their respective claims. The proposed measure would be in the line of securing recognition of the fact that in many strikes the public has itself an interest which cannot wisely be disregarded; an interest not merely of general convenience, for the question of a just and proper public policy must also be considered. In all legislation of this kind it is well to advance cautiously, testing each step by the actual results; the step proposed can surely be safely taken for the decisions of the commission would not bind the parties in legal fashion, and yet would give a chance for public opinion to crystallize and thus to exert its full force for the right.

COAL-LANDS

It is not wise that the nation should alienate its remaining coal-lands. I have temporarily withdrawn from settlement all the lands which the Geological Survey has indicated as containing, or in all probability containing, coal. The question, however, can be properly settled only by legislation, which in my judgment should provide for the withdrawal of these lands from sale or from entry, save in certain especial circumstances. The ownership would then remain in the United States, which should not, however, attempt to work them, but permit them to be worked by private individuals under a royalty system, the government keeping such control as to permit it to see that no excessive price was charged consumers. It would, of course, be as necessary to supervise the rates charged by the common carriers to transport the product as the rates charged by those who mine it; and the supervision must extend to the conduct of the common carriers, so that they shall in no way favor one competitor at the expense of another. The withdrawal of these coal-lands would constitute a policy analogous to that which has been followed in withdrawing the forest-lands from ordinary settlement. The coal, like the forests, should be treated as the property of the public and its disposal should be under conditions which would inure to the benefit of the public as a whole.

REGULATION OF CORPORATIONS

The present Congress has taken long strides in the direction of securing proper supervision and control by the National Government over corporations engaged in interstate business —and the enormous majority of corporations of any size are engaged in interstate business. The passage of the railway-rate bill, and only to a less degree the passage of the pure-food bill, and the provision for increasing and rendering more effective national control over the beef-packing industry, mark an important advance in the proper direction. In the short session it will perhaps be difficult to do much further along this line; and it may be best to wait until the laws have been in operation for a number of months before endeavoring to increase their scope, because only operation will show with exactness their merits and their shortcomings and thus give opportunity to define what further remedial legislation is needed. Yet in my judgment it will in the end be advisable in con-

nection with the packing-house-inspection law to provide for
putting a date on the label and for charging the cost of inspection to the packers. All these laws have already justified
their enactment. The interstate commerce law, for instance,
has rather amusingly falsified the predictions, both of those
who asserted that it would ruin the railroads and of those who
asserted that it did not go far enough and would accomplish
nothing. During the last five months the railroads have shown
increased earnings and some of them unusual dividends; while
during the same period the mere taking effect of the law has
produced an unprecedented, a hitherto unheard-of, number
of voluntary reductions in freights and fares by the railroads.
Since the founding of the commission there has never been
a time of equal length in which anything like so many reduced
tariffs have been put into effect. On August 27, for instance,
two days before the new law went into effect, the commission
received notices of over 5,000 separate tariffs which represented
reductions from previous rates.

It must not be supposed, however, that with the passage of
these laws it will be possible to stop progress along the line of
increasing the power of the National Government over the
use of capital in interstate commerce. For example, there will
ultimately be need of enlarging the powers of the Interstate
Commerce Commission along several different lines, so as to
give it a larger and more efficient control over the railroads.

It cannot too often be repeated that experience has conclusively shown the impossibility of securing by the actions of
nearly half a hundred different State legislatures anything but
ineffective chaos in the way of dealing with the great corporations which do not operate exclusively within the limits of any
one State. In some method, whether by a national license law
or in other fashion, we must exercise, and that at an early
date, a far more complete control than at present over these
great corporations—a control that will among other things prevent the evils of excessive overcapitalization, and that will
compel the disclosure by each big corporation of its stockholders

and of its properties and business, whether owned directly or through subsidiary or affiliated corporations. This will tend to put a stop to the securing of inordinate profits by favored individuals at the expense whether of the general public, the stockholders, or the wage-workers. Our effort should be not so much to prevent consolidation as such, but so to supervise and control it as to see that it results in no harm to the people. The reactionary or ultraconservative apologists for the misuse of wealth assail the effort to secure such control as a step toward socialism. As a matter of fact it is these reactionaries and ultraconservatives who are themselves most potent in increasing socialistic feeling. One of the most efficient methods of averting the consequences of a dangerous agitation, which is eighty per cent wrong, is to remedy the twenty per cent of evil as to which the agitation is well founded. The best way to avert the very undesirable move for the government ownership of railways is to secure by the government on behalf of the people as a whole such adequate control and regulation of the great interstate common carriers as will do away with the evils which give rise to the agitation against them. So the proper antidote to the dangerous and wicked agitation against the men of wealth as such is to secure by proper legislation and executive action the abolition of the grave abuses which actually do obtain in connection with the business use of wealth under our present system—or rather no system—of failure to exercise any adequate control at all. Some persons speak as if the exercise of such governmental control would do away with the freedom of individual initiative and dwarf individual effort. This is not a fact. It would be a veritable calamity to fail to put a premium upon individual initiative, individual capacity and effort; upon the energy, character, and foresight which it is so important to encourage in the individual. But as a matter of fact the deadening and degrading effect of pure socialism, and especially of its extreme form, communism, and the destruction of individual character which they would bring about, are in part achieved by the wholly unregulated competition which results in a single individual or corporation rising at the expense of all others until his or its rise effectually checks all competition and reduces former competitors to a position of utter inferiority and subordination.

In enacting and enforcing such legislation as this Congress already has to its credit, we are working on a coherent plan, with the steady endeavor to secure the needed reform by the joint action of the moderate men, the plain men who do not wish anything hysterical or dangerous, but who do intend to deal in resolute common-sense fashion with the real and great evils of the present system. The reactionaries and the violent extremists show symptoms of joining hands against us. Both assert, for instance, that, if logical, we should go to government ownership of railroads and the like; the reactionaries, because on such an issue they think the people would stand with them, while the extremists care rather to preach discontent and agitation than to achieve solid results. As a matter of fact, our position is as remote from that of the Bourbon reactionary as from that of the impracticable or sinister visionary. We hold that the government should not conduct the business of the nation, but that it should exercise such supervision as will insure its being conducted in the interest of the nation. Our aim is, so far as may be, to secure, for all decent, hard-working men, equality of opportunity and equality of burden.

The actual working of our laws has shown that the effort to prohibit all combination, good or bad, is noxious where it is not ineffective. Combination of capital like combination of labor is a necessary element of our present industrial system. It is not possible completely to prevent it; and if it were possible, such complete prevention would do damage to the body politic. What we need is not vainly to try to prevent all combination, but to secure such rigorous and adequate control and supervision of the combinations as to prevent their injuring the public, or existing in such form as inevitably to threaten injury—for the mere fact that a combination has secured practically complete control of a necessary of life would under any circumstances show that such combination was to be presumed to be adverse to the public interest. It is unfortunate that our present laws should forbid all combinations, instead of sharply discriminating between those combinations which do good and those combinations which do evil. Rebates, for instance, are as often due to the pressure of big shippers (as was shown in the investigation of the Standard Oil Company and as has been shown since by the investigation of the tobacco and sugar trusts) as to the initiative of big railroads. Often railroads would like to combine for the purpose of preventing a big shipper from maintaining improper advantages at the expense of small shippers and of the general public. Such a combination, instead of being forbidden by law, should be favored. In other words, it should be permitted to railroads to make agreements, provided these agreements were sanctioned by the Interstate Commerce Commission and were published. With these two conditions complied with it is impossible to see what harm such a combination could do to the public at large. It is a public evil to have on the statute-books a law incapable of full enforcement because both judges and juries realize that its full enforcement would destroy the business of the country; for the result is to make decent railroad men violators of the law against their will, and to put a premium on the behavior of the wilful wrong-doers. Such a result in turn tends to throw the decent man and the wilful wrong-doer into close association, and in the end to drag down the former to the latter's level; for the man who becomes a lawbreaker in one way unhappily tends to lose all respect for law and to be willing to break it in many ways. No more scathing condemnation could be visited upon a law than is contained in the words of the Interstate Commerce Commission when, in commenting upon the fact that the numerous joint traffic associations do technically violate the law, they say: "The decision of the United States Supreme Court in the Trans-Missouri case and the Joint Traffic Association case has produced no practical effect upon the railway operations of the country. Such associations, in fact, exist now as they did before these decisions, and with the same general effect. In justice to all parties, we ought probably to add that it is difficult to see how our interstate railways could be operated with due regard to the interest of the shipper and the railway without concerted action of the kind afforded through these associations."

This means that the law as construed by the Supreme Court is such that the business of the country cannot be conducted without breaking it. I recommend that you give careful and early consideration to this subject, and if you find the opinion of the Interstate Commerce Commission justified, that you amend the law so as to obviate the evil disclosed.

FEDERAL TAXATION

The question of taxation is difficult in any country, but it is especially difficult in ours with its Federal system of government. Some taxes should on every ground be levied in a small district for use in that district. Thus the taxation of real estate is peculiarly one for the immediate locality in which the real estate is found. Again, there is no more legitimate tax for any State than a tax on the franchises conferred by that State upon street railroads and similar corporations which operate wholly within the State boundaries, sometimes in one and sometimes in several municipalities or other minor divisions of the State. But there are many kinds of taxes which can only be levied by the general government so as to produce the best results, because, among other reasons, the attempt to impose them in one particular State too often results merely in driving the corporation or individual affected to some other locality or other State. The National Government has long derived its chief revenue from a tariff on imports and from an internal or excise tax. In addition to these there is every reason why, when next our system of taxation is revised, the National Government should impose a graduated inheritance tax, and, if possible, a graduated income tax. The man of great wealth owes a peculiar obligation to the State, because he derives special advantages from the mere existence of government. Not only should he recognize this obligation in the way he leads his daily life and in the way he earns and spends his money, but it should also be recognized by the way in which he pays for the protection the State gives him. On the one hand, it is desirable that he should assume his full and proper share of the burden of taxation; on the other hand, it is quite as necessary that in this kind of taxation, where the men who vote the tax pay but little of it, there should be clear recognition of the danger of inaugurating any such system save in a spirit of entire justice and moderation. Whenever we, as a people, undertake to remodel our taxation system along the lines suggested, we must make it clear beyond peradventure that our aim is to distribute the burden of supporting the government more equitably than at present; that we intend to treat rich man and poor man on a basis of absolute equality, and that we regard it as equally fatal to true democracy to do or permit injustice to the one as to do or permit injustice to the other.

I am well aware that such a subject as this needs long and careful study in order that the people may become familiar with what is proposed to be done, may clearly see the necessity of proceeding with wisdom and self-restraint, and may make up their minds just how far they are willing to go in the matter; while only trained legislators can work out the project in necessary detail. But I feel that in the near future our national legislators should enact a law providing for a graduated inheritance tax by which a steadily increasing rate of duty should be put upon all moneys or other valuables coming by gift, bequest, or devise to any individual or corporation. It may be well to make the tax heavy in proportion as the individual benefited is remote of kin. In any event, in my judgment the pro rata of the tax should increase very heavily with the increase of the amount left to any one individual after a certain point has been reached. It is most desirable to encourage thrift and ambition, and a potent source of thrift and ambition is the desire on the part of the bread-winner to leave his children well off. This object can be attained by making the tax very small on moderate amounts of property left; because the prime object should be to put a constantly increasing burden on the inheritance of those swollen fortunes which it is certainly of no benefit to this country to perpetuate.

There can be no question of the ethical propriety of the government thus determining the conditions upon which any gift or inheritance should be received. Exactly how far the inheritance tax would, as an incident, have the effect of limiting the transmission by devise or gift of the enormous fortunes in question it is not necessary at present to discuss. It is wise that progress in this direction should be gradual. At first a permanent national inheritance tax, while it might be more substantial than any such tax has hitherto been, need not approximate, either in amount or in the extent of the increase by graduation, to what such a tax should ultimately be.

This species of tax has again and again been imposed, although only temporarily, by the National Government. It was first imposed by the act of July 6, 1797, when the makers of the Constitution were alive and at the head of affairs. It was a graduated tax; though small in amount, the rate was increased with the amount left to any individual, exceptions being made in the case of certain close kin. A similar tax was again imposed by the act of July 1, 1862; a minimum sum of $1,000 in personal property being excepted from taxation, the tax then becoming progressive according to the remoteness of kin. The war-revenue act of June 13, 1898, provided for an inheritance tax on any sum exceeding the value of $10,000, the rate of the tax increasing both in accordance with the amounts left and in accordance with the legatee's remoteness of kin. The Supreme Court has held that the succession tax imposed at the time of the Civil War was not a direct tax but an impost or excise which was both constitutional and valid. More recently the court, in an opinion delivered by Mr. Justice White, which contained an exceedingly able and elaborate discussion of the powers of the Congress to impose death duties, sustained the constitutionality of the inheritance-tax feature of the war-revenue act of 1898.

In its incidents, and apart from the main purpose of raising revenue, an income tax stands on an entirely different footing from an inheritance tax; because it involves no question of the perpetuation of fortunes swollen to an unhealthy size. The question is in its essence a question of the proper adjustment of burdens to benefits. As the law now stands it is undoubtedly difficult to devise a national income tax which shall be constitutional. But whether it is absolutely impossible is another question; and if possible it is most certainly desirable. The first purely income-tax law was passed by the Congress in 1861, but the most important law dealing with the subject was that of 1894. This the court held to be unconstitutional.

The question is undoubtedly very intricate, delicate, and troublesome. The decision of the court was only reached by one majority. It is the law of the land, and of course is accepted as such and loyally obeyed by all good citizens. Nevertheless, the hesitation evidently felt by the court as a whole in coming to a conclusion, when considered together with the previous decisions on the subject, may perhaps indicate the possibility of devising a constitutional income-tax law which shall substantially accomplish the results aimed at. The difficulty of amending the Constitution is so great that only real necessity can justify a resort thereto. Every effort should be made in dealing with this subject, as with the subject of the proper control by the National Government over the use of corporate wealth in interstate business, to devise legislation which without such action shall attain the desired end; but if this fails, there will ultimately be no alternative to a constitutional amendment.

THE WELFARE OF THE WAGE-WORKER

It would be impossible to overstate (though it is of course difficult quantitatively to measure) the effect upon a nation's growth to greatness of what may be called organized patriotism, which necessarily includes the substitution of a national feeling for mere local pride; with as a resultant a high ambition for the whole country. No country can develop its full strength so long as the parts which make up the whole each put a feeling of loyalty to the part above the feeling of loyalty to the whole. This is true of sections and it is just as true of classes. The industrial and agricultural classes must work together, capitalists and wage-workers must work together, if the best work of which the country is capable is to be done. It is probable that a thoroughly efficient system of education comes next to the influence of patriotism in bringing about national success of this kind. Our Federal form of government, so fruitful of advantage to our people in certain ways, in other ways undoubtedly limits our national effectiveness. It is not possible, for instance, for the National Government to take the lead in technical industrial education, to see that the public-school system of this country develops on all its technical, industrial, scientific, and commercial sides. This must be left primarily to the several States. Nevertheless, the National Government has control of the schools of the District of Columbia, and it should see that these schools promote and encourage the fullest development of the scholars in both commercial and industrial training. The commercial training should in one of its branches deal with foreign trade. The industrial training is even more important. It shou'd be one of our prime objects as a nation, so far as feasible, constantly to work toward putting the mechanic, the wage-worker who works with his hands, on a higher plane of efficiency and reward, so as to increase his effectiveness in the economic world, and the dignity, the remuneration, and the power of his position in the social world. Unfortunately, at present the effect of some of the work in the public schools is in the exactly opposite direction. If boys and girls are trained merely in literary accomplishments, to the total exclusion of industrial, manual, and technical training, the tendency is to unfit them for industrial work and to make them reluctant to go into it, or unfitted to do well if they do go into it. This is a tendency which should be strenuously combated. Our industrial development depends largely upon technical education, including in this term all industrial education, from that which fits a man to be a good mechanic, a good carpenter, or blacksmith, to that which fits a man to do the greatest engineering feat. The skilled mechanic, the skilled workman, can best become such by technical industrial education. The far-reaching usefulness of institutes of technology and schools of mines or of engineering is now universally acknowledged, and no less far-reaching is the effect of a good building or mechanical trades-school, a textile, or watchmaking, or engraving school. All such training must develop not only manual dexterity but industrial intelligence. In international rivalry this country does not have to fear the competition of pauper labor as much as it has to fear the educated labor of specially trained competitors; and we should have the education of the hand, eye, and brain which will fit us to meet such competition.

In every possible way we should help the wage-worker who toils with his hands and who must (we hope in a constantly increasing measure) also toil with his brain. Under the Constitution the national legislature can do but little of direct importance for his welfare save where he is engaged in work which permits it to act under the interstate commerce clause of the Constitution; and this is one reason why I so earnestly hope that both the legislative and judicial branches of the government will construe this clause of the Constitution in the broadest possible manner. We can, however, in such a matter as industrial training, in such a matter as child-labor and factory laws, set an example to the States by enacting the most advanced legislation that can wisely be enacted for the District of Columbia.

THE WELFARE OF THE FARMER

The only other persons whose welfare is as vital to the welfare of the whole country as is the welfare of the wage-workers, are the tillers of the soil, the farmers. It is a mere truism to say that no growth of cities, no growth of wealth, no industrial development can atone for any falling off in the character and standing of the farming population. During the last few decades this fact has been recognized with ever-increasing clearness. There is no longer any failure to realize that farming, at least in certain branches, must become a technical and scientific profession. This means that there must be open to farmers the chance for technical and scientific training, not theoretical merely but of the most severely practical type. The farmer represents a peculiarly high type of American citizenship, and he must have the same chance to rise and develop as other American citizens have. Moreover, it is exactly as true of the farmer, as it is of the business man and the wage-worker, that the ultimate success of the nation of which he forms a part must be founded not alone on material prosperity but upon high moral, mental, and physical development. This education of the farmer—self-education by preference, but also education from the outside, as with all other men—is peculiarly necessary here in the United States, where the frontier conditions even in the newest States have now nearly vanished, where there must be a substitution of a more intensive system of cultivation for the old wasteful farm management, and where there must be a better business organization among the farmers themselves.

Several factors must co-operate in the improvement of the farmer's condition. He must have the chance to be educated in the widest possible sense—in the sense which keeps ever in view the intimate relationship between the theory of education and the facts of life. In all education we should widen our aims. It is a good thing to produce a certain number of trained scholars and students; but the education superintended by the State must seek rather to produce a hundred good citizens than merely one scholar, and it must be turned now and then from the class-book to the study of the great book of nature itself. This is especially true of the farmer, as has been pointed out again and again by all observers most competent to pass practical judgment on the problems of our country life. All students now realize that education must seek to train the executive powers of young people and to confer more real significance upon the phrase "dignity of labor," and to prepare the pupils so that, in addition to each developing in the highest degree his individual capacity for work, they may together help create a right public opinion, and show in many ways social and co-operative spirit. Organization has become necessary in the business world; and it has accomplished much for good in the world of labor. It is no less necessary for farmers. Such a movement as the grange movement is good in itself and is capable of a well-nigh infinite further extension for good so long as it is kept to its own legitimate business. The benefits to be derived by the association of farmers for mutual advantage are partly economic and partly sociological.

Moreover, while in the long run voluntary efforts will prove more efficacious than government assistance, while the farmers must primarily do most for themselves, yet the government can also do much. The Department of Agriculture has broken new ground in many directions, and year by year it finds how it can improve its methods and develop fresh usefulness. Its constant effort is to give the governmental assistance in the most effective way; that is, through associations of farmers rather than to or through individual farmers. It is also striving to co-ordinate its work with the agricultural departments of the several States, and so far as its own work is educational to co-ordinate it with the work of other educational authorities. Agricultural education is necessarily based upon general education, but our agricultural educational institutions are wisely specializing themselves, making their courses relate to the actual teaching of the agricultural and kindred sciences to young country people or young city people who wish to live in the country.

Great progress has already been made among farmers by the creation of farmers' institutes, of dairy associations, of breeders' associations, horticultural associations, and the like. A striking example of how the government and the farmers can co-operate is shown in connection with the menace offered to the cotton-growers of the Southern States by the advance of the boll-weevil. The department is doing all it can to organize the farmers in the threatened districts, just as it has been doing all it can to organize them in aid of its work to eradicate the cattle-fever tick in the South. The department can and will co-operate with all such associations, and it must have their help if its own work is to be done in the most efficient style.

CONSERVATION

Much is now being done for the States of the Rocky Mountains and great plains through the development of the national policy of irrigation and forest-preservation; no government policy for the betterment of our internal conditions has been more fruitful of good than this. The forests of the White Mountains and southern Appalachian regions should also be preserved; and they cannot be unless the people of the States in which they lie, through their representatives in the Congress, secure vigorous action by the National Government.

ARLINGTON NATIONAL CEMETERY

I invite the attention of the Congress to the estimate of the secretary of war for an appropriation to enable him to begin the preliminary work for the construction of a memorial amphitheatre at Arlington. The Grand Army of the Republic in its national encampment has urged the erection of such an amphitheatre as necessary for the proper observance of Memorial Day and as a fitting monument to the soldier and sailor dead buried there. In this I heartily concur and commend the matter to the favorable consideration of the Congress.

MARRIAGE AND DIVORCE

I am well aware how difficult it is to pass a constitutional amendment. Nevertheless in my judgment the whole question of marriage and divorce should be relegated to the authority of the National Congress. At present the wide differences in the laws of the different States on this subject result in scandals and abuses; and surely there is nothing so vitally essential to the welfare of the nation, nothing around which the nation should so bend itself to throw every safeguard, as the home life of the average citizen. The change would be good from every standpoint. In particular it would be good because it would confer on the Congress the power at once to deal radically and efficiently with polygamy; and this should be done whether or not marriage and divorce are dealt with. It is neither safe nor proper to leave the question of polygamy to be dealt with by the several States. Power to deal with it should be conferred on the National Government.

When home ties are loosened; when men and women cease to regard a worthy family life, with all its duties fully performed, and all its responsibilities lived up to, as the life best worth living; then evil days for the commonwealth are at hand. There are regions in our land, and classes of our population, where the birth-rate has sunk below the death-rate. Surely it should need no demonstration to show that wilful sterility is, from the standpoint of the nation, from the standpoint of the human race, the one sin for which the penalty is national death, race death; a sin for which there is no atonement; a sin which is the more dreadful exactly in proportion as the men and women guilty thereof are in other respects, in character, and bodily and mental powers, those whom for the sake of the State it would be well to see the fathers and mothers of many healthy children, well brought up in homes made happy by their presence. No man, no woman, can shirk the primary duties of life, whether for love of ease and pleasure, or for any other cause, and retain his or her self-respect.

MERCHANT MARINE

Let me once again call the attention of the Congress to two subjects concerning which I have frequently before communicated with them. One is the question of developing American shipping. I trust that a law embodying in substance the views, or a major part of the views, expressed in the report on this subject laid before the House at its last session will be passed. I am well aware that in former years objectionable measures have been proposed in reference to the encouragement of American shipping; but it seems to me that the proposed measure is as nearly unobjectionable as any can be. It will of course benefit primarily our seaboard States, such as Maine, Louisiana, and Washington; but what benefits part of our people in the end benefits all; just as government aid to irrigation and forestry in the West is really of benefit, not only to the Rocky Mountain States, but to all our country. If it prove impracticable to enact a law for the encouragement of shipping generally, then at least provision should be made for better communication with South America, notably for fast mail lines to the chief South American ports. It is discreditable to us that our business people, for lack of direct communication in the shape of lines of steamers with South America, should in that great sister continent be at a disadvantage compared to the business people of Europe.

THE CURRENCY

I especially call your attention to the second subject, the condition of our currency laws. The National Bank Act has ably served a great purpose in aiding the enormous business development of the country; and within ten years there has been an increase in circulation per capita from $21.41 to $33.08.

For several years evidence has been accumulating that additional legislation is needed. The recurrence of each crop season emphasizes the defects of the present laws. There must soon be a revision of them, because to leave them as they are means to incur liability of business disaster. Since your body adjourned there has been a fluctuation in the interest on call money from two per cent to thirty per cent; and the fluctuation was even greater during the preceding six months. The secretary of the treasury had to step in and by wise action put a stop to the most violent period of oscillation. Even worse than such fluctuation is the advance in commercial rates and the uncertainty felt in the sufficiency of credit even at high rates. All commercial interests suffer during each crop period. Excessive rates for call money in New York attract money from the interior banks into the speculative field; this depletes the fund that would otherwise be available for commercial uses, and commercial borrowers are forced to pay abnormal rates; so that each fall a tax, in the shape of increased interest charges, is placed on the whole commerce of the country.

The mere statement of these facts shows that our present system is seriously defective. There is need of a change. Unfortunately, however, many of the proposed changes must be ruled from consideration because they are complicated, are not easy of comprehension, and tend to disturb existing rights and interests. We must also rule out any plan which would materially impair the value of the United States two per cent bonds now pledged to secure circulation, the issue of which was made under conditions peculiarly creditable to the Treasury. I do not press any especial plan. Various plans have recently been proposed by expert committees of bankers. Among the plans which are possibly feasible and which certainly should receive your consideration is that repeatedly brought to your attention by the present secretary of the treasury, the essential features of which have been approved by many prominent bankers and business men. According to this plan national banks should be permitted to issue a specified proportion of their capital in notes of a given kind, the issue to be taxed at so high a rate as to drive the notes back when not wanted in legitimate trade. This plan would not permit the issue of currency to give banks additional profits, but to meet the emergency presented by times of stringency.

I do not say that this is the right system. I only advance it to emphasize my belief that there is need for the adoption of some system which shall be automatic and open to all sound banks, so as to avoid all possibility of discrimination and favoritism. Such a plan would tend to prevent the spasms of high money and speculation which now obtain in the New York market; for at present there is too much currency at certain seasons of the year, and its accumulation at New York tempts bankers to lend it at low rates for speculative purposes; whereas at other times when the crops are being moved there is urgent need for a large but temporary increase in the currency supply. It must never be forgotten that this question concerns business men generally quite as much as bankers; especially is this true of stockmen, farmers, and business men in the West; for at present at certain seasons of the year the difference in interest rates between the East and the West is from six to ten per cent, whereas in Canada the corresponding difference is but two per cent. Any plan must of course, guard the interests of Western and Southern bankers as carefully as it guards the interests of New York or Chicago bankers; and must be drawn from the standpoints of the farmer and the merchant no less than from the standpoints of the city banker and the country banker.

The law should be amended so as specifically to provide that the funds derived from customs duties may be treated by the secretary of the treasury as he treats funds obtained under the internal-revenue laws. There should be a considerable increase in bills of small denominations. Permission should be given banks, if necessary under settled restrictions, to retire their circulation to a larger amount than $3,000,000 a month.

THE PHILIPPINES

I most earnestly hope that the bill to provide a lower tariff for or else absolute free trade in Philippine products will become a law. No harm will come to any American industry; and while there will be some small but real material benefit to the Filipinos, the main benefit will come by the showing made as to our purpose to do all in our power for their welfare. So far our action in the Philippines has been abundantly justified, not mainly and indeed not primarily because of the added dignity it has given us as a nation by proving that we are capable honorably and efficiently to bear the international burdens which a mighty people should bear, but even more because of the immense benefit that has come to the people of the Philippine Islands. In these islands we are steadily introducing both liberty and order, to a greater degree than their people have ever before known. We have secured justice. We have provided an efficient police force, and have put down ladronism. Only in the islands of Leyte and Samar is the authority of our government resisted and this by wild mountain tribes under the superstitious inspiration of fakirs and pseudo-religious leaders. We are constantly increasing the measure of liberty accorded the islanders, and next spring, if conditions warrant, we shall take a great stride forward in testing their capacity for self-government by summoning the first Filipino legislative assembly; and the way in which they stand this test will largely determine whether the self-government thus granted will be increased or decreased; for if we have erred at all in the Philippines it has been in proceeding too rapidly in the direction of granting a large measure of self-government. We are building roads. We have, for the immeasurable good of the people, arranged for the building of railroads. Let us also see to it that they are given free access to our markets. This nation owes no more imperative duty to itself and mankind than the duty of managing the affairs of all the islands under the American flag—the Philippines, Porto Rico, and Hawaii—so as to make it evident that it is in every way to their advantage that the flag should fly over them.

PORTO RICO

American citizenship should be conferred on the citizens of Porto Rico. The harbor of San Juan in Porto Rico should be dredged and improved. The expenses of the Federal court of Porto Rico should be met from the Federal Treasury. The administration of the affairs of Porto Rico, together with those of the Philippines, Hawaii, and our other insular possessions, should all be directed under one executive department; by preference the Department of State or the Department of War.

HAWAII

The needs of Hawaii are peculiar; every aid should be given the islands; and our efforts should be unceasing to develop them along the lines of a community of small freeholders, not of great planters with coolie-tilled estates. Situated as this Territory is, in the middle of the Pacific, there are duties imposed upon this small community which do not fall in like degree or manner upon any other American community. This warrants our treating it differently from the way in which we treat Territories contiguous to or surrounded by sister Territories or other States, and justifies the setting aside of a portion of our revenues to be expended for educational and internal improvements therein. Hawaii is now making an effort to secure immigration fit in the end to assume the duties and burdens of full American citizenship, and whenever the leaders in the various industries of those islands finally adopt our ideals and heartily join our administration in endeavoring to develop a middle class of substantial citizens, a way will then be found to deal with the commercial and industrial problems which now appear to them so serious. The best Americanism is that which aims for stability and permanency of prosperous citizenship, rather than immediate returns on large masses of capital.

ALASKA

Alaska's needs have been partially met, but there must be a complete reorganization of the governmental system, as I have before indicated to you. I ask your especial attention to this. Our fellow citizens who dwell on the shores of Puget Sound with characteristic energy are arranging to hold in Seattle the Alaska Yukon Pacific Exposition. Its special aims include the upbuilding of Alaska and the development of American commerce on the Pacific Ocean. This exposition, in its purposes and scope, should appeal not only to the people of the Pacific slope, but to the people of the United States at large. Alaska since it was bought has yielded to the government eleven millions of dollars of revenue, and has produced nearly three hundred millions of dollars in gold, furs, and fish. When properly developed it will become in large degree a land of homes. The countries bordering the Pacific Ocean have a population more numerous than that of all the countries of Europe; their annual foreign commerce amounts to over three billions of dollars, of which the share of the United States is some seven hundred millions of dollars. If this trade were thoroughly understood and pushed by our manufacturers and producers, the industries not only of the Pacific slope, but of all our country, and particularly of our cotton-growing States, would be greatly benefited. Of course, in order to get these benefits, we must treat fairly the countries with which we trade.

INTERNATIONAL GOOD-WILL

It is a mistake, and it betrays a spirit of foolish cynicism, to maintain that all international governmental action is, and must ever be, based upon mere selfishness, and that to advance ethical reasons for such action is always a sign of hypocrisy. This is no more necessarily true of the action of governments than of the action of individuals. It is a sure sign of a base nature always to ascribe base motives for the actions of others. Unquestionably no nation can afford to disregard proper considerations of self-interest, any more than a private individual can so do. But it is equally true that the average private individual in any really decent community does many actions with reference to other men in which he is guided, not by self-interest, but by public spirit, by regard for the rights of others, by a disinterested purpose to do good to others, and to raise the tone of the community as a whole. Similarly, a really great nation must often act, and as a matter of fact often does act, toward other nations in a spirit not in the least of mere self-interest, but paying heed chiefly to ethical reasons; and as the centuries go by this disinterestedness in international action, this tendency of the individuals comprising a nation to require that nation to act with justice toward its neighbors, steadily grows and strengthens. It is neither wise nor right for a nation to disregard its own needs, and it is foolish—and may be wicked—to think that other nations will disregard theirs. But it is wicked for a nation only to regard its own interest, and foolish to believe that such is the sole motive that actuates any other nation. It should be our steady aim to raise the ethical standard of national action just as we strive to raise the ethical standard of individual action.

Not only must we treat all nations fairly, but we must treat with justice and good-will all immigrants who come here under the law. Whether they are Catholic or Protestant, Jew or Gentile; whether they come from England or Germany, Russia, Japan, or Italy, matters nothing. All we have a right to question is the man's conduct. If he is honest and upright in his dealings with his neighbor and with the State, then he is entitled to respect and good treatment. Especially do we need to remember our duty to the stranger within our gates. It is the sure mark of a low civilization, a low morality, to abuse or discriminate against or in any way humiliate such stranger who has come here lawfully and who is conducting himself properly. To remember this is incumbent on every American citizen, and it is of course peculiarly incumbent on every government official, whether of the nation or of the several States.

ANTI-JAPANESE AGITATION

I am prompted to say this by the attitude of hostility here and there assumed toward the Japanese in this country. This hostility is sporadic and is limited to a very few places. Nevertheless, it is most discreditable to us as a people, and it may be fraught with the gravest consequences to the nation. The friendship between the United States and Japan has been continuous since the time, over half a century ago, when Commodore Perry, by his expedition to Japan, first opened the islands to Western civilization. Since then the growth of Japan has been literally astounding. There is not only nothing to parallel it, but nothing to approach it in the history of civilized mankind. Japan has a glorious and ancient past. Her civilization is older than that of the nations of northern Europe—the nations from whom the people of the United States have chiefly sprung. But fifty years ago Japan's development was still that of the Middle Ages. During that fifty years the progress of the country in every walk in life has been a marvel to mankind, and she now stands as one of the greatest of civilized nations; great in the arts of war and in the arts of peace; great in military, in industrial, in artistic development and achievement. Japanese soldiers and sailors have shown themselves equal in combat to any of whom history makes note. She has produced great generals and mighty admirals; her fighting men, afloat and ashore, show all the heroic courage, the unquestioning, unfaltering loyalty, the splendid indifference to hardship and death, which marked the Loyal Ronins; and they show also that they possess the highest ideal of patriotism. Japanese artists of every kind see their products eagerly sought for in all lands. The industrial and commercial development of Japan has been phenomenal; greater than that of any other country during the same period. At the same time the advance in science and philosophy is no less marked. The admirable management of the Japanese Red Cross during the late war, the efficiency and humanity of the Japanese officials, nurses, and doctors, won the respectful admiration of all acquainted with the facts. Through the Red Cross the Japanese people sent over $100,000 to the sufferers of San Francisco, and the gift was accepted with gratitude by our people. The courtesy of the Japanese, nationally and individually, has become proverbial. To no other country has there been such an increasing number of visitors from this land as to Japan. In return, Japanese have come here in great numbers. They are welcome, socially and intellectually, in all our colleges and institutions of higher learning, in all our professional and social bodies. The Japanese have won in a single generation the right to stand abreast of the foremost and most enlightened peoples of Europe and America; they have won on their own merits and by their own exertions the right to treatment on a basis of full and frank equality. The overwhelming mass of our people cherish a lively regard and respect for the people of Japan, and in almost every quarter of the Union the stranger from Japan is treated as he deserves; that is, he is treated as the stranger from any part of civilized Europe is and deserves to be treated. But here and there a most unworthy feeling has manifested itself toward the Japanese—the feeling that has been shown in shutting them out from the common schools in San Francisco, and in mutterings against them in one or two other places, because of their efficiency as workers. To shut them out from the public schools is a wicked absurdity, when there are no first-class colleges in the land, including the universities and colleges of California, which do not gladly welcome Japanese students and on which Japanese students do not reflect credit. We have as much to learn from Japan as Japan has to learn from us; and no nation is fit to teach unless it is also willing to learn. Throughout Japan Americans are well treated, and any failure on the part of Americans at home to treat the Japanese with a like courtesy and consideration is by just so much a confession of inferiority in our civilization.

Our nation fronts on the Pacific, just as it fronts on the Atlantic. We hope to play a constantly growing part in the great ocean of the Orient. We wish, as we ought to wish, for a great commercial development in our dealings with Asia; and it is out of the question that we should permanently have such development unless we freely and gladly extend to other nations the same measure of justice and good treatment which we expect to receive in return. It is only a very small body of our citizens that act badly. Where the Federal Government has power it will deal summarily with any such. Where the several States have power I earnestly ask that they also deal wisely and promptly with such conduct, or else this small body of wrong-doers may bring shame upon the great mass of their innocent and right-thinking fellows—that is, upon our nation as a whole. Good manners should be an international no less than an individual attribute. I ask fair treatment for the Japanese as I would ask fair treatment for Germans or Englishmen, Frenchmen, Russians, or Italians. I ask it as due to humanity and civilization. I ask it as due to ourselves because we must act uprightly toward all men.

NATURALIZATION OF JAPANESE

I recommend to the Congress that an act be passed specifically providing for the naturalization of Japanese who come here intending to become American citizens. One of the great embarrassments attending the performance of our international obligations is the fact that the statutes of the United States are entirely inadequate. They fail to give to the National Government sufficiently ample power, through United States courts and by the use of the army and navy, to protect aliens in the rights secured to them under solemn treaties which are the law of the land. I therefore earnestly recommend that the criminal and civil statutes of the United States be so amended and added to as to enable the President, acting for the United States Government, which is responsible in our international relations, to enforce the rights of aliens under treaties. Even as the law now is something can be done by the Federal Government toward this end, and in the matter now before me affecting the Japanese everything that it is in my power to do will be done, and all of the forces, military and civil, of the United States which I may lawfully employ will be so employed. There should, however, be no particle of doubt as to the power of the National Government completely to perform and enforce its own obligations to other nations. The mob of a single city may at any time perform acts of lawless violence against some class of foreigners which would plunge us into war. That city by itself would be powerless to make defense against the foreign power thus assaulted, and if independent of this government it would never venture to perform or permit the performance of the acts complained of. The entire power and the whole duty to protect the offending city or the offending community lies in the hands of the United States Government. It is unthinkable that we should continue a policy under which a given locality may be allowed to commit a crime against a friendly nation, and the United States Government limited, not to preventing the commission of the crime, but, in the last resort, to defending the people who have committed it against the consequences of their own wrong-doing.

CUBA

Last August an insurrection broke out in Cuba which it speedily grew evident that the existing Cuban Government was powerless to quell. This government was repeatedly asked by the then Cuban Government to intervene, and finally was notified by the President of Cuba that he intended to resign; that his decision was irrevocable; that none of the other constitutional officers would consent to carry on the government, and that he was powerless to maintain order. It was evident that chaos was impending, and there was every probability that if steps were not immediately taken by this government to try to restore order the representatives of various European nations in the island would apply to their respective governments for armed intervention in order to protect the lives and property of their citizens. Thanks to the preparedness of our navy, I was able immediately to send enough ships to Cuba to prevent the situation from becoming hopeless; and I furthermore despatched to Cuba the secretary of war and the assistant secretary of state, in order that they might grapple with the situation on the ground. All efforts to secure an agreement between the contending factions, by which they should themselves come to an amicable understanding and settle upon some modus vivendi—some provisional government of their own—failed. Finally the President of the republic resigned. The quorum of Congress assembled failed by deliberate purpose of its members, so that there was no power to act on his resignation, and the government came to a halt. In accordance with the so-called Platt amendment, which was embodied in the constitution of Cuba, I thereupon proclaimed a provisional government for the island, the secretary of war acting as provisional governor until he could be replaced by Mr. Magoon, the late minister to Panama and governor of the Canal Zone on the Isthmus; troops were sent to support them and to relieve the navy, the expedition being handled with most satisfactory speed and efficiency. The insurgent chiefs immediately agreed that their troops should lay down their arms and disband; and the agreement was carried out. The provisional government has left the personnel of the old government and the old laws, so far as might be, unchanged, and will thus administer the island for a few months until tranquillity can be restored, a new election properly held, and a new government inaugurated. Peace has come in the island; and the harvesting of the sugar-cane crop, the great crop of the island, is about to proceed.

When the election has been held and the new government inaugurated in peaceful and orderly fashion the provisional government will come to an end. I take this opportunity of expressing upon behalf of the American people, with all possible solemnity, our most earnest hope that the people of Cuba will realize the imperative need of preserving justice and keeping order in the island. The United States wishes nothing of Cuba except that it shall prosper morally and materially, and wishes nothing of the Cubans save that they shall be able to preserve order among themselves and therefore to preserve their independence. If the elections become a farce, and if the insurrectionary habit becomes confirmed in the island, it is absolutely out of the question that the island should continue independent; and the United States, which has assumed the sponsorship before the civilized world for Cuba's career as a nation, would again have to intervene and to see that the government was managed in such orderly fashion as to secure the safety of life and property. The path to be trodden by those who exercise self-government is always hard, and we should have every charity and patience with the Cubans as they tread this difficult path. I have the utmost sympathy with, and regard for, them; but I most earnestly adjure them solemnly to weigh their responsibilities and to see that when their new government is started it shall run smoothly, and with freedom from flagrant denial of right on the one hand, and from insurrectionary disturbances on the other.

CONFERENCE OF AMERICAN REPUBLICS

The Second International Conference of American Republics, held in Mexico in the years 1901–2, provided for the holding of the third conference within five years, and committed the fixing of the time and place and the arrangements for the conference to the governing board of the Bureau of American Republics, composed of the representatives of all the American nations in Washington. That board discharged the duty imposed upon it with marked fidelity and painstaking care, and upon the courteous invitation of the United States of Brazil the conference was held at Rio de Janeiro, continuing from the 23d of July to the 29th of August last. Many subjects of common interest to all the American nations were discussed by the conference, and the conclusions reached, embodied in a series of resolutions and proposed conventions, will be laid before you upon the coming in of the final report of the American delegates. They contain many matters of importance relating to the extension of trade, the increase of communication, the smoothing away of barriers to free intercourse, and the promotion of a better knowledge and good understanding between the different countries represented. The meetings of the conference were harmonious and the conclusions were reached with substantial unanimity. It is interesting to observe that in the successive conferences which have been held the representatives of the different American nations have been learning to work together effectively, for, while the First Conference in Washington in 1889, and the Second Conference in Mexico in 1901–2, occupied many months, with much time wasted in an unregulated and fruitless discussion, the Third Conference at Rio exhibited much of the facility in the practical despatch of business which characterizes permanent deliberative bodies, and completed its labors within the period of six weeks orignally allotted for its sessions.

Quite apart from the specific value of the conclusions reached by the conference, the example of the representatives of all the American nations engaging in harmonious and kindly consideration and discussion of subjects of common interest is itself of great and substantial value for the promotion of reasonable and considerate treatment of all international questions. The thanks of this country are due to the government of Brazil and to the people of Rio de Janeiro for the generous hospitality with which our delegates, in common with the others, were received, entertained, and facilitated in their work.

RELATIONS WITH CENTRAL AND SOUTH AMERICA

Incidentally to the meeting of the conference, the secretary of state visited the city of Rio de Janeiro and was cordially received by the conference, of which he was made an honorary president. The announcement of his intention to make this visit was followed by most courteous and urgent invitations from nearly all the countries of South America to visit them as the guest of their governments. It was deemed that by the acceptance of these invitations we might appropriately express the real respect and friendship in which we hold our sister republics of the southern continent, and the secretary, accordingly, visited Brazil, Uruguay, Argentina, Chile, Peru, Panama, and Colombia. He refrained from visiting Paraguay, Bolivia, and Ecuador only because the distance of their capitals from the seaboard made it impracticable with the time at his disposal. He carried with him a message of peace and friendship, and of strong desire for good understanding and mutual helpfulness; and he was everywhere received in the spirit of his message. The members of government, the press, the learned professions, the men of business, and the great masses of the people united everywhere in emphatic response to his friendly expressions and in doing honor to the country and cause which he represented.

In many parts of South America there has been much misunderstanding of the attitude and purposes of the United States toward the other American republics. An idea had become prevalent that our assertion of the Monroe Doctrine implied, or carried with it, an assumption of superiority, and of a right to exercise some kind of protectorate over the countries to whose territory that doctrine applies. Nothing could be farther from the truth. Yet that impression continued to be a serious barrier to good understanding, to friendly intercourse, to the introduction of American capital and the extension of American trade. The impression was so wide-spread that apparently it could not be reached by any ordinary means.

It was part of Secretary Root's mission to dispel this unfounded impression, and there is just cause to believe that he has succeeded. In an address to the Third Conference at Rio on the 31st of July—an address of such note that I send it in, together with this message—he said:

"We wish for no victories but those of peace; for no territory except our own; for no sovereignty except the sovereignty over ourselves. We deem the independence and equal rights of the smallest and weakest member of the family of nations entitled to as much respect as those of the greatest empire, and we deem the observance of that respect the chief guarantee of the weak against the oppression of the strong. We neither claim nor desire any rights or privileges or powers that we do not freely concede to every American republic. We wish to increase our prosperity, to extend our trade, to grow in wealth, in wisdom, and in spirit, but our conception of the true way to accomplish this is not to pull down others and profit by their ruin, but to help all friends to a common prosperity and a common growth, that we may all become greater and stronger together. Within a few months for the first time the recognized possessors of every foot of soil upon the American continents can be and I hope will be represented with the acknowledged rights of equal sovereign states in the great World Congress at The Hague. This will be the world's formal and final acceptance of the declaration that no part of the American continents is to be deemed subject to colonization. Let us pledge ourselves to aid each other in the full performance of the duty to humanity which that accepted declaration implies, so that in time the weakest and most unfortunate of our republics may come to march with equal step by the side of the stronger and more fortunate. Let us help each other to show that for all the races of men the liberty for which we have fought and labored is the twin sister of justice and peace. Let us unite in creating and maintaining and making effective an all-American public opinion, whose power shall influence international conduct and prevent international wrong, and narrow the causes of war, and forever preserve our free lands from the burden of such armaments as are massed behind the frontiers of Europe, and bring us ever nearer to the perfection of ordered liberty. So shall come security and prosperity, production and trade, wealth, learning, the arts, and happiness for us all."

These words appear to have been received with acclaim in every part of South America. They have my hearty approval, as I am sure they will have yours, and I cannot be wrong in the conviction that they correctly represent the sentiments of the whole American people. I cannot better characterize the true attitude of the United States in its assertion of the Monroe Doctrine than in the words of the distinguished former minister of foreign affairs of Argentina, Doctor Drago, in his speech welcoming Mr. Root at Buenos Ayres. He spoke of

"The traditional policy of the United States (which) without accentuating superiority or seeking preponderance, condemned the oppression of the nations of this part of the world and the control of their destinies by the great powers of Europe."

It is gratifying to know that in the great city of Buenos Ayres, upon the arches which spanned the streets, entwined with Argentine and American flags for the reception of our representative, there were emblazoned not only the names of Washington and Jefferson and Marshall, but also, in appreciative recognition of their services to the cause of South American independence, the names of James Monroe, John Quincy Adams, Henry Clay, and Richard Rush. We take especial pleasure in the graceful courtesy of the government of Brazil, which has given to the beautiful and stately building first used for the meeting of the conference the name of "Palacio Monroe." Our grateful acknowledgments are due to the governments and the people of all the countries visited by the secretary of state for the courtesy, the friendship, and the honor shown to our country in their generous hospitality to him.

In my message to you on the 5th of December, 1905, I called your attention to the embarrassment that might be caused to this government by the assertion by foreign nations of the right to collect by force of arms contract debts due by American republics to citizens of the collecting nation, and to the danger that the process of compulsory collection might result in the occupation of territory tending to become permanent. I then said:

"Our own government has always refused to enforce such contractual obligations on behalf of its citizens by an appeal to arms. It is much to be wished that all foreign governments would take the same view."

This subject was one of the topics of consideration at the conference at Rio and a resolution was adopted by that conference recommending to the respective governments represented "to consider the advisability of asking the Second Peace Conference at The Hague to examine the question of the compulsory collection of public debts, and, in general, means tending to diminish among nations conflicts of purely pecuniary origin."

This resolution was supported by the representatives of the United States in accordance with the following instructions:

"It has long been the established policy of the United States not to use its armed forces for the collection of ordinary contract debts due to its citizens by other governments. We have not considered the use of force for such a purpose consistent with that respect for the independent sovereignty of other members of the family of nations which is the most important principle of international law and the chief protection of weak nations against the oppression of the strong. It seems to us that the practice is injurious in its general effect upon the relations of nations and upon the welfare of weak and disordered states, whose development ought to be encouraged in the interests of civilization; that it offers frequent temptation to bullying and oppression and to unnecessary and unjustifiable warfare. We regret that other powers, whose opinions and sense of justice we esteem highly, have at times taken a different view and have permitted themselves, though we believe with reluctance, to collect such debts by force. It is doubtless true that the non-payment of public debts may be accompanied by such circumstances of fraud and wrongdoing or violation of treaties as to justify the use of force. This government would be glad to see an international consideration of the subject which shall discriminate between such cases and the simple non-performance of a contract with a private person, and a resolution in favor of reliance upon peaceful means in cases of the latter class.

"It is not felt, however, that the conference at Rio should undertake to make such a discrimination or to resolve upon such a rule. Most of the American countries are still debtor nations, while the countries of Europe are the creditors. If the Rio conference, therefore, were to take such action it would have the appearance of a meeting of debtors resolving how their creditors should act, and this would not inspire respect. The true course is indicated by the terms of the programme, which proposes to request the Second Hague Conference, where both creditors and debtors will be assembled, to consider the subject."

Last June trouble which had existed for some time between the republics of Salvador, Guatemala, and Honduras culminated in war—a war which threatened to be ruinous to the countries involved and very destructive to the commercial interests of Americans, Mexicans, and other foreigners who are taking an important part in the development of these countries. The thoroughly good understanding which exists between the United States and Mexico enabled this government and that of Mexico to unite in effective mediation between the warring republics; which mediation resulted, not without long-continued and patient effort, in bringing about a meeting of the representatives of the hostile powers on board a United States war-ship as neutral territory, and peace was there concluded; a peace which resulted in the saving of thousands of lives and in the prevention of an incalculable amount of misery and the destruction of property and of the means of livelihood. The Rio conference passed the following resolution in reference to this action:

"That the Third International American Conference shall address to the Presidents of the United States of America and of the United States of Mexico a note in which the conference which is being held at Rio expresses its satisfaction at the happy results of their mediation for the celebration of peace between the republics of Guatemala, Honduras, and Salvador."

This affords an excellent example of one way in which the influence of the United States can properly be exercised for the benefit of the peoples of the western hemisphere; that is, by action taken in concert with other American republics and therefore free from those suspicions and prejudices which might attach if the action were taken by one alone. In this way it is possible to exercise a powerful influence toward the substitution of considerate action in the spirit of justice for the insurrectionary or international violence which has hitherto been so great a hindrance to the development of many of our neighbors. Repeated examples of united action by several or many American republics in favor of peace, by urging cool and reasonable, instead of excited and belligerent, treatment of international controversies, cannot fail to promote the growth of a general public opinion among the American nations which will elevate the standards of international action, strengthen the sense of international duty among governments, and tell in favor of the peace of mankind.

PANAMA

I have just returned from a trip to Panama and shall report to you at length later on the whole subject of the Panama Canal.

COMMERCIAL RIGHTS IN MOROCCO

The Algeciras Convention, which was signed by the United States as well as by most of the powers of Europe, supersedes the previous convention of 1880, which was also signed both by the United States and a majority of the European powers. This treaty confers upon us equal commercial rights with all European countries and does not entail a single obligation of any kind upon us, and I earnestly hope it may be speedily ratified. To refuse to ratify it would merely mean that we forfeited our commercial rights in Morocco and would not achieve another object of any kind. In the event of such refusal we would be left for the first time in a hundred and twenty years without any commercial treaty with Morocco; and this at a time when we are everywhere seeking new markets and outlets for trade.

DESTRUCTION OF SEALS

The destruction of the Pribilof Islands fur-seals by pelagic sealing still continues. The herd which, according to the surveys made in 1874 by direction of the Congress, numbered 4,700,000, and which, according to the survey of both American and Canadian commissioners in 1891, amounted to 1,000,-000, has now been reduced to about 180,000. This result has been brought about by Canadian and some other sealing vessels killing the female seals while in the water during their annual pilgrimage to and from the south, or in search of food. As a rule the female seal when killed is pregnant, and also has an unweaned pup on land, so that, for each skin taken by pelagic sealing, as a rule, three lives are destroyed—the mother, the unborn offspring, and the nursing pup, which is left to starve to death. No damage whatever is done to the herd by the carefully regulated killing on land; the custom of pelagic sealing is solely responsible for all of the present evil, and is alike indefensible from the economic standpoint and from the standpoint of humanity.

In 1896 over 16,000 young seals were found dead from starvation on the Pribilof Islands. In 1897 it was estimated that since pelagic sealing began upward of 400,000 adult female seals had been killed at sea, and over 300,000 young seals had died of starvation as the result. The revolting barbarity of such a practice, as well as the wasteful destruction which it involves, needs no demonstration and is its own condemnation. The Bering Sea Tribunal, which sat in Paris in 1893, and which decided against the claims of the United States to exclusive jurisdiction in the waters of Bering Sea and to a property right in the fur-seals when outside of the three-mile limit, determined also upon certain regulations which the Tribunal considered sufficient for the proper protection and preservation of the fur-seal in, or habitually resorting to, the Bering Sea. The Tribunal by its regulations established a close season, from the 1st of May to the 31st of July, and excluded all killing in the waters within sixty miles around the Pribilof Islands. They also provided that the regulations which they had determined upon, with a view to the protection and preservation of the seals, should be submitted every five years to new examination, so as to enable both interested governments to consider whether, in the light of past experience, there was occasion for any modification thereof.

The regulations have proved plainly inadequate to accomplish the object of protection and preservation of the fur-seals, and for a long time this government has been trying in vain to secure from Great Britain such revision and modification of the regulations as were contemplated and provided for by the award of the Tribunal of Paris.

The process of destruction has been accelerated during recent years by the appearance of a number of Japanese vessels engaged in pelagic sealing. As these vessels have not been bound even by the inadequate limitations prescribed by the Tribunal of Paris, they have paid no attention either to the close season or to the sixty-mile limit imposed upon the Canadians, and have prosecuted their work up to the very islands themselves. On July 16 and 17 the crews from several Japanese vessels made raids upon the island of St. Paul, and before they were beaten off by the very meagre and insufficiently armed guard, they succeeded in killing several hundred seals and carrying off the skins of most of them. Nearly all the seals killed were females and the work was done with frightful barbarity. Many of the seals appear to have been skinned alive and many were found half-skinned and still alive. The raids were repelled only by the use of firearms, and five of the raiders were killed, two were wounded, and twelve captured, including the two wounded. Those captured have since been tried and sentenced to imprisonment. An attack of this kind has been wholly unlooked for, but such provision of vessels, arms, and ammunition will now be made that its repetition will not be found profitable.

Suitable representations regarding the incident have been made to the government of Japan, and we are assured that all practicable measures will be taken by that country to prevent any recurrence of the outrage. On our part, the guard on the island will be increased and better equipped and organized, and a better revenue-cutter patrol service about the islands will be established; next season a United States war-vessel will also be sent there.

We have not relaxed our efforts to secure an agreement with Great Britain for adequate protection of the seal-herd, and negotiations with Japan for the same purpose are in progress.

The laws for the protection of the seals within the jurisdiction of the United States need revision and amendment. Only the islands of St. Paul and St. George are now, in terms, included in the government reservation, and the other islands are also to be included. The landing of aliens as well as citizens upon the islands, without a permit from the Department of Commerce and Labor, for any purpose except in case of stress of weather or for water, should be prohibited under adequate penalties. The approach of vessels for the excepted purposes should be regulated. The authority of the government agents on the islands should be enlarged, and the chief agent should have the powers of a committing magistrate. The entrance of a vessel into the territorial waters surrounding the islands with intent to take seals should be made a criminal offense and cause of forfeiture. Authority for seizures in such cases should be given and the presence on any such vessel of seals or sealskins, or the paraphernalia for taking them, should be made *prima-facie* evidence of such intent. I recommend what legislation is needed to accomplish these ends; and I commend to your attention the report of Mr. Sims, of the Department of Commerce and Labor, on this subject.

In case we are compelled to abandon the hope of making arrangements with other governments to put an end to the hideous cruelty now incident to pelagic sealing, it will be a question for your serious consideration how far we should continue to protect and maintain the seal-herd on land with the result of continuing such a practice, and whether it is not better to end the practice by exterminating the herd ourselves in the most humane way possible.

SECOND HAGUE CONFERENCE

In my last message I advised you that the Emperor of Russia had taken the initiative in bringing about a second peace conference at The Hague. Under the guidance of Russia the arrangement of the preliminaries for such a conference has been progressing during the past year. Progress has necessarily been slow, owing to the great number of countries to be consulted upon every question that has arisen. It is a matter of satisfaction that all of the American republics have now, for the first time, been invited to join in the proposed conference.

The close connection between the subjects to be taken up by the Red Cross Conference held at Geneva last summer and the subjects which naturally would come before the Hague Conference made it apparent that it was desirable to have the work of the Red Cross Conference completed and considered by the different powers before the meeting at The Hague. The Red Cross Conference ended its labors on the 6th day of July, and the revised and amended convention, which was signed by the American delegates, will be promptly laid before the Senate.

By the special and highly appreciated courtesy of the governments of Russia and the Netherlands, a proposal to call the Hague Conference together at a time which would conflict with the Conference of the American Republics at Rio de Janeiro in August was laid aside. No other date has yet been suggested. A tentative programme for the conference has been proposed by the government of Russia, and the subjects which it enumerates are undergoing careful examination and consideration in preparation for the conference.

THE PEACE OF JUSTICE

It must ever be kept in mind that war is not merely justifiable, but imperative, upon honorable men, upon an honorable nation, where peace can only be obtained by the sacrifice of conscientious conviction or of national welfare. Peace is normally a great good, and normally it coincides with righteousness; but it is righteousness and not peace which should bind the conscience of a nation as it should bind the conscience of an individual; and neither a nation nor an individual can surrender conscience to another's keeping. Neither can a nation, which is an entity, and which does not die as individuals die, refrain from taking thought for the interest of the generations that are to come, no less than for the interest of the generation of to-day; and no public men have a right, whether from short-sightedness, from selfish indifference, or from sentimentality, to sacrifice national interests which are vital in character. A just war is in the long run far better for a nation's soul than the most prosperous peace obtained by acquiescence in wrong or injustice. Moreover, though it is criminal for a nation not to prepare for war, so that it may escape the dreadful consequences of being defeated in war, yet it must always be remembered that even to be defeated in war may be far better than not to have fought at all. As has been well and finely said, a beaten nation is not necessarily a disgraced nation; but the nation or man is disgraced if the obligation to defend right is shirked.

We should as a nation do everything in our power for the cause of honorable peace. It is morally as indefensible for a nation to commit a wrong upon another nation, strong or weak, as for an individual thus to wrong his fellows. We should do all in our power to hasten the day when there shall be peace among the nations—a peace based upon justice and not upon cowardly submission to wrong. We can accomplish a good deal in this direction, but we cannot accomplish everything, and the penalty of attempting to do too much would almost inevitably be to do worse than nothing; for it must be remembered that fantastic extremists are not in reality leaders of the causes which they espouse, but are ordinarily those who do most to hamper the real leaders of the cause and to damage the cause itself. As yet there is no likelihood of establishing any kind of international power, of whatever sort, which can effectively check wrong-doing, and in these circumstances it would be both a foolish and an evil thing for a great and free nation to deprive itself of the power to protect its own rights and even in exceptional cases to stand up for the rights of others. Nothing would more promote iniquity, nothing would further defer the reign upon earth of peace and righteousness, than for the free and enlightened peoples which, though with much stumbling and many shortcomings, nevertheless strive toward justice, deliberately to render themselves powerless while leaving every despotism and barbarism armed and able to work their wicked will. The chance for the settlement of disputes peacefully, by arbitration, now depends mainly upon the possession by the nations that mean to do right of sufficient armed strength to make their purpose effective.

THE NAVY

The United States navy is the surest guarantor of peace which this country possesses. It is earnestly to be wished that we would profit by the teachings of history in this matter. A strong and wise people will study its own failures no less than its triumphs, for there is wisdom to be learned from the study of both, of the mistake as well as of the success. For this purpose nothing could be more instructive than a rational study of the War of 1812, as it is told, for instance, by Captain Mahan. There was only one way in which that war could have been avoided. If during the preceding twelve years a navy relatively as strong as that which this country now has had been built up, and an army provided relatively as good as that which the country now has, there never would have been the slightest necessity of fighting the war; and if the necessity had arisen the war would under such circumstances have ended with our speedy and overwhelming triumph. But our people during those twelve years refused to make any preparations whatever, regarding either the army or the navy. They saved a million or two of dollars by so doing; and in mere money paid a hundredfold for each million they thus saved during the three years of war which followed—a war which brought untold suffering upon our people, which at one time threatened the gravest national disaster, and which, in spite of the necessity of waging it, resulted merely in what was in effect a drawn battle, while the balance of defeat and triumph was almost even.

I do not ask that we continue to increase our navy. I ask merely that it be maintained at its present strength; and this can be done only if we replace the obsolete and outworn ships by new and good ones, the equals of any afloat in any navy. To stop building ships for one year means that for that year the navy goes back instead of forward. The old battleship *Texas,* for instance, would now be of little service in a stand-up fight with a powerful adversary. The old double-turret monitors have outworn their usefulness, while it was a waste of money to build the modern single-turret monitors. All these ships should be replaced by others; and this can be done by a well-settled programme of providing for the building each year of at least one first-class battleship equal in size and speed to any that any nation is at the same time building; the armament presumably to consist of as large a number as possible of very heavy guns of one caliber, together with smaller guns to repel torpedo attack; while there should be heavy armor, turbine-engines, and in short, every modern device. Of course, from time to time, cruisers, colliers, torpedo-boat destroyers or torpedo-boats, will have to be built also. All this, be it remembered, would not increase our navy, but would merely keep it at its present strength. Equally of course, the ships will be absolutely useless if the men aboard them are not so trained that they can get the best possible service out of the formidable but delicate and complicated mechanisms intrusted to their care. The marksmanship of our men has so improved during the last five years that I deem it within bounds to say that the navy is more than twice as efficient, ship for ship, as half a decade ago. The navy can only attain proper efficiency if enough officers and men are provided, and if these officers and men are given the chance (and required to take advantage of it) to stay continually at sea and to exercise the fleets singly and above all in squadron, the exercise to be of every kind and to include unceasing practice at the guns, conducted under conditions that will test marksmanship in time of war.

MILITARY AND NAVAL TRAINING

In both the army and the navy there is urgent need that everything possible should be done to maintain the highest standard for the personnel, alike as regards the officers and the enlisted men. I do not believe that in any service there is a finer body of enlisted men and of junior officers than we have in both the army and the navy, including the Marine

Corps. All possible encouragement to the enlisted men should be given, in pay and otherwise, and everything practicable done to render the service attractive to men of the right type. They should be held to the strictest discharge of their duty, and in them a spirit should be encouraged which demands not the mere performance of duty, but the performance of far more than duty, if it conduces to the honor and the interest of the American nation; and in return the amplest consideration should be theirs.

West Point and Annapolis already turn out excellent officers. We do not need to have these schools made more scholastic. On the contrary we should never lose sight of the fact that the aim of each school is to turn out a man who shall be above everything else a fighting man. In the army in particular it is not necessary that either the cavalry or infantry officer should have special mathematical ability. Probably in both schools the best part of the education is the high standard of character and of professional morale which it confers.

But in both services there is urgent need for the establishment of a principle of selection which will eliminate men after a certain age if they cannot be promoted from the subordinate ranks, and which will bring into the higher ranks fewer men, and these at an earlier age. This principle of selection will be objected to by good men of mediocre capacity, who are fitted to do well while young in the lower positions, but who are not fitted to do well when at an advanced age they come into positions of command and of great responsibility. But the desire of these men to be promoted to positions which they are not competent to fill should not weigh against the interest of the navy and the country. At present our men, especially in the navy, are kept far too long in the junior grades, and then, at much too advanced an age, are put quickly through the senior grades, often not attaining to these senior grades until they are too old to be of real use in them; and if they are of real use, being put through them so quickly that little benefit to the navy comes from their having been in them at all.

The navy has one great advantage over the army in the fact that the officers of high rank are actually trained in the continual performance of their duties; that is, in the management of the battleships and armored cruisers gathered into fleets. This is not true of the army officers, who rarely have corresponding chances to exercise command over troops under service conditions. The conduct of the Spanish War showed the lamentable loss of life, the useless extravagance, and the inefficiency certain to result, if during peace the high officials of the War and Navy Departments are praised and rewarded only if they save money at no matter what cost to the efficiency of the service, and if the higher officers are given no chance whatever to exercise and practise command. For years prior to the Spanish War the secretaries of war were praised chiefly if they practised economy; while economy, especially in connection with the Quartermaster, Commissary, and Medical Departments, was directly responsible for most of the mismanagement that occurred in the war itself—and parenthetically be it observed that the very people who clamored for the misdirected economy in the first place were foremost to denounce the mismanagement, loss, and suffering which were primarily due to this same misdirected economy and to the lack of preparation it involved. There should soon be an increase in the number of men for our coast defenses; these men should be of the right type and properly trained; and there should therefore be an increase of pay for certain skilled grades, especially in the coast artillery. Money should be appropriated to permit troops to be massed in body and exercised in manœuvres, particularly in marching. Such exercise during the summer just passed has been of incalculable benefit to the army and should under no circumstances be discontinued. If on these practice marches and in these manœuvres elderly officers prove unable to bear the strain, they should be retired at once, for the fact is conclusive as to their unfitness for war; that is, for the only purpose because of which they should be allowed to stay in the service. It is a real misfortune to have scores of small company or regimental posts scattered throughout the country; the army should be gathered in a few brigade or division posts; and the generals should be practised in handling the men in masses. Neglect to provide for all of this means to incur the risk of future disaster and disgrace.

The readiness and efficiency of both the army and navy in dealing with the recent sudden crisis in Cuba illustrate afresh their value to the nation. This readiness and efficiency would have been very much less had it not been for the existence of the general staff in the army and the general board in the navy; both are essential to the proper development and use of our military forces afloat and ashore. The troops that were sent to Cuba were handled flawlessly. It was the swiftest mobilization and despatch of troops oversea ever accomplished by our government. The expedition landed completely equipped and ready for immediate service, several of its organizations hardly remaining in Havana overnight before splitting up into detachments and going to their several posts. It was a fine demonstration of the value and efficiency of the general staff. Similarly, it was owing in large part to the general board that the navy was able at the outset to meet the Cuban crisis with such instant efficiency; ship after ship appearing on the shortest notice at any threatened point, while the Marine Corps in particular performed indispensable service. The army and navy war colleges are of incalculable value to the two services, and they co-operate with constantly increasing efficiency and importance.

The Congress has most wisely provided for a national board for the promotion of rifle practice. Excellent results have already come from this law, but it does not go far enough. Our Regular Army is so small that in any great war we would have to trust mainly to volunteers; and in such event these volunteers should already know how to shoot; for if a soldier has the fighting edge, and ability to take care of himself in the open, his efficiency on the line of battle is almost directly proportionate to excellence in marksmanship. We should establish shooting-galleries in all the large public and military schools, should maintain national target ranges in different parts of the country, and should in every way encourage the formation of rifle-clubs throughout all parts of the land. The little republic of Switzerland offers us an excellent example in all matters connected with building up an efficient citizen soldiery.

VIII

SEVENTH ANNUAL MESSAGE[1]

To the Senate and House of Representatives:
No nation has greater resources than ours, and I think it can be truthfully said that the citizens of no nation possess greater energy and industrial ability. In no nation are the fundamental business conditions sounder than in ours at this very moment; and it is foolish, when such is the case, for people to hoard money instead of keeping it in sound banks; for it is such hoarding that is the immediate occasion of money stringency. Moreover, as a rule, the business of our people is conducted with honesty and probity, and this applies alike to farm and factories, to railroads and banks, to all our legitimate commercial enterprises.

REGULATION OF CORPORATIONS

In any large body of men, however, there are certain to be some who are dishonest, and if the conditions are such that these men prosper or commit their misdeeds with impunity, their example is a very evil thing for the community. Where these men are business men of great sagacity and of temperament both unscrupulous and reckless, and where the conditions are such that they act without supervision or control and at first without effective check from public opinion, they delude many innocent people into making investments or embarking in kinds of business that are really unsound. When the misdeeds of these successfully dishonest men are discovered, suffering comes not only upon them, but upon the innocent men whom they have misled. It is a painful awakening, whenever it oc-

[1] Dated, the White House, December 3, 1907.

410

curs; and, naturally, when it does occur those who suffer are apt to forget that the longer it was deferred the more painful it would be. In the effort to punish the guilty it is both wise and proper to endeavor so far as possible to minimize the distress of those who have been misled by the guilty. Yet it is not possible to refrain because of such distress from striving to put an end to the misdeeds that are the ultimate causes of the suffering, and, as a means to this end, where possible to punish those responsible for them. There may be honest differences of opinion as to many governmental policies; but surely there can be no such differences as to the need of unflinching perseverance in the war against successful dishonesty.

In my message to the Congress on December 5, 1905, I said:

"If the folly of man mars the general well-being, then those who are innocent of the folly will have to pay part of the penalty incurred by those who are guilty of the folly. A panic brought on by the speculative folly of part of the business community would hurt the whole business community; but such stoppage of welfare, though it might be severe, would not be lasting. In the long run, the one vital factor in the permanent prosperity of the country is the high individual character of the average American worker, the average American citizen, no matter whether his work be mental or manual, whether he be farmer or wage-worker, business man or professional man.

"In our industrial and social system the interests of all men are so closely intertwined that in the immense majority of cases a straight-dealing man, who by his efficiency, by his ingenuity and industry, benefits himself, must also benefit others. Normally, the man of great productive capacity who becomes rich by guiding the labor of many other men does so by enabling them to produce more than they could produce without his guidance; and both he and they share in the benefit, which comes also to the public at large. The superficial fact that the sharing may be unequal must never blind us to the underlying fact that there is this sharing, and that the benefit comes in some degree to each man concerned. Normally, the wage-worker, the man of small means, and the average consumer, as well as the average producer, are all alike helped by making conditions such that the man of exceptional business ability receives an exceptional reward for his ability. Something can be done by legislation to help the general prosperity; but no such help of a permanently beneficial character can be given to the less able and less fortunate save as the results of a policy which shall inure to the advantage of all industrious and efficient people who act decently; and this is only another way of saying that any benefit which comes to the less able and less fortunate must of necessity come even more to the more able and more fortunate. If, therefore, the less fortunate man is moved by envy of his more fortunate brother to strike at the conditions under which they have both, though unequally, prospered, the result will assuredly be that while damage may come to the one struck at, it will visit with an even heavier load the one who strikes the blow. Taken as a whole, we must all go up or go down together.

"Yet, while not merely admitting, but insisting upon this, it is also true that where there is no governmental restraint or supervision some of the exceptional men use their energies, not in ways that are for the common good, but in ways which tell against this common good. The fortunes amassed through corporate organization are now so large, and vest such power in those that wield them, as to make it a matter of necessity to give to the sovereign—that is, to the government, which represents the people as a whole—some effective power of supervision over their corporate use. In order to insure a healthy social and industrial life, every big corporation should be held responsible by, and be accountable to, some sovereign strong enough to control its conduct. I am in no sense hostile to corporations. This is an age of combination, and any effort to prevent all combination will be not only useless, but in the end vicious, because of the contempt for law which the failure to enforce law inevitably produces. We should, more-over, recognize in cordial and ample fashion the immense good effected by corporate agencies in a country such as ours, and the wealth of intellect, energy, and fidelity devoted to their service, and therefore normally to the service of the public, by their officers and directors. The corporaton has come to stay, just as the trade-union has come to stay. Each can do and has done great good. Each should be favored so long as it does good. But each should be sharply checked where it acts against law and justice.

". . . The makers of our National Constitution pro-vided especially that the regulation of interstate commerce should come within the sphere of the general government. The arguments in favor of their taking this stand were even then overwhelming. But they are far stronger to-day, in view of the enormous development of great business agencies, usually corporate in form. Experience has shown conclusively that it is useless to try to get any adequate regulations and supervision of these great corporations by State action. Such regulation and supervision can only be effectively exercised by a sovereign whose jurisdiction is coextensive with the field of work of the corporations—that is, by the National Government. I believe that this regulation and supervision can be obtained by the enactment of law by the Congress. . . . Our steady aim should be by legislation, cautiously and carefully under-taken, but resolutely persevered in, to assert the sovereignty of the National Government by affirmative action.

"This is only in form an innovation. In substance it is merely a restoration; for from the earliest time such regula-tion of industrial activities has been recognized in the action of the lawmaking bodies; and all that I propose is to meet the changed conditions in such manner as will prevent the commonwealth abdicating the power it has always possessed, not only in this country, but also in England before and since this country became a separate nation.

"It has been a misfortune that the national laws on this

subject have hitherto been of a negative or prohibitive rather than an affirmative kind, and still more that they have in part sought to prohibit what could not be effectively prohibited, and have in part in their prohibitions confounded what should be allowed and what should not be allowed. It is generally useless to try to prohibit all restraint on competition, whether this restraint be reasonable or unreasonable; and where it is not unless it is generally hurtful. . . . The successful prosecution of one device to evade the law immediately develops another device to accomplish the same purpose. What is needed is not sweeping prohibition of every arrangement, good or bad, which may tend to restrict competition, but such adequate supervision and regulation as will prevent any restriction of competition from being to the detriment of the public, as well as such supervision and regulation as will prevent other abuses in no way connected with restriction of competition."

I have called your attention in these quotations to what I have already said because I am satisfied that it is the duty of the National Government to embody in action the principles thus expressed.

No small part of the trouble that we have comes from carrying to an extreme the national virtue of self-reliance, of independence in initiative and action. It is wise to conserve this virtue and to provide for its fullest exercise, compatible with seeing that liberty does not become a liberty to wrong others. Unfortunately, this is the kind of liberty that the lack of all effective regulation inevitably breeds. The founders of the Constitution provided that the National Government should have complete and sole control of interstate commerce. There was then practically no interstate business save such as was conducted by water, and this the National Government at once proceeded to regulate in thoroughgoing and effective fashion. Conditions have now so wholly changed that the interstate commerce by water is insignificant compared with the amount that goes by land, and almost all big business concerns are now engaged in interstate commerce. As a result, it can be but partially and imperfectly controlled or regulated by the action of any one of the several States; such action inevitably tending to be either too drastic or else too lax, and in either case ineffective for purposes of justice. Only the National Government can in thoroughgoing fashion exercise the needed control. This does not mean that there should be any extension of Federal authority, for such authority already exists under the Constitution in amplest and most far-reaching form; but it does mean that there should be an extension of Federal activity. This is not advocating centralization. It is merely looking facts in the face, and realizing that centralization in business has already come and cannot be avoided or undone, and that the public at large can only protect itself from certain evil effects of this business centralization by providing better methods for the exercise of control through the authority already centralized in the National Government by the Constitution itself. There must be no halt in the healthy constructive course of action which this nation has elected to pursue, and has steadily pursued, during the last six years, as shown both in the legislation of the Congress and the administration of the law by the Department of Justice. The most vital need is in connection with the railroads. As to these, in my judgment there should now be either a national incorporation act or a law licensing railway companies to engage in interstate commerce upon certain conditions. The law should be so framed as to give to the Interstate Commerce Commission power to pass upon the future issue of securities, while ample means should be provided to enable the commission, whenever in its judgment it is necessary, to make a physical valuation of any railroad. As I stated in my message to the Congress a year ago, railroads should be given power to enter into agreements, subject to these agreements being made public in minute detail and to the consent of the Interstate Commerce Commission being first obtained. Until the National Government assumes proper control of interstate commerce, in the exercise of the authority it already possesses, it will be impossible either to give or to get from the railroads full justice. The railroads and all other great corporations will do well to recognize that this control must come; the only question is as to what governmental body can most wisely exercise it. The courts will determine the limits within which the Federal authority can exercise it, and there will still remain ample work within each State for the railway commission of that State; and the National Interstate Commission will work in harmony with the several State commissions, each within its own province, to achieve the desired end.

Moreover in my judgment there should be additional legislation looking to the proper control of the great business concerns engaged in interstate business, this control to be exercised for their own benefit and prosperity no less than for the protection of investors and of the general public. As I have repeatedly said in messages to the Congress and elsewhere, experience has definitely shown not merely the unwisdom but the futility of endeavoring to put a stop to all business combinations. Modern industrial conditions are such that combination is not only necessary but inevitable. It is so in the world of business just as it is so in the world of labor, and it is as idle to desire to put an end to all corporations, to all big combinations of capital, as to desire to put an end to combinations of labor. Corporation and labor-union alike have come to stay. Each if properly managed is a source of good and not evil. Whenever in either there is evil, it should be promptly held to account; but it should receive hearty encouragement so long as it is properly managed. It is profoundly immoral to put or keep on the statute-books a law, nominally in the interest of public morality that really puts a premium upon public immorality, by undertaking to forbid honest men from doing what must be done under modern business conditions, so that the law itself provides that its own infraction must be the condition precedent upon business success. To aim at the accomplishment of too much usually means the accomplishment of too little, and often the doing of positive damage. In my message to the Congress a year ago, in speaking of the antitrust laws, I said:

"The actual working of our laws has shown that the effort to prohibit all combination, good or bad, is noxious where it is not ineffective. Combination of capital, like combination of labor, is a necessary element in our present industrial system. It is not possible completely to prevent it; and if it were possible, such complete prevention would do damage to the body politic. What we need is not vainly to try to prevent all combination, but to secure such rigorous and adequate control and supervision of the combinations as to prevent their injuring the public, or existing in such forms as inevitably to threaten injury. . . . It is unfortunate that our present laws should forbid all combinations instead of sharply discriminating between those combinations which do evil. . . . Often railroads would like to combine for the purpose of preventing a big shipper from maintaining improper advantages at the expense of small shippers and of the general public. Such a combination, instead of being forbidden by law, should be favored. . . . It is a public evil to have on the statute-books a law incapable of full enforcement, because both judges and juries realize that its full enforcement would destroy the business of the country; for the result is to make decent men violators of the law against their will, and to put a premium on the behavior of the wilful wrong-doers. Such a result in turn tends to throw the decent man and the wilful wrong-doer into close association, and in the end to drag down the former to the latter's level; for the man who becomes a lawbreaker in one way unhappily tends to lose all respect for law and to be willing to break it in many ways. No more scathing condemnation could be visited upon a law than is contained in the words of the Interstate Commerce Commission when, in commenting upon the fact that the numerous joint traffic associations do technically violate the law, they say: 'The decision of the United States Supreme Court in the trans-Missouri case and the Joint Traffic Association case has produced no practical effect upon the railway operations of the country. Such associations, in fact, exist now as they did before these decisions, and with the same general effect. In justice to all parties, we ought probably to add that it is difficult to see how our interstate railways could be operated with due regard to the interest of the shipper and the railway without concerted action of the kind afforded through these associations.'

"This means that the law as construed by the Supreme Court is such that the business of the country cannot be conducted without breaking it."

As I have elsewhere said:

"All this is substantially what I have said over and over again. Surely it ought not to be necessary to say that it in no shape or way represents any hostility to corporations as such. On the contrary, it means a frank recognition of the fact that combinations of capital, like combinations of labor, are a natural result of modern conditions and of our national development. As far as in my ability lies my endeavor is and will be to prevent abuse of power by either and to favor both so long as they do well. The aim of the National Government is quite as much to favor and protect honest corporations, honest business men of wealth, as to bring to justice those individuals and corporations representing dishonest methods. Most certainly there will be no relaxation by the government authorities in the effort to get at any great railroad wrecker —any man who by clever swindling devices robs investors, oppresses wage-workers, and does injustice to the general public. But any such move as this is in the interest of honest railway operators, of honest corporations, and of those who, when they invest their small savings in stocks and bonds, wish to be assured that these will represent money honestly expended for legitimate business purposes. To confer upon the National Government the power for which I ask would be a check upon over-capitalization and upon the clever gamblers who benefit by overcapitalization. But it alone would mean an increase in the value, an increase in the safety of the stocks and bonds of law-abiding, honestly managed railroads, and would render it far easier to market their securities. I believe in proper publicity. There has been complaint of some of the investigations recently carried on, but those who complain should put the blame where it belongs—upon the misdeeds which are done in darkness and not upon the investigations which brought them to light. The Administration is responsible for turning on the light, but it is not responsible for what the light showed. I ask for full power to be given the Federal Government, because no single State can by legislation effectually cope with these powerful corporations engaged in interstate commerce, and, while doing them full justice, exact from them in return full justice to others. The conditions of railroad activity, the conditions of our immense interstate commerce, are such as to make the central government alone competent to exercise full supervision and control.

"The grave abuses in individual cases of railroad management in the past represent wrongs not merely to the general public, but, above all, wrongs to fair-dealing and honest corporations and men of wealth, because they excite a popular anger and distrust which from the very nature of the case tends to include in the sweep of its resentment good and bad alike. From the standpoint of the public I cannot too earnestly say that as soon as the natural and proper resentment aroused by these abuses becomes indiscriminate and unthinking, it also becomes not merely unwise and unfair, but calculated to defeat the very ends which those feeling it have in view. There has been plenty of dishonest work by corporations in the past. There will not be the slightest let-up in the effort to hunt down and punish every dishonest man. But the bulk of our business is honestly done. In the natural indignation the people feel over the dishonesty, it is essential that they should not lose their heads and get drawn into an indiscriminate raid upon all corporations, all people of wealth, whether they do well or ill. Out of any such wild movement good will not come, cannot come, and never has come. On the contrary, the surest way to invite reaction is to follow the lead of either demagogue or visionary in a sweeping assault upon property values and upon public confidence, which would work incalculable damage in the business world and would produce such distrust of the agitators that in the revulsion the distrust would extend to honest men who, in sincere and sane fashion, are trying to remedy the evils."

The antitrust law should not be repealed; but it should be made both more efficient and more in harmony with actual conditions. It should be so amended as to forbid only the kind of combination which does harm to the general public, such amendment to be accompanied by, or to be an incident of, a grant of supervisory power to the government over these big concerns engaged in interstate business. This should be accompanied by provision for the compulsory publication of accounts and the subjection of books and papers to the inspection of the government officials. A beginning has already been made for such supervision by the establishment of the Bureau of Corporations.

The antitrust law should not prohibit combinations that do no injustice to the public, still less those the existence of which is on the whole of benefit to the public. But even if this feature of the law were abolished, there would remain as an equally objectionable feature the difficulty and delay now incident to its enforcement. The government must now submit to irksome and repeated delay before obtaining a final decision of the courts upon proceedings instituted, and even a favorable decree may mean an empty victory. Moreover, to attempt to control these corporations by lawsuits means to impose upon both the Department of Justice and the courts an impossible burden; it is not feasible to carry on more than a limited number of such suits. Such a law to be really effective must of course be administered by an executive body, and not merely by means of lawsuits. The design should be to prevent the abuses incident to the creation of unhealthy and improper combinations, instead of waiting until they are in existence and then attempting to destroy them by civil or criminal proceedings.

A combination should not be tolerated if it abuse the power acquired by combination to the public detriment. No corporation or association of any kind should be permitted to engage in foreign or interstate commerce that is formed for the purpose of, or whose operations create, a monoply or general control of the production, sale, or distribution of any one or more of the prime necessities of life or articles of general use and necessity. Such combinations are against public policy; they violate the common law; the doors of the courts are closed to those who are parties to them, and I believe the Congress can close the channels of interstate commerce against them for its protection. The law should make its prohibitions and permissions as clear and definite as possible, leaving the least possible room for arbitrary action, or allegation of such action, on the part of the Executive, or of divergent interpretations by the courts. Among the points to be aimed at should be the prohibition of unhealthy competition, such as by rendering service at an actual loss for the purpose of crushing out competition, the prevention of inflation of capital, and the prohibition of a corporation's making exclusive trade with itself a condition of having any trade with itself. Reasonable agreements between, or combination of, corporations should be permitted, provided they are submitted to and approved by some appropriate government body.

The Congress has the power to charter corporations to engage in interstate and foreign commerce, and a general law can be enacted under the provisions of which existing corporations could take out Federal charters and new Federal corporations could be created. An essential provision of such a law should be a method of predetermining by some Federal board or commission whether the applicant for a Federal charter was an association or combination within the restrictions of the Federal law. Provision should also be made for complete publicity in all matters affecting the public and complete protection to the investing public and the shareholders in the matter of issuing corporate securities. If an incorporation law is not deemed advisable, a license act for big interstate corporations might be enacted; or a combination of the two might be tried. The supervision established might be analogous to that now exercised over national banks. At least, the antitrust act should be supplemented by specific prohibitions of the methods which experience has shown have been of most service in enabling monopolistic combinations to crush out competition. The real owners of a corporation should be compelled to do business in their own name. The right to hold stock in other corporations should hereafter be denied to interstate corporations, unless on approval by the government officials, and a prerequisite to such approval should be the listing with the government of all owners and stockholders, both by the corporation owning such stock and by the corporation in which such stock is owned.

To confer upon the National Government, in connection with the amendment I advocate in the antitrust law, power of supervision over big business concerns engaged in interstate commerce, would benefit them as it has benefited the national banks. In the recent business crisis it is noteworthy that the institutions which failed were institutions which were not under the supervision and control of the National Government. Those which were under national control stood the test.

National control of the kind above advocated would be to the benefit of every well-managed railway. From the standpoint of the public there is need for additional tracks, additional terminals, and improvements in the actual handling of the railroads, and all this as rapidly as possible. Ample, safe, and speedy transportation facilities are even more necessary than cheap transportation. Therefore, there is need for the investment of money which will provide for all these things while at the same time securing as far as is possible better wages and shorter hours for their employees. Therefore, while there must be just and reasonable regulation of rates, we should be the first to protest against any arbitrary and unthinking movement to cut them down without the fullest and most careful consideration of all interests concerned and of the actual needs of the situation. Only a special body of men acting for the National Government under authority conferred upon it by the Congress is competent to pass judgment on such a matter.

Those who fear, from any reason, the extension of Federal activity will do well to study the history not only of the national banking act but of the pure-food law, and notably the meat-inspection law recently enacted. The pure-food law was opposed so violently that its passage was delayed for a decade; yet it has worked unmixed and immediate good. The meat-inspection law was even more violently assailed; and the same men who now denounce the attitude of the National Government in seeking to oversee and control the workings of interstate common carriers and business concerns, then asserted that we were "discrediting and ruining a great American industry." Two years have not elapsed, and already it has become evident that the great benefit the law confers upon the public is accompanied by an equal benefit to the reputable packing establishments. The latter are better off under the law than they were without it. The benefit to interstate common carriers and business concerns from the legislation I advocate would be equally marked.

Incidentally, in the passage of the pure-food law the action of the various State food and dairy commissioners showed in striking fashion how much good for the whole people results from the hearty co-operation of the Federal and State officials in securing a given reform. It is primarily to the action of these State commissioners that we owe the enactment of this law; for they aroused the people, first to demand the enactment and enforcement of State laws on the subject, and then the enactment of the Federal law, without which the State laws were largely ineffective. There must be the closest co-operation between the National and State governments in administering these laws.

THE CURRENCY

In my message to the Congress a year ago I spoke as follows of the currency:

"I especially call your attention to the condition of our currency laws. The national-bank act has ably served a great purpose in aiding the enormous business development of the country, and within ten years there has been an increase in circulation per capita from $21.41 to $33.08. For several years evidence has been accumulating that additional legislation is needed. The recurrence of each crop season emphasizes the defects of the present laws. There must soon be a revision of them, because to leave them as they are means to incur liability of business disaster. Since your body adjourned there has been a fluctuation in the interest on call money from two per cent to thirty per cent, and the fluctuation was even greater during the preceding six months. The secretary of the treasury had to step in and by wise action put a stop to the most violent period of oscillation. Even worse than such fluctuation is the advance in commercial rates and the uncertainty felt in the sufficiency of credit even at high rates. All commercial interests suffer during each crop period. Excessive rates for call money in New York attract money from the interior banks into the speculative field. This depletes the fund that would otherwise be available for commercial uses, and commercial borrowers are forced to pay abnormal rates, so that each fall a tax, in the shape of increased interest charges, is placed on the whole commerce of the country.

"The mere statement of these facts shows that our present system is seriously defective. There is need of a change. Unfortunately, however, many of the proposed changes must be ruled from consideration because they are complicated, are not easy of comprehension, and tend to disturb existing rights and interests. We must also rule out any plan which would materially impair the value of the United States two per cent bonds now pledged to secure circulation, the issue of which was made under conditions peculiarly creditable to the Treasury. I do not press any especial plan. Various plans have recently been proposed by expert committees of bankers. Among the plans which are possibly feasible and which certainly should receive your consideration is that repeatedly brought to your attention by the present secretary of the treasury, the essential features of which have been approved by many prominent bankers and business men. According to this plan national banks should be permitted to issue a specified proportion of their capital in notes of a given kind, the issue to be taxed at so high a rate as to drive the notes back when not wanted in legitimate trade. This plan would not permit the issue of currency to give banks additional profits, but to meet the emergency presented by times of stringency.

"I do not say that this is the right system. I only advance it to emphasize my belief that there is need for the adoption of some system which shall be automatic and open to all sound banks, so as to avoid all possibility of discrimination and favoritism. Such a plan would tend to prevent the spasms of high money and speculation which now obtain in the New York market; for at present there is too much currency at certain seasons of the year, and its accumulation at New York tempts bankers to lend it at low rates for speculative purposes; whereas at other times when the crops are being moved there is urgent need for a large but temporary increase in the currency supply. It must never be forgotten that this question concerns business men generally quite as much as bankers; especially is this true of stockmen, farmers, and business men in the West; for at present at certain seasons of the year the difference in interest rates between the East and the West is from six to ten per cent, whereas in Canada the corresponding difference is but two per cent. Any plan must, of course, guard the interests of Western and Southern bankers as carefully as it guards the interests of New York or Chicago bankers, and must be drawn from the standpoints of the farmer and the merchant no less than from the standpoints of the city banker and the country banker."

I again urge on the Congress the need of immediate attention to this matter. We need a greater elasticity in our currency; provided, of course, that we recognize the even greater need of a safe and secure currency. There must always be the most rigid examination by the national authorities. Provision should be made for an emergency currency. The emergency issue should, of course, be made with an effective guarantee, and upon conditions carefully prescribed by the government. Such emergency issue must be based on adequate securities approved by the government, and must be issued under a heavy tax. This would permit currency being issued when the demand for it was urgent, while securing its requirement as the demand fell off. It is worth investigating to determine whether officers and directors of national banks should ever be allowed to loan to themselves. Trust companies should be subject to the same supervision as banks; legislation to this effect should be enacted for the District of Columbia and the Territories.

Yet we must also remember that even the wisest legislation on the subject can only accomplish a certain amount. No legislation can by any possibility guarantee the business community against the results of speculative folly any more than it can guarantee an individual against the results of his extravagance. When an individual mortgages his house to buy an automobile he invites disaster; and when wealthy men, or men who pose as such, or are unscrupulously or foolishly eager to become such, indulge in reckless speculation—especially if it is accompanied by dishonesty—they jeopardize not only their own future but the future of all their innocent fellow citizens, for they expose the whole business community to panic and distress.

REVISION OF THE TARIFF

The income account of the nation is in a most satisfactory condition. For the six fiscal years ending with the 1st of July last, the total expenditures and revenues of the National Government, exclusive of the postal revenues and expenditures, were, in round numbers, revenues, $3,465,000,000, and expenditures, $3,275,000,000. The net excess of income over expenditures, including in the latter the $50,000,000 expended for the Panama Canal, was $190,000,000 for the six years, an average of about $31,000,000 a year. This represents an approximation between income and outgo which it would be hard to improve. The satisfactory working of the present tariff law has been chiefly responsible for this excellent showing. Nevertheless, there is an evident and constantly growing feeling among our people that the time is rapidly approaching when our system of revenue legislation must be revised.

This country is definitely committed to the protective system and any effort to uproot it could not but cause wide-spread industrial disaster. In other words, the principle of the present tariff law could not with wisdom be changed. But in a country of such phenomenal growth as ours it is probably well that every dozen years or so the tariff laws should be carefully scrutinized so as to see that no excessive or improper benefits are conferred thereby, that proper revenue is provided, and that our foreign trade is encouraged. There must always be as a minimum a tariff which will not only allow for the collection of an ample revenue but which will at least make good the difference in cost of production here and abroad; that is, the difference in the labor cost here and abroad, for the well-being of the wage-worker must ever be a cardinal point of American policy. The question should be approached purely from a business standpoint; both the time and the manner of the change being such as to arouse the minimum of agitation and disturbance in the business world, and to give the least play for selfish and factional motives. The sole consideration should be to see that the sum total of changes represents the public good. This means that the subject cannot with wisdom be dealt with in the year preceding a presidential election, because as a matter of fact experience has conclusively shown that at such a time it is impossible to get men to treat it from the standpoint of the public good. In my judgment the wise time to deal with the matter is immediately after such election.

TAXATION

When our tax laws are revised the question of an income tax and an inheritance tax should receive the careful attention of our legislators. In my judgment both of these taxes should be part of our system of Federal taxation. I speak diffidently about the income tax because one scheme for an income tax was declared unconstitutional by the Supreme Court; while in addition it is a difficult tax to administer in its practical working, and great care would have to be exercised to see that it was not evaded by the very men whom it was most desirable to have taxed, for if so evaded it would, of course, be worse than no tax at all; as the least desirable of all taxes is the tax which bears heavily upon the honest as compared with the dishonest man. Nevertheless, a graduated income tax of the proper type would be a desirable feature of Federal taxation, and it is to be hoped that one may be devised which the Supreme Court will declare constitutional. The inheritance tax, however, is both a far better method of taxation, and far more important for the purpose of having fortunes of the country bear in proportion to their increase in size a corresponding increase and burden of taxation. The government has the absolute right to decide as to the terms upon which a man shall receive a bequest or devise from another, and this point in the devolution of property is especially appropriate for the imposition of a tax. Laws imposing such taxes have repeatedly been placed upon the national statute-books and as repeatedly declared constitutional by the courts; and these laws contained the progressive principle, that is, after a certain amount is reached the bequest or gift, in life or death, is increasingly burdened and the rate of taxation is increased in proportion to the remoteness of blood of the man receiving the bequest. These principles are recognized already in the leading civilized nations of the world. In Great Britain all the estates worth $5,000 or less are practically exempt from death duties, while the increase is such that when an estate exceeds five millions of dollars in value and passes to a distant kinsman or stranger in blood the government receives all told an amount equivalent to nearly a fifth of the whole estate. In France so much of an inheritance as exceeds $10,000,000 pays over a fifth to the state if it passes to a distant relative. The German law is especially interesting to us because it makes the inheritance tax an imperial measure while allotting to the individual states of the empire a portion of the proceeds and permitting them to impose taxes in addition to those imposed by the imperial government. Small inheritances are exempt, but the tax is so sharply progressive that when the inheritance is still not very large, provided it is not an agricultural or a forest land, it is taxed at the rate of twenty-five per cent if it goes to distant relatives. There is no reason why in the United States the National Government should not impose inheritance taxes in addition to those imposed by the States, and when we last had an inheritance tax about one-half of the States levied such taxes concurrently with the National Government, making a combined maximum rate, in some cases as high as twenty-five per cent. The French law has one feature which is to be heartily commended. The progressive principle is so applied that each higher rate is imposed only on the excess above the amount subject to the next lower rate; so that each increase of rate will apply only to a certain amount above a certain maximum. The tax should if possible be made to bear more heavily upon those residing without the country than within it. A heavy progressive tax upon a very large fortune is in no way such a tax upon thrift or industry as a like would be on a small fortune. No advantage comes either to the country as a whole or to the individuals inheriting the money by permitting the transmission in their entirety of the enormous fortunes which would be affected by such a tax; and as an incident to its function of revenue raising, such a tax would help to preserve a measurable equality of opportunity for the people of the generations growing to manhood. We have not the slightest sympathy with that socialistic idea which would try to put laziness, thriftlessness, and inefficiency on a par with industry, thrift, and efficiency; which would strive to break up not merely private property, but what is far more important, the home, the chief prop upon which our whole civilization stands. Such a theory, if ever adopted, would mean the ruin of the entire country—a ruin which would bear heaviest upon the weakest, upon those least able to shift for themselves. But proposals for legislation such as this herein advocated are directly opposed to this class of socialistic theories. Our aim is to recognize what Lincoln pointed out: The fact that there are some respects in which men are obviously not equal; but also to insist that there should be an equality of self-respect and of mutual respect, an equality of rights before the law, and at least an approximate equality in the conditions under which each man obtains the chance to show the stuff that is in him when compared to his fellows.

THE CRIMINAL LAW

A few years ago there was loud complaint that the law could not be invoked against wealthy offenders. There is no such complaint now. The course of the Department of Justice during the last few years has been such as to make it evident that no man stands above the law, that no corporation is so wealthy that it cannot be held to account. The Department of Justice has been as prompt to proceed against the wealthiest malefactor whose crime was one of greed and cunning as to proceed against the agitator who incites to brutal violence. Everything that can be done under the existing law, and with the existing state of public opinion, which so profoundly influences both the courts and juries, has been done. But the laws themselves need strengthening in more than one important point; they should be made more definite, so that no honest man can be led unwittingly to break them, and so that the real wrong-doer can be readily punished.

Moreover, there must be the public opinion back of the laws or the laws themselves will be of no avail. At present, while the average juryman undoubtedly wishes to see trusts broken up, and is quite ready to fine the corporation itself, he is very reluctant to find the facts proven beyond a reasonable doubt when it comes to sending to jail a member of the business community for indulging in practices which are profoundly unhealthy, but which, unfortunately, the business community has grown to recognize as well-nigh normal. Both the present condition of the law and the present temper of juries render it a task of extreme difficulty to get at the real wrong-doer in any such case, especially by imprisonment. Yet it is from every standpoint far preferable to punish the prime offender by imprisonment rather than to fine the corporation, with the attendant damage to stockholders.

The two great evils in the execution of our criminal laws to-day are sentimentality and technicality. For the latter the remedy must come from the hands of the legislatures, the courts, and the lawyers. The other must depend for its cure upon the gradual growth of a sound public opinion which shall insist that regard for the law and the demands of reason shall control all other influences and emotions in the jury-box. Both of these evils must be removed or public discontent with the criminal law will continue.

INJUNCTIONS

Instances of abuse in the granting of injunctions in labor disputes continue to occur, and the resentment in the minds of those who feel that their rights are being invaded and their liberty of action and of speech unwarrantably restrained continues likewise to grow. Much of the attack on the use of the process of injunction is wholly without warrant; but I am constrained to express the belief that for some of it there is warrant. This question is becoming more and more one of prime importance, and unless the courts will themselves deal with it in effective manner, it is certain ultimately to demand some form of legislative action. It would be most unfortunate for our social welfare if we should permit many honest and law-abiding citizens to feel that they had just cause for regarding our courts with hostility. I earnestly commend to the attention of the Congress this matter, so that some way may be devised which will limit the abuse of injunctions and protect those rights which from time to time it unwarrantably invades. Moreover, discontent is often expressed with the use of the process of injunction by the courts, not only in labor disputes, but where State laws are concerned. I refrain from discussion of this question as I am informed that it will soon receive the consideration of the Supreme Court.

The Federal courts must of course decide ultimately what are the respective spheres of State and nation in connection with any law, State or national, and they must decide definitely and finally in matters affecting individual citizens, not only as to the rights and wrongs of labor but as to the rights and wrongs of capital; and the National Government must always see that the decision of the court is put into effect. The process of injunction is an essential adjunct of the court's doing its work well; and as preventive measures are always better than remedial, the wise use of this process is from every standpoint commendable. But where it is recklessly or unnecessarily used, the abuse should be censured, above all by the very men who are properly anxious to prevent any effort to shear the courts of this necessary power. The court's decision must be final; the protest is only against the conduct of individual judges in needlessly anticipating such final decision, or in the tyrannical use of what is nominally a temporary injunction to accomplish what is in fact a permanent decision.

RAILROAD ACCIDENTS

The loss of life and limb from railroad accidents in this country has become appalling. It is a subject of which the National Government should take supervision. It might be well to begin by providing for a Federal inspection of interstate railroads somewhat along the lines of Federal inspection of steamboats, although not going so far; perhaps at first all that it would be necessary to have would be some officer whose duty would be to investigate all accidents on interstate railroads and report in detail the causes thereof. Such an officer should make it his business to get into close touch with railroad operating men so as to become thoroughly familiar with every side of the question, the idea being to work along the lines of the present steamboat-inspection law.

EMPLOYER'S LIABILITY LAW

The National Government should be a model employer. It should demand the highest quality of service from each of its employees and it should care for all of them properly in return. Congress should adopt legislation providing limited but definite compensation for accidents to all workmen within the scope of the Federal power, including employees of navy-yards and arsenals. In other words, a model employers' liability act, far-reaching and thoroughgoing, should be enacted which should apply to all positions, public and private, over which the National Government has jurisdiction. The number of accidents to wage-workers, including those that are preventable and those that are not, has become appalling in the mechanical, manufacturing, and transportation operations of the day. It works grim hardship to the ordinary wage-worker and his family to have the effect of such an accident fall solely upon him; and, on the other hand, there are whole classes of attorneys who exist only by inciting men who may or may not have been wronged to undertake suits for negligence. As a matter of fact a suit for negligence is generally an inadequate remedy for the person injured, while it often causes altogether disproportionate annoyance to the employer. The law should be made such that the payment for accidents by the employer would be automatic instead of being a matter for lawsuits. Workmen should receive certain and definite compensation for all accidents in industry irrespective of negligence. The employer is the agent of the public and on his own responsibility and for his own profit he serves the public. When he starts in motion agencies which create risks for others, he should take all the ordinary and extraordinary risks involved; and the risk he thus at the moment assumes will ultimately be assumed, as it ought to be, by the general public. Only in this way can the shock of the accident be diffused, instead of falling upon the man or woman least able to bear it, as is now the case. The community at large should share the burdens as well as the benefits of industry. By the proposed law, employers would gain a desirable certainty of obligation and get rid of litigation to determine it, while the workman and his family would be relieved from a crushing load. With such a policy would come increased care, and accidents would be reduced in number. The national laws providing for employers' liability on railroads engaged in interstate commerce and for safety appliances, as well as for diminishing the hours any employee of a railroad should be permitted to work, should all be strengthened wherever in actual practice they have shown weakness; they should be kept on the statute-books in thoroughgoing form.

The constitutionality of the employers' liability act passed by the preceding Congress has been carried before the courts. In two jurisdictions the law has been declared unconstitutional, and in three jurisdictions its constitutionality has been affirmed. The question has been carried to the Supreme Court, the case has been heard by that tribunal, and a decision is expected at an early date. In the event that the court should affirm the constitutionality of the act, I urge further legislation along the lines advocated in my message to the preceding Congress. The practice of putting the entire burden of loss of life or limb upon the victim or the victim's family is a form of social injustice in which the United States stands in unenviable prominence. In both our Federal and State legislation we have, with few exceptions, scarcely gone farther than the repeal of the fellow-servant principle of the old law of liability, and in some of our States even this slight modification of a completely outgrown principle has not yet been secured. The legislation of the rest of the industrial world stands out in striking contrast to our backwardness in this respect. Since 1895 practically every country of Europe, together with Great Britain, New Zealand, Australia, British Columbia, and the Cape of Good Hope has enacted legislation embodying in one form or another the complete recognition of the principle which places upon the employer the entire trade risk in the various lines of industry. I urge upon the Congress the enactment of a law which will at the same time bring Federal legislation up to the standard already established by all the European countries, and which will serve as a stimulus to the various States to perfect their legislation in this regard.

HOURS OF LABOR

The Congress should consider the extension of the eight-hour law. The constitutionality of the present law has recently been called into question, and the Supreme Court has decided that the existing legislation is unquestionably within the powers of the Congress. The principle of the eight-hour day should as rapidly and as far as practicable be extended to the entire work carried on by the government; and the present law should be amended to embrace contracts on those public works which the present wording of the act has been construed to exclude. The general introduction of the eight-hour day should be the goal toward which we should steadily tend and the government should set the example in this respect.

INVESTIGATION OF INDUSTRIAL CONTROVERSIES

Strikes and lockouts, with their attendant loss and suffering, continue to increase. For the five years ending December 31, 1905, the number of strikes was greater than those in any previous ten years and was double the number in the preceding five years. These figures indicate the increasing need of providing some machinery to deal with this class of disturbance in the interest alike of the employer, the employee, and the general public. I renew my previous recommendation that the Congress favorably consider the matter of creating the machinery for compulsory investigation of such industrial controversies as are of sufficient magnitude and of sufficient concern to the people of the country as a whole to warrant the Federal Government in taking action.

The need for some provision for such investigation was forcibly illustrated during the past summer. A strike of telegraph operators seriously interfered with telegraphic communication, causing great damage to business interests and serious inconvenience to the general public. Appeals were made to me from many parts of the country, from city councils, from boards of trade, from chambers of commerce, and from labor organizations, urging that steps be taken to terminate the strike. Everything that could with any propriety be done by a representative of the government was done, without avail, and for weeks the public stood by and suffered without recourse of any kind. Had the machinery existed and had there been authority for compulsory investigation of the dispute, the public would have been placed in possession of the merits of the controversy, and public opinion would probably have brought about a prompt adjustment.

Each successive step creating machinery for the adjustment of labor difficulties must be taken with caution, but we should endeavor to make progress in this direction.

The provisions of the act of 1898 creating the chairman of the Interstate Commerce Commission and the commissioner of labor a board of mediation in controversies between interstate railroads and their employees has, for the first time, been subjected to serious tests within the past year, and the wisdom of the experiment has been fully demonstrated. The creation of a board for compulsory investigation in cases where mediation fails and arbitration is rejected is the next logical step in a progressive programme.

CONDITIONS OF LABOR

It is certain that for some time to come there will be a constant increase absolutely, and perhaps relatively, of those among our citizens who dwell in cities or towns of some size and who work for wages. This means that there will be an ever-increasing need to consider the problems inseparable from a great industrial civilization. Where an immense and complex business, especially in those branches relating to manufacture and transportation, is transacted by a large number of capitalists who employ a very much larger number of wage-earners, the former tend more and more to combine into corporations and the latter into unions. The relations of the capitalist and wage-worker to one another, and of each to the general public, are not always easy to adjust; and to put them and keep them on a satisfactory basis is one of the most important and one of the most delicate tasks before our whole civilization. Much of the work for the accomplishment of this end must be done by the individuals concerned themselves, whether singly or in combination; and the one fundamental fact that must never be lost track of is that the character of the average man, whether he be a man of means or a man who works with his hands, is the most important factor in solving the problem aright. But it is almost equally important to remember that without good laws it is also impossible to reach the proper solution. It is idle to hold that without good laws evils such as child labor, as the overworking of women, as the failure to protect employees from loss of life or limb, can be effectively reached, any more than the evils of rebates and stock-watering can be reached without good laws. To fail to stop these practices by legislation means to force honest men into them, because otherwise the dishonest who surely will take advantage of them will have everything their own way. If the States will correct these evils, well and good; but the nation must stand ready to aid them.

No question growing out of our rapid and complex industrial development is more important than that of the employment of women and children. The presence of women in industry reacts with extreme directness upon the character of the home and upon family life, and the conditions surrounding the employment of children bear a vital relation to our future citizenship. Our legislation in those areas under the control of the Congress is very much behind the legislation of our more progressive States. A thorough and comprehensive measure should be adopted at this session of the Congress relating to the employment of women and children in the District of Columbia and the Territories. The investigation into the condition of women and children wage-earners recently authorized and directed by the Congress is now being carried on in the various States, and I recommend that the appropriation made last year for beginning this work be renewed, in order that we may have the thorough and comprehensive investigation which the subject demands. The National Government has as an ultimate resort for control of child labor the use of the interstate commerce clause to prevent the products of child labor from entering into interstate commerce. But before using this it ought certainly to enact model laws on the subject for the Territories under its own immediate control.

There is one fundamental proposition which can be laid down as regards all these matters, namely: While honesty by itself will not solve the problem, yet the insistence upon honesty—not merely technical honesty, but honesty in purpose and spirit—is an essential element in arriving at a right conclusion. Vice in its cruder and more archaic forms shocks everybody; but there is very urgent need that public opinion should be just as severe in condemnation of the vice which hides itself behind class or professional loyalty, or which denies that it is vice if it can escape conviction in the courts. The public and the representatives of the public, the high officials, whether on the bench or in executive or legislative positions, need to remember that often the most dangerous criminals, so far as the life of the nation is concerned, are not those who commit the crimes known to and condemned by the popular conscience for centuries, but those who commit crimes only rendered possible by the complex conditions of our modern industrial life. It makes not a particle of difference whether these crimes are committed by a capitalist or by a laborer, by a leading banker or manufacturer or railroad man, or by a leading representative of a labor-union. Swindling in stocks, corrupting legislatures, making fortunes by the inflation of securities, by wrecking railroads, by destroying competitors through rebates— these forms of wrong-doing in the capitalist, are far more infamous than any ordinary form of embezzlement or forgery; yet it is a matter of extreme difficulty to secure the punishment of the man most guilty of them, most responsible for them. The business man who condones such conduct stands on a level with the labor man who deliberately supports a corrupt demagogue and agitator, whether head of a union or head of some municipality, because he is said to have "stood by the union." The members of the business community, the educators, or clergymen, who condone and encourage the first kind of wrong-doing, are no more dangerous to the community, but are morally even worse, than the labor men who are guilty of the second type of wrong-doing, because less is to be pardoned those who have no such excuse as is furnished either by ignorance or by dire need.

THE WELFARE OF THE FARMER

When the Department of Agriculture was founded there was much sneering as to its usefulness. No department of the government, however, has more emphatically vindicated its usefulness, and none save the Post-Office Department comes so continually and intimately into touch with the people. The two citizens whose welfare is in the aggregate most vital to the welfare of the nation, and therefore to the welfare of all other citizens, are the wage-worker who does manual labor and the tiller of the soil, the farmer. There are, of course, kinds of labor where the work must be purely mental, and there are other kinds of labor where, under existing conditions, very little demand indeed is made upon the mind, though I am glad to say that the proportion of men engaged in this kind of work is diminishing. But in any community with the solid, healthy qualities which make up a really great nation the bulk of the people should do work which calls for the exercise of both body and mind. Progress cannot permanently exist in the abandonment of physical labor, but in the development of physical labor, so that it shall represent more and more the work of the trained mind in the trained body. Our school system is gravely defective in so far as it puts a premium upon mere literary training and tends therefore to train the boy away from the farm and the workshop. Nothing is more needed than the best type of industrial school, the school for mechanical industries in the city, the school for practically teaching agriculture in the country. The calling of the skilled tiller of the soil, the calling of the skilled mechanic, should alike be recognized as professions, just as emphatically as the callings of lawyer, doctor, merchant, or clerk. The schools recognize this fact and it should equally be recognized in popular opinion. The young man who has the far-sightedness and courage to recognize it and to get over the idea that it makes a difference whether what he earns is called salary or wages, and who refuses to enter the crowded field of the so-called professions, and takes to constructive industry instead, is reasonably sure of an ample reward in earnings, in health, in opportunity to marry early, and to establish a home with a fair amount of freedom from worry. It should be one of our prime objects to put both the farmer and the mechanic on a higher plane of efficiency and reward, so as to increase their effectiveness in the economic world, and therefore the dignity, the remuneration, and the power of their positions in the social world.

No growth of cities, no growth of wealth, can make up for any loss in either the number or the character of the farming population. We of the United States should realize this above almost all other peoples. We began our existence as a nation of farmers, and in every great crisis of the past a peculiar dependence has had to be placed upon the farming population; and this dependence has hitherto been justified. But it cannot be justified in the future if agriculture is permitted to sink in the scale as compared with other employments. We cannot afford to lose that pre-eminently typical American, the farmer who owns his own medium-sized farm. To have his place taken by either a class of small peasant proprietors, or by a class of great landlords with tenant-farmed estates, would be a veritable calamity. The growth of our cities is a good thing but only in so far as it does not mean a growth at the expense of the country farmer. We must welcome the rise of physical sciences in their application to agricultural practices, and we must do all we can to render country conditions more easy and pleasant. There are forces which now tend to bring about both these results, but they are, as yet, in their infancy. The National Government through the Department of Agriculture should do all it can by joining with the State governments and with independent associations of farmers to encourage the growth in the open farming country of such institutional and social movements as will meet the demand of the best type of farmers, both for the improvement of their farms and for the betterment of the life itself. The Department of Agriculture has in many places, perhaps especially in certain districts of the South, accomplished an extraordinary amount by co-operating with and teaching the farmers through their associations, on their own soil, how to increase their income by managing their farms better than they were hitherto managed.

The farmer must not lose his independence, his initiative, his rugged self-reliance, yet he must learn to work in the heartiest co-operation with his fellows, exactly as the business man has learned to work; and he must prepare to use to constantly better advantage the knowledge that can be obtained from agricultural colleges, while he must insist upon a practical curriculum in the schools in which his children are taught. The Department of Agriculture and the Department of Commerce and Labor both deal with the fundamental needs of our people in the production of raw material and its manufacture and distribution, and, therefore, with the welfare of those who produce it in the raw state, and of those who manufacture and distribute it. The Department of Commerce and Labor has but recently been founded but has already justified its existence; while the Department of Agriculture yields to no other in the government in the practical benefits which it produces in proportion to the public money expended. It must continue in the future to deal with growing crops as it has dealt in the past, but it must still further extend its field of usefulness hereafter by dealing with live men, through a far-reaching study and treatment of the problems of farm life alike from the industrial and economic and social standpoint. Farmers must co-operate with one another and with the government, and the government can best give its aid through associations of farmers, so as to deliver to the farmer the large body of agricultural knowledge which has been accumulated by the National and State governments and by the agricultural colleges and schools.

GRAIN

The grain-producing industry of the country, one of the most important in the United States, deserves special consideration at the hands of the Congress. Our grain is sold almost exclusively by grades. To secure satisfactory results in our home markets and to facilitate our trade abroad, these grades should approximate the highest degree of uniformity and certainty. The present diverse methods of inspection and grading throughout the country under different laws and boards, result in confusion and lack of uniformity, destroying that confidence which is necessary for healthful trade. Complaints against the present methods have continued for years and they are growing in volume and intensity, not only in this country but abroad. I therefore suggest to the Congress the advisability of a national system of inspection and grading of grain entering into the interstate and foreign commerce as a remedy for the present evils.

CONSERVATION

The conservation of our natural resources and their proper use constitute the fundamental problem which underlies almost every other problem of our national life. We must maintain for our civilization the adequate material basis without which that civilization cannot exist. We must show foresight, we must look ahead. As a nation we not only enjoy a wonderful measure of present prosperity but if this prosperity is used aright it is an earnest of future success such as no other nation will have. The reward of foresight for this nation is great and easily foretold. But there must be the look ahead, there must be a realization of the fact that to waste, to destroy, our natural resources, to skin and exhaust the land instead of using it so as to increase its usefulness, will result in undermining in the days of our children the very prosperity which we ought by right to hand down to them amplified and developed. For the last few years, through several agencies, the government has been endeavoring to get our people to look ahead and to substitute a planned and orderly development of our resources in place of a haphazard striving for immediate profit. Our great river systems should be developed as national water highways, the Mississippi, with its tributaries, standing first in importance, and the Columbia second, although there are many others of importance on the Pacific, the Atlantic, and the Gulf slopes. The National Government should undertake this work, and I hope a beginning will be made in the present Congress; and the greatest of all our rivers, the Mississippi, should receive especial attention. From the Great Lakes to the mouth of the Mississippi there should be a deep waterway, with deep waterways leading from it to the East and the West. Such a waterway would practically mean the extension of our coastline into the very heart of our country. It would be of incalculable benefit to our people. If begun at once it can be carried through in time appreciably to relieve the congestion of our great freight-carrying lines of railroads. The work should be systematically and continuously carried forward in accordance with some well-conceived plan. The main streams should be improved to the highest point of efficiency before the improvement of the branches is attempted; and the work should be kept free from every taint of recklessness or jobbery. The inland waterways which lie just back of the whole Eastern and Southern coasts should likewise be developed. Moreover, the development of our waterways involves many other important water problems, all of which should be considered as part of the same general scheme. The government dams should be used to produce hundreds of thousands of horse-power as an incident to improving navigation; for the annual value of the unused water-power of the United States perhaps exceeds the annual value of the products of all our mines. As an incident to creating the deep waterways down the Mississippi, the government should build along its whole lower length levees which, taken together with the control of the headwaters, will at once and forever put a complete stop to all threat of floods in the immensely fertile delta region. The territory lying adjacent to the Mississippi along its lower course will thereby become one of the most prosperous and populous, as it already is one of the most fertile farming regions in all the world. I have appointed an inland waterways commission to study and outline a comprehensive scheme of development along all the lines indicated. Later I shall lay its report before the Congress.

IRRIGATION

Irrigation should be far more extensively developed than at present, not only in the States of the great plains and the Rocky Mountains, but in many others, as, for instance, in large portions of the South Atlantic and Gulf States, where it should go hand in hand with the reclamation of swamp-land. The Federal Government should seriously devote itself to this task, realizing that utilization of waterways and water-power, forestry, irrigation, and the reclamation of lands threatened with overflow, are all interdependent parts of the same problem. The work of the Reclamation Service in developing the larger opportunities of the Western half of our country for irrigation is more important than almost any other movement. The constant purpose of the government in connection with the Reclamation Service has been to use the water resources of the public lands for the ultimate greatest good of the greatest number; in other words, to put upon the land permanent homemakers, to use and develop it for themselves and for their children and children's children. There has been, of course, opposition to this work; opposition from some interested men who desire to exhaust the land for their own immediate profit without regard to the welfare of the next generation, and opposition from honest and well-meaning men who did not fully understand the subject or who did not look far enough ahead. This opposition is, I think, dying away, and our people are understanding that it would be utterly wrong to allow a few individuals to exhaust for their own temporary personal profit the resources which ought to be developed through use so as to be conserved for the permanent common advantage of the people as a whole.

PUBLIC LANDS

The effort of the government to deal with the public land has been based upon the same principle as that of the Reclamation Service. The land law system which was designed to meet the needs of the fertile and well-watered regions of the Middle West has largely broken down when applied to the drier regions of the great plains, the mountains, and much of the Pacific slope, where a farm of 160 acres is inadequate for self-support. In these regions the system lent itself to fraud, and much land passed out of the hands of the government without passing into the hands of the home-maker. The Department of the Interior and the Department of Justice joined in prosecuting the offenders against the law; and they have accomplished much, while where the administration of the law has been defective it has been changed. But the laws themselves are defective. Three years ago a public-lands commission was appointed to scrutinize the law, and defects, and recommend a remedy. Their examination specifically showed the existence of great fraud upon the public domain, and their recommendations for changes in the law were made with the design of conserving the national resources of every part of the public lands by putting it to its best use. Especial attention was called to the prevention of settlement by the passage of great areas of public land into the hands of a few men, and to the enormous waste caused by unrestricted grazing upon the open range. The recommendations of the Public-Lands Commission are sound, for they are especially in the interest of the actual home-maker; and where the small home-maker cannot at present utilize the land they provide that the government shall keep control of it so that it may not be monopolized by a few men. The Congress has not yet acted upon these recommendations; but they are so just and proper, so essential to our national welfare, that I feel confident, if the Congress will take time to consider them, that they will ultimately be adopted.

THE OPEN RANGE

Some such legislation as that proposed is essential in order to preserve the great stretches of public grazing-land which are unfit for cultivation under present methods and are valuable only for the forage which they supply. These stretches amount in all to some 300,000,000 acres, and are open to the free grazing of cattle, sheep, horses, and goats, without restriction. Such a system, or lack of system, means that the range is not so much used as wasted by abuse. As the West settles, the range becomes more and more overgrazed. Much of it cannot be used to advantage unless it is fenced, for fencing is the only way by which to keep in check the owners of nomad flocks which roam hither and thither, utterly destroying the pastures and leaving a waste behind so that their presence is incompatible with the presence of home-makers. The existing fences are all illegal. Some of them represent the improper exclusion of actual settlers, actual home-makers, from territory which is usurped by great cattle companies. Some of them represent what is in itself a proper effort to use the range for those upon the land, and to prevent its use by nomadic outsiders. All these fences, those that are hurtful and those that are beneficial, are alike illegal and must come down. But it is an outrage that the law should necessitate such action on the part of the Administration. The unlawful fencing of public lands for private grazing must be stopped, but the necessity which occasioned it must be provided for. The Federal Government should have control of the range, whether by permit or lease, as local necessities may determine. Such control could secure the great benefit of legitimate fencing, while at the same time securing and promoting the settlement of the country. In some places it may be that the tracts of range adjacent to the homesteads of actual settlers should be allotted to them severally or in common for the summer grazing of their stock. Elsewhere it may be that a lease system would serve the purpose; the leases to be temporary and subject to the rights of settlement, and the amount charged being large enough merely to permit of the efficient and beneficial control of the range by the government, and of the payment to the county of the equivalent of what it would otherwise receive in taxes. The destruction of the public range will continue until some such laws as these are enacted. Fully to prevent the fraud in the public lands which, through the joint action of the Interior Department and the Department of Justice, we have been endeavoring to prevent, there must be further legislation, and especially a sufficient appropriation to permit the Department of the Interior to examine certain classes of entries on the ground before they pass into private ownership. The government should part with its title only to the actual home-maker, not to the profit-maker who does not care to make a home. Our prime object is to secure the rights and guard the interests of the small ranchman, the man who ploughs and pitches hay for himself. It is this small ranchman, this actual settler and home-maker, who in the long run is most hurt by permitting thefts of the public land in whatever form.

FOREST PRESERVATION

Optimism is a good characteristic, but if carried to an excess it becomes foolishness. We are prone to speak of the resources of this country as inexhaustible; this is not so. The mineral wealth of the country, the coal, iron, oil, gas, and the like, does not reproduce itself, and therefore is certain to be exhausted ultimately; and wastefulness in dealing with it to-day means that our descendants will feel the exhaustion a generation or two before they otherwise would. But there are certain other forms of waste which could be entirely stopped— the waste of soil by washing, for instance, which is among the most dangerous of all wastes now in progress in the United States, is easily preventable, so that this present enormous loss of fertility is entirely unnecessary. The preservation or replacement of the forests is one of the most important means of preventing this loss. We have made a beginning in forest preservation, but it is only a beginning. At present lumbering is the fourth greatest industry in the United States; and yet, so rapid has been the rate of exhaustion of timber in the United States in the past, and so rapidly is the remainder being exhausted, that the country is unquestionably on the verge of a timber famine which will be felt in every household in the land. There has already been a rise in the price of lumber, but there is certain to be a more rapid and heavier rise in the future. The present annual consumption of lumber is certainly three times as great as the annual growth; and if the consumption and growth continue unchanged, practically all our lumber will be exhausted in another generation, while long before the limit to complete exhaustion is reached the growing scarcity will make itself felt in many blighting ways upon our national welfare. About twenty per cent of our forested territory is now reserved in national forests; but these do not include the most valuable timber-lands, and in any event the proportion is too small to expect that the reserves can accomplish more than a mitigation of the trouble which is ahead for the nation. Far more drastic action is needed. Forests can be lumbered so as to give to the public the full use of their mercantile timber without the slightest detriment to the forest, any more than it is a detriment to a farm to furnish a harvest; so that there is no parallel between forests and mines, which can only be completely used by exhaustion. But forests, if used as all our forests have been used in the past and as most of them are still used, will be either wholly destroyed, or so damaged that many decades have to pass before effective use can be made of them again. All these facts are so obvious that it is extraordinary that it should be necessary to repeat them. Every business man in the land, every writer in the newspapers, every man or woman of an ordinary school education, ought to be able to see that immense quantities of timber are used in the country, that the forests which supply this timber are rapidly being exhausted, and that, if no change takes place, exhaustion will come comparatively soon, and that the effects of it will be felt severely in the everyday life of our people. Surely, when these facts are so obvious, there should be no delay in taking preventive measures. Yet we seem as a nation to be willing to proceed in this matter with happy-go-lucky indifference even to the immediate future. It is this attitude which permits the self-interest of a very few persons to weigh for more than the ultimate interest of all our people. There are persons who find it to their immense pecuniary benefit to destroy the forests by lumbering. They are to be blamed for thus sacrificing the future of the nation as a whole to their own self-interest of the moment; but heavier blame attaches to the people at large for permitting such action, whether in the White Mountains, in the southern Alleghanies, or in the Rockies and Sierras. A big lumbering company, impatient for immediate returns and not caring to look far enough ahead, will often deliberately destroy all the good timber in a region, hoping afterward to move on to some new country. The shiftless man of small means, who does not care to become an actual home-maker but would like immediate profit, will find it to his advantage to take up timber-land simply to turn it over to such a big company, and leave it valueless for future settlers. A big mine-owner, anxious only to develop his mine at the moment, will care only to cut all the timber that he wishes without regard to the future—probably not looking ahead to the condition of the country when the forests are exhausted, any more than he does to the condition when the mine is worked out. I do not blame these men nearly as much as I blame the supine public opinion, the indifferent public opinion, which permits their action to go unchecked. Of course to check the waste of timber means that there must be on the part of the public the acceptance of a temporary restriction in the lavish use of the timber, in order to prevent the total loss of this use in the future. There are plenty of men in public and private life who actually advocate the continuance of the present system of unchecked and wasteful extravagance, using as an argument the fact that to check it will of course mean interference with the ease and comfort of certain people who now get lumber at less cost than they ought to pay, at the expense of the future generations. Some of these persons actually demand that the present forest reserves be thrown open to destruction, because, forsooth, they think that thereby the price of lumber could be put down again for two or three or more years. Their attitude is precisely like that of an agitator protesting against the outlay of money by farmers on manure and in taking care of their farms generally. Undoubtedly, if the average farmer were content absolutely to ruin his farm, he could for two or three years avoid spending any money on it, and yet make a good deal of money out of it. But only a savage would, in his private affairs, show such reckless disregard of the future; yet it is precisely this reckless disregard of the future which the opponents of the forestry system are now endeavoring to get the people of the United States to show. The only trouble with the movement for the preservation of our forests is that it has not gone nearly far enough, and was not begun soon enough. It is a most fortunate thing, however, that we began it when we did. We should acquire in the Appalachian and White Mountain regions all the forest-lands that it is possible to acquire for the use of the nation. These lands, because they form a national asset, are as emphatically national as the rivers which they feed, and which flow through so many States before they reach the ocean.

There should be no tariff on any forest product grown in this country; and, in especial, there should be no tariff on wood-pulp; due notice of the change being of course given to those engaged in the business so as to enable them to adjust themselves to the new conditions. The repeal of the duty on wood-pulp should if possible be accompanied by an agreement with Canada that there shall be no export duty on Canadian pulp-wood.

COAL AND OIL

In the Eastern United States the mineral fuels have already passed into the hands of large private owners, and those of the West are rapidly following. It is obvious that these fuels should be conserved and not wasted, and it would be well to protect the people against unjust and extortionate prices, so far as that can still be done. What has been accomplished in the great oil-fields of the Indian Territory by the action of the Administration offers a striking example of the good results of such a policy. In my judgment the government should have the right to keep the fee of the coal, oil, and gas fields in its own possession and to lease the rights to develop them under proper regulations; or else, if the Congress will not adopt this method, the coal deposits should be sold under limitations, to conserve them as public utilities, the right to mine coal being separated from the title to the soil. The regulations should permit coal-lands to be worked in sufficient quantity by the several corporations. The present limitations have been absurd, excessive, and serve no useful purpose, and often render it necessary that there should be either fraud or close abandonment of the work of getting out the coal.

PANAMA CANAL

Work on the Panama Canal is proceeding in a highly satisfactory manner. In March last, John F. Stevens, chairman of the commission and chief engineer, resigned, and the commission was reorganized and consituted as follows: Lieutenant-Colonel George W. Goethals, Corps of Engineers, U. S. Army, chairman and chief engineer; Major D. D. Gaillard, Corps of Engineers, U. S. Army; Major William L. Sibert, Corps of Engineers, U. S. Army; Civil Engineer H. H. Rousseau, U. S. Navy; Mr. J. C. S. Blackburn; Colonel W. C. Gorgas, U. S. Army; and Mr. Jackson Smith, commissioners. This change of authority and direction went into effect on April 1, without causing a perceptible check to the progress of the work. In March the total excavation in the Culebra Cut, where effort was chiefly concentrated, was 815,270 cubic yards. In April this was increased to 879,527 cubic yards. There was a considerable decrease in the output for May and June owing partly to the advent of the rainy season and partly to temporary trouble with the steam-shovel men over the question of wages. This trouble was settled satisfactorily to all parties, and in July the total excavation advanced materially, and in August the grand total from all points in the Canal prism by steam-shovels and dredges exceeded all previous United States records, reaching 1,274,404 cubic yards. In September this record was eclipsed and a total of 1,517,412 cubic yards was removed. Of this amount 1,481,307 cubic yards were from the Canal prism and 36,105 cubic yards were from accessory works. These results were achieved in the rainy season with a rainfall in August of 11.89 inches and in September of 11.65 inches. Finally, in October, the record was again eclipsed, the total excavation being 1,868,729 cubic yards; a truly extraordinary record, especially in view of the heavy rainfall, which was 17.1 inches. In fact, experience during the last two rainy seasons demonstrates that the rains are a less serious obstacle to progress than has hitherto been supposed.

Work on the locks and dams at Gatun, which began actively in March last, has advanced so far that it is thought that masonry work on the locks can be begun within fifteen months. In order to remove all doubt as to the satisfactory character of the foundations for the locks of the Canal, the secretary of war requested three eminent civil engineers, of special experience in such construction, Alfred Noble, Frederic P. Stearns, and John R. Freeman, to visit the Isthmus and make thorough personal investigations of the sites. These gentlemen went to the Isthmus in April and by means of test pits which had been dug for the purpose, they inspected the proposed foundations, and also examined the borings that had been made. In their report to the secretary of war, under date of May 2, 1907, they said: "We found that all of the locks, of the dimensions now proposed, will rest upon rock of such character that it will furnish a safe and stable foundation." Subsequent new borings, conducted by the present commission, have fully confirmed this verdict. They show that the locks will rest on rock for their entire strength. The cross-section of the dam and method of construction will be such as to insure against any slip or sloughing off. Similar examination of the foundations of the locks and dams on the Pacific side are in progress. I believe that the locks should be made of a width of 120 feet.

Last winter bids were requested and received for doing the work of canal construction by contract. None of them was found to be satisfactory and all were rejected. It is the unanimous opinion of the present commission that the work can be done better, more cheaply, and more quickly by the government than by private contractors. Fully eighty per cent of the entire plant needed for construction has been purchased or contracted for; machine-shops have been erected and equipped for making all needed repairs to the plant; many thousands of employees have been secured; an effective organization has been perfected; a recruiting system is in operation which is capable of furnishing more labor than can be used advantageously; employees are well sheltered and well fed; salaries paid are satisfactory, and the work is not only going forward smoothly, but it is producing results far in advance of the most sanguine anticipations. Under these favorable conditions, a change in the method of prosecuting the work would be unwise and unjustifiable, for it would inevitably disorganize existing conditions, check progress, and increase the cost and lengthen the time of completing the Canal.

The chief engineer and all his professional associates are firmly convinced that the eighty-five-feet-level lock-canal which they are constructing is the best that could be desired. Some of them had doubts on this point when they went to the Isthmus. As the plans have developed under their direction their doubts have been dispelled. While they may decide upon changes in detail as construction advances they are in hearty accord in approving the general plan. They believe that it provides a canal not only adequate to all demands that will be made upon it but superior in every way to a sea-level canal. I concur in this belief.

POSTAL SAVINGS-BANK

I commend to the favorable consideration of the Congress a postal savings-bank system, as recommended by the post-master-general. The primary object is to encourage among our people economy and thrift and by the use of postal savings-banks to give them an opportunity to husband their resources, particularly those who have not the facilities at hand for depositing their money in savings-banks. Viewed, however, from the experience of the past few weeks, it is evident that the advantages of such an institution are still more far-reaching. Timid depositors have withdrawn their savings for the time being from national banks, trust companies, and savings-banks; individuals have hoarded their cash and the working men their earnings; all of which money has been withheld and kept in hiding or in safe-deposit box to the detriment of prosperity. Through the agency of the postal savings-banks such money would be restored to the channels of trade, to the mutual benefit of capital and labor.

POSTAL SERVICE

I further commend to the Congress the consideration of the postmaster-general's recommendation for an extension of the parcel-post, especially on the rural routes. There are now 38,215 rural routes, serving nearly 15,000,000 people who do not have the advantages of the inhabitants of cities in obtaining their supplies. These recommendations have been drawn up to benefit the farmer and the country storekeeper; otherwise, I should not favor them, for I believe that it is good policy for our government to do everything possible to aid the small town and the country district. It is desirable that the country merchant should not be crushed out.

The fourth-class postmasters' convention has passed a very strong resolution in favor of placing the fourth-class post-masters under the civil-service law. The Administration has already put into effect the policy of refusing to remove any fourth-class postmasters save for reasons connected with the good of the service; and it is endeavoring so far as possible to remove them from the domain of partisan politics. It would be a most desirable thing to put the fourth-class postmasters in the classified service. It is possible that this might be done without congressional action, but, as the matter is debatable, I earnestly recommend that the Congress enact a law providing that they be included under the civil-service law and put in the classified service.

OKLAHOMA

Oklahoma has become a State, standing on a full equality with her elder sisters, and her future is assured by her great natural resources. The duty of the National Government to guard the personal and property rights of the Indians within her borders remains of course unchanged.

ALASKA

I reiterate my recommendations of last year as regards Alaska. Some form of local self-government should be provided, as simple and inexpensive as possible; it is impossible for the Congress to devote the necessary time to all the little details of necessary Alaskan legislation. Road-building and railway-building should be encouraged. The governor of Alaska should be given an ample appropriation wherewith to organize a force to preserve the public peace. Whiskey-selling to the natives should be made a felony. The coal-land laws should be changed so as to meet the peculiar needs of the Territory. This should be attended to at once; for the present laws permit individuals to locate large areas of the public domain for speculative purposes; and cause an immense amount of trouble, fraud, and litigation. There should be another judicial division established. As early as possible lighthouses and buoys should be established as aids to navigation, especially in and about Prince William Sound, and the survey of the coast completed. There is need of liberal appropriations for lighting and buoying the southern coast and improving the aids to navigation in south-eastern Alaska. One of the great industries of Alaska, as of Puget Sound and the Columbia, is salmon-fishing. Gradually, by reason of lack of proper laws, this industry is being ruined; it should now be taken in charge, and effectively protected, by the United States Government.

The courage and enterprise of the citizens of the far Northwest in their projected Alaskan-Yukon-Pacific Exposition, to be held in 1909, should receive liberal encouragement. This exposition is not sentimental in its conception, but seeks to exploit the natural resources of Alaska and to promote the commerce, trade, and industry of the Pacific States with their neighboring States and with our insular possessions and the neighboring countries of the Pacific. The exposition asks no loan from the Congress but seeks appropriations for national exhibits and exhibits of the Western dependencies of the general government. The State of Washington and the city of Seattle have shown the characteristic Western enterprise in large donations for the conduct of this exposition in which other States are lending generous assistance.

HAWAII

The unfortunate failure of the shipping bill at the last session of the last Congress was followed by the taking off of certain Pacific steamships, which has greatly hampered the movement of passengers between Hawaii and the mainland. Unless the Congress is prepared by positive encouragement to secure proper facilities in the way of shipping between Hawaii and the mainland, then the coastwise shipping laws should be so far relaxed as to prevent Hawaii suffering as it is now suffering. I again call your attention to the capital importance from every standpoint of making Pearl Harbor available for the largest deep-water vessels, and of suitably fortifying the island.

PHILIPPINES

The secretary of war has gone to the Philippines. On his return I shall submit to you his report on the islands.

PORTO RICO

I again recommend that the rights of citizenship be conferred upon the people of Porto Rico.

BUREAU OF MINES

A bureau of mines should be created under the control and direction of the secretary of the interior; the bureau to have power to collect statistics and make investigations in all matters pertaining to mining and particularly to the accidents and dangers of the industry. If this cannot now be done, at least additional appropriations should be given the Interior Department to be used for the study of mining conditions, for the prevention of fradulent mining schemes, for carrying on the work of mapping the mining districts, for studying methods for minimizing the accidents and dangers in the industry; in short, to aid in all proper ways the development of the mining industry.

MEMORIALS

I strongly recommend to the Congress to provide funds for keeping up the Hermitage, the home of Andrew Jackson; these funds to be used through the existing Hermitage Association for the preservation of a historic building which should ever be dear to Americans. I further recommend that a naval monument be established in the Vicksburg National Park. This national park gives a unique opportunity for commemorating the deeds of those gallant men who fought on water, no less than of those who fought on land, in the great Civil War.

CENSUS

Legislation should be enacted at the present session of the Congress for the Thirteenth Census. The establishment of the permanent Census Bureau affords the opportunity for a better census than we have ever had, but in order to realize the full advantage of the permanent organization, ample time must be given for preparation.

PUBLIC HEALTH

There is a constantly growing interest in this country in the question of the public health. At last the public mind is awake to the fact that many diseases, notably tuberculosis, are national scourages. The work of the State and city boards of health should be supplemented by a constantly increasing interest on the part of the national government. The Congress has already provided a bureau of public health and has provided for a hygienic laboratory. There are other valuable laws relating to the public health connected with the various departments. This whole branch of the government should be strengthened and aided in every way.

REORGANIZATION OF GOVERNMENTAL METHODS

I call attention to two governmental commissions which I have appointed and which have already done excellent work. The first of these has to do with the organization of the scientific work of the government, which has grown up wholly without plan and is in consequence so unwisely distributed among the executive departments that much of its effect is lost for the lack of proper co-ordination. The commission's chief object is to introduce a planned and orderly development and operation in the place of the ill-assorted and often ineffective grouping and methods of work which have prevailed. This cannot be done without legislation, nor would it be feasible to deal in detail with so complex an administrative problem by specific provisions of law. I recommend that the President be given authority to concentrate related lines of work and reduce duplication by Executive order through transfer and consolidation of lines of work.

The second committee, that on department methods, was instructed to investigate and report upon the changes needed to place the conduct of the executive force of the government on the most economical and effective basis in the light of the best modern business practice. The committee has made very satisfactory progress. Antiquated practices and bureaucratic ways have been abolished, and a general renovation of departmental methods has been inaugurated. All that can be done by Executive order has already been accomplished or will be put into effect in the near future. The work of the main committee and its several assistant committees has produced a wholesome awakening on the part of the great body of officers and employees engaged in government work. In nearly every department and office there has been a careful self-inspection for the purpose of remedying any defects before they could be made the subject of adverse criticism. This has led individuals to a wider study of the work on which they were engaged, and this study has resulted in increasing their efficiency in their respective lines of work. There are recommendations of special importance from the committee on the subject of personnel and the classification of salaries which will require legislative action before they can be put into effect. It is my intention to submit to the Congress in the near future a special message on those subjects.

CAMPAIGN EXPENSES

Under our form of government voting is not merely a right but a duty, and moreover, a fundamental and necessary duty if a man is to be a good citizen. It is well to provide that corporations shall not contribute to presidential or national campaigns, and furthermore to provide for the publication of both contributions and expenditures. There is, however, always danger in laws of this kind, which from their very nature are difficult of enforcement; the danger being lest they be obeyed only by the honest, and disobeyed by the unscrupulous, so as to act only as a penalty upon honest men. Moreover, no such law would hamper an unscrupulous man of unlimited means from buying his own way into office. There is a very radical measure which would, I believe, work a substantial improvement in our system of conducting a campaign, although I am well aware that it will take some time for people so to familiarize themselves with such a proposal as to be willing to consider its adoption. The need for collecting large campaign funds would vanish if Congress provided an appropriation for the proper and legitimate expenses of each of the great national parties, an appropriation ample enough to meet the necessity for thorough organization and machinery, which requires a large expenditure of money. Then the stipulation should be made that no party receiving campaign funds from the Treasury should accept more than a fixed amount from any individual subscriber or donor; and the necessary publicity for receipts and expenditures could without difficulty be provided.

NATIONAL GALLERY OF ART

There should be a national gallery of art established in the capital city of this country. This is important not merely to the artistic but to the material welfare of the country; and the people are to be congratulated on the fact that the movement to establish such a gallery is taking definite form under the guidance of the Smithsonian Institution. So far from there being a tariff on works of art brought into the country, their importation should be encouraged in every way. There have been no sufficient collections of objects of art by the government, and what collections have been acquired are scattered and are generally placed in unsuitable and imperfectly lighted galleries.

THE BIOLOGICAL SURVEY

The Biological Survey is quietly working for the good of our agricultural interests, and is an excellent example of a government bureau which conducts original scientific research the findings of which are of much practical utility. For more than twenty years it has studied the food habits of birds and mammals that are injurious or beneficial to agriculture, horticulture, and forestry; has distributed illustrated bulletins on the subject, and has labored to secure legislative protection for the beneficial species. The cotton boll-weevil, which has recently overspread the cotton belt of Texas and is steadily extending its range, is said to cause an annual loss of about $3,000,000. The Biological Survey has ascertained and gives wide publicity to the fact that at least forty-three kinds of birds prey upon this destructive insect. It has discovered that fifty-seven species of birds feed upon scale-insects—dreaded enemies of the fruit-grower. It has shown that woodpeckers as a class, by destroying the larvæ of wood-boring insects, are so essential to tree life that it is doubtful if our forests could exist without them. It has shown that cuckoos and orioles are the natural enemies of the leaf-eating caterpillars that destroy our shade and fruit trees; that our quails and sparrows consume annually hundreds of tons of seeds of noxious weeds; that hawks and owls as a class (excepting the few that kill poultry and game-birds) are markedly beneficial, spending their lives in catching grasshoppers, mice, and other pests that prey upon the products of husbandry. It has conducted field experiments for the purpose of devising and perfecting simple methods for holding in check the hordes of destructive rodents—rats, mice, rabbits, gophers, prairie-dogs, and ground-squirrels—which annually destroy crops worth many millions of dollars; and it has published practical directions for the destruction of wolves and coyotes on the stock-ranges of the West, resulting during the past year in an estimated saving of cattle and sheep valued at upward of a million dollars.

It has inaugurated a system of inspection at the principal ports of entry on both Atlantic and Pacific coasts by means of which the introduction of noxious mammals and birds is prevented, thus keeping out the mongoose and certain birds which are as much to be dreaded as the previously introduced English sparrow and the house rats and mice.

In the interest of game protection it has co-operated with local officials in every State in the Union, has striven to promote uniform legislation in the several States, has rendered important service in enforcing the Federal law regulating inter-state traffic in game, and has shown how game protection may be made to yield a large revenue to the State—a revenue amounting in the case of Illinois to $128,000 in a single year.

The Biological Survey has explored the faunas and floras of America with reference to the distribution of animals and plants; it has defined and mapped the natural life areas—areas in which, by reason of prevailing climatic conditions, certain kinds of animals and plants occur—and has pointed out the adaptability of these areas to the cultivation of particular crops. The results of these investigations are not only of high educational value but are worth each year to the progressive farmers of the country many times the cost of maintaining the survey, which, it may be added, is exceedingly small. I recommend to Congress that this bureau, whose usefulness is seriously handicapped by lack of funds, be granted an appropriation in some degree commensurate with the importance of the work it is doing.

OCEAN-MAIL SERVICE

I call your especial attention to the unsatisfactory condition of our foreign-mail service, which, because of the lack of American steamship-lines is now largely done through foreign lines, and which, particularly so far as South and Central America are concerned, is done in a manner which constitutes a serious barrier to the extension of our commerce.

The time has come, in my judgment, to set to work seriously to make our ocean-mail service correspond more closely with our recent commercial and political development. A beginning was made by the ocean-mail act of March 3, 1891, but even at that time the act was known to be inadequate in various particulars. Since that time events have moved rapidly in our history. We have acquired Hawaii, the Philippines, and lesser islands in the Pacific. We are steadily prosecuting the great work of uniting at the Isthmus the waters of the Atlantic and the Pacific. To a greater extent than seemed probable even a dozen years ago we may look to an American future on the sea worthy of the traditions of our past. As the first step in that direction, and the step most feasible at the present time, I recommend the extension of the ocean-mail act of 1891. This act has stood for some years free from successful criticism of its principle and purpose. It was based on theories of the obligations of a great maritime nation, undisputed in our own land and followed by other nations since the beginning of steam navigation. Briefly those theories are, that it is the duty of a first-class power so far as practicable to carry its ocean mails under its own flag; that the fast ocean steamships and their crews, required for such mail service, are valuable auxiliaries to the sea-power of a nation. Furthermore, the construction of such steamships insures the maintenance in an efficient condition of the shipyards in which our battleships must be built.

The expenditure of public money for the performance of such necessary functions of government is certainly warranted, nor is it necessary to dwell upon the incidental benefits to our foreign commerce, to the ship-building industry, and to ship-owning and navigation which will accompany the discharge of these urgent public duties, though they, too, should have weight.

The only serious question is whether at this time we can afford to improve our ocean-mail service as it should be improved. All doubt on this subject is removed by the reports of the Post-Office Department. For the fiscal year ended June 30, 1907, that department estimates that the postage collected on the articles exchanged with foreign countries other than Canada and Mexico amounted to $6,579,043.48, or $3,637,-226.81 more than the net cost of the service exclusive of the cost of transporting the articles between the United States exchange post-offices and the United States post-offices at which they were mailed or delivered. In other words, the government of the United States, having assumed a monopoly of carrying the mails for the people, is making a profit of over

$3,600,000 by rendering a cheap and inefficient service. That profit I believe should be devoted to strengthening our maritime power in those directions where it will best promote our prestige. The country is familiar with the facts of our maritime impotence in the harbors of the great and friendly republics of South America. Following the failure of the shipbuilding bill we lost our only American line of steamers to Australasia, and that loss on the Pacific has become a serious embarrassment to the people of Hawaii, and has wholly cut off the Samoan Islands from regular communication with the Pacific coast. Puget Sound, in the year, has lost over half (four out of seven) of its American steamers trading with the Orient.

We now pay under the act of 1891 four dollars a statute mile outward to twenty-knot American mail steamships, built according to naval plans, available as cruisers, and manned by Americans. Steamships of that speed are confined exclusively to transatlantic trade with New York. To steamships of sixteen knots or over only two dollars a mile can be paid, and it is steamships of this speed and type which are needed to meet the requirements of mail service to South America, Asia (including the Philippines), and Australia. I strongly recommend, therefore, a simple amendment to the ocean-mail act of 1891 which shall authorize the postmaster-general in his discretion to enter into contracts for the transportation of mails to the republics of South America, to Asia, the Philippines, and Australia at a rate not to exceed four dollars a mile for steamships of sixteen knots speed or upward, subject to the restrictions and obligations of the act of 1891. The profit of $3,600,000 which has been mentioned will fully cover the maximum annual expenditure involved in this recommendation, and it is believed will in time establish the lines so urgently needed. The proposition involves no new principle, but permits the efficient discharge of public functions now inadequately performed or not performed at all.

THE ARMY

Not only there is not now, but there never has been, any other nation in the world so wholly free from the evils of militarism as is ours. There never has been any other large nation, not even China, which for so long a period has had relatively to its numbers so small a regular army as has ours. Never at any time in our history has this nation suffered from militarism or been in the remotest danger of suffering from militarism. Never at any time of our history has the Regular Army been of a size which caused the slightest appreciable tax upon the taxpaying citizens of the nation. Almost always it has been too small in size and underpaid. Never in our entire history has the nation suffered in the least particular because too much care has been given to the army, too much prominence given it, too much money spent upon it, or because it has been too large. But again and again we have suffered because enough care has not been given to it, because it has been too small, because there has not been sufficient preparation in advance for possible war. Every foreign war in which we have engaged has cost us many times the amount which, if wisely expended during the preceding years of peace on the Regular Army, would have insured the war ending in but a fraction of the time and but for a fraction of the cost that was actually the case. As a nation we have always been short-sighted in providing for the efficiency of the army in time of peace. It is nobody's especial interest to make such provision and no one looks ahead to war at any period, no matter how remote, as being a serious possibility; while an improper economy, or rather niggardliness, can be practised at the expense of the army with the certainty that those practising it will not be called to account therefor, but that the price will be paid by the unfortunate persons who happen to be in office when a war does actually come.

I think it is only lack of foresight that troubles us, not any hostility to the army. There are, of course, foolish people who denounce any care of the army or navy as "militarism," but I do not think that these people are numerous. This country has to contend now, and has had to contend in the past, with many evils, and there is ample scope for all who would work for reform. But there is not one evil that now exists, or that ever has existed in this country, which is, or ever has been, owing in the smallest part to militarism. Declamation against militarism has no more serious place in an earnest and intelligent movement for righteousness in this country than declamation against the worship of Baal or Astaroth. It is declamation against a non-existent evil, one which never has existed in this country, and which has not the slightest chance of appearing here. We are glad to help in any movement for international peace, but this is because we sincerely believe that it is our duty to help all such movements provided they are sane and rational, and not because there is any tendency toward militarism on our part which needs to be cured. The evils we have to fight are those in connection with industrialism, not militarism. Industry is always necessary, just as war is sometimes necessary. Each has its price, and industry in the United States now exacts, and has always exacted, a far heavier toll of death than all our wars put together. The statistics of the railroads of this country for the year ended June 30, 1906, the last contained in the annual statistical report of the Interstate Commerce Commission, show in that one year a total of 108,324 casualties to persons, of which 10,618 represent the number of persons killed. In that wonderful hive of human activity, Pittsburgh, the deaths due to industrial accidents in 1906 were 919, all the result of accidents in mills, mines, or on railroads. For the entire country, therefore, it is safe to say that the deaths due to industrial accidents aggregate in the neighborhood of 20,000 a year. Such a record makes the death-rate in all our foreign wars utterly trivial by comparison. The number of deaths in battle in all the foreign wars put together, for the last century and a quarter, aggregate considerably less than one year's death record for our industries.

A mere glance at these figures is sufficient to show the absurdity of the outcry against militarism.

But again and again in the past our little Regular Army has rendered service literally vital to the country, and it may at any time have to do so in the future. Its standard of efficiency and instruction is higher now than ever in the past. But it is too small. There are not enough officers; and it is impossible to secure enough enlisted men. We should maintain in peace a fairly complete skeleton of a large army. A great and long-continued war would have to be fought by volunteers. But months would pass before any large body of efficient volunteers could be put in the field, and our Regular Army should be large enough to meet any immediate need. In particular it is essential that we should possess a number of extra officers trained in peace to perform efficiently the duties urgently required upon the breaking out of war.

The medical corps should be much larger than the needs of our Regular Army in war. Yet at present it is smaller than the needs of the service demand even in peace. The Spanish War occurred less than ten years ago. The chief loss we suffered in it was by disease among the regiments which never left the country. At the moment the nation seemed deeply impressed by this fact; yet seemingly it has already been forgotten, for not the slightest effort has been made to prepare a medical corps of sufficient size to prevent the repetition of the same disaster on a much larger scale if we should ever be engaged in a serious conflict. The trouble in the Spanish War was not with the then existing officials of the War Department; it was with the representatives of the people as a whole who, for the preceding thirty years, had declined to make the necessary provision for the army. Unless ample provision is now made by Congress to put the medical corps where it should be put disaster in the next war is inevitable, and the responsibility will not lie with those then in charge of the War Department, but with those who now decline to make the necessary provision. A well-organized medical corps, thoroughly trained before the advent of war in all the important administrative duties of a military sanitary corps, is essential to the efficiency of any large army, and especially of a large volunteer army. Such knowledge of medicine and surgery as is possessed by the medical profession generally will not alone suffice to make an efficient military surgeon. He must have, in addition, knowledge of the administration and sanitation of large field hospitals and camps, in order to safeguard the health and lives of men intrusted in great numbers to his care. A bill has long been pending before the Congress for the reorganization of the medical corps; its passage is urgently needed.

But the Medical Department is not the only department for which increased provision should be made. The rate of pay for the officers should be greatly increased; there is no higher type of citizen than the American regular officer, and he should have a fair reward for his admirable work. There should be a relatively even greater increase in the pay for the enlisted men. In especial provision should be made for establishing grades equivalent to those of warrant officers in the navy which should be open to the enlisted men who serve sufficiently long and who do their work well. Inducements should be offered sufficient to encourage really good men to make the army a life occupation. The prime need of our present army is to secure and retain competent non-commissioned officers. This difficulty rests fundamentally on the question of pay. The non-commissioned officer does not correspond with an unskilled laborer; he corresponds to the best type of skilled workman or to the subordinate official in civil institutions. Wages have greatly increased in outside occupations in the last forty years and the pay of the soldier, like the pay of the officers, should be proportionately increased. The first sergeant of a company, if a good man, must be one of such executive and administrative ability, and such knowledge of his trade, as to be worth far more than we at present pay him. The same is true of the regimental sergeant-major. These men should be men who had fully resolved to make the army a life occupation and they should be able to look forward to ample reward; while only men properly qualified should be given a chance to secure these final rewards. The increase over the present pay need not be great in the lower grades for the first one or two enlistments, but the increase should be marked for the non-commissioned officers of the upper grades who serve long enough to make it evident that they intend to stay permanently in the army, while additional pay should be given for high qualifications in target practice. The position of warrant officer should be established and there should be not only an increase of pay, but an increase of privileges and allowances and dignity, so as to make the grade open to non-commissioned officers capable of filling them desirably from every standpoint. The rate of desertion in our army now in time of peace is alarming. The deserter should be treated by public opinion as a man guilty of the greatest crime; while on the other hand the man who serves steadily in the army should be treated as what he is, that is, as pre-eminently one of the best citizens of this Republic. After twelve years' service in the army my own belief is that the man should be given a preference according to his ability for certain types of office over all civilian applicants without examination. This should also apply, of course, to the men who have served twelve years in the navy. A special corps should be provided to do the manual labor now necessarily demanded of the privates themselves.

Among the officers there should be severe examinations to weed out the unfit up to the grade of major. From that position on appointments should be solely by selection and it should be understood that a man of merely average capacity could never get beyond the position of major, while every man who serves in any grade a certain length of time prior to promotion to the next grade without getting the promotion to the next grade should be forthwith retired. The practice marches and field manœuvres of the last two or three years have been invaluable to the army. They should be continued and extended. A rigid and not a perfunctory examination of physical capacity has been provided for the higher grade officers. This will work well. Unless an officer has a good physique, unless he can stand hardship, ride well, and walk fairly, he is not fit for any position, even after he has become a colonel. Before he has become a colonel the need for physical fitness in the officers is almost as great as in the enlisted man. I hope speedily to see introduced into the army a far more rigid and thorough-going test of horsemanship for all field-officers than at present. There should be a chief of cavalry just as there is a chief of artillery.

Perhaps the most important of all legislation needed for the benefit of the army is a law to equalize and increase the pay of officers and enlisted men of the army, navy, marine corps, and Revenue-Cutter Service. Such a bill has been prepared, which it is hoped will meet with your favorable consideration. The next most essential measure is to authorize a number of extra officers as mentioned above. To make the army more attractive to enlisted men, it is absolutely essential to create a service corps, such as exists in nearly every modern army in the world, to do the skilled and unskilled labor, inseparably connected with military administration, which is now exacted, without just compensation, of enlisted men who voluntarily entered the army to do service of an altogether different kind. There are a number of other laws necessary to so organize the army as to promote its efficiency and facilitate its rapid expansion in time of war; but the above are the most important.

THE NAVY

It was hoped the Hague Conference might deal with the question of the limitation of armaments. But even before it had assembled informal inquiries had developed that as regards naval armaments, the only one in which this country had any interest, it was hopeless to try to devise any plan for which there was the slightest possibility of securing the assent of the nations gathered at The Hague. No plan was even proposed which would have had the assent of more than one first-class power outside of the United States. The only plan that seemed at all feasible, that of limiting the size of battleships, met with no favor at all. It is evident, therefore, that it is folly for this nation to base any hope of securing peace on any international agreement as to the limitations of armaments. Such being the fact it would be most unwise for us to stop the upbuilding of our navy. To build one battleship of the best and most advanced type a year would barely keep our fleet up to its present force. This is not enough. In my judgment, we should this year provide for four battleships. But it is idle to build battleships unless in addition to providing the men, and the means for thorough training, we provide the auxiliaries for them, unless we provide docks, the coaling-stations, the colliers and supply-ships that they need. We are extremely deficient in coaling-stations and docks on the Pacific, and this deficiency should not longer be permitted to exist. Plenty of torpedo-boats and destroyers should be built. Both on the Atlantic and Pacific coasts, fortifications of the best type should be provided for all our greatest harbors.

We need always to remember that in time of war the navy is not to be used to defend harbors and seacoast cities; we should perfect our system of coast fortifications. The only efficient use for the navy is for offense. The only way in which it can efficiently protect our own coast against the possible action of a foreign navy is by destroying that foreign navy. For defense against a hostile fleet which actually attacks them, the coast cities must depend upon their forts, mines, torpedoes, submarines and torpedo-boats and destroyers. All of these together are efficient for defensive purposes, but they in no way supply the place of a thoroughly efficient navy capable of acting on the offensive; for parrying never yet won a fight. It can only be won by hard hitting, and an aggressive seagoing navy alone can do this hard hitting of the offensive type. But the forts and the like are necesary so that the navy may be foot-loose. In time of war there is sure to be demand, under pressure, of fright, for the ships to be scattered so as to defend all kind of ports. Under penalty of terrible disaster, this demand must be refused. The ships must be kept together, and their objective made the enemies' fleet. If fortifications are sufficiently strong, no modern navy will venture to attack them, so long as the foe has in existence a hostile navy of anything like the same size or efficiency. But unless there exists such a navy then the fortifications are powerless by themselves to secure the victory. For of course the mere deficiency means that any resolute enemy can at his leisure combine all his forces upon one point with the certainty that he can take it.

Until our battle fleet is much larger than at present it should never be split into detachments so far apart that they could not in event of emergency be speedily united. Our coast-line is on the Pacific just as much as on the Atlantic. The interests of California, Oregon, and Washington are as emphatically the interests of the whole Union as those of Maine and New York, of Louisiana and Texas. The battle fleet should now and then be moved to the Pacific, just as at other times it should be kept in the Atlantic. When the Isthmian Canal is built the transit of the battle fleet from one ocean to the other will be comparatively easy. Until it is built I earnestly hope that the battle fleet will be thus shifted between the two oceans every year or two. The marksmanship on all our ships has improved phenomenally during the last five years. Until within the last two or three years it was not possible to train a battle fleet in squadron manœuvres under service conditions, and it is only during these last two or three years that the training under these conditions has become really effective. Another and most necessary stride in advance is now being taken. The battle fleet is about starting by the Straits of Magellan to visit the Pacific coast. Sixteen battleships are going under the command of Rear-Admiral Evans, while eight armored cruisers and two other battleships will meet him at San Francisco, whither certain torpedo destroyers are also going. No fleet of such size has ever made such a voyage, and it will be of very great educational use to all engaged in it. The only way by which to teach officers and men how to handle the fleet so as to meet every possible strain and emergency in time of war is to have them practise under similar conditions in time of peace. Moreover, the only way to find out our actual needs is to perform in time of peace whatever manœuvres might be necessary in time of war. After war is declared it is too late to find out the needs; that means to invite disaster. This trip to the Pacific will show what some of our needs are and will enable us to provide for them. The proper place for an officer to learn his duty is at sea, and the only way in which a navy can ever be made efficient is by practice at sea, under all the conditions which would have to be met if war existed.

I bespeak the most liberal treatment for the officers and enlisted men of the navy. It is true of them, as likewise of the officers and enlisted men of the army, that they form a body whose interests should be close to the heart of every good American. In return the most rigid performance of duty should be exacted from them. The reward should be ample when they do their best; and nothing less than their best should be tolerated. It is idle to hope for the best results when the men in the senior grades come to those grades late in life and serve too short a time in them. Up to the rank of lieutenant-commander promotion in the navy should be as now, by seniority, subject, however, to such rigid tests as would eliminate the unfit. After the grade of lieutenant-commander, that is, when we come to the grade of command rank, the unfit should be eliminated in such manner that only the conspicuously fit would remain, and sea service should be a principle test of fitness. Those who are passed by should, after a certain length of service in their respective grades, be retired. Of a given number of men it may well be that almost all would make good lieutenants and most of them good lieutenant-commanders, while only a minority be fit to be captains, and but three or four to be admirals. Those who object to promotion otherwise than by mere seniority should reflect upon the elementary fact that no business in private life could be successfully managed if those who enter at the lowest rungs of the ladder should each in turn, if he lived, become the head of the firm, its active director, and retire after he had held the position a few months. On its face such a scheme is an absurdity. Chances for improper favoritism can be minimized by a properly formed board; such as the board of last June, which did such conscientious and excellent work in elimination.

If all that ought to be done cannot now be done, at least let a beginning be made. In my last three annual messages, and in a special message to the last Congress, the necessity for legislation that will cause officers of the line of the navy to reach the grades of captain and rear-admiral at less advanced ages and which will cause them to have more sea training and experience in the highly responsible duties of those grades, so that they may become thoroughly skilful in handling battleships, divisions, squadrons, and fleets in action, has been fully explained and urgently recommended. Upon this subject the secretary of the navy has submitted detailed and definite recommendations which have received my approval, and which, if enacted into law, will accomplish what is immediately necessary, and will, as compared with existing law, make a saving of more than five millions of dollars during the next seven years. The navy personnel act of 1899 has accomplished all that was expected of it in providing satisfactory periods of service in the several subordinate grades, from the grade of ensign to the grade of lieutenant-commander, but the law is inadequate in the upper grades and will continue to be inadequate on account of the expansion of the personnel since its enactment. Your attention is invited to the following quotations from the report of the personnel board of 1906, of which the assistant secretary of the navy was president:

"Congress has authorized a considerable increase in the number of midshipmen at the Naval Academy, and these midshipmen upon graduation are promoted to ensign and lieutenant (junior grade). But no provision has been made for a corresponding increase in the upper grades, the result being that the lower grades will become so congested that a midshipman now in one of the lowest classes at Annapolis may possibly not be promoted to lieutenant until he is between forty-five and fifty years of age. So it will continue under the present law, congesting at the top and congesting at the bottom. The country fails to get from the officers of the service the best that is in them by not providing opportunity for their normal development and training. The board believes that this works a serious detriment to the efficiency of the navy and is a real menace to the public safety."

As stated in my special message to the last Congress: "I am firmly of the opinion that unless the present condition of the higher commissioned personnel is rectified by judicious legislation the future of our navy will be gravely compromised." It is also urgently necessary to increase the efficiency of the medical corps of the navy. Special legislation to this end has already been proposed; and I trust it may be enacted without delay.

It must be remembered that everything done in the navy to fit it to do well in time of war must be done in time of peace. Modern wars are short; they do not last the length of time requisite to build a battleship; and it takes longer to train the officers and men to do well on a battleship than it takes to build it. Nothing effective can be done for the navy once war has begun, and the result of the war, if the combatants are otherwise equally matched, will depend upon which power has prepared best in time of peace. The United States navy is the best guarantee the nation has that its honor and interest will not be neglected; and in addition it offers by far the best insurance for peace that can by human ingenuity be devised.

I call attention to the report of the official board of visitors to the Naval Academy at Annapolis which has been forwarded to the Congress. The report contains this paragraph:

"Such revision should be made of the courses of study and methods of conducting and marking examinations as will develop and bring out the average all-round ability of the midshipman rather than to give him prominence in any one particular study. The fact should be kept in mind that the Naval Academy is not a university but a school, the primary object of which is to educate boys to be efficient naval officers. Changes in curriculum, therefore, should be in the direction of making the course of instruction less theoretical and more practical. No portion of any future class should be graduated in advance of the full four years' course, and under no circumstances should the standard of instruction be lowered. The Academy in almost all of its departments is now magnificiently equipped, and it would be very unwise to make the course of instruction less exacting than it is to-day."

Acting upon this suggestion I designated three seagoing officers, Captain Richard Wainwright, Commander Robert S. Griffin, and Lieutenant-Commander Albert L. Key, all graduates of the Academy, to investigate conditions and to recommend to me the best method of carrying into effect this general recommendation. These officers performed the duty promptly and intelligently, and, under the personal direction of Captain Charles J. Badger, superintendent of the Academy, such of the proposed changes as were deemed to be at present advisable were put into effect at the beginning of the academic year, October 1, last. The results, I am confident, will be most beneficial to the Academy, to the midshipmen, and to the navy.

SECOND HAGUE CONFERENCE

In foreign affairs this country's steady policy is to behave toward other nations as a strong and self-respecting man should behave toward the other men with whom he is brought into contact. In other words, our aim is disinterestedly to help other nations where such help can be wisely given without the appearance of meddling with what does not concern us; to be careful to act as a good neighbor; and at the same time, in good-natured fashion, to make it evident that we do not intend to be imposed upon.

The Second International Peace Conference was convened at

The Hague on the 15th of June last and remained in session until the 18th of October. For the first time the representatives of practically all the civilized countries of the world united in a temperate and kindly discussion of the methods by which the causes of war might be narrowed and its injurious effects reduced.

Although the agreements reached in the conference did not in any direction go to the length hoped for by the more sanguine, yet in many directions important steps were taken, and upon every subject on the programme there was such full and considerate discussion as to justify the belief that substantial progress has been made toward further agreements in the future. Thirteen conventions were agreed upon embodying the definite conclusions which had been reached, and resolutions were adopted marking the progress made in matters upon which agreement was not yet sufficiently complete to make conventions practicable.

The delegates of the United States were instructed to favor an agreement for obligatory arbitration, the establishment of a permanent court of arbitration to proceed judicially in the hearing and decision of international causes, the prohibition of force for the collection of contract debts alleged to be due from governments to citizens of other countries until after arbitration as to the justice and amount of the debt and the time and manner of payment, the immunity of private property at sea, the better definition of the rights of neutrals, and, in case any measure to that end should be introduced, the limitation of armaments.

In the field of peaceful disposal of international differences several important advances were made. First, as to obligatory arbitration. Although the conference failed to secure a unanimous agreement upon the details of a convention for obligatory arbitration, it did resolve as follows:

"It is unanimous: (1) In accepting the principle for obligatory arbitration; (2) in declaring that certain differences, and notably those relating to the interpretation and application of international conventional stipulations are susceptible of being submitted to obligatory arbitration without any restriction."

In view of the fact that as a result of the discussion the vote upon the definite treaty of obligatory arbitration, which was proposed, stood thirty-two in favor to nine against the adoption of the treaty, there can be little doubt that the great majority of the countries of the world have reached a point where they are now ready to apply practically the principles thus unanimously agreed upon by the conference.

The second advance, and a very great one, is the agreement which relates to the use of force for the collection of contract debts. Your attention is invited to the paragraphs upon this subject in my message of December, 1906, and to the resolution of the Third American Conference at Rio in the summer of 1906. The convention upon this subject adopted by the conference substantially as proposed by the American delegates is as follows:

"In order to avoid between nations armed conflicts of a purely pecuniary origin arising from contractual debts claimed of the government of one country by the government of another country to be due to its nationals, the signatory powers agree not to have recourse to armed force for the collection of such contractual debts.

"However, this stipulation shall not be applicable when the debtor State refuses or leaves unanswered an offer to arbitrate, or, in case of acceptance, makes it impossible to formulate the terms of submission, or, after arbitration, fails to comply with the award rendered.

"It is further agreed that arbitration here contemplated shall be in conformity, as to procedure, with Chapter III of the Convention for the Pacific Settlement of International Disputes adopted at The Hague, and that it shall determine, in so far as there shall be no agreement between the parties, the justice and the amount of the debt, the time and mode of payment thereof."

Such a provision would have prevented much injustice and

extortion in the past, and I cannot doubt that its effect in the future will be most salutary.

A third advance has been made in amending and perfecting the convention of 1899 for the voluntary settlement of international disputes, and particularly the extension of those parts of that convention which relate to commissions of inquiry. The existence of those provisions enabled the governments of Great Britain and Russia to avoid war, notwithstanding great public excitement, at the time of the Dogger Bank incident, and the new convention agreed upon by the conference gives practical effect to the experience gained in that inquiry.

Substantial progress was also made toward the creation of a permanent judicial tribunal for the determination of international causes. There was very full discussion of the proposal for such a court and a general agreement was finally reached in favor of its creation. The conference recommended to the signatory powers the adoption of a draft upon which it agreed for the organization of the court, leaving to be determined only the method by which the judges should be selected. This remaining unsettled question is plainly one which time and good temper will solve.

A further agreement of the first importance was that for the creation of an international prize-court. The constitution, organization, and procedure of such a tribunal were provided for in detail. Any one who recalls the injustices under which this country suffered as a neutral power during the early part of the last century cannot fail to see in this provision for an international prize-court the great advance which the world is making toward the substitution of the rule of reason and justice in place of simple force. Not only will the international prize-court be the means of protecting the interests of neutrals, but it is in itself a step toward the creation of the more general court for the hearing of international controversies to which reference has just been made. The organization and action of such a prize-court cannot fail to accustom the different countries to the submission of international questions to the decision of an international tribunal, and we may confidently expect the results of such submission to bring about a general agreement upon the enlargement of the practice.

Numerous provisions were adopted for reducing the evil effects of war and for defining the rights and duties of neutrals.

The conference also provided for the holding of a third conference within a period similar to that which elapsed between the First and Second Conferences.

The delegates of the United States worthily represented the spirit of the American people and maintained with fidelity and ability the policy of our government upon all the great questions discussed in the conference.

The report of the delegation, together with authenticated copies of the conventions signed, when received, will be laid before the Senate for its consideration.

When we remember how difficult it is for one of our own legislative bodies, composed of citizens of the same country, speaking the same language, living under the same laws, and having the same customs, to reach an agreement, or even to secure a majority upon any difficult and important subject which is proposed for legislation, it becomes plain that the representatives of forty-five different countries, speaking many different languages, accustomed to different methods of procedure, with widely diverse interests, who discussed so many different subjects and reached agreements upon so many, are entitled to grateful appreciation for the wisdom, patience, and moderation with which they have discharged their duty. The example of this temperate discussion, and the agreements and the efforts to agree, among representatives of all the nations of the earth, acting with universal recognition of the supreme obligation to promote peace, cannot fail to be a powerful influence for good in future international relations.

CUBA

A year ago in consequence of a revolutionary movement in Cuba which theatened the immediate return to chaos of the island, the United States intervened, sending down an army and establishing a provisional government under Governor Magoon. Absolute quiet and prosperity have returned to the island because of this action. We are now taking steps to provide for elections in the island and our expectation is within the coming year to be able to turn the island over again to a government chosen by the people thereof. Cuba is at our doors. It is not possible that this nation should permit Cuba again to sink into the condition from which we rescued it. All that we ask of the Cuban people is that they be prosperous, that they govern themselves so as to bring content, order, and progress to their island, the Queen of the Antilles; and our only interference has been and will be to help them achieve these results.

JAPAN

An invitation has been extended by Japan to the government and people of the United States to participate in a great national exposition to be held at Tokyo from April 1 to October 31, 1912, and in which the principal countries of the world are to be invited to take part. This is an occasion of special interest to all the nations of the world, and peculiarly so to us; for it is the first instance in which such a great national exposition has been held by a great power dwelling on the Pacific; and all the nations of Europe and America will, I trust, join in helping to success this first great exposition ever held by a great nation of Asia. The geographical relations of Japan and the United States as the possessors of such large portions of the coasts of the Pacific, the intimate trade relations already existing between the two countries, the warm friendship which has been maintained between them without break since the opening of Japan to intercourse with the Western nations, and her increasing wealth and production, which we regard with hearty good-will and wish to make the occasion of mutually beneficial commerce, all unite in making it eminently desirable that this invitation should be accepted. I heartily recommend such legislation as will provide in generous fashion for the representation of this government and its people in the proposed exposition. Action should be taken now. We are apt to underestimate the time necesary for preparation in such cases. The invitation to the French Exposition of 1900 was brought to the attention of the Congress by President Cleveland in December, 1895; and so many are the delays necessary to such proceedings that the period of four years and a half which then intervened before the exposition proved none too long for the proper preparation of the exhibits.

THE TARIFF

The adoption of a new tariff by Germany, accompanied by conventions for reciprocal tariff concessions between that country and most of the other countries of Continental Europe, led the German Government to give the notice necessary to terminate the reciprocal commercial agreement with this country proclaimed July 13, 1900. The notice was to take effect on the 1st of March, 1906, and in default of some other arrangements this would have left the exports from the United States to Germany subject to the general German tariff duties, from twenty-five to fifty per cent higher than the conventional duties imposed upon the goods of most of our competitors for German trade.

Under a special agreement made between the two governments in February, 1906, the German Government postponed the operation of their notice until the 30th of June, 1907. In the meantime, deeming it to be my duty to make every possible effort to prevent a tariff war between the United States and Germany arising from misunderstanding by either country of the conditions existing in the other, and acting upon the invitation of the German Government, I sent to Berlin a commission composed of competent experts in the operation and administration of the customs tariff, from the Departments of the Treasury and Commerce and Labor. This commission was engaged for several months in conference with a similar commission appointed by the German Government, under instructions, so far as practicable, to reach a common understanding as to all the facts regarding the tariffs of the United States and Germany material and relevant to the trade relations between the two countries. The commission reported, and upon the basis of the report, a further temporary commercial agreement was entered into by the two countries, pursuant to which, in the exercise of the authority conferred upon the President by the third section of the tariff act of July 24, 1897, I extended the reduced tariff rates provided for in that section to champagne and all other sparkling wines, and pursuant to which the German conventional or minimum tariff rates were extended to about 96½ per cent of all the exports from the United States to Germany. This agreement is to remain in force until the 30th of June, 1908, and until six months after notice by either party to terminate it.

The agreement and the report of the commission on which it is based will be laid before the Congress for its information.

CUSTOMS ADMINISTRATION

This careful examination into the tariff relations between the United States and Germany involved an inquiry into certain of our methods of administration which had been the cause of much complaint on the part of German exporters. In this inquiry I became satisfied that certain vicious and unjustifiable practices had grown up in our customs administration, notably the practice of determining values of imports upon detective reports never disclosed to the persons whose interests were affected. The use of detectives, though often necessary, tends toward abuse, and should be carefully guarded. Under our practice as I found it to exist in this case, the abuse had become gross and discreditable. Under it, instead of seeking information as to the market value of merchandise from the well-known and respected members of the commerical community in the country of its production, secret statements were obtained from informers and discharged employees and business rivals, and upon this kind of secret evidence the values of imported goods were frequently raised and heavy penalities were frequently imposed upon importers who were never permitted to know what the evidence was and who never had an opportunity to meet it. It is quite probable that this system tended toward an increase of the duties collected upon imported goods, but I conceive it to be a violation of law to exact more duties than the law provides, just as it is a violation to admit goods upon the payment of less than the legal rate of duty. This practice was repugnant to the spirit of American law and to American sense of justice. In the judgment of the most competent experts of the Treasury Department and the Department of Commerce and Labor it was wholly unnecessary for the due collection of the customs revenues, and the attempt to defend it merely illustrates the demoralization which naturally follows from a long-continued course of reliance upon such methods. I accordingly caused the regulations governing this branch of the customs service to be modified so that values are determined upon a hearing in which all the parties interested have an opportunity to be heard and to know the evidence against them. Moreover our treasury agents are accredited to the government of the country in which they seek information, and in Germany receive the assistance of the quasi-official chambers of commerce in determining the actual market value of goods, in accordance with what I am advised to be the true construction of the law.

These changes of regulations were adapted to the removal of such manifest abuses that I have not felt that they ought to be confined to our relations with Germany; and I have extended their operation to all other countries which have expressed a desire to enter into similar administrative relations.

CHINESE BOXER INDEMNITY

I ask for authority to reform the agreement with China under which the indemnity of 1900 was fixed, by remitting and cancelling the obligation of China for the payment of all that part of the stipulated indemnity which is in excess of the sum of $11,665,492.69, and interest at four per cent. After the rescue of the foreign legations in Peking during the Boxer troubles in 1900 the powers required from China the payment of equitable indemnities to the several nations, and the final protocol under which the troops were withdrawn, signed at Peking, September 7, 1901, fixed the amount of this indemnity allotted to the United States at over $20,000,000, and China paid, up to and including the 1st day of June last, a little over $6,000,000. It was the first intention of this government at the proper time, when all claims had beeen presented and all expenses ascertained as fully as possible, to revise the estimates and account, and as a proof of sincere friendship for China voluntarily to release that country from its legal liability for all payments in excess of the sum which should prove to be necessary for actual indemnity to the United States and its citizens.

This nation should help in every practicable way in the education of the Chinese people, so that the vast and populous empire of China may gradually adapt itself to modern conditions. One way of doing this is by promoting the coming of Chinese students to this country and making it attractive to them to take courses at our universities and higher educational institutions. Our educators should, so far as possible, take concerted action toward this end.

CENTRAL AND SOUTH AMERICA

On the courteous invitation of the president of Mexico, the secretary of state visited that country in September and October and was received everywhere with the greatest kindness and hospitality.

He carried from the government of the United States to our southern neighbor a message of respect and good-will and of desire for better acquaintance and increasing friendship. The response from the government and the people of Mexico was hearty and sincere. No pains were spared to manifest the most friendly attitude and feeling toward the United States.

In view of the close neighborhood of the two countries the relations which exist between Mexico and the United States are just cause for gratification. We have a common boundary of over 1,500 miles from the Gulf of Mexico to the Pacific. Much of it is marked only by the shifting waters of the Rio Grande. Many thousands of Mexicans are residing upon our side of the line and it is estimated that over 40,000 Americans are resident in Mexican territory and that American investments in Mexico amount to over $700,000,000. The extraordinary industrial and commercial prosperity of Mexico has been greatly promoted by American enterprise, and Americans are sharing largely in its results. The foreign trade of the republic already exceeds $240,000,000 per annum, and of this two-thirds both of exports and imports are exchanged with the United States. Under these circumstances numerous questions necessarily arise between the two countries. These questions are always approached and disposed of in a spirit of mutual courtesy and fair dealing. Americans carrying on business in Mexico testify uniformly to the kindness and consideration with which they are treated and their sense of the security of their property and enterprises under the wise administration of the great statesman who has so long held the office of chief magistrate of that republic.

The two governments have been uniting their efforts for a considerable time past to aid Central America in attaining the degree of peace and order which have made possible the prosperity of the northern ports of the Continent. After the peace between Guatemala, Honduras, and Salvador, celebrated under the circumstances described in my last message, a new war broke out between the republics of Nicaragua, Honduras, and

Salvador. The effort to compose this new difficulty has resulted in the acceptance of the joint suggestion of the presidents of Mexico and of the United States for a general peace conference between all the countries of Central America. On the 17th day of September last a protocol was signed between the representatives of the five Central American countries accredited to this government agreeing upon a conference to be held in the city of Washington "in order to devise the means of preserving the good relations among said republics and bringing about permanent peace in those countries." The protocol includes the expression of a wish that the presidents of the United States and Mexico should appoint "representatives to lend their good and impartial offices in a purely friendly way toward the realization of the objects of the conference." The conference is now in session and will have our best wishes and, where it is practicable, our friendly assistance.

One of the results of the Pan-American Conference at Rio Janeiro in the summer of 1906 has been a great increase in the activity and usefulness of the International Bureau of American Republics. That institution, which includes all the American republics in its membership and brings all their representatives together, is doing a really valuable work in informing the people of the United States about the other republics and in making the United States known to them. Its action is now limited by appropriations determined when it was doing a work on a much smaller scale and rendering much less valuable service. I recommend that the contribution of this government to the expenses of the bureau be made commensurate with its increased work.

IX

EIGHTH ANNUAL MESSAGE[1]

To the Senate and House of Representatives

FINANCES

THE financial standing of the nation at the present time is excellent and the financial management of the nation's interests by the government during the last seven years has shown the most satisfactory results. But our currency system is imperfect and it is earnestly to be hoped that the Currency Commission will be able to propose a thoroughly good system which will do away with the existing defects.

During the period from July 1, 1901, to September 30, 1908, there was an increase in the amount of money in circulation of $902,991,399. The increase in the per capita during this period was 7.06. Within this time there were several occasions when it was necessary for the Treasury Department to come to the relief of the money market by purchases or redemptions of United States bonds; by increasing deposits in national banks; by stimulating additional issues of national-bank notes, and by facilitating importations from abroad of gold. Our imperfect currency system has made these proceedings necessary, and they were effective until the monetary disturbance in the fall of 1907 immensely increased the difficulty of ordinary methods of relief. By the middle of November the available working balance in the Treasury had been reduced to approximately $5,000,000. Clearing-house associations throughout the country had been obliged to resort to the expedient of issuing clearing-house certificates, to be used

[1] Dated, the White House, December 8, 1908.

as money. In this emergency it was determined to invite subscriptions for $50,000,000 Panama Canal bonds, and $100,000,000 three per cent certificates of indebtedness authorized by the act of June 13, 1898. It was proposed to redeposit in the national banks the proceeds of these issues, and to permit their use as a basis for additional circulating notes of national banks. The moral effect of this procedure was so great that it was necessary to issue only $24,631,980 of the Panama Canal bonds and $15,436,500 of the certificates of indebtedness.

During the period from July 1, 1901, to September 30, 1908, the balance between the net ordinary receipts and the net ordinary expenses of the government showed a surplus in the four years 1902, 1903, 1906, and 1907, and a deficit in the years 1904, 1905, 1908, and a fractional part of the fiscal year 1909. The net result was a surplus of $99,233,413.54. The financial operations of the government during this period, based upon these differences between receipts and expenditures, resulted in a net reduction of the interest-bearing debt of the United States from $987,141,040 to $897,253,990, notwithstanding that there had been two sales of Panama Canal bonds amounting in the aggregate to $54,631,980, and an issue of three per cent certificates of indebtedness under the act of June 13, 1898, amounting to $15,436,500. Refunding operations of the Treasury Department under the act of March 14, 1900, resulted in the conversion into two per cent consols of 1930 of $200,309,400 bonds bearing higher rates of interest. A decrease of $8,687,956 in the annual interest charge resulted from these operations.

In short, during the seven years and three months there has been a net surplus of nearly $100,000,000 of receipts over expenditures, a reduction of the interest-bearing debt by $90,000,000, in spite of the extraordinary expense of the Panama Canal, and a saving of nearly $9,000,000 on the annual interest charge. This is an exceedingly satisfactory showing, especially in view of the fact that during this period the nation has never hesitated to undertake any expenditure that it regarded as necessary. There have been no new taxes and no increase of taxes; on the contrary, some taxes have been taken off; there has been a reduction of taxation.

CORPORATIONS

As regards the great corporations engaged in interstate business, and especially the railroad, I can only repeat what I have already again and again said in my messages to the Congress. I believe that under the interstate clause of the Constitution the United States has complete and paramount right to control all agencies of interstate commerce; and I believe that the National Government alone can exercise this right with wisdom and effectiveness so as both to secure justice from, and to do justice to, the great corporations which are the most important factors in modern business. I believe that it is worse than folly to attempt to prohibit all combinations as is done by the Sherman antitrust law, because such a law can be enforced only imperfectly and unequally, and its enforcement works almost as much hardship as good. I strongly advocate that instead of an unwise effort to prohibit all combinations there shall be substituted a law which shall expressly permit combinations which are in the interest of the public, but shall at the same time give to some agency of the National Government full power of control and supervision over them. One of the chief features of this control should be securing entire publicity in all matters which the public has a right to know, and furthermore, the power, not by judicial but by executive action, to prevent or put a stop to every form of improper favoritism or other wrong-doing.

The railways of the country should be put completely under the Interstate Commerce Commission and removed from the domain of the antitrust law. The power of the commission should be made thoroughgoing, so that it could exercise complete supervision and control over the issue of securities as well as over the raising and lowering of rates. As regards rates, at least, this power should be summary. The power to investigate the financial operations and accounts of the railways has been one of the most valuable features in recent legislation. Power to make combinations and traffic agreements should be explicitly conferred upon the railroads, the permission of the commission being first gained and the combination or agreement being published in all its details. In the interest of the public the representatives of the public should have complete power to see that the railroads do their duty by the public, and as a matter of course this power should also be exercised so as to see that no injustice is done to the railroads. The shareholders, the employees, and the shippers all have interests that must be guarded. It is to the interest of all of them that no swindling stock speculation should be allowed, and that there should be no improper issuance of securities. The guiding intelligences necessary for the successful building and successful management of railroads should receive ample remuneration; but no man should be allowed to make money in connection with railroads out of fraudulent overcapitalization and kindred stock-gambling performances; there must be no defrauding of investors, oppression of the farmers and business men who ship freight, or callous disregard of the rights and needs of the employees. In addition to this the interests of the shareholders, of the employees, and of the shippers should all be guarded as against one another. To give any one of them undue and improper consideration is to do injustice to the others. Rates must be made as low as is compatible with giving proper returns to all the employees of the railroad, from the highest to the lowest, and proper returns to the shareholders; but they must not, for instance, be reduced in such fashion as to necessitate a cut in the wages of the employees or the abolition of the proper and legitimate profits of honest shareholders.

Telegraph and telephone companies engaged in interstate business should be put under the jurisdiction of the Interstate Commerce Commission.

It is very earnestly to be wished that our people, through their representatives, should act in this matter. It is hard to say whether most damage to the country at large would come from entire failure on the part of the public to supervise and control the actions of the great corporations, or from the exercise of the necessary governmental power in a way which would do injustice and wrong to the corporations. Both the preachers of an unrestricted individualism, and the preachers of an oppression which would deny to able men of business the just reward of their initiative and business sagacity, are advocating policies that would be fraught with the gravest harm to the whole country. To permit every lawless capitalist, every law-defying corporation, to take any action, no matter how iniquitous, in the effort to secure an improper profit and to build up privilege, would be ruinous to the Republic and would mark the abandonment of the effort to secure in the industrial world the spirit of democratic fair dealing. On the other hand, to attack these wrongs in that spirit of demagogy which can see wrong only when committed by the man of wealth, and is dumb and blind in the presence of wrong committed against men of property or by men of no property, is exactly as evil as corruptly to defend the wrong-doing of men of wealth. The war we wage must be waged against misconduct, against wrong-doing wherever it is found; and we must stand heartily for the rights of every decent man, whether he be a man of great wealth or a man who earns his livelihood as a wage-worker or a tiller of the soil.

It is to the interest of all of us that there should be a premium put upon individual initiative and individual capacity, and an ample reward for the great directing intelligences alone competent to manage the great business operations of to-day. It is well to keep in mind that exactly as the anarchist is the worst enemy of liberty and the reactionary the worst enemy of order, so the men who defend the rights of property have most to fear from the wrong-doers of great wealth, and the men who are championing popular rights have most to fear from the demagogues who in the name of popular rights would do wrong to and oppress honest business men, honest men of wealth; for the success of either type of wrong-doer necessarily invites a violent reaction against the cause the wrong-doer nominally upholds. In point of danger to the nation there is nothing to choose between on the one hand the corruptionist, the bribe-giver, the bribe-taker, the man who employs his great talent to swindle his fellow citizens on a large scale, and, on the other hand, the preacher of class hatred, the man who, whether from ignorance or from willingness to sacrifice his country to his ambition, persuades well-meaning but wrong-headed men to try to destroy the instruments upon which our prosperity mainly rests. Let each group of men beware of and guard against the shortcomings to which that group is itself most liable. Too often we see the business community in a spirit of unhealthy class consciousness deplore the effort to hold to account under the law the wealthy men who in their management of great corporations, whether railroads, street-railways, or other industrial enterprises, have behaved in a way that revolts the conscience of the plain, decent people. Such an attitude cannot be condemned too severely, for men of property should recognize that they jeopardize the rights of property when they fail heartily to join in the effort to do away with the abuses of wealth. On the other hand, those who advocate proper control on behalf of the public, through the State, of these great corporations, and of the wealth engaged on a giant scale in business operations, must ever keep in mind that unless they do scrupulous justice to the corporation, unless they permit ample profit, and cordially encourage capable men of business so long as they act with honesty, they are striking at the root of our national well being; for in the long run, under the mere pressure of material distress, the people as a whole would probably go back to the reign of an unrestricted individualism rather than submit to a control by the State so drastic and so foolish, conceived in a spirit of such unreasonable and narrow hostility to wealth, as to prevent business operations from being profitable, and therefore to bring ruin upon the entire business community, and ultimately upon the entire body of citizens.

The opposition to government control of these great corporations makes its most effective effort in the shape of an appeal to the old doctrine of States' rights. Of course there are many sincere men who now believe in unrestricted individualism in business, just as there were formerly many sincere men who believed in slavery—that is, in the unrestricted right of an individual to own another individual. These men do not by themselves have great weight, however. The effective fight against adequate government control and supervision of individual, and especially of corporate, wealth engaged in interstate business is chiefly done under cover; and especially under cover of an appeal to States' rights. It is not at all infrequent to read in the same speech a denunciation of predatory wealth fostered by special privilege and defiant of both the public welfare and law of the land, and a denunciation of centralization in the centralized and organized wealth. Of course the policy set forth in such twin denunciations amounts to absolutely nothing, for the first half is nullified by the second half. The chief reason, among the many sound and compelling reasons, that led to the formation of the National Government was the absolute need that the Union, and not the several States, should deal with interstate and foreign commerce; and the power to deal with interstate commerce was granted absolutely and plenarily to the central government and was exercised completely as regards the only instruments of interstate commerce known in those days—the waterways, the highroads, as well as the partnerships of individuals who then conducted all of what business there was. Interstate commerce is now chiefly conducted by railroads; and the great corporation has supplanted the mass of small partnerships or individuals. The proposal to make the National Government supreme over, and therefore to give it complete control over, the railroads and other instruments of interstate commerce is merely a proposal to carry out to the letter one of the prime purposes, if not the prime purpose, for which the Constitution was founded. It does not represent centralization. It represents merely the acknowledgment of the patent fact that centralization has already come in business. If this irresponsible outside business power is to be controlled in the interest of the general public it can only be controlled in one way—by giving adequate power of control to the one sovereignty capable of exercising such power—the National Government. Forty or fifty separate State governments cannot exercise that power over corporations doing business in most or all of them; first, because they absolutely lack the authority to deal with interstate business in any form; and second, because of the inevitable conflict of authority sure to arise in the effort to enforce different kinds of State regulation, often inconsistent with one another and sometimes oppressive in themselves. Such divided authority cannot regulate commerce with wisdom and effect. The central government is the only power which, without oppression, can nevertheless thoroughly and adequately control and supervise the large corporations. To abandon the effort for national control means to abandon the effort for all adequate control and yet to render likely continual bursts of action by State legislatures, which cannot achieve the purpose sought for, but which can do a great deal of damage to the corporation without conferring any real benefit on the public.

I believe that the more far-sighted corporations are themselves coming to recognize the unwisdom of the violent hostility they have displayed during the last few years to regulation and control by the National Government of combinations engaged in interstate business. The truth is that we who believe in this movement of asserting and exercising a genuine control, in the public interest, over these great corporations have to contend against two sets of enemies, who, though nominally opposed to one another, are really allies in preventing a proper solution of the problem. There are, first, the big corporation men, and the extreme individualists among business men, who genuinely believe in utterly unregulated business—that is, in the reign of plutocracy; and, second, the men who, being blind to the economic movements of the day, believe in a movement of repression rather than of regulation of corporations, and who denounce both the power of the railroads and the exercise of the Federal power which alone can really control the railroads. Those who believe in efficient national control, on the other hand, do not in the least object to combinations; do not in the least object to concentration in business administration. On the contrary, they favor both, with the all-important proviso that there shall be such publicity about their workings, and such thoroughgoing control over them, as to insure their being in the interest, and not against the interest, of the general public. We do not object to the concentration of wealth and administration; but we do believe in the distribution of the wealth in profits to the real owners, and in securing to the public the full benefit of the concentrated administration. We believe that with concentration in administration there can come both the advantage of a larger ownership and of a more equitable distribution of profits, and at the same time a better service to the commonwealth. We believe that the administration should be for the benefit of the many; and that greed and rascality, practised on a large scale, should be punished as relentlessly as if practised on a small scale.

We do not for a moment believe that the problem will be solved by any short and easy method. The solution will come only by pressing various concurrent remedies. Some of these remedies must lie outside the domain of all government. Some must lie outside the domain of the Federal Government. But there is legislation which the Federal Government alone can enact and which is absolutely vital in order to secure the attainment of our purpose. Many laws are needed. There should be regulation by the National Government of the great interstate corporations, including a simple method of account-keeping, publicity, supervision of the issue of securities, abolition of rebates, and of special privileges. There should be short-time franchises for all corporations engaged in public business; including the corporations which get power from water rights. There should be national as well as State guardianship of mines and forests. The labor legislation hereinafter referred to should concurrently be enacted into law.

To accomplish this, means of course a certain increase in the use of—not the creation of—power, by the central government. The power already exists; it does not have to be created; the only question is whether it shall be used or left idle—and meanwhile the corporations over which the power ought to be exercised will not remain idle. Let those who object to this increase in the use of the only power available, the national power, be frank, and admit openly that they propose to abandon any effort to control the great business corporations and to exercise supervision over the accumulation and distribution of wealth; for such supervision and control can only come through this particular kind of increase of power. We no more believe in that empiricism which demands absolutely unrestrained individualism than we do in that empiricism which clamors for a deadening socialism which would destroy all individual initiative and would ruin the country with a completeness that not even an unrestrained individualism itself could achieve. The danger to American democracy lies not in the least in the concentration of administrative power in responsible and accountable hands. It lies in having the power insufficiently concentrated, so that no one can be held responsible to the people for its use. Concentrated power is palpable, visible, responsible, easily reached, quickly held to account. Power scattered through many administrators, many legislators, many men who work behind and through legislators and administrators, is impalpable, is unseen, is irresponsible, cannot be reached, cannot be held to account. Democracy is in peril wherever the administration of political power is scattered among a variety of men who work in secret, whose very names are unknown to the common people. It is not in peril from any man who derives authority from the people, who exercises it in sight of the people, and who is from time to time compelled to give an account of its exercise to the people.

LABOR

There are many matters affecting labor and the status of the wage-worker to which I should like to draw your attention, but an exhaustive discussion of the problem in all its aspects is not now necessary. This administration is nearing its end; and, moreover, under our form of government the solution of the problem depends upon the action of the States as much as upon the action of the nation. Nevertheless, there are certain considerations which I wish to set before you, because I hope that our people will more and more keep them in mind. A blind and ignorant resistance to every effort for the reform of abuses and for the readjustment of society to modern industrial conditions represents not true conservatism, but an incitement to the wildest radicalism; for wise radicalism and wise conservatism go hand in hand, one bent on progress, the other bent on seeing that no change is made unless in the right direction. I believe in a steady effort, or perhaps it would be more accurate to say in steady efforts in many different directions, to bring about a condition of affairs under which the men who work with hand or with brain, the laborers, the superintendents, the men who produce for the market and the men who find a market for the articles produced, shall own a far greater share than at present of the wealth they produce, and be enabled to invest it in the tools and instruments by which all work is carried on. As far as possible I hope to see a frank recognition of the advantages conferred by machinery, organization, and division of labor, accompanied by an effort to bring about a larger share in the ownership by wage-worker of railway, mill, and factory. In farming, this simply means that we wish to see the farmer own his own land; we do not wish to see the farms so large that they become the property of absentee landlords who farm them by tenants, nor yet so small that the farmer becomes like a European peasant. Again, the depositors in our savings-banks now number over one-tenth of our entire population. These are all capitalists, who through the savings-banks loan their money to the workers —that is, in many cases to themselves—to carry on their various industries. The more we increase their number, the more we introduce the principle of co-operation into our industry. Every increase in the number of small stockholders in corporations is a good thing, for the same reasons; and where the employees are the stockholders the result is particularly good. Very much of this movement must be outside of anything that can be accomplished by legislation; but legislation can do a good deal. Postal savings-banks will make it easy for the poorest to keep their savings in absolute safety. The regulation of the national highways must be such that they shall serve all people with equal justice. Corporate finances must be supervised so as to make it far safer than at present for the man of small means to invest his money in stocks. There must be prohibition of child labor, diminution of woman labor, shortening of hours of all mechanical labor; stock watering should be prohibited, and stock gambling so far as is possible discouraged. There should be a progressive inheritance tax on large fortunes. Industrial education should be encouraged. As far as possible we should lighten the burden of taxation on the small man. We should put a premium upon thrift, hard work, and business energy; but these qualities cease to be the main factors in accumulating a fortune long before that fortune reaches a point where it would be seriously affected by any inheritance tax such as I propose. It is eminently right that the nation should fix the terms upon which the great fortunes are inherited. They rarely do good and they often do harm to those who inherit them in their entirety.

PROTECTION FOR WAGE-EARNERS

The above is the merest sketch, hardly even a sketch in outline, of the reforms for which we should work. But there is one matter with which the Congress should deal at this session. There should no longer be any paltering with the question of taking care of the wage-workers who, under our present industrial system, become killed, crippled, or worn out as part of the regular incidents of a given business. The majority of wage-workers must have their rights secured for them by State action; but the National Government should legislate in thoroughgoing and far-reaching fashion not only for all employees of the National Government, but for all persons engaged in interstate commerce. The object sought for could be achieved to a measurable degree, as far as those killed or crippled are concerned, by proper employers' liability laws. As far as concerns those who have been worn out, I call your attention to the fact that definite steps toward providing old-age pensions have been taken in many of our private industries. These may be indefinitely extended through voluntary association and contributory schemes, or through the agency of savings-banks, as under the recent Massachusetts plan. To strengthen these practical measures should be our immediate duty; it is not at present necessary to consider the larger and more general governmental schemes that most European governments have found themselves obliged to adopt.

Our present system, or rather no system, works dreadful wrong, and is of benefit to only one class of people—the lawyers. When a workman is injured what he needs is not an expensive and doubtful lawsuit, but the certainty of relief through immediate administrative action. The number of accidents which result in the death or crippling of wage-workers, in the Union at large, is simply appalling; in a very few years it runs up a total far in excess of the aggregate of the dead and wounded in any modern war. No academic theory about "freedom of contract" or "constitutional liberty to contract" should be permitted to interfere with this and similar movements. Progress in civilization has everywhere meant a limitation and regulation of contract. I call your especial attention to the bulletin of the Bureau of Labor which gives a statement of the methods of treating the unemployed in European countries, as this is a subject which in Germany, for instance, is treated in connection with making provision for worn-out and crippled workmen.

Pending a thoroughgoing investigation and action there is certain legislation which should be enacted at once. The law, passed at the last session of the Congress, granting compensation to certain classes of employees of the government, should be extended to include all employees of the government, and should be made more liberal in its terms. There is no good ground for the distinction made in the law between those engaged in hazardous occupations and those not so engaged. If a man is injured or killed in any line of work, it was hazardous in his case. Whether one per cent or ten per cent of those following a given occupation actually suffer injury or death ought not to have any bearing on the question of their receiving compensation. It is a grim logic which says to an injured employee or to the dependents of one killed that he or they are entitled to no compensation because very few people other than he have been injured or killed in that occupation. Perhaps one of the most striking omissions in the law is that it does not embrace peace officers and others whose lives may be sacrificed in enforcing the laws of the United States. The terms of the act providing compensation should be made more liberal than in the present act. A year's compensation is not adequate for a wage-earner's family in the event of his death by accident in the course of his employment. And in the event of death occurring, say, ten or eleven months after the accident, the family would only receive as compensation the equivalent of one or two months' earnings. In this respect the generosity of the United States toward its employees compares most unfavorably with that of every country in Europe—even the poorest.

The terms of the act are also a hardship in prohibiting payment in cases where the accident is in any way due to the negligence of the employee. It is inevitable that daily familiarity with danger will lead men to take chances that can be construed into negligence. So well is this recognized that in practically all countries in the civilized world, except the United States, only a great degree of negligence acts as a bar to securing compensation. Probably in no other respect is our legislation, both State and national, so far behind practically the entire civilized world as in the matter of liability and compensation for accidents in industry. It is humiliating that at European international congresses on accidents the United States should be singled out as the most belated among the nations in respect to employers' liability legislation. This government is itself a large employer of labor, and in its dealings with its employees it should set a standard in this country which would place it on a par with the most progressive countries in Europe. The laws of the United States in this respect and the laws of European countries have been summarized in a recent Bulletin of the Bureau of Labor, and no American who reads this summary can fail to be struck by the great contrast between our practices and theirs—a contrast not in any sense to our credit.

The Congress should without further delay pass a model employers' liability law for the District of Columbia. The employers' liability act recently declared unconstitutional, on account of apparently including in its provisions employees engaged in intrastate commerce as well as those engaged in interstate commerce, has been held by the local courts to be still in effect so far as its provisions apply to the District of Columbia. There should be no ambiguity on this point. If there is any doubt on the subject, the law should be re-enacted with special reference to the District of Columbia. This act, however, applies only to employees of common carriers. In all other occupations the liability law of the District is the old common law. The severity and injustice of the common law in this matter has been in some degree or another modified in the majority of our States, and the only jurisdiction under the exclusive control of the Congress should be ahead and not behind the States of the Union in this respect. A comprehensive employers' liability law should be passed for the District of Columbia.

I renew my recommendation made in a previous message that half-holidays be granted during summer to all wage-workers in government employ.

I also renew my recommendation that the principle of the eight-hour day should as rapidly and as far as practicable be extended to the entire work being carried on by the government; the present law should be amended to embrace contracts on those public works which the present wording of the act seems to exclude.

THE COURTS

I most earnestly urge upon the Congress the duty of increasing the totally inadequate salaries now given to our judges. On the whole there is no body of public servants who do as valuable work, nor whose moneyed reward is so inadequate compared to their work. Beginning with the Supreme Court, the judges should have their salaries doubled. It is not befitting the dignity of the nation that its most honored public servants should be paid sums so small compared to what they would earn in private life that the performance of public service by them implies an exceedingly heavy pecuniary sacrifice.

It is earnestly to be desired that some method should be devised for doing away with the long delays which now obtain in the administration of justice, and which operate with peculiar severity against persons of small means, and favor only the very criminals whom it is most desirable to punish. These long delays in the final decisions of cases make in the aggregate a crying evil; and a remedy should be devised. Much of this intolerable delay is due to improper regard paid to technicalities which are a mere hindrance to justice. In some noted recent cases this overregard for technicalities has resulted in a striking denial of justice, and flagrant wrong to the body politic.

At the last election certain leaders of organized labor made a violent and sweeping attack upon the entire judiciary of the country, an attack couched in such terms as to include the most upright, honest, and broad-minded judges, no less than those of narrower mind and more restricted outlook. It was the kind of attack admirably fitted to prevent any successful attempt to reform abuses of the judiciary, because it gave the champions of the unjust judge their eagerly desired opportunity to shift their ground into a championship of just judges who were unjustly assailed. Last year, before the House Committee on the Judiciary, these same labor leaders formulated their demands, specifying the bill that contained them, refusing all compromise, stating they wished the principle of that bill or nothing. They insisted on a provision that in a labor dispute no injunction should issue except to protect a property right, and specifically provided that the right to carry on business should not be construed as a property right; and in a second provision their bill made legal in a labor dispute any act or agreement by or between two or more persons that would not have been unlawful if done by a single person. In other words, this bill legalized blacklisting and boycotting in every form, legalizing, for instance, those forms of the secondary boycott which the anthracite-coal strike commission so unreservedly condemned; while the right to carry on a business was explicitly taken out from under that protection which the law throws over property. The demand was made that there should be trial by jury in contempt cases, thereby most seriously impairing the authority of the courts. All this represented a course of policy which, if carried out, would mean the enthronement of class privilege in its crudest and most brutal form, and the destruction of one of the most essential functions of the judiciary in all civilized lands.

The violence of the crusade for this legislation, and its complete failure, illustrate two truths which it is essential our people should learn. In the first place, they ought to teach the working man, the laborer, the wage-worker, that by demanding what is improper and impossible he plays into the hands of his foes. Such a crude and vicious attack upon the courts, even if it were temporarily successful, would inevitably in the end cause a violent reaction and would band the great mass of citizens together, forcing them to stand by all the judges, competent and incompetent alike, rather than to see the wheels of justice stopped. A movement of this kind can ultimately result in nothing but damage to those in whose behalf it is nominally undertaken. This is a most healthy truth, which it is wise for all our people to learn. Any movement based on that class hatred which at times assumes the name of "class consciousness" is certain ultimately to fail, and if it temporarily succeeds, to do far-reaching damage. "Class consciousness," where it is merely another name for the odious vice of class selfishness, is equally noxious whether in an employer's association or in a working man's association. The movement in question was one in which the appeal was made to all working men to vote primarily, not as American citizens, but as individuals of a certain class in society. Such an appeal in the first place revolts the more high-minded and far-sighted among the persons to whom it is addressed, and in the second place tends to arouse a strong antagonism among all other classes of citizens, whom it therefore tends to unite against the very organization on whose behalf it is issued. The result is therefore unfortunate from every standpoint. This healthy truth, by the way, will be learned by the Socialists if they ever succeed in establishing in this country an important national party based on such class consciousness and selfish class interest.

The wage-workers, the working men, the laboring men of

the country, by the way in which they repudiated the effort to get them to cast their votes in response to an appeal to class hatred, have emphasized their sound patriotism and Americanism. The whole country has cause to feel pride in this attitude of sturdy independence, in this uncompromising insistence upon acting simply as good citizens, as good Americans, without regard to fancied—and improper—class interests. Such an attitude is an object-lesson in good citizenship to the entire nation.

JUDICIAL DECISIONS

But the extreme reactionaries, the persons who blind themselves to the wrongs now and then committed by the courts on laboring men, should also think seriously as to what such a movement as this portends. The judges who have shown themselves able and willing effectively to check the dishonest activity of the very rich man who works iniquity by the mismanagement of corporations, who have shown themselves alert to do justice to the wage-worker, and sympathetic with the needs of the mass of our people, so that the dweller in the tenement-houses, the man who practises a dangerous trade, the man who is crushed by excessive hours of labor, feel that their needs are understood by the courts—these judges are the real bulwark of the courts; these judges, the judges of the stamp of the President-elect, who have been fearless in opposing labor when it has gone wrong, but fearless also in holding to strict account corporations that work iniquity, and far-sighted in seeing that the working man gets his rights, are the men of all others to whom we owe it that the appeal for such violent and mistaken legislation has fallen on deaf ears, that the agitation for its passage proved to be without substantial basis. The courts are jeopardized primarily by the action of those Federal and State judges who show inability or unwillingness to put a stop to the wrong-doing of very rich men under modern industrial conditions, and inability or unwillingness to give relief to men of small means or wage-workers who are crushed down by these modern industrial conditions; who, in other words, fail to understand and apply the needed remedies for the new wrongs produced by the new and highly complex social and industrial civilization which has grown up in the last half-century.

The rapid changes in our social and industrial life which have attended this rapid growth have made it necessary that, in applying to concrete cases the great rule of right laid down in our Constitution, there should be a full understanding and appreciation of the new conditions to which the rules are to be applied. What would have been an infringement upon liberty half a century ago may be the necessary safeguard of liberty to-day. What would have been an injury to property then may be necessary to the enjoyment of property now. Every judicial decision involves two terms—one, as interpretation of the law; the other, the understanding of the facts to which it is to be applied. The great mass of our judicial officers are, I believe, alive to those changes of conditions which so materially affect the performance of their judicial duties. Our judicial system is sound and effective at core, and it remains, and must ever be maintained, as the safeguard of those principles of liberty and justice which stand at the foundation of American institutions; for, as Burke finely said, when liberty and justice are separated, neither is safe. There are, however, some members of the judicial body who have lagged behind in their understanding of these great and vital changes in the body politic, whose minds have never been opened to the new applications of the old principles made necessary by the new conditions. Judges of this stamp do lasting harm by their decisions, because they convince poor men in need of protection that the courts of the land are profoundly ignorant of and out of sympathy with their needs, and profoundly indifferent or hostile to any proposed remedy. To such men it seems a cruel mockery to have any court decide against them on the ground that it desires to preserve "liberty" in a purely technical form, by withholding liberty in any real and constructive sense. It is desirable that the legislative body should possess, and wherever necessary exercise, the power to determine whether in a given case employers and employees are not on an equal footing, so that the necessities of the latter compel them to submit to such exactions as to hours and conditions of labor as unduly to tax their strength; and only mischief can result when such determination is upset on the ground that there must be no "interference with the liberty to contract"—often a merely academic "liberty," the exercise of which is the negation of real liberty.

There are certain decisions by various courts which have been exceedingly detrimental to the rights of wage-workers. This is true of all the decisions that decide that men and women are, by the Constitution, "guaranteed their liberty" to contract to enter a dangerous occupation, or to work an undesirable or improper number of hours, or to work in unhealthy surroundings; and therefore cannot recover damages when maimed in that occupation and cannot be forbidden to work what the legislature decides is an excessive number of hours, or to carry on the work under conditions which the legislature decides to be unhealthy. The most dangerous occupations are often the poorest paid and those where the hours of work are longest; and in many cases those who go into them are driven by necessity so great that they have practically no alternative. Decisions such as those alluded to above nullify the legislative effort to protect the wage-workers who most need protection from those employers who take advantage of their grinding need. They halt or hamper the movement for securing better and more equitable conditions of labor. The talk about preserving to the misery-hunted beings who make contracts for such service their "liberty" to make them, is either to speak in a spirit of heartless irony or else to show an utter lack of knowledge of the conditions of life among the great masses of our fellow countrymen, a lack which unfits a judge to do good service just as it would unfit any executive or legislative officer.

There is also, I think, ground for the belief that substantial injustice is often suffered by employees in consequence of the custom of courts issuing temporary injunctions without notice to them, and punishing them for contempt of court in instances where, as a matter of fact, they have no knowledge of any proceedings. Outside of organized labor there is a wide-spread feeling that this system often works great injustice to wage-workers when their efforts to better their working condition result in industrial disputes. A temporary injunction procured ex parte may as a matter of fact have all the effect of a permanent injunction in causing disaster to the wage-workers' side in such a dispute. Organized labor is chafing under the unjust restraint which comes from repeated resort to this plan of procedure. Its discontent has been unwisely expressed, and often improperly expressed, but there is a sound basis for it, and the orderly and law-abiding people of a community would be in a far stronger position for upholding the courts if the undoubtedly existing abuses could be provided against.

Such proposals as those mentioned above as advocated by the extreme labor leaders contain the vital error of being class legislation of the most offensive kind, and even if enacted into law I believe that the law would rightly be held unconstitutional. Moreover, the labor people are themselves now beginning to invoke the use of the power of injunction. During the last ten years, and within my own knowledge, at least fifty injunctions have been obtained by labor-unions in New York City alone, most of them being to protect the union label (a "property right"), but some being obtained for other reasons against employers. The power of injunction is a great equitable remedy, which should on no account be destroyed. But safeguards should be erected against its abuse. I believe that some such provisions as those I advocated a year ago for checking the abuse of the issuance of temporary injunctions should be adopted. In substance, provision should be made that no injunction or temporary restraining order issue otherwise than on notice, except where irreparable injury would otherwise result; and in such case a hearing on the merits of the order should be had within a short fixed period, and, if not then continued after hearing, it should forthwith lapse. Decisions should be rendered immediately, and the chance of delay minimized in every way. Moreover, I believe that the procedure should be sharply defined, and the judge required minutely to state the particulars both of his action and of his reasons therefor, so that the Congress can, if it desires, examine and investigate the same.

The chief lawmakers in our country may be, and often are, the judges, because they are the final seat of authority. Every time they interpret contract, property, vested rights, due process of law, liberty, they necessarily enact into law parts of a system of social philosophy; and as such interpretation is fundamental, they give direction to all lawmaking. The decisions of the courts on economic and social questions depend upon their economic and social philosophy; and for the peaceful progress of our people during the twentieth century we shall owe most to those judges who hold to a twentieth-century economic and social philosophy and not to a long outgrown philosophy, which was itself the product of primitive economic conditions. Of course a judge's views on progressive social philosophy are entirely second in importance to his possession of a high and fine character; which means the possession of such elementary virtues as honesty, courage, and fair-mindedness. The judge who owes his election to pandering to demagogic sentiments or class hatreds and prejudices, and the judge who owes either his election or his appointment to the money or the favor of a great corporation, are alike unworthy to sit on the bench, are alike traitors to the people; and no profundity of legal learning, or correctness of abstract conviction on questions of public policy, can serve as an offset to such shortcomings. But it is also true that judges, like executives and legislators, should hold sound views on the questions of public policy which are of vital interest to the people.

The legislators and executives are chosen to represent the people in enacting and administering the laws. The judges are not chosen to represent the people in this sense. Their function is to interpret the laws. The legislators are responsible for the laws; the judges for the spirit in which they interpret and enforce the laws. We stand aloof from the reckless agitators who would make the judges mere pliant tools of popular prejudice and passion; and we stand aloof from those equally unwise partisans of reaction and privilege who deny the proposition that, inasmuch as judges are chosen to serve the interests of the whole people, they should strive to find out what those interests are, and, so far as they conscientiously can, should strive to give effect to popular conviction when deliberately and duly expressed by the lawmaking body. The courts are to be highly commended and stanchly upheld when they set their faces against wrong-doing or tyranny by a majority; but they are to be blamed when they fail to recognize under a government like ours the deliberate judgment of the majority as to a matter of legitimate policy, when duly expressed by the legislature. Such lawfully expressed and deliberate judgment should be given effect by the courts, save in the extreme and exceptional cases where there has been a clear violation of a constitutional provision. Anything like frivolity or wantonness in upsetting such clearly taken governmental action is a grave offense against the Republic. To protest against tyranny, to protect minorities from oppression, to nullify an act committed in a spasm of popular fury, is to render a service to the Republic. But for the courts to arrogate to themselves functions which properly belong to the legislative bodies is all wrong, and in the end works mischief. The people should not be permitted to pardon evil and slipshod legislation on the theory that the court will set it right; they should be taught that the right way to get rid of a bad law is to have the legislature repeal it, and not to have the courts by ingenious hair-splitting nullify it. A law may be unwise and improper; but it should not for these reasons be declared unconstitutional by a strained interpretation, for the result of such action is to take away from the people at large their sense of responsibility and ultimately to destroy their capacity for orderly self-restraint and self-government. Under such a popular government as ours, founded on the theory that in the long run the will of the people is supreme, the ultimate safety of the nation can only rest in training and guiding the people so that what they will shall be right, and not in devising means to defeat their will by the technicalities of strained construction.

For many of the shortcomings of justice in our country our people as a whole are themselves to blame, and the judges and juries merely bear their share together with the public as a whole. It is discreditable to us as a people that there should be difficulty in convicting murderers, or in bringing to justice men who as public servants have been guilty of corruption, or who have profited by the corruption of public servants. The result is equally unfortunate, whether due to hair-splitting technicalities in the interpretation of law by judges, to sentimentality and class consciousness on the part of juries, or to hysteria and sensationalism in the daily press. For much of this failure of justice no responsibility whatever lies on rich men as such. We who make up the mass of the people cannot shift the responsibility from our own shoulders. But there is an important part of the failure which has specially to do with inability to hold to proper account men of wealth who behave badly.

The chief breakdown is in dealing with the new relations that arise from the mutualism, the interdependence of our time. Every new social relation begets a new type of wrong-doing —of sin, to use an old-fashioned word—and many years always elapse before society is able to turn this sin into crime which can be effectively punished at law. During the lifetime of the older men now alive the social relations have changed far more rapidly than in the preceding two centuries. The immense growth of corporations, of business done by associations, and the extreme strain and pressure of modern life, have produced conditions which render the public confused as to who its really dangerous foes are; and among the public servants who have not only shared this confusion, but by some of their acts have increased it, are certain judges. Marked inefficiency has been shown in dealing with corporations and in resettling the proper attitude to be taken by the public not only toward corporations, but toward labor and toward the social questions arising out of the factory system and the enormous growth of our great cities.

The huge wealth that has been accumulated by a few individuals of recent years, in what has amounted to a social and industrial revolution, has been as regards some of these individuals made possible only by the improper use of the modern corporation. A certain type of modern corporation, with its officers and agents, its many issues of securities, and its constant consolidation with allied undertakings, finally becomes an instrument so complex as to contain a greater number of elements that, under various judicial decisions, lend themselves to fraud and oppression than any device yet evolved in the human brain. Corporations are necessary instruments of modern business. They have been permitted to become a menace largely because the governmental representatives of the people have worked slowly in providing for adequate control over them.

The chief offender in any given case may be an executive, a legislature, or a judge. Every executive head who advises violent, instead of gradual, action, or who advocates ill-considered and sweeping measures of reform (especially if they are tainted with vindictiveness and disregard for the rights of the minority) is particularly blameworthy. The several legislatures are responsible for the fact that our laws are often prepared with slovenly haste and lack of consideration. Moreover, they are often prepared, and still more frequently amended during passage, at the suggestion of the very parties against whom they are afterward enforced. Our great clusters of corporations, huge trusts and fabulously wealthy multimillionaires, employ the very best lawyers they can obtain to pick flaws in these statutes after their passage; but they also employ a class of secret agents who seek, under the advice of experts, to render hostile legislation innocuous by making it unconstitutional, often through the insertion of what appear on their face to be drastic and sweeping provisions against the interests of the parties inspiring them; while the demagogues, the corrupt creatures who introduce blackmailing schemes to "strike" corporations, and all who demand extreme, and undesirably radical, measures, show themselves to be the worst enemies of the very public whose loud-mouthed champions they profess to be. A very striking illustration of the consequences of carelessness in the preparation of a statute was the employers' liability law of 1906. In the cases arising under that law, four out of six courts of first instance held it unconstitutional; six out of nine justices of the Supreme Court held that its subject-matter was within the province of congressional action; and four of the nine justices held it valid. It was, however, adjudged unconstitutional by a bare majority of the court—five to four. It was surely a very slovenly piece of work to frame the legislation in such shape as to leave the question open at all.

Real damage has been done by the manifold and conflicting interpretations of the interstate commerce law. Control over the great corporations doing interstate business can be effective only if it is vested with full power in an administrative department, a branch of the Federal executive, carrying out a Federal law; it can never be effective if a divided responsibility is left in both the States and the nation; it can never be effective if left in the hands of the courts to be decided by lawsuits.

The courts hold a place of peculiar and deserved sanctity under our form of government. Respect for the law is essential to the permanence of our institutions; and respect for the law is largely conditioned upon respect for the courts. It is an offense against the Republic to say anything which can weaken this respect, save for the gravest reason and in the most carefully guarded manner. Our judges should be held in peculiar honor; and the duty of respectful and truthful comment and criticism, which should be binding when we speak of anybody, should be especially binding when we speak of them. On an average they stand above any other servants of the community, and the greatest judges have reached the high level held by those few greatest patriots whom the whole country delights to honor. But we must face the fact that there are wise and unwise judges, just as there are wise and unwise executives and legislators. When a president or a governor behaves improperly or unwisely, the remedy is easy, for his term is short; the same is true with the legislator, although not to the same degree, for he is one of many who belong to some given legislative body, and it is therefore less easy to fix his personal responsibility and hold him accountable therefor. With a judge, who, being human, is also likely to err, but whose tenure is for life, there is no similar way of holding him to responsibility. Under ordinary conditions the only forms of pressure to which he is in any way amenable are public opinion and the action of his fellow judges. It is the last which is most immediately effective, and to which we should look for the reform of abuses. Any remedy applied from without is fraught with risk. It is far better, from every standpoint, that the remedy should come from within. In no other nation in the world do the courts wield such vast and far-reaching power as in the United States. All that is necessary is that the courts as a whole should exercise this power with the far-sighted wisdom already shown by those judges who scan the future while they act in the present. Let them exercise this great power not only honestly and bravely, but with wise insight into the needs and fixed purposes of the people, so that they may do justice and work equity, so that they may protect all persons in their rights, and yet break down the barriers of privilege, which is the foe of right.

FORESTS

If there is any one duty which more than another we owe it to our children and our children's children to perform at once, it is to save the forests of this country, for they constitute the first and most important element in the conservation of the natural resources of the country. There are of course two kinds of natural resources. One is the kind which can only be used as part of a process of exhaustion; this is true of mines, natural oil and gas wells, and the like. The other, and of course ultimately by far the most important, includes the resources which can be improved in the process of wise use; the soil, the rivers, and the forests come under this head. Any really civilized nation will so use all of these three great national assets that the nation will have their benefit in the future. Just as a farmer, after all his life making his living from his farm, will, if he is an expert farmer, leave it as an asset of increased value to his son, so we should leave our national domain to our children, increased in value and not worn out. There are small sections of our own country, in the East and the West, in the Adirondacks, the White Mountains, and the Appalachians, and in the Rocky Mountains, where we can already see for ourselves the damage in the shape of permanent injury to the soil and the river systems which comes from reckless deforestation. It matters not whether this deforestation is due to the actual reckless cutting of timber, to the fires that inevitably follow such reckless cutting of timber, or to reckless and uncontrolled grazing, especially by the great migratory bands of sheep, the unchecked wandering of which over the country means destruction to forests and disaster to the small home-makers, the settlers of limited means.

Short-sighted persons, or persons blinded to the future by desire to make money in every way out of the present, sometimes speak as if no great damage would be done by the reckless destruction of our forests. It is difficult to have patience with the arguments of these persons. Thanks to our own recklessness in the use of our splendid forests, we have already crossed the verge of a timber famine in this country, and no measures that we now take can, at least for many years, undo the mischief that has already been done. But we can prevent further mischief being done; and it would be in the highest degree reprehensible to let any consideration of temporary convenience or temporary cost interfere with such action, especially as regards the national forests which the nation can *now,* at this very moment, control.

All serious students of the question are aware of the great damage that has been done in the Mediterranean countries of Europe, Asia, and Africa by deforestation. The similar damage that has been done in eastern Asia is less well known. A recent investigation into conditions in North China by Mr. Frank N. Meyer, of the Bureau of Plant Industry of the United States Department of Agriculture, has incidentally furnished in very striking fashion proof of the ruin that comes from reckless deforestation of mountains, and of the further fact that the damage once done may prove practically irreparable. So important are these investigations that I herewith attach as an appendix to my message certain photographs showing present conditions in China. They show in vivid fashion the appalling desolation, taking the shape of barren mountains and gravel and sand-covered plains, which immediately follows and depends upon the deforestation of the mountains. Not many centuries ago the country of northern China was one of the most fertile and beautiful spots in the entire world, and was heavily forested. We know this not only from the old Chinese records, but from the accounts given by the traveller Marco Polo. He, for instance, mentions that in visiting the provinces of Shansi and Shensi he observed many plantations of mulberry-trees. Now there is hardly a single mulberry-tree in either of these provinces, and the culture of the silkworm has moved farther south, to regions of atmospheric moisture. As an illustration of the complete change in the rivers, we may take Polo's statement that a certain river, the Hun Ho, was so large and deep that merchants ascended it from the sea with heavily laden boats; to-day this river is simply a broad sandy bed, with shallow, rapid currents wandering hither and thither across it, absolutely unnavigable. But we do not have to depend upon written records. The dry wells, and the wells with water far below the former watermark, bear testimony to the good days of the past and the evil days of the present. Wherever the native vegetation has been allowed to remain, as, for instance, here and there around a sacred temple or imperial burying-ground, there are still huge trees and tangled jungle, fragments of the glorious ancient forests. The thick, matted forest growth formerly covered the mountains to their summits. All natural factors favored this dense forest growth, and as long as it was permitted to exist the plains at the foot of the mountains were among the most fertile on the globe, and the whole country was a garden. Not the slightest effort was made, however, to prevent the unchecked cutting of the trees, or to secure reforestation. Doubtless for many centuries the tree-cutting by the inhabitants of the mountains worked but slowly in bringing about the changes that have now come to pass; doubtless for generations the inroads were scarcely noticeable. But there came a time when the forest had shrunk sufficiently to make each year's cutting a serious matter, and from that time on the destruction proceeded with appalling rapidity; for of course each year of destruction rendered the forest less able to recuperate, less able to resist next year's inroad. Mr. Meyer describes the ceaseless progress of the destruction even now, when there is so little left to destroy. Every morning men and boys go out armed with mattox or axe, scale the steepest mountainsides, and cut down and grub out, root and branch, the small trees and shrubs still to be found. The big trees disappeared centuries ago, so that now one of these is never seen save in the neighborhood of temples, where they are artificially protected; and even here it takes all the watch and care of the tree-loving priests to prevent their destruction.

Each family, each community, where there is no common care exercised in the interest of all of them to prevent deforestation, finds its profit in the immediate use of the fuel which would otherwise be used by some other family or some other community. In the total absence of regulation of the matter in the interest of the whole people, each small group is inevitably pushed into a policy of destruction which cannot afford to take thought for the morrow. This is just one of those matters which it is fatal to leave to unsupervised individual control. The forest can only be protected by the State, by the nation; and the liberty of action of individuals must be conditioned upon what the State or nation determines to be necessary for the common safety.

The lesson of deforestation in China is a lesson which mankind should have learned many times already from what has occurred in other places. Denudation leaves naked soil; then gullying cuts down to the bare rock; and meanwhile the rock waste buries the bottom-lands. When the soil is gone, men must go; and the process does not take long.

This ruthless destruction of the forests in northern China has brought about, or has aided in bringing about, desolation, just as the destruction of the forests in central Asia aided in bringing ruin to the once rich central Asian cities; just as the destruction of the forests in northern Africa helped toward the ruin of a region that was a fertile granary in Roman days. Short-sighted man, whether barbaric, semicivilized, or what he mistakenly regards as fully civilized, when he has destroyed the forests, has rendered certain the ultimate destruction of the land itself. In northern China the mountains are now such as are shown by the accompanying photographs, absolutely barren peaks. Not only have the forests been destroyed, but because of their destruction the soil has been washed off the naked rock. The terrible consequence is that it is impossible now to undo the damage that has been done. Many centuries would have to pass before soil would again collect, or could be made to collect, in sufficient quantity once more to support the old-time forest growth. In consequence the Mongol Desert is practically extending eastward over northern China. The climate has changed and is still changing. It has changed even within the last half-century, as the work of tree destruction has been consummated. The great masses of arboreal vegetation on the mountains formerly absorbed the heat of the sun and sent up currents of cool air which brought the moisture-laden clouds lower and forced them to precipitate in rain a part of their burden of water. Now that there is no vegetation, the barren mountains, scorched by the sun, send up currents of heated air which drive away instead of attracting the rain-clouds, and cause their moisture to be disseminated. In consequence, instead of the regular and plentiful rains which existed in these regions of China when the forests were still in evidence, the unfortunate inhabitants of the deforested lands now see their crops wither for lack of rainfall, while the seasons grow more and more irregular; and as the air becomes drier certain crops refuse longer to grow at all. That everything dries out faster than formerly is shown by the fact that the level of the wells all over the land has sunk perceptibly, many of them having become totally dry. In addition to the resulting agricultural distress, the watercourses have changed. Formerly they were narrow and deep, with an abundance of clear water the year around; for the roots and humus of the forests caught the rain-water and let it escape by slow, regular seepage. They have now become broad, shallow stream-beds, in which muddy water trickles in slender currents during the dry seasons, while when it rains there are freshets, and roaring muddy torrents come tearing down, bringing disaster and destruction everywhere. Moreover, these floods and freshets, which diversify the general dryness, wash away from the mountainsides, and either wash away or cover in the valleys, the rich fertile soil which it took tens of thousands of years for nature to form; and it is lost forever, and until the forests grow again it cannot be replaced. The sand and stones from the mountainsides are washed loose and come rolling down to cover the arable lands, and in consequence, throughout this part of China, many formerly rich districts are now sandy wastes, useless for human cultivation and even for pasture. The cities have been of course seriously affected, for the streams have gradually ceased to be navigable. There is testimony that even within the memory of men now living there has been a serious diminution of the rainfall of northeastern China. The level of the Sungari River in northern Manchuria has been sensibly lowered during the last fifty years, at least partly as the result of the indiscriminate cutting of the forests forming its watershed. Almost all the rivers of northern China have become uncontrollable, and very dangerous to the dwellers along their banks, as a direct result of the destruction of the forests. The journey from Peking to Jehol shows in melancholy fashion how the soil has been washed away from whole valleys, so that they have been converted into deserts.

In northern China this disastrous process has gone on so long and has proceeded so far that no complete remedy could be applied. There are certain mountains in China from which the soil is gone so utterly that only the slow action of the ages could again restore it; although of course much could be done to prevent the still further eastward extension of the Mongolian Desert if the Chinese Government would act at once. The accompanying cuts from photographs show the inconceivable desolation of the barren mountains in which certain of these rivers rise—mountains, be it remembered, which formerly supported dense forests of larches and firs, now unable to produce any wood, and because of their condition a source of danger to the whole country. The photographs also show the same rivers after they have passed through the mountains, the beds having become broad and sandy because of the deforestation of the mountains. One of the photographs shows a caravan passing through a valley. Formerly, when the mountains were forested, it was thickly peopled by prosperous peasants. Now the floods have carried destruction all over the land and the valley is a stony desert. Another photograph shows a mountain road covered with the stones and rocks that are brought down in the rainy season from the mountains which have already been deforested by human hands. Another shows a pebbly river-bed in southern Manchuria where what was once a great stream has dried up owing to the deforestation in the mountains. Only some scrub-wood is left, which will disappear within a half-century. Yet another shows the effect of one of the washouts, destroying an arable mountainside, these washouts being due to the removal of all vegetation; yet in this photograph the foreground shows that reforestation is still a possibility in places.

What has thus happened in northern China, what has happened in central Asia, in Palestine, in North Africa, in parts of the Mediterranean countries of Europe, will surely happen in our country if we do not exercise that wise forethought which should be one of the chief marks of any people calling itself civilized. Nothing should be permitted to stand in the way of the preservation of the forests, and it is criminal to permit individuals to purchase a little gain for themselves through the destruction of forests when this destruction is fatal to the well-being of the whole country in the future.

INLAND WATERWAYS

Action should be begun forthwith, during the present session of the Congress, for the improvement of our inland waterways—action which will result in giving us not only navigable but navigated rivers. We have spent hundreds of millions of dollars upon these waterways, yet the traffic on nearly all of them is steadily declining. This condition is the direct result of the absence of any comprehensive and far-seeing plan of waterway improvement. Obviously we cannot continue thus to expend the revenues of the government without return. It is poor business to spend money for inland navigation unless we get it.

Inquiry into the condition of the Mississippi and its principal tributaries reveals very many instances of the utter waste caused by the methods which have hitherto obtained for the so-called "improvement" of navigation. A striking instance is supplied by the "improvement" of the Ohio, which, begun in 1824, was continued under a single plan for half a century. In 1875 a new plan was adopted and followed for a quarter of a century. In 1902 still a different plan was adopted and has since been pursued at a rate which only promises a navigable river in from twenty to one hundred years longer.

Such short-sighted, vacillating, and futile methods are accompanied by decreasing water-borne commerce and increasing traffic congestion on land, by increasing floods, and by the waste of public money. The remedy lies in abandoning the methods which have so signally failed and adopting new ones in keeping with the needs and demands of our people.

In a report on a measure introduced at the first session of the present Congress, the secretary of war said: "The chief defect in the methods hitherto pursued lies in the absence of executive authority for originating comprehensive plans covering the country or natural divisions thereof." In this opinion I heartily concur. The present methods not only fail to give us inland navigation, but they are injurious to the army as well. What is virtually a permanent detail of the corps of engineers to civilian duty necessarily impairs the efficiency of our military establishment. The military engineers have undoubtedly done efficient work in actual construction, but they are necessarily unsuited by their training and traditions to take the broad view, and to gather and transmit to the Congress the commercial and industrial information and forecasts, upon which waterway improvement must always so largely rest. Furthermore, they have failed to grasp the great underlying fact that every stream is a unit from its source to its mouth, and that all its uses are interdependent. Prominent officers of the engineer corps have recently even gone so far as to assert in print that waterways are not dependent upon the conservation of the forests about their headwaters. This position is opposed to all the recent work of the scientific bureaus of the government and to the general experience of mankind. A physician who disbelieved in vaccination would not be the right man to handle an epidemic of smallpox, nor should we leave a doctor sceptical about the transmission of yellow fever by the Stegomyia mosquito in charge of sanitation at Havana or Panama. So with the improvement of our rivers; it is no longer wise or safe to leave this great work in the hands of men who fail to grasp the essential relations between navigation and general development and to assimilate and use the central facts about our streams.

Until the work of river improvement is undertaken in a modern way it cannot have results that will meet the needs of this modern nation. These needs should be met without further dilly-dallying or delay. The plan which promises the best and quickest results is that of a permanent commission authorized to co-ordinate the work of all the government departments relating to waterways, and to frame and supervise the execution of a comprehensive plan. Under such a commission the actual work of construction might be intrusted to the reclamation service; or to the military engineers acting with a sufficient number of civilians to continue the work in time of war; or it might be divided between the reclamation service and the corps of engineers. Funds should be provided from current revenues if it is deemed wise—otherwise from the sale of bonds. The essential thing is that the work should go forward under the best possible plan, and with the least possible delay. We should have a new type of work and a new organization for planning and directing it. The time for playing with our waterways is past. The country demands results.

NATIONAL PARKS

I urge that all our national parks adjacent to national forests be placed completely under the control of the forest service of the Agricultural Department, instead of leaving them as they now are, under the Interior Department and policed by the army. The Congress should provide for superintendents with adequate corps of first-class civilian scouts, or rangers, and, further, place the road construction under the superintendent instead of leaving it with the War Department. Such a change in park management would result in economy and avoid the difficulties of administration which now arise from having the responsibility of care and protection divided between different departments. The need for this course is peculiarly great in the Yellowstone Park. This, like the Yosemite, is a great wonderland, and should be kept as a national playground. In both, all wild things should be protected and the scenery kept wholly unmarred.

I am happy to say that I have been able to set aside in various parts of the country small, well-chosen tracts of ground to serve as sanctuaries and nurseries for wild creatures.

DENATURED ALCOHOL

I had occasion in my message of May 4, 1906, to urge the passage of some law putting alcohol, used in the arts, industries, and manufactures, upon the free list—that is, to provide for the withdrawal free of tax of alcohol which is to be denatured for those purposes. The law of June 7, 1906, and its amendment of March 2, 1907, accomplished what was desired in that respect, and the use of denatured alcohol, as intended, is making a fair degree of progress and is entitled to further encouragement and support from the Congress.

PURE FOOD

The pure-food legislation has already worked a benefit difficult to overestimate.

INDIAN SERVICE

It has been my purpose from the beginning of my administration to take the Indian Service completely out of the atmosphere of political activity, and there has been steady progress toward that end. The last remaining stronghold of politics in that service was the agency system, which had seen its best days and was gradually falling to pieces from natural or purely evolutionary causes, but, like all such survivals, was decaying slowly in its later stages. It seems clear that its extinction had better be made final now, so that the ground can be cleared for larger constructive work on behalf of the Indians, preparatory to their induction into the full measure of responsible citizenship. On November 1 only eighteen agencies were left on the roster; with two exceptions, where some legal questions seemed to stand temporarily in the way, these have been changed to superintendencies, and their heads brought into the classified civil service.

SECRET SERVICE

Last year an amendment was incorporated in the measure providing for the Secret Service, which provided that there should be no detail from the Secret Service and no transfer therefrom. It is not too much to say that this amendment has been of benefit only, and could be of benefit only, to the criminal classes. If deliberately introduced for the purpose of diminishing the effectiveness of war against crime it could not have been better devised to this end. It forbade the practices that had been followed to a greater or less extent by the executive heads of various departments for twenty years. To these practices we owe the securing of the evidence which enabled us to drive great lotteries out of business and secure a quarter of a million of dollars in fines from their promoters. These practices have enabled us to get some of the evidence in connection with the theft of government land and government timber by great corporations and by individuals. These practices have enabled us to get some of the evidence indispensable in order to secure the conviction of the wealthiest and most formidable criminals with whom the government has to deal, both those operating in violation of the antitrust law and others. The amendment in question was of benefit to no one excepting to these criminals, and it seriously hampers the government in the detection of crime and the securing of justice. Moreover, it not only affects departments outside of the Treasury, but it tends to hamper the secretary of the treasury himself in the effort to utilize the employees of his department so as to best meet the requirements of the public service. It forbids him from preventing frauds upon the customs service, from investigating irregularities in branch mints and assay offices, and has seriously crippled him. It prevents the promotion of employees in the Secret Service, and this further discourages good effort. In its present form the restriction operates only to the advantage of the criminal, of the wrong-doer. The chief argument in favor of the provision was that the congressmen did not themselves wish to be investigated by Secret-Service men. Very little of such investigation has been done in the past; but it is true that the work of the Secret-Service agents was partly responsible for the indictment and conviction of a senator and a congressman for land frauds in Oregon. I do not believe that it is in the public interest to protect criminals in any branch of the public service, and exactly as we have again and again during the past seven years prosecuted and convicted such criminals who were in the executive branch of the government, so in my belief we should be given ample means to prosecute them if found in the legislative branch. But if this is not considered desirable a special exception could be made in the law prohibiting the use of the Secret-Service force in investigating members of the Congress. It would be far better to do this than to do what actually was done, and strive to prevent or at least to hamper effective action against criminals by the executive branch of the government.

POSTAL SAVINGS-BANKS

I again renew my recommendation for postal savings-banks, for depositing savings with the security of the government behind them. The object is to encourage thrift and economy in the wage-earner and person of moderate means. In fourteen States the deposits in savings-banks as reported to the comptroller of the currency amount to $3,590,245,402, or 98.4 per cent of the entire deposits, while in the remaining thirty-two States there are only $70,308,543, or 1.6 per cent, showing conclusively that there are many localities in the United States where sufficient opportunity is not given to the people to deposit their savings. The result is that money is kept in hiding and unemployed. It is believed that in the aggregate vast sums of money would be brought into circulation through the instrumentality of the postal savings-banks. While there are only 1,453 savings-banks reporting to the comptroller, there are more than 61,000 post-offices, 40,000 of which are money-order offices. Postal savings-banks are now in operation in practically all of the great civilized countries with the exception of the United States.

PARCEL-POST

In my last annual message I commended the postmaster-general's recommendation for an extension of the parcel-post on the rural routes. The establishment of a local parcel-post on rural routes would be to the mutual benefit of the farmer and the country storekeeper, and it is desirable that the routes, serving more than 15,000,000 people, should be utilized to the fullest practicable extent. An amendment was proposed in the Senate at the last session, at the suggestion of the postmaster-general, providing that, for the purpose of ascertaining the practicability of establishing a special local parcel-post system on the rural routes throughout the United States, the postmaster-general be authorized and directed to experiment and report to the Congress the result of such experiment by establishing a special local parcel-post system on rural-delivery routes in not to exceed four counties in the United States for packages of fourth-class matter originating on a rural route or at the distributing post-office for delivery by rural carriers. It would seem only proper that such an experiment should be tried in order to demonstrate the practicability of the proposition, especially as the postmaster-general estimates that the revenue derived from the operation of such a system on all the rural routes would amount to many million dollars.

EDUCATION

The share that the National Government should take in the broad work of education has not received the attention and the care it rightly deserves. The immediate responsibility for the support and improvement of our educational systems and institutions rests and should always rest with the people of the several States acting through their State and local governments, but the nation has an opportunity in educational work which must not be lost and a duty which should no longer be neglected.

The National Bureau of Education was established more than forty years ago. Its purpose is to collect and diffuse such information "as shall aid the people of the United States in the establishment and maintenance of efficient school systems and otherwise promote the cause of education throughout the country." This purpose in no way conflicts with the educational work of the States, but may be made of great advantage to the States by giving them the fullest, most accurate, and hence the most helpful information and suggestion regarding the best educational systems. The nation, through its broader field of activities, its wider opportunity for obtaining information from all the States and from foreign countries, is able to do that which not even the richest States can do, and with the distinct additional advantage that the information thus obtained is used for the immediate benefit of all our people.

With the limited means hitherto provided, the Bureau of Education has rendered efficient service, but the Congress has neglected to adequately supply the bureau with means to meet the educational growth of the country. The appropriations for the general work of the bureau, outside education in Alaska, for the year 1909 are but $87,500—an amount less than they were ten years ago, and some of the important items in these appropriations are less than they were thirty years ago. It is an inexcusable waste of public money to appropriate an amount which is so inadequate as to make it impossible properly to do the work authorized, and it is unfair to the great educational interests of the country to deprive them of the value of the results which can be obtained by proper appropriations.

I earnestly recommend that this unfortunate state of affairs as regards the national educational office be remedied by adequate appropriations. This recommendation is urged by the representatives of our common schools and great State universities and the leading educators, who all unite in requesting favorable consideration and action by the Congress upon this subject.

CENSUS

I strongly urge that the request of the director of the census in connection with the decennial work so soon to be begun be complied with and that the appointments to the census force be placed under the civil-service law, waiving the geographical requirements as requested by the director of the census. The supervisors and enumerators should not be appointed under the civil-service law, for the reasons given by the director. I commend to the Congress the careful consideration of the admirable report of the director of the census, and I trust that his recommendations will be adopted and immediate action thereon taken.

PUBLIC HEALTH

It is highly advisable that there should be intelligent action on the part of the nation on the question of preserving the health of the country. Through the practical extermination in San Francisco of disease-bearing rodents our country has thus far escaped the bubonic plague. This is but one of the many achievements of American health officers; and it shows what can be accomplished with a better organization than at present exists. The dangers to public health from food adulteration and from many other sources, such as the menace to the physical, mental, and moral development of children from child labor, should be met and overcome. There are numerous diseases, which are now known to be preventable, which are, nevertheless, not prevented. The recent International Congress on Tuberculosis has made us painfully aware of the inadequacy of American public-health legislation. This nation cannot afford to lag behind in the world-wide battle now being waged by all civilized people with the microscopic foes of mankind, nor ought we longer to ignore the reproach that this government takes more pains to protect the lives of hogs and of cattle than of human beings.

REDISTRIBUTION OF BUREAUS

The first legislative step to be taken is that for the concentration of the proper bureaus into one of the existing departments. I therefore urgently recommend the passage of a bill which shall authorize a redistribution of the bureaus which shall best accomplish this end.

GOVERNMENT PRINTING OFFICE

I recommend that legislation be enacted placing under the jurisdiction of the Department of Commerce and Labor the Government Printing Office. At present this office is under the combined control, supervision, and administrative direction of the President and of the Joint Committee on Printing of the two houses of the Congress. The advantage of having the 4,069 employees in this office and the expenditure of the $5,761,377.57 appropriated therefor supervised by an executive department is obvious, instead of the present combined supervision.

SOLDIERS' HOMES

All Soldiers' Homes should be placed under the complete jurisdiction and control of the War Department.

INDEPENDENT BUREAUS AND COMMISSIONS

Economy and sound business policy require that all existing independent bureaus and commissions should be placed under the jurisdiction of appropriate executive departments. It is unwise from every standpoint, and results only in mischief, to have any executive work done save by the purely executive bodies, under the control of the President; and each such executive body should be under the immediate supervision of a Cabinet minister.

STATEHOOD

I advocate the immediate admission of New Mexico and Arizona as States. This should be done at the present session of the Congress. The people of the two Territories have made it evident by their votes that they will not come in as one State. The only alternative is to admit them as two, and I trust that this will be done without delay.

INTERSTATE FISHERIES

I call the attention of the Congress to the importance of the problem of the fisheries in the interstate waters. On the Great Lakes we are now, under the very wise treaty of April 11th of this year, endeavoring to come to an international agreement for the preservation and satisfactory use of the fisheries of these waters which cannot otherwise be achieved. Lake Erie, for example, has the richest fresh-water fisheries in the world; but it is now controlled by the statutes of two nations, four States, and one province, and in this province by different ordinances in different counties. All these political divisions work at cross-purposes, and in no case can they achieve protection to the fisheries, on the one hand, and justice to the localities and individuals, on the other. The case is similar in Puget Sound.

But the problem is quite as pressing in the interstate waters of the United States. The salmon-fisheries of the Columbia

River are now but a fraction of what they were twenty-five years ago, and what they would be now if the United States Government had taken complete charge of them by intervening between Oregon and Washington. During these twenty-five years the fishermen of each State have naturally tried to take all they could get, and the two legislatures have never been able to agree on joint action of any kind adequate in degree for the protection of the fisheries. At the moment the fishing on the Oregon side is practically closed, while there is no limit on the Washington side of any kind, and no one can tell what the courts will decide as to the very statutes under which this action and non-action result. Meanwhile very few salmon reach the spawning-grounds, and probably four years hence the fisheries will amount to nothing; and this comes from a struggle between the associated, or gill-net, fishermen, on the one hand, and the owners of the fishing-wheels up the river. The fisheries of the Mississippi, the Ohio, and the Potomac are also in a bad way. For this there is no remedy except for the United States to control and legislate for the interstate fisheries as part of the business of interstate commerce. In this case the machinery for scientific investigation and for control already exists in the United States Bureau of Fisheries. In this as in similar problems the obvious and simple rule should be followed of having those matters which no particular State can manage taken in hand by the United States; problems which in the seesaw of conflicting State legislatures are absolutely unsolvable are easy enough for Congress to control.

FISHERIES AND FUR-SEALS

The Federal statute regulating interstate traffic in game should be extended to include fish. New Federal fish-hatcheries should be established. The administration of the Alaskan fur-seal service should be vested in the Bureau of Fisheries.

FOREIGN AFFAIRS

This nation's foreign policy is based on the theory that right must be done between nations precisely as between individuals, and in our actions for the last ten years we have in this matter proven our faith by our deeds. We have behaved, and are behaving, toward other nations as in private life an honorable man would behave toward his fellows.

LATIN-AMERICAN REPUBLICS

The commercial and material progress of the twenty Latin-American republics is worthy of the careful attention of the Congress. No other section of the world has shown a greater proportionate development of its foreign trade during the last ten years and none other has more special claims on the interest of the United States. It offers to-day probably larger opportunities for the legitimate expansion of our commerce than any other group of countries. These countries will want our products in greatly increased quantities, and we shall correspondingly need theirs. The International Bureau of the American Republics is doing a useful work in making these nations and their resources better known to us, and in acquainting them not only with us as a people and with our purposes toward them, but with what we have to exchange for their goods. It is an international institution supported by all the governments of the two Americas.

PANAMA CANAL

The work on the Panama Canal is being done with a speed, efficiency, and entire devotion to duty which make it a model for all work of the kind. No task of such magnitude has ever before been undertaken by any nation; and no task of the kind has ever been better performed. The men on the Isthmus, from Colonel Goethals and his fellow commissioners through the entire list of employees who are faithfully doing their duty, have won their right to the ungrudging respect and gratitude of the American people.

OCEAN-MAIL LINERS

I again recommend the extension of the ocean-mail act of 1891 so that satisfactory American ocean-mail lines to South America, Asia, the Philippines, and Australasia may be established. The creation of such steamship-lines should be the natural corollary of the voyage of the battle fleet. It should precede the opening of the Panama Canal. Even under favorable conditions several years must elapse before such lines can be put into operation. Accordingly I urge that the Congress act promptly where foresight already shows that action sooner or later will be inevitable.

HAWAII

I call particular attention to the Territory of Hawaii. The importance of those islands is apparent, and the need of improving their condition and developing their resources is urgent. In recent years industrial conditions upon the islands have radically changed. The importation of coolie labor has practically ceased, and there is now developing such a diversity in agricultural products as to make possible a change in the land conditions of the Territory, so that an opportunity may be given to the small landowner similar to that on the mainland. To aid these changes, the National Government must provide the necessary harbor improvements on each island, so that the agricultural products can be carried to the markets of the world. The coastwise shipping laws should be amended to meet the special needs of the islands, and the alien contract labor law should be so modified in its application to Hawaii as to enable American and European labor to be brought thither.

We have begun to improve Pearl Harbor for a naval base and to provide the necessary military fortifications for the protection of the islands, but I cannot too strongly emphasize the need of appropriations for these purposes of such an amount as will within the shortest possible time make those islands practically impregnable. It is useless to develop the industrial conditions of the islands and establish there bases of supply for our naval and merchant fleets unless we insure, as far as human ingenuity can, their safety from foreign seizure.

One thing to be remembered with all our fortifications is that it is almost useless to make them impregnable from the sea if they are left open to land attack. This is true even of our own coast, but it is doubly true of our insular possessions. In Hawaii, for instance, it is worse than useless to establish a naval station unless we establish it behind fortifications so strong that no landing force can take them save by regular and long-continued siege operations.

THE PHILIPPINES

Real progress toward self-government is being made in the Philippine Islands. The gathering of a Philippine legislative body and Philippine assembly marks a process absolutely new in Asia, not only as regards Asiatic colonies of European powers but as regards Asiatic possessions of other Asiatic powers; and, indeed, always excepting the striking and wonderful example afforded by the great empire of Japan, it opens an entirely new departure when compared with anything which has happened among Asiatic powers which are their own masters. Hitherto this Philippine legislature has acted with moderation and self-restraint, and has seemed in practical fashion to realize the eternal truth that there must always be government, and that the only way in which any body of individuals can escape the necessity of being governed by outsiders is to show that they are able to restrain themselves, to keep down wrong-doing and disorder. The Filipino people, through their officials, are therefore making real steps in the direction of self-government. I hope and believe that these steps mark the beginning of a course which will continue till the Filipinos become fit to decide for themselves whether they desire to be an independent nation. But it is well for them (and well also for those Americans who during the past decade have done so much damage to the Filipinos by agitation for an immediate independence for which they were totally unfit) to remember that self-government depends, and must depend, upon the Filipinos themselves. All we can do is to give them the opportunity to develop the capacity for self-government. If we had followed the advice of the foolish doctrinaires who wished us at any time during the last ten years to turn the Filipino people adrift, we should have shirked the plainest possible duty and have inflicted a lasting wrong upon the Filipino people. We have acted in exactly the opposite spirit. We have given the Filipinos constitutional government—a government based upon justice—and we have shown that we have governed them for their good and not for our aggrandizement. At the present time, as during the past ten years, the inexorable logic of facts shows that this government must be supplied by us and not by them. We must be wise and generous; we must help the Filipinos to master the difficult art of self-control, which is simply another name for self-government. But we cannot give them self-government save in the sense of governing them so that gradually they may, if they are able, learn to govern themselves. Under the present system of just laws and sympathetic administration, we have every reason to believe that they are gradually acquiring the character which lies at the basis of self-government, and for which, if it be lacking, no system of laws, no paper constitution, will in any wise serve as a substitute. Our people in the Philippines have achieved what may legitimately be called a marvellous success in giving to them a government which marks on the part of those in authority both the necessary understanding of the people and the necessary purpose to serve them disinterestedly and in good faith. I trust that within a generation the time will arrive when the Philippines can decide for themselves whether it is well for them to become independent, or to continue under the protection of a strong and disinterested power, able to guarantee to the islands order at home and protection from foreign invasion. But no one can prophesy the exact date when it will be wise to consider independence as a fixed and definite policy. It would be worse than folly to try to set down such a date in advance, for it must depend upon the way in which the Philippine people themselves develop the power of self-mastery.

PORTO RICO

I again recommend that American citizenship be conferred upon the people of Porto Rico.

CUBA

In Cuba our occupancy will cease in about two months' time; the Cubans have in orderly manner elected their own governmental authorities, and the island will be turned over to them. Our occupation on this occasion has lasted a little over two years, and Cuba has thriven and prospered under it. Our earnest hope and one desire is that the people of the island shall now govern themselves with justice, so that peace and order may be secure. We will gladly help them to this end; but I would solemnly warn them to remember the great truth that the only way a people can permanently avoid being governed from without is to show that they both can and will govern themselves from within.

JAPANESE EXPOSITION

The Japanese Government has postponed until 1917 the date of the great international exposition, the action being taken so as to insure ample time in which to prepare to make the exposition all that it should be made. The American commissioners have visited Japan and the postponement will merely give ampler opportunity for America to be represented at the exposition. Not since the first international exposition has there been one of greater importance than this will be, marking as it does the fiftieth anniversary of the ascension to the throne of the Emperor of Japan. The extraordinary leap to a foremost place among the nations of the world made by Japan during this half-century is something unparalleled in all previous history. This exposition will fitly commemorate and signalize the giant progress that has been achieved. It is the first exposition of its kind that has ever been held in Asia. The United States, because of the ancient friendship between the two peoples, because each of us fronts on the Pacific, and because of the growing commercial relations between this country and Asia, takes a peculiar interest in seeing the exposition made a success in every way.

I take this opportunity publicly to state my appreciation of the way in which in Japan, in Australia, in New Zealand, and in all the states of South America, the battle fleet has been received on its practice voyage around the world. The American Government cannot too strongly express its appreciation of the abounding and generous hospitality shown our ships in every port they visited.

THE ARMY

As regards the army I call attention to the fact that while our junior officers and enlisted men stand very high, the present system of promotion by seniority results in bringing into the higher grades many men of mediocre capacity who have but a short time to serve. No man should regard it as his vested right to rise to the highest rank in the army any more than in any other profession. It is a curious and by no means creditable fact that there should be so often a failure on the part of the public and its representatives to understand the great need, from the standpoint of the service and the nation, of refusing to promote respectable, elderly incompetents. The higher places should be given to the most deserving men without regard to seniority; at least seniority should be treated as only one consideration. In the stress of modern industrial competition no business firm could succeed if those responsible for its management were chosen simply on the ground that they were the oldest people in its employment; yet this is the course advocated as regards the army, and required by law for all grades except those of general officer. As a matter of fact, all of the best officers in the highest ranks of the army are those who have attained their present position wholly or in part by a process of selection.

The scope of retiring-boards should be extended so that they could consider general unfitness to command for any cause, in order to secure a far more rigid enforcement than at present in the elimination of officers for mental, physical, or temperamental disabilities. But this plan is recommended only if the Congress does not see fit to provide what in my judgment is far better; that is, for selection in promotion, and for elimination for age. Officers who fail to attain a certain rank by a certain age should be retired—for instance, if a man should not attain field rank by the time he is forty-five he should of course be placed on the retired list. General officers should be selected as at present, and one-third of the other promotions should be made by selection, the selection to be made by the President or the secretary of war from a list of at least two candidates proposed for each vacancy by a board of officers from the arm of the service from which the promotion is to be made. A bill is now before the Congress having for its object to secure the promotion of officers to various grades at reasonable ages through a process of selection, by boards of officers, of the least efficient for retirement with a percentage of their pay depending upon length of service. The bill, although not accomplishing all that should be done, is a long step in the right direction; and I earnestly recommend its passage, or that of a more completely effective measure.

The cavalry arm should be reorganized upon modern lines. This is an arm in which it is peculiarly necessary that the field-officers should not be old. The cavalry is much more difficult to form than infantry, and it should be kept up to the maximum both in efficiency and in strength, for it cannot be made in a hurry. At present both infantry and artillery are too few in number for our needs. Especial attention should be paid to development of the machine-gun. A general service corps should be established. As things are now the average soldier has far too much labor of a non-military character to perform.

NATIONAL GUARD

Now that the organized militia, the National Guard, has been incorporated with the army as a part of the national forces, it behooves the government to do every reasonable thing in its power to perfect its efficiency. It should be assisted in its instruction and otherwise aided more liberally than heretofore. The continuous services of many well-trained regular officers will be essential in this connection. Such officers must be specially trained at service schools best to qualify them as instructors of the National Guard. But the detailing of officers for training at the service schools and for duty with the National Guard entails detaching them from their regiments which are already greatly depleted by detachment of officers for assignment to duties prescribed by acts of the Congress.

A bill is now pending before the Congress creating a number of extra officers in the army, which if passed, as it ought to be, will enable more officers to be trained as instructors of the National Guard and assigned to that duty. In case of war it will be of the utmost importance to have a large number of trained officers to use for turning raw levies into good troops.

There should be legislation to provide a complete plan for organizing the great body of volunteers behind the Regular Army and National Guard when war has come. Congressional assistance should be given those who are endeavoring to promote rifle practice so that our men, in the services or out of them, may know how to use the rifle. While teams representing the United States won the rifle and revolver championships of the world against all comers in England this year, it is unfortunately true that the great body of our citizens shoot less and less as time goes on. To meet this we should encourage rifle practice among schoolboys, and indeed among all classes, as well as in the military services, by every means in our power. Thus, and not otherwise, may we be able to assist in preserving the peace of the world. Fit to hold our own against the strong nations of the earth, our voice for peace will carry to the ends of the earth. Unprepared, and therefore unfit, we must sit dumb and helpless to defend ourselves, protect others, or preserve peace. The first step—in the direction of preparation to avert war if possible, and to be fit for war if it should come—is to teach our men to shoot.

THE NAVY

I approve the recommendations of the general board for the increase of the navy, calling especial attention to the need of additional destroyers and colliers, and, above all, of the four battleships. It is desirable to complete as soon as possible a squadron of eight battleships of the best existing type. The *North Dakota, Delaware, Florida,* and *Utah* will form the first division of this squadron. The four vessels proposed will form the second division. It will be an improvement on the first, the ships being of the heavy, single-caliber, all big-gun type. All the vessels should have the same tactical qualities —that is, speed and turning circle—and as near as possible these tactical qualities should be the same as in the four vessels before named now being built.

I most earnestly recommend that the general board be by law turned into a general staff. There is literally no excuse whatever for continuing the present bureau organization of the navy. The navy should be treated as a purely military organization, and everything should be subordinated to the one object of securing military efficiency. Such military efficiency can only be guaranteed in time of war if there is the most thorough previous preparation in time of peace—a preparation, I may add, which will in all probability prevent any need of war. The secretary must be supreme, and he should have as his official advisers a body of line-officers who should themselves have the power to pass upon and co-ordinate all the work and all the proposals of the several bureaus. A system of promotion by merit, either by selection or by exclusion, or by both processes, should be introduced. It is out of the question, if the present principle of promotion by mere seniority is kept, to expect to get the best results from the higher officers. Our men come too old, and stay for too short a time, in the high-command positions.

Two hospital ships should be provided. The actual experience of the hospital ship with the fleet in the Pacific has shown the invaluable work which such a ship does, and has also proved that it is well to have it kept under the command of a medical officer. As was to be expected, all of the anticipations of trouble from such a command have proved completely baseless. It is as absurd to put a hospital ship under a line-officer as it would be to put a hospital on shore under such a command. This ought to have been realized before, and there is no excuse for failure to realize it now.

Nothing better for the navy from every standpoint has ever occurred than the cruise of the battle fleet around the world. The improvement of the ships in every way has been extraordinary, and they have gained far more experience in battle tactics than they would have gained if they had stayed in the Atlantic waters. The American people have cause for profound gratification, both in view of the excellent condition of the fleet as shown by this cruise, and in view of the improvement the cruise has worked in this already high condition. I do not believe that there is any other service in the world in which the average of character and efficiency in the enlisted men is as high as is now the case in our own. I believe that the same statement can be made as to our officers, taken as a whole; but there must be a reservation made in regard to those in the highest ranks—as to which I have already spoken—and in regard to those who have just entered the service; because we do not now get full benefit from our excellent naval school at Annapolis. It is absurd* not to graduate the midshipmen as ensigns; to keep them for two years in such an anomalous position as at present the law requires is detrimental to them and to the service. In the Academy itself, every first class-man should be required in turn to serve as petty officer and officer; his ability to discharge his duties as such should be a prerequisite to his going into the line, and his success in commanding should largely determine his standing at graduation. The Board of Visitors should be appointed in January, and each member should be required to give at least six days' service, only from one to three days' to be performed during June week, which is the least desirable time for the board to be at Annapolis so far as benefiting the navy by their observations is concerned.

BIBLIOGRAPHICAL NOTE

BY R. W. G. VAIL

LIBRARIAN OF ROOSEVELT HOUSE

Many of these addresses and messages were first published in separate form. In this volume, however, no attempt has been made to trace the first editions of the various chapters, as it has seemed of more practical reference value to give here the more readily accessible collected forms of Colonel Roosevelt's public papers as the sources of the present compilation. The volumes listed below include many of Colonel Roosevelt's less important public addresses and papers not included in this edition. They will be found in all the larger public libraries and in the Roosevelt Memorial Library, at Roosevelt House, 28 East 20th Street, New York City.

STATE OF NEW YORK. PUBLIC PAPERS OF THEODORE ROOSEVELT, GOVERNOR, 1899 [1900]. Albany, N. Y.: Brandow Printing Company. Department Printers, 1899 [1900]. 2 vols., 8vo, olive cloth. (Hereafter referred to as: PUBLIC PAPERS.)

STATE OF NEW YORK. MESSAGES FROM THE GOVERNORS . . . 1683 to 1906. With notes. Edited by Charles Z. Lincoln. Published by authority of the State. Volume X, 1899-1906. Albany: J. B. Lyon Company, State Printers, 1909. This is Volume X of an eleven-volume, illustrated, 8vo, tan cloth bound set, and contains the messages, etc., of Governors Roosevelt, Odell, and Higgins. (Hereafter referred to as: MESSAGES FROM THE GOVERNORS.)

SUPPLEMENT TO THE MESSAGES AND PAPERS OF THE PRESIDENTS COVERING THE PRESIDENTIAL TERMS OF THEODORE ROOSEVELT, September 14, 1901, to March 4, 1909. With index. . . . New York: Bureau of National Literature (Inc.). This 8vo volume appears in various bindings. It is a supplement to the standard edition of the MESSAGES AND PAPERS OF THE PRESIDENTS, but was issued as a separate volume. As the pagination of all recent editions of this work is the same, the following references to the supplementary volume will also refer to whichever edition happens to be available to the student. (Hereafter referred to as: MESSAGES AND PAPERS.)

PRESIDENTIAL ADDRESSES AND STATE PAPERS. New York: The Review of Reviews Company, 1910. This eight-volume set will be found described in full in an earlier bibliographical note. It is of value for its addresses rather than for the more strictly official State papers. (Hereafter referred to as: PRESIDENTIAL ADDRESSES.)

Descriptive titles have, for the most part, been added by the editor. The contents of this volume have been reprinted from the following sources:

GOVERNOR

I.　PUBLIC PAPERS, I :247–249.

II.　PUBLIC PAPERS, I :5–34.
　　MESSAGES FROM THE GOVERNORS, X :1–30.

III.　PUBLIC PAPERS, II :7–60.
　　MESSAGES FROM THE GOVERNORS, X :74–126.

VICE-PRESIDENT

I.　MESSAGES AND PAPERS, 6638–6639.

PRESIDENT

I.　MESSAGES AND PAPERS, 6641–6680.

II.　MESSAGES AND PAPERS, 6709–6729.
　　PRESIDENTIAL ADDRESSES, II :606–645.

III.　MESSAGES AND PAPERS, 6784–6815.
　　PRESIDENTIAL ADDRESSES, II :648–709.

IV.　MESSAGES AND PAPERS, 6894–6930.
　　PRESIDENTIAL ADDRESSES, III :119–189.

V.　MESSAGES AND PAPERS, 6930–6932.
　　PRESIDENTIAL ADDRESSES, III :269–272.

VI.　MESSAGES AND PAPERS, 6973–7023.
　　PRESIDENTIAL ADDRESSES, IV :560–658.

VII.　MESSAGES AND PAPERS, 7023–7070.
　　PRESIDENTIAL ADDRESSES, V :898–990.

VIII.　MESSAGES AND PAPERS, 7070–7125.
　　PRESIDENTIAL ADDRESSES, VII :1488–1597.

IX.　MESSAGES AND PAPERS, 7198–7238.
　　PRESIDENTIAL ADDRESSES, VIII :1893–1968.